The Black Republic

AMERICA IN THE NINETEENTH CENTURY

Series editors:
Brian DeLay, Steven Hahn, Amy Dru Stanley

America in the Nineteenth Century proposes a rigorous rethinking of this most formative period in U.S. history. Books in the series will be wide-ranging and eclectic, with an interest in politics at all levels, culture and capitalism, race and slavery, law, gender, the environment, and regional and transnational history. The series aims to expand the scope of nineteenth-century historiography by bringing classic questions into dialogue with innovative perspectives, approaches, and methodologies.

A complete list of books in the series
is available from the publisher.

The BLACK REPUBLIC

African Americans and the Fate of Haiti

Brandon R. Byrd

PENN

UNIVERSITY OF PENNSYLVANIA PRESS

PHILADELPHIA

Published by
University of Pennsylvania Press
Philadelphia, Pennsylvania 19104-4112
www.upenn.edu/pennpress

Printed in the United States of America
on acid-free paper
3 5 7 9 10 8 6 4

Library of Congress Cataloging-in-Publication Data

Names: Byrd, Brandon R., author.
Title: The black republic: African Americans and the fate of Haiti / Brandon R. Byrd.
Other titles: America in the nineteenth century.
Description: First edition. | Philadelphia: University of Pennsylvania Press, [2020] | Series: America in the nineteenth century. | Includes bibliographical references and index.
Identifiers: LCCN 2019016630| ISBN 9780812251708 (hardcover: alk. paper) | ISBN 0812251709 (hardcover: alk. paper)
Subjects: LCSH: African Americans—Civil rights—History—19th century. | African Americans—Intellectual life—19th century. | Haiti—History—Revolution, 1791–1804—Influence. | Haiti—Relations—United States. | United States—Relations—United States. | Haiti—Foreign relations—United States. | United States—Foreign relations—Haiti.
Classification: LCC E185.61.B985 2020 | DDC 323.1196/07309034—dc23
LC record available at https://lccn.loc.gov/2019016630

To Mom, for the gifts of writing and history

CONTENTS

PROLOGUE

Growing up, Hayti was close. Less than a gallon of gas away. From our home in Swift Creek, you just drove past some horse farms, a strawberry field, and two elementary schools before hopping on the highway.

It's not clear how the historic black section of Durham, North Carolina, got its name. Its earliest surviving documented use is from 1877, when a property owner sold a plot of land "near the town of Durham in the settlement of colored people near the South East end of the Corporation of said town known as Hayti."[1] Did white southerners who thought of the Republic of Haiti as nothing more than black and inferior impose its name upon the "settlement of colored people" relegated across the tracks? Maybe. At least that's what some people say. Yet African Americans in the Bull City claim it as a badge of honor in the past and today. Their ancestors were proud of the Haitian Revolution, they proclaim. Hayti, established by freedpeople following the Civil War, took its name from the Black Republic, whose independence they not only admired but expected to emulate.

For much of its history, Hayti *was* a site of black self-determination and economic success. Residents of what became the main black residential district in Durham, many of them workers in the local tobacco factories, became landowners, built schools, and formed churches. Some established businesses. Located on Parrish Street, the North Carolina Mutual Life Insurance Company and the Mechanics and Farmers Bank formed the heart of what prominent black intellectuals including Booker T. Washington, W. E. B. Du Bois, and E. Franklin Frazier praised as "Black Wall Street" and "the capital of the black middle class."[2] They, along with the North Carolina College for Negroes (NCCN), the first state-supported black liberal arts college in the United States, were spaces of real black empowerment within the confines of Jim Crow.[3]

In many ways, integration and urban renewal ensured that the Hayti I knew was different than the one that once existed. During the first two-thirds of the twentieth century, a grassroots civil rights movement led by black women tore down the walls of racial segregation in Durham.[4] It could have achieved even more for the working-class residents of Hayti were it not for the foreseeable consequences of urban renewal. As Durham grew in size and economic strength, local and state officials, including some black elites, concluded that the city needed an interstate to stimulate further growth. In 1967, construction began on the Durham Freeway. It cut right through Hayti, leaving hundreds of displaced families and a demolished community in its wake.[5]

Most Sundays, our family took that freeway on our way to mass at Durham's Holy Cross Catholic Church. Sitting in the back seat, I didn't think about the inseparable histories of racism and capitalism that bulldozed the way to our diocese's lone black Catholic congregation and one of the oldest in the state.[6] I didn't ask what ideas about black self-determination bound our unique church to its surrounding community let alone to Haiti, the latter's historical namesake.

In the summer before my senior year of college, I began research for my honors thesis. My subject was a fellow Tar Heel, Charles Clinton Spaulding. It was close to home, or so I thought.

Born in 1874, Spaulding grew up on a farm in Whiteville, North Carolina, a town dwarfed in size and about an hour southeast of the town of ten thousand people where I was born. He was, from a young age, drawn to Booker T. Washington's philosophies and convinced that black economic achievement was a sound solution to discrimination. At the age of twenty, Spaulding moved from the country to Durham, believing that the bustling city offered better educational and economic opportunities for an aspirational black man. His efforts matching his ambitions, Spaulding soon earned a job at North Carolina Mutual. By the 1920s, he was its president and helped make it into the largest black-owned life insurance company in the United States.[7]

For most of his life, Spaulding emulated and echoed Washington, the famous black educator for whom he named one son. But a shift to more direct action in support of black civil and political rights came in the decade and a half before his death in 1952. In 1935, two years after undermining an attempt to integrate the University of North Carolina at Chapel Hill in order to avoid white backlash to black activism and obtain more financial support for black education, Spaulding became the founding president of the Durham Committee on Negro Affairs (DCNA). Under his leadership, the DCNA registered thousands of black voters and drove them to the polls. It gave electoral power to the rising civil rights activism in Durham, even getting several black candidates elected to local public offices in which only white men had served before.[8]

Accordingly, in Spaulding, I thought I had a subject that was local and personal. In studying his life, I hoped to better understand black leadership in the Jim Crow South. I wanted to capture the changes that made modern Durham and learn more about North Carolina, the state where my enslaved ancestors toiled before the American Revolution. I expected to find myself.

It was a surprise, then, to stumble upon Spaulding's trip to Haiti. In April 1937, three years after the United States ended a destructive military occupation of the Western Hemisphere's lone black nation-state, the North Carolina Mutual president left his home in Durham's principal black residential district and joined a group of black businessmen, attorneys, and one radio evangelist on a self-proclaimed Good Neighbor Tour of Haiti. For more than a week, Spaulding and his colleagues met with coffee exporters and government officials, toured the National Bank of Haiti, and enjoyed the hospitality of the Hotel Splendid. According to Spaulding, the "goodwill ambassadors" simply wanted "to study economic conditions . . . and build as much goodwill as possible."[9] Their goal was to "throw up a highway so that there would be a better understanding between the black Republic of Haiti and the American Negroes."[10]

The call, the question, was impossible to ignore. There were inescapable connections among Spaulding's highway and the Durham Freeway, postoccupation Haiti and postemancipation Hayti. There was obvious proof that Haiti, or at least ideas about it, had mattered a whole lot to black Tar Heels, my people, in 1877 and 1937 and, presumably, in the decades in between.

But how? And why? I've since pursued those questions, all the while trying to figure out what exactly Haiti means to me.

INTRODUCTION

The Ideas of Haiti and Black Internationalism

Haiti would not exist had it been up to France, Great Britain, Spain, or the United States. Certainly not if George Washington had had his way. In September 1791, mere weeks after the Vodou ceremony that started the slave insurrection in Saint-Domingue, the slaveholding U.S. president wrote to the French ambassador to the United States pledging to help restore France's control over its richest colony. "I am happy in the opportunity of testifying how well disposed the United States are to render every aid . . . to quell the alarming insurrection of Negroes in Hispanola [*sic*]," he told his ally.[1] Having just won his country's independence from a colonial power, Washington wanted to see that black people in Saint-Domingue did not secure their own.

Of course, Haitians did just that. They did the unthinkable.[2] In the United States, the so-called Founding Fathers, educated men of the Enlightenment with lofty ideals of representative government and natural rights, had no tools for understanding an actual revolution. Not one initiated by Africans said to lack history, will, and a love for freedom. Not one that overthrew colonialism *and* slavery in one fell swoop. So instead of celebrating the Haitian Revolution as the most radical declaration of human rights the world had ever known, they characterized it as a savage race war and an unjustifiable attack on (white) property rights. They tried to silence the Haitian Revolution—to speak out of existence the incomprehensible black nation that it birthed.[3]

Haiti, the first black nation and second independent republic in the Western Hemisphere thus became shorthand for a host of evils. In the antebellum United States, Haiti became synonymous with slave insurrection and black barbarism. It came to mean the specter of abolitionism, and for that sin it was shunned.[4] Explaining why the United States refused to grant diplomatic recognition to Haiti, Senator Thomas Hart Benton of Missouri proclaimed that "the peace of eleven states in this Union will not permit the fruits of a successful negro insurrection to be exhibited among them." White southerners, he continued, would "not permit black Consuls and Ambassadors to establish themselves in our cities, and to parade through our country, and give their fellow blacks in the United States, proof in hand of the honors which await them, for a like successful effort on their part." They could not acknowledge Haitian independence, at least not without entertaining dangerous questions about the "rights of Africans in *this* hemisphere."[5]

For men like Benton, to control U.S. foreign policy was to command the marketplace of ideas about slavery and freedom and about Haiti and the Haitian Revolution. From their perspective, to cede ownership of policies or thought would ensure the realization of abolitionist nightmares. It would mean the collapse of a slaveholding empire already built on lands seized from Native Americans and Mexicans—the end of the world that slaveholders dreamed.[6]

Proslavery internationalists had reason for concern. As they knew and scholars have since shown, the concurrent, subversive idea of Haiti was a legitimate cause of worry for white men, women, and children invested in racial slavery. The symbolic power of a black nation-state birthed in a successful slave insurrection undermined the power of white planters and businessmen who reaped from black labor the greatest profits that the world had ever seen. In fact, it encouraged other visions of emancipation and emboldened champions of racial equality.

News of the Haitian Revolution spread like wildfire among black people throughout the Americas. From its outset, free and enslaved black people monitored newspaper coverage of the slave rebellion in Saint-Domingue and solicited reports of its progress by word of mouth. Black sailors on U.S. trading vessels that conducted business in the French colony were more than happy to comply. As they confirmed that slavery was, in fact, under assault in the Caribbean, thousands of planters fleeing Saint-Domingue landed in New Orleans, Philadelphia, Norfolk, and Charleston.[7] While they brought warnings of the so-called Horrors of Saint-Domingue, their enslaved people imported inspirational stories about the rebellious origins of Haiti meant to stimulate similar struggles for black liberation.[8] As Booker T. Washington wrote, African Americans came to appreciate "the Haytian struggle for liberty." They knew of its example even if they were "ignorant of everything except [their] master and the plantation."[9] In fact, they equated it with their most profound aspirations.[10]

For free and enslaved black people, Haiti became a singular beacon of liberty. Enslaved revolutionaries including Gabriel, Denmark Vesey, and Nat Turner tried to emulate the Haitian Revolution, the lone successful slave rebellion in modern global history.[11] Free black northerners fought for the diplomatic recognition of Haiti, the black nation that they understood to be the embodiment of racial equality.[12] Thousands more accepted the invitations of the Haitian presidents Jean-Pierre Boyer and Fabre Geffrard and fled to Haiti's shores.[13] One black man who emigrated from Washington, D.C., to Port-au-Prince during the 1820s explained the reasons for that refugee movement in a letter sent to friends in his former home. "I have adopted myself a Haytian; and I bid eternal farewell to America," he wrote. "Here I repose under my vine and banana tree, contented with Hayti . . . determined to live and die under the safe-guard of her constitution."[14]

In the minds of antebellum African Americans, Haiti was haven and inspiration.[15] It was imitable, too. In the decades before the Civil War, militant black abolitionists including David Walker and Henry Highland Garnet proclaimed that the Haitian Revolution proved the righteousness and efficacy of slave rebellion.[16] They welcomed what they called the Abolition War. During the conflict caused by secessionists who predicted that Abraham Lincoln's election would bring about "San Domingo and Hayti, with all their attendant horrors," black recruiters and soldiers invoked and imitated Haitians.[17] As one chaplain in the Union Army observed, "The name of Toussaint L'Overture has been passed from mouth to mouth until it has become a secret household word." It had encouraged the hundreds of thousands of black soldiers and sailors who enlisted in the Union Army and Navy because they "felt it was right for the colored Haytiens to fight to be free [so] it is equally right for colored Americans."[18]

These "American Toussaints" ended U.S. slavery and put white supremacy on its heels.[19] They did not secure uncontested freedom, though. How could they when their white counterparts still litigated what should have been the incontestable outcome of the Haitian Revolution? No, U.S. black activists, intellectuals, soldiers, and enslaved people won the war but quickly found themselves embroiled in another fight. Like Haitians, they had to grapple with freedom's varied and contested meanings in a world founded on racial slavery and white supremacy.

The Black Republic begins with this premise: there existed multiple and sometimes conflicting ideas of Haiti that changed over time but remained critical to African Americans during the long postemancipation era following the U.S. Civil War. It is a premise that has received little to no consideration to date. For the most part, historians have drawn attention either to white fear of or black fascination with the Haitian Revolution during the eras of slavery and the Civil War. Their works have ended at the conclusion of the Civil War, when numerous black intellectuals identified new and urgent connections among Haiti, freedom, and black self-determination.[20]

This forgotten period of black interest in Haiti overlaps with a significant gap in the scholarship on black internationalism. In recent decades, historians have paid closer attention to the global dimensions of local and national black freedom struggles, compared collective experiences across the African Diaspora, and examined how black organizations, intellectuals, and activists shaped international politics. They have advanced our understanding of black internationalism, an insurgent political and intellectual response to slavery, colonialism, and white imperialism.[21] Still, studies of black internationalism tend to focus on three eras: the Age of Revolutions, at the end of the eighteenth century, when black internationalism emerged as an evangelical and revolutionary struggle for universal emancipation; World War I, when black leftists and nationalists gave black internationalism greater organizational structure and increased geographic scope; and what the scholars Michael O. West and William G. Martin call the "long black Sixties," a period when global Black Power advocates challenged a post–World War II liberal order that betrayed the promises of desegregation and decolonization.[22] By comparison, little attention has been given to global visions of black freedom in the tumultuous decades that followed the U.S. Civil War.

And yet black internationalism was very much alive in that period. Haiti was its heart. For late nineteenth- and early twentieth-century African Americans, Haiti demonstrated the opportunity that freedom presented: black self-determination (or black self-government), a malleable idea centered on the demand for individual and collective independence from the political, economic, and social structures that perpetuated white supremacy and limited the opportunities for black people to dictate their own lives.[23]

In fact, Haiti confirmed that self-determination and freedom went hand in hand, that the former was a necessary condition of the latter. Accordingly, even African Americans who expressed ambivalence about the political and social conditions of Haiti, characterized it as an incomplete project of black self-government and social development in need of their civilizing influence, or sanitized what they considered to be disreputable aspects of the Haitian Revolution still expressed a deep and enduring investment in Haiti and Haitians. There was no other choice. To them, Haiti was what Frederick Douglass called it: "the only self-made Black Republic in the world";[24] a black "city set on a hill."[25]

That analogy suggests the complexities of the association of Haiti with black freedom and self-determination. Douglass and other black intellectuals in the United States often imagined Haiti much as John Winthrop and the Puritans had thought of Massachusetts.[26] From their perspective, Haiti was unique albeit imitable, exemplary but imperfect, symbolic though real. It was an experiment in black self-government, distinct yet inseparable from the flawed world that its singular example had the power to change.

In other words, the multiple powerful ideas of Haiti were not evidence of ideological uniformity but rather the product of much debate and scrutiny amid great uncertainty. Across the Civil War, Reconstruction, post-Reconstruction, and early Jim Crow eras, black artists, educators, diplomats, missionaries, clergy, clubwomen, activists, and students—all of them intellectuals in their own right—considered the possibilities of meaningful black freedom in light of the forms of racial oppression that emerged after the end of slavery. They thought about Haiti, a country that the inheritors of proslavery internationalism misrepresented as culturally backward, politically unstable, and proof that black people were incapable of freedom and self-government. Although black men, women, and occasionally children from across the political spectrum believed in Haiti's significance, they did not always agree on how to realize the promises associated with it. Instead, their public engagement with that country and its people, as found in hundreds of untapped sources, including plays, poems, speeches, convention proceedings, letters, periodicals, and books, often revealed significant disagreement and occasional incoherence about culture, nationalism, history, race, gender, politics, imperialism, colonialism, and other pressing subjects.

It was therefore the long-standing production *and* constant reproduction of the ideas of Haiti that proved instrumental to broader black intellectual change. When the United States began its devastating military occupation of Haiti, which lasted from 1915 to 1934, African Americans had long ago reached a consensus that Haiti mattered because it was black and free and self-governing. They had to take interest in the occupation even though there were divergent understandings of its initial meaning. Eventually, opposition to the occupation coalesced among a diverse collection of black intellectuals who saw the attack on Haitian sovereignty as a symptom of broader problems that plagued the entire colored world. Their anti-occupation protests and, by extension, their ideas of Haiti thus became a cornerstone of the anti-capitalist, anti-colonial, and anti-racist radical black internationalism that arose in the period between the two world wars.

Put another way, what historians understand as an interwar radical black internationalism has its roots in, even if it did not emerge during, a long postemancipation era that featured black intellectuals' complex albeit consistent debates about Haiti. Tracking these varied responses to Haiti, which ranged from seemingly conservative to quite radical for their day, takes us down a winding and sometimes unpredictable path through changing social and political terrains.

Chapter 1 recounts the initially optimistic and ultimately frustrated international visions of black freedom and self-determination that emerged during the Civil War and Reconstruction eras. It draws particular attention to African Americans' concurrent celebrations of the Emancipation Proclamation and the U.S. diplomatic recognition of Haiti and U.S. president Ulysses S. Grant's appointment of Ebenezer Don Carlos Bassett as the U.S. minister resident and consul general to Haiti and the first black diplomat in U.S. history. For numerous black writers, orators, abolitionists, and freedpeople, these were signs of collective black progress from slavery to freedom to full citizenship. They not only reinvigorated interest in the Haitian Revolution, now viewed as the inspirational story of a slave rebellion that won Haitians freedom *and* international recognition of their right to self-determination, but also encouraged genuine faith in the United States, the country that now seemed to welcome black citizens as its representatives.

Still, there was cause for concern. The real and imagined descendants of pro-slavery internationalists maligned Haiti in order to undermine the black civil and political rights encoded in the Thirteenth, Fourteenth, and Fifteenth Amendments to the U.S. Constitution and resurrect the racial hierarchies of the antebellum era. Once synonymous with slave insurrection and abolitionism, Haiti became racist shorthand for the looming evils of social equality and "Negro rule."[27]

Accordingly, Chapter 1 also introduces readers to two additional, related topics: black intellectuals' response to the simultaneous backlash to Radical Reconstruction, the pursuit of U.S. empire, and the ascension of scientific racism; and the attendant birth of black missionary work in Haiti. As white Americans maligned Haitians and African Americans in the same breath, some middle-class black ministers and church members concluded that Haiti had to be improved. Influenced by scientific racism, they pronounced themselves the leaders of the black race, supported U.S. political intervention in Haiti, and sent missionaries to civilize Haitians. They belied their confidence in their country's supposed racial egalitarianism. Unsure about the security of their improved social and political status, black intellectuals tried to manipulate their connection to Haiti, a country that they understood as an imperfect model of black political capacity that had to be sound, according to middle-class U.S. standards, for the sake of the entire race.

So critical to the since-overlooked global visions of black freedom that emerged in the Civil War and Reconstruction eras, Haiti maintained its symbolic and practical value to African Americans in the aftermath of Redemption, the violent process through which white southerners returned to power. Chapter 2 highlights how black politicians, missionaries, educators, and would-be emigrationists viewed Haiti as a place where black diplomats could still participate in U.S. politics despite the loss of Reconstruction's gains and an inspiring albeit imperfect model of black self-determination. It draws attention to their response to Spenser St. John. In 1884, in the midst of a transatlantic dialogue on black potential in post-emancipation societies, the British diplomat published a widely read book about Haiti that denied the possibilities of any sound black government. Black journalists were prominent among the African Americans who responded. To them, the intensifying rhetorical assaults and military threats to Haiti mirrored the violent efforts to restrict black rights in the United States. They articulated a nascent anti-imperial critique in defense of the Black Republic.

If black intellectuals increasingly saw similarities between their precarious status and the contempt for Haiti in the post-Reconstruction era, that connection became even clearer during the 1890s. Chapter 3 advances our understanding of two well-known events involving Frederick Douglass: what became known as the Môle-Saint-Nicolas affair and the Chicago

World's Fair. As the U.S. government tried to seize Môle-Saint-Nicolas, a port town in Haiti, Douglass, a proponent of U.S. expansion in the Caribbean during the promising days of Reconstruction who then served the U.S. government as its minister resident and consul general to Haiti, tried to encourage racial egalitarianism rather than racial domination as the foundations of U.S. foreign policy. He failed. The heavy-handed negotiations for Haitian territory, occurring as Europeans solidified their control over Africa and the United States pursued its own empire in the Caribbean and the Pacific, clarified the intensified threats to the freedom of the colored world during the Age of Imperialism and Jim Crow.

The expansion of U.S. and European empire also showed the heightened importance of Haiti. The belief that Haiti was a shining beacon of militant black resistance to white oppression and virile black manhood during the emasculating depths of racial segregation and colonialism was front and center at the Chicago World's Fair. At that event, African Americans flocked to the Haitian Pavilion, where Douglass now proudly represented the Haitian government, not the United States. More artistic and journalistic representations of Haiti and the Haitian Revolution soon followed. They presented both as models of black resistance that embattled African Americans could and should emulate.

By the turn of the twentieth century, Haiti was thus central to a transnational politics of defiance.[28] Black journalists were foremost among the African Americans who contrasted the real crimes committed by white southerners with the invented tales of barbarism in Haiti. In bearing witness to the victims of racial violence at home, they vindicated black independence abroad. Theirs was a burgeoning anti-imperial politics in defense of Haiti that contrasted with the concurrent efforts by some black elites to claim citizenship through participation in U.S. empire.[29]

Chapter 4 links those politics to the seemingly disconnected ones that took root amid intensifying investigations of the "Negro problem." As white social scientists continued to insist that Haitians proved that black people were incapable of assimilation into a modern, industrialized society, black spokesmen such as Booker T. Washington relied on Haiti to disprove racist stereotypes used to justify lynching, black disfranchisement, and racial segregation. These proponents of racial uplift, an intraracial *and* international politics of self-help and self-improvement, encouraged Haitians to pursue industrial education in the United States and called for skilled African Americans to move to Haiti and modernize that country.

They were adamant that through these efforts Haiti would become an unassailable model of black self-determination in an era when segregationists and imperialists in the United States and Europe drew the global color line.

To be sure, informed by the stereotyping of black people in Africa and the African Diaspora and often functioning as a civilizing mission, racial uplift ideology buttressed a host of ineffective and detrimental pursuits.[30] It reinforced intraracial class differences and Afro-diasporic hierarchies. It reified U.S. models of development in the United States and overseas. In fact, it motivated William Pickens, a future leader of the National Association for the Advancement of Colored People (NAACP), to lead the call for the annexation of Haiti by the United States.

Still, the transnational politics of racial uplift rested on potentially subversive foundations. Rather than turning inward as historians have suggested, fin de siècle U.S. black intellectuals looked abroad as they attempted to rehabilitate the image of black people, affirm black respectability, and achieve black progress at a time when white supremacists demanded black subordination. They looked to Haiti and Haitians. Outside of a few strident voices espousing cultural relativism, advancing anti-imperialism, and demanding Afro-diasporic political solidarities, most U.S. black intellectuals struggled to reconcile their imagined connection to Haiti with their strivings for the rights associated with national citizenship. Still, the continued attempts to link domestic and global issues reinforced the enduring idea that U.S. birth was compatible with Afro-diasporic belonging. They provided the most immediate foundations of a reenvisioning of Haiti in a new moment of radical black internationalism.

As Chapter 5 shows, the long-standing importance assigned to and ambivalence about Haiti produced widespread interest among African Americans in the ensuing U.S. occupation of Haiti. When U.S. Marines landed outside of Port-au-Prince, African Americans were undecided about what to do. Could U.S. intervention stabilize Haitian politics? Would African Americans strengthen their claims to political and civil rights by participating in the occupation government? Was it possible to make the U.S. government live up to its progressive ideals?

The ensuing violence of and Haitian resistance to an occupation motivated by the belief that black people could not govern themselves clarified the answer: no. As Haiti groaned under the U.S. occupation that censored the Haitian press, conscripted Haitians to forced labor, seized control of the Haitian treasury, and waged war on the Haitian peasantry, W. E. B.

Du Bois, once a proponent of U.S. intervention in that country, changed course. In his mind, the occupation became evidence of the destructive impact of racism, capitalism, militarism, and imperialism on the entire colored world. He, with the encouragement of Haitian freedom fighters, joined an emerging group of radical black internationalists who, during and after the First World War, imagined the free Black Republic as the foundation of black and working-class emancipation.[31]

Ultimately, *The Black Republic* advances our understanding of black political thought and the ideas of Haiti that have long preoccupied the Western world. Throughout the nineteenth and twentieth centuries, North American and European politicians, diplomats, and military personnel banded together and "produced discourses that intensify the [modern] notion of a progress-resistant, deviant and childlike [Haiti] unaware of the material and ideological benefits of democracy and capitalism."[32] White travel writers and journalists consistently added their own prejudices to those discourses. Time after time, they rendered the creolized religion of Vodou as nothing more than cannibalism, witchcraft, and paganism while characterizing the Haitian state as the bastardized product of the unholy marriage between black inferiority and military despotism. Taken together, these foreign actors popularized an enduring notion of an "enigmatic Haiti, largely produced by the gravitational forces of North American and Western European ideologies of Christianity, capitalism, and whiteness."[33] They rendered Haiti ahistorical and irrational, characterizing it as a black nation with dark pathologies that transcended time.

African Americans participated in those discourses, too. For nineteenth- and early twentieth-century African Americans, the Haitian Revolution confirmed the possibility of freedom from slavery and the ability—perhaps even the necessity or destiny—of all black people to seize their freedom through militant action. The subsequent establishment and long-awaited U.S. recognition of the independent government of Haiti demonstrated the opportunities that freedom presented: self-determination, both communally and personally. African Americans understood the Black Republic as a singular site of and litmus test for black potential.

It was potentially exceptional, too. Reflecting on the modern transformations of deeply rooted historical ideas about Haiti, the late Haitian scholar Michel-Rolph Trouillot wrote that when "we are being told over and over again that Haiti is unique, bizarre, unnatural, odd, queer, freakish, or grotesque, we are also being told, in varying degrees, that it is unnatural, erratic and therefore unexplainable"—or, at the very least, extraordinary.[34] African Americans have been no less complicit in those renderings of Haiti, often representing Haiti as singular (although imitable) in an attempt to manipulate or challenge the more damaging and pejorative assessments of its unique world-historical meaning and its standing in global affairs. Their representations of Haiti and the Haitian Revolution raise a question: What is the historical impact of African American (as distinct from Western) imaginings and articulations of Haitian singularity? Have they simply encouraged the placement of outsized, even unattainable, burdens on Haiti, the much-needed model of black freedom and self-determination? Or have they produced powerful intellectual change, a new envisioning of how black people might replicate the Haitian Revolution and resist the forces that built the racial inequalities of the modern world?

The answer presented in this book is both. From the 1860s to the 1930s, over the course of the long postemancipation era, African Americans offered their own thoughts about Haiti and its people. They did not just react to white racial thought, though. Their ideas—found in the visual and dramatic arts, newspapers and literature, and everyday acts and extraordinary celebrations—sometimes derived from considerable time spent in Haiti and among Haitians. At other times, they came less from amateur ethnographic research or transnational exchange and more from what those black intellectuals thought was true about Haiti: it was black and free and self-governing and that was what mattered. And, ultimately, Haiti *did* matter. It mattered a great deal for African Americans thinking about emancipation and Reconstruction, the uncertain years that preceded the onset of Jim Crow, and the ensuing challenges that rose from the depths of racial segregation and white imperialism. It influenced their imaginings of the means and ends of achieving black freedom in a world that demanded black subservience, imaginings that tended to come full circle and birth new thoughts about Haiti and its people.

In the end, this preoccupation with and reproduction of the ideas of Haiti was not just another piece of a diasporic consciousness or a single moment in a long tradition of black engagement with the world. Instead, it transformed that global engagement and stimulated the rise of the radical black internationalism that took root in the interwar period. Even before the ink had dried on the Emancipation Proclamation, African Americans thought deeply about the connections between freedom and self-determination. Although interpretations of both would differ in the ensuing decades, changing alongside the shifting methods of and threats to achieving what was often characterized as black progress, the conviction that both were connected to Haiti remained. The strength of that conviction produced considerable interest in the U.S. occupation of Haiti. African Americans who condemned Wall Street, the U.S. Marines, and the U.S. government for stripping Haitians of their sovereignty did so in an era when black intellectuals across the African Diaspora reconsidered the conditions and ideologies that would bring about complete black liberation rather than incremental black progress. They knew from a wealth of literature, art, oral traditions, and family history about the importance of Haiti, the singular example of black self-determination that had fallen under white rule. They had long-standing ideas about Haiti from which to draw their own. For those black men and women who would help tear down the U.S. occupation while transforming black thought, there was no doubt about the inspiration for the world they sought to build. It was Haiti. The Black Republic.

CHAPTER 1

Emancipation, Reconstruction, and the Quandary of Haiti

The thousands of enslaved people escaping to Union lines irked James Gordon Bennett, Jr.[1] In January 1863, the *New York Herald*'s editor complained to his readers that the problem or "question of the largely increasing numbers of contrabands now entirely dependent on the United States government for support is becoming a rather perplexing one." "In New Orleans alone, and along the borders of the Mississippi now in the hands of the federal government," the Democrat and anti-abolitionist editor wrote, "there are probably as many negroes as Union soldiers—amounting, necessarily to several thousands." Those "contrabands" placed a great burden on white northerners, he continued. To Bennett, there was no value in "spending such large sums of money to support the slaves who escape from their masters" or voting for "radical" politicians "who sanction these proceedings." There was no honor in helping "fugitives" including the "full colony of blacks, numbering some eight or ten thousand," formed "at a place very appropriately called New Hayti, near Newbern, N.C."[2]

New Hayti. It is possible that the name came from a descendant of one of the "French gentlemen at New Bern who," according to a founder of the University of North Carolina, "are really gentleman and unfortunate refugees from St. Domingo."[3] It might have escaped from the nightmares of white Tar Heels who hated black freedom just as much as they loved slavery. Still, it is at least as likely that the name emerged from the dreams of enslaved people nurtured on tales of the Haitian Revolution. It seemed apt to one Union soldier who found the "fragrant breezes" and "generally intelligent and . . . greatly elated" freedmen of war-torn New Bern reminiscent of "Port-au-Princc, Hayti, its aspect and its mixed population, and its luxuriant breezes."[4]

Whatever the case, the fleeting glimpse of New Hayti highlights the connections among Haiti, emancipation, and the concerns that shaped African Americans' ideas about both. In the final years of the Civil War, freedom became a public experience for countless African Americans. In a variety of intellectual spaces, including contraband camps, emancipation day celebrations, lecture halls, and colored conventions, African Americans shared their ideas about the postemancipation future. In doing so, they often identified relevance in Haiti's past and present. As books addressing Haitian history found a receptive audience among black readers forging new social institutions and embracing new opportunities for education, African Americans across the United States praised the extension of diplomatic relations from their country to Haiti, tried to welcome the first Haitian diplomat sent to Washington, D.C., and paid homage to the Haitian Revolution. From their perspective, those events taking place across time and space were no less urgent than the Emancipation Proclamation. All were signs of collective black progress from bondage and oppression toward freedom and equality.

Such optimism would falter over the course of Reconstruction, though. Black public figures, many of them churchgoing northerners free(d) before the Civil War, often sympathized with black southerners' demands for landownership and labor rights, but they also worried about the extent to which the black freedom, citizenship, and enfranchisement now codified in law would exist in practice. This anxiety shaped their uses of Haiti. Aware of and influenced by the rising tide of scientific racism, the looming discourse and practice of U.S. imperialism, and the prejudices of white Americans who identified Haiti as proof of black inferiority, some African Americans attempted to reform Haiti through U.S. political intervention, missionary work, or both.[5] In fact, by 1877, the African Methodist Episcopal (AME) Church, then the largest black denomination in the United States, developed a foreign mission field meant to imbue Haitians with U.S. middle-class cultural norms, rehabilitate the international image of Haiti, elevate the status of all black people, and place their fitness for self-governance beyond reproach.

This complex intellectual and material engagement with Haiti, an important aspect of the overlooked, international histories of the Reconstruction era, demonstrates the confidence and competing apprehension of African Americans contemplating freedom's meanings. Emboldened by the appointment of a black man as U.S. minister resident and consul general to Haiti and sensing that the end of slavery might presage an era of unprecedented racial egalitarianism, black religious and political leaders expressed a more pronounced patriotism while announcing that they had ascended to the vanguard of their race, surpassing Haitians who worshipped a pantheon of gods and used violence to make political change. The audacity of such statements obscured more substantial anxieties. Unsure about the security of their ascendant status, black spokespersons assigned the much-maligned Haitian "experiment in self-government" great importance. They not only endeavored to speak for an emergent black citizenry in the United States but also tried to renegotiate old racial hierarchies, strengthen their fragile political status, and improve their relationship with the U.S. government by manipulating their connection to Haiti, a nation that they sometimes embraced, otherwise critiqued, but ultimately needed.

The idea that a watershed moment for black people had arrived in 1863 resonated in Washington, D.C. Throughout that year, Caroline Eliot Kasson, a native white southerner married to the representative of Iowa's Fifth Congressional District, maintained a detailed correspondence with the Des Moines–based *Iowa State Register*. Her letters provided Iowans with unique insights into social life and political developments in wartime Washington. They could not avoid race. That subject became more pressing once the United States offered diplomatic recognition to Haiti and Ernest Roumain, the first Haitian consul general and chargé d'affaires to the United States, joined Kasson in the U.S. capital.

In March 1863, Kasson told readers of the *Register* about a "very brilliant" party that she attended at the home of an "aristocratic" Boston congressman. Building up to her stunning revelation, she asked her audience who they thought attended the dinner besides the usual white military officers, diplomats, politicians, and foreign dignitaries. "Guess, and guess again," she teased. "Not right yet? Well! Who indeed but the Haytien Embassy." Kasson wrote as if she was still recovering from the shock too. "It is so," she wrote. "There they were, guests and honored guests, and unmistakably *colored* at that!—It was a new sensation." Kasson noted that she "felt queerly, as though I were having a very funny dream. Two elegant colored gentlemen, white kid gloves, Parisian toilet, conversing in Spanish, French and English, yet most unmistakably darkey." The presence of Roumain's secretary was of particular amazement. The bewildered Kasson told her fellow Iowans that, unlike the "bright copper colored" Roumain, the other Haitian official was a darker-skinned "regular colored representative." His hair even kinked.[6]

Unwittingly, Kasson revealed why the establishment of diplomatic relations between Haiti and the United States mattered to African Americans. She still identified with the white South and, "like any one . . . raised in a slave State," she found it "a little ludicrous to be entertaining people from Hayti." Indeed, Kasson confessed to her readers that she "stared more at them than was quite polite, and found it a little hard to keep my face straight." Yet she did keep her face straight and her manners in mind. Although she found it "droll to see them in society," Kasson reported that she showed Roumain and his secretary respect and admitted that both were "*gentlemen*." Her fellow partygoers allegedly did the same. The European diplomats in attendance "entered into cordial conversation with them," the host "waited upon his dark guests at supper," and no attendee expressed "repugnance to the men whose manners were so gentlemanly."[7] As represented by Kasson, the event held in honor of the Haitian legation was a realization of the visions of citizenship articulated by black abolitionists in the previous decades. It was, in essence, a fulfillment of their hopes that white Americans could see black people not only as voters or public officials but also as compatriots bound to them by ties of mutual affection.[8]

African Americans confirmed as much as they, too, marveled at the injection of blackness into the lily-whiteness of U.S. politics and Washington society. According to white newspaper correspondents in the capital, black Washingtonians disagreed with white residents who insisted that Roumain, an educated "mulatto" who had recently helped Haitian president Fabre Geffrard overthrow Emperor Faustin I and return republicanism to Haiti, was not a "negro."[9] The "colored folks hereabouts," their derisive reports noted, "insist that [Roumain and his secretary] are veritable darkies."[10] In fact, they continued, the "upper ten of the African persuasion" had tried to "effect an *entente cordiale*" with Roumain and get the Haitian diplomat to "champion their cause."[11]

That cause—moving from slavery to freedom to full citizenship—animated the black elite, but freedpeople were no less invested in Roumain. Soon after the Haitian diplomat and his secretary arrived in Washington, D.C., a white newspaper correspondent reported that black Washingtonians "held a meeting, and decided to establish intimate relations with them by sending their ministers to wait upon them first, and then the common negroes were to follow."[12] Henry McNeal Turner, the famous pastor of Washington, D.C.'s Union Bethel Church who later championed black emigration from the United States to Liberia, corroborated that account. In March 1863, he told readers of the *Christian Recorder*, the organ of the AME Church and the most-circulated black paper in the country, that Roumain was "attracting no little attention among all classes of society," including "several of our people [who] have called on him." Even more had apparently come to see Turner. "I have been asked by fifty person [*sic*], Why, have you not called on the Haytien minister?," the prominent AME minister complained. "Ain't you going to," the "pride-touched parties" demanded, the main clue to their identity the vernacular in which Turner rendered their speech.[13]

Unfortunately, the Haitian diplomat appears to have been no more sympathetic than Turner to the overtures from African Americans who felt empowered by his egalitarian relationship with their federal government. The same white journalists who complained about the "Abolitionists" who tried to introduce Roumain and his secretary "into white society" also circulated reports that the Haitian legation quickly "sent a message to the negro preachers, the purpose being that 'They were not receiving calls from negroes just yet.' "[14] Again, Turner substantiated those allegations. He informed readers of the *Christian Recorder* that Roumain "confines himself strictly to the society of his diplomatic peers" and "sternly refused to receive visiters [*sic*], unless those who rank equally with himself."[15] His social circle was apparently at the majority-white St. Matthews Catholic Church, not the Union Bethel or any other black church in the city.[16]

What were African Americans to make of this snub? White newspapers, many of them eager to diminish the changes wrought by emancipation, reported that the "cool proceeding took the darkies aback, and some of them have since then made no reserve in venting their indignation at this treatment." That airing of grievances allegedly took place during a meeting at a black church in Washington, D.C., where attendees concluded "that the Haytiens were negroes, and had no right to act like white men." In fact, one widespread article purported, a "venerable old contraband . . . a preacher before he came out of the land of slavery . . . wound up a long strain of invective as follows: 'Dese d—d furrin niggers tink demselbs better dan de President. Massa Ole Abe let de cullered folks come into de White House, and talks to them like a fader, and here's dese cusses won't look at 'em. I isn't gwine to hab nuffin more to do wid 'em,' the old contraband concluded. 'I isn't.' "[17]

It is plausible that a freedman reacted with anger to a rebuke that reeked of colorism and elitism. It is just as possible, though, that the reported response, absent from black-authored sources, was the product of white imaginations, not black indignation. While the words of the "venerable old contraband" cohere with how some freedpeople venerated Abraham Lincoln after his signing of the Emancipation Proclamation, they also exalt "Massa Ole Abe" at the expense of "d—d furrin niggers."[18] That unique juxtaposition diminished Afro-diasporic solidarities, assuring readers that Haitians might have a seat at the table but African Americans would still receive nothing but scraps. It presented white politicians as paternalistic fathers who could dole out freedom as they saw fit and black people as helpless children reliant on white benevolence.

While the actual reaction of "contraband" to Roumain's reclusiveness is ambiguous, the response of elite black Washingtonians and the reasoning for it is clear. Turner insisted that it was not only "justifiable, but highly commendable" for the Haitian diplomat to refuse social calls that might hamper his ability to conduct his professional duties. He had not come to Washington on a "visiting excursion." For Turner, excusing Roumain did not amount to "advocating a policy looking to an aristocratical isolation of a man of my race, simply upon the ground that he holds a rank of elevation." Instead, it did the exact opposite. The AME minister argued that Roumain's "uninjuring separateness will effect an object far more advantageous to whom the isolation is made than could be by an open armed embrace."[19] It would allow the Haitian diplomat to focus on his work, demonstrate black political acumen, and advance the national interests of Haiti. It would benefit African Americans in need of strong representations of black self-government.[20]

Turner was not alone in agreeing with the *Christian Recorder* that, regardless of Roumain's behavior, it remained the right moment to emphasize Afro-diasporic solidarities and give "all hail and honor to Hayti."[21] Like Haitians, African Americans had now secured their emancipation in large part due to their own efforts. They wanted more than freedom, however. For a great number of African Americans, the diplomatic recognition of Haiti by the United States was a portent of greater appreciation of their own changing status. It presaged unprecedented respect for their rights and privileges as people born and raised in the United States. It augured greater acknowledgment of their humanity. To honor Haiti was thus earnest and self-serving. It was a means of congratulating the lone black nation-state in the Western Hemisphere for its entrance into the sisterhood of nations while also encouraging African Americans who hoped for an analogous inclusion as free citizens in U.S. public life.

A celebration at the Fifteenth Street Presbyterian Church in Washington, D.C., helped make that connection clear. In April 1863, a crowd filled the "cushioned seats, carpeted aisles, [and] gold-lettered pews" of the prestigious black church pastored by Henry Highland Garnet, a well-known abolitionist and former agent of the Haytian Bureau of Emigration, the agency that the Haitian government and U.S.-based abolitionists founded three years earlier to promote black emigration from the United States to Haiti. They had come there to celebrate the first anniversary of the District of Columbia Compensated Emancipation Act.[22] The commemoration of legislation that freed more than three thousand enslaved people in the nation's capital while compensating their former owners featured a number of prominent speakers, including William E. Matthews, a leading black activist and educator from Baltimore. Standing on the elevated platform before the large audience, Matthews proclaimed that African Americans "should celebrate . . . Toussaint L'Ouverture, who worked successfully the greater than mathematical problem that they who would be free must first strike the blow." African Americans, he continued between eruptions of applause from the pews, had to appreciate that Louverture "turned Hayti from a hell of slavery to a paradise of freedom, and America had been forced to recognize her nationality, and to-day we have a black man representing her here." Those developments were clear signs "that this is the beginning of a better time for the race."[23]

To Frederick Douglass, the most famous black man in the United States, the symbolic importance of Roumain was just as obvious. In an editorial appearing in his *Douglass' Monthly*, Douglass called the diplomatic recognition of Haiti by the United States one of the most remarkable developments "in the history of the relation of this Government to the colored part of mankind." That claim rested on his familiarity with the denial of Haiti's independence during the antebellum era. Douglass reminded his readers of Haiti's diplomatic isolation, remembering that southern politicians had dismissed the "thought of receiving at Washington a colored minister, from a colored Republic." Their objections, he continued, carried great weight as the U.S.

government acquiesced to the belief that "the introduction of a colored diplomatist at the Capital would be a direct insult to slavery, and an open invitation to an Insurrection of the slaves." The status quo had changed, though. Douglass rejoiced that Haiti was now "recognized, and her minister, an accomplished gentleman and scholar, is received, and will be treated with the respectful consideration due to himself and his country." Like his contemporaries, Douglass knew that it was the right time to "hail the recognition of Haiti." In his estimation, Roumain was not just the long-awaited representative of a sovereign black republic but also an "unmistakable sign of the doom of caste and dawn of higher civilization."[24]

Douglass's editorial advanced long-standing discourses that equated the nation-state with racial capacity and reflected rhetorical traditions that encouraged hyperbole and argumentation.[25] Still, it cohered with a current, widespread response to Haiti's diplomatic recognition that extended far beyond the boundaries of the nation's capital. In the same moment that Douglass offered his reflections in *Douglass' Monthly*, black Chicagoans came together for an annual celebration. For decades, hundreds of men, women, and children, like black people in other cities and towns throughout the U.S. North, had celebrated the anniversary of the 1833 Slavery Abolition Act, which abolished slavery throughout Great Britain's colonies.[26] In August 1863, however, the enthusiasm reached new heights. That summer morning, scores of black Chicagoans crowded onto six railroad cars bound for a suburban grove, where they met large delegations of black people from Detroit, St. Louis, and Milwaukee. After arriving at the festival grounds, the attendees listened to speeches, sang hymns, and played sports. The jubilation was palpable as the crowd celebrated not only the anniversary of freedom in the British West Indies but also the Emancipation Proclamation and the long-awaited diplomatic recognition of Haiti by the United States.[27]

For one black Midwesterner, the year of jubilee was nothing less than the beginning of an era prophesied in the Bible. In a letter to the *Christian Recorder*, W. J. Davis, an Indiana-based AME minister enslaved before the Civil War, wrote that he once called on Abraham Lincoln at his Springfield law office. The future president, after hearing about Davis's sale at auction, offered a strong condemnation of the "wretched system" of slavery. This encounter, Davis continued, made him unsurprised by what Lincoln had "done to free so many millions of our poor down-trodden people in the South." Indeed, it made him optimistic about the potential impact of a politician who commiserated in private with black people, issued the Emancipation Proclamation, and authorized the diplomatic recognition of Haiti. Davis asked readers of the *Recorder* whether any president had ever considered the prospect of general emancipation or entertained the thought of acknowledging Haitian independence. Certainly not, he replied. Implying that the recent acts of his old acquaintance were just the start of a renaissance of black social and political life, Davis rejoiced that "Ethiopia [was] stretching out her hands to God."[28]

Davis's reference to Psalm 68:31, the prediction that "Princes shall come out of Egypt; Ethiopia shall soon stretch out her hands unto God," would have been widely understood given its ubiquity during the antebellum era.[29] The Ethiopian Prophecy was a central part of nineteenth-century black nationalism, a malleable ideology centered on the belief that people of African descent were a distinct nation that had to unite on the principles of racial pride, political and economic self-determination, and civilized progress. For proponents of it, Psalm 68:31 confirmed that God had a greater purpose for allowing the Transatlantic Slave Trade. It encouraged their belief in the Fortunate Fall, the idea that God sanctioned the enslavement of black people in order to bring them civilization and prepare them to redeem Africa from its fallen condition.[30]

Still, even African Americans who knew of the Ethiopian Prophecy and had long found personal meaning in the stories and prophecies of the Old Testament knew that God's work sometimes warranted further explication. Accordingly, black writers and readers, orators and audiences, educators, and political representatives throughout and even outside of the United States clarified individual and collective understandings of freedom that were intertwined with ideas about Haiti. They often did so for themselves, their black and white compatriots, and international audiences alike. All of those public acts of speaking and writing about Haiti were crafted to confirm that, in the words of Frederick Douglass, the diplomatic recognition of Haiti was just one of "Freedom's gains" emboldening the "friends of Freedom" throughout the Atlantic World. They were aspirational words and actions meant to highlight the international "irreversible results" that had supposedly placed racial slavery and caste on an inevitable path to extinction.[31]

Black authors who hoped to cement racial equality as the foundation of a new era published favorable narratives of the Haitian Revolution. In 1863, the abolitionist William Wells Brown completed *The Black Man: His Antecedents, His Genius, and His Achievements*. The formerly enslaved writer described his work as a direct challenge to "the calumniators and traducers of the Negro" who claimed that black people "were destined only for a servile condition, entitled neither to liberty nor the legitimate pursuit of happiness." He wanted to show that African Americans could meet all the responsibilities of citizenship by presenting biographical sketches of "individuals who, by their own genius, capacity, and intellectual development, have surmounted the many obstacles which slavery and prejudice have thrown in their way."[32] Brown could have relied on the achievements of African Americans to prove his point, yet he chose to highlight Haitians.

The Black Man contains biographies of Toussaint Louverture, Jean Jacques Dessalines, and six other men of African descent who shaped Haitian history. The account of Louverture, taken from one of Brown's earlier works, *St. Domingo: Its Revolution and Its Patriots*, describes the governor-general of Saint-Domingue from 1796 to 1801 as a man of great "humanity, generosity, and courage" who attained that position due to his unsurpassed "genius." Moreover, it contends that Louverture achieved success not only because he possessed "high qualities of mind" but also because he had great capacity for self-development. The latter point was especially critical. Brown's treatment of Louverture emphasizes that "from ignorance [Louverture] became educated by his own exertions" and "from a slave he rose to be a soldier, a general, and a governor."[33] Louverture, then, did not merely demonstrate individual black genius and achievement—he made obvious the collective ability of black people to rise from slavery, thrive in freedom, and exercise a central right of male citizens: political leadership.

While his description of Louverture complemented standard treatments of the "first of the blacks," Brown's interpretation of Dessalines, the first head of state of independent Haiti, was more exceptional. According to Brown, the "untamed ferocity" that drove Dessalines to condemn thousands to death also made him a laudable example of black intelligence. In particular, the "savage" and "barbarous" tactics employed by Dessalines matched the "ferocious and sanguinary spirit" of the French and proved vital to the defense of his fledgling country. Brown concluded that Dessalines's vindication of "the rights of the oppressed in that unfortunate island" was evidence that a free and autonomous black people could replicate the force and cunning that white people considered effective means of political and military leadership.[34]

There is little doubt that external interests influenced *The Black Man*. At the outset of the 1860s, Brown worked for the Haytian Emigration Bureau, the U.S.-based immigration agency that the Haitian government financed to bring black refugees from the United States to Haiti. James Redpath, a Scottish abolitionist, was the head of the bureau, which collapsed with the waning interest in emigration during what abolitionists called the Abolition War. Since the "Haitian fever" broke and one-time supporters including Henry Highland Garnet and Brown distanced themselves from the bureau, Redpath had turned his energies to publishing works that presented Haitian history in a manner that would not only justify emancipation but also bolster the Union recruitment of black soldiers.[35] *The Black Man* was one of his projects. It stands to reason that, as its publisher, he played a role in how Brown presented Louverture and Dessalines.

Nonetheless, Brown's representations of Haiti's founding fathers ultimately reflect the thoughts and priorities of a once enslaved man turned author who was attempting to establish a usable past for navigating the uncertain path from slavery to freedom to full citizenship. Haiti was vital to his efforts in this regard. Brown made it clear that noteworthy Haitians had become remarkable statesmen—even leaders of nations—despite feeling the callous whip of slavery and the harsh stings of racism. As he looked to a future in which African Americans might have to fight for full political and civil equality after transcending bondage, Brown asked white Americans a simple question: If Haitians could rise to such heights then what might be the potential of African Americans?

While often aimed at white audiences, *The Black Man* and similar works still found a receptive readership among literate African Americans. Throughout 1863 and 1864, the *Christian Recorder* kept Brown's work on its list of recommended books while *Douglass' Monthly* maintained that it "should find its way into every school library—and indeed, every house in the land."[36] The *Recorder* also included a biography of Toussaint Louverture on its list of recommended books for sale until the demand for it exceeded their supply.[37] In January 1864, the AME organ capitalized on this clear interest in Haitian history by offering a copy of the "work that every colored lady and gentleman ought to have" to the first person who could guarantee the paper twenty-five new subscribers.[38] Unsurprisingly, the offer proved irresistible. Three months later, a black Missourian preaching along the Mississippi River took the prize.[39]

In fact, even as the life of Louverture obtained special relevance for a minister working in a border state where the transition away from slavery remained contested, African Americans living abroad expressed a similar yearning for books on Haiti. Daniel and James Adger were the sons of a formerly enslaved man who had moved from South Carolina to Philadelphia and became a successful furniture dealer. After attending the Lombard Street School, a public school for black pupils founded by two white educators, the brothers decided to venture to Australia rather than join the family business.[40] James opened a profitable hairdressing salon in Melbourne while Daniel wrote as the *Christian Recorder's* Australian correspondent when he found time away from his shopkeeping job. In May 1864, he ended one of his earliest reports on his experiences in Australia with a request for books on Toussaint Louverture, Fabre Geffrard, and "many others of distinguished negroes, and any pertaining to Liberia, Africa, and St. Domingo, written by colored men, or of Hayti."[41] It is possible that Daniel intended to sell the books to a colony of African Americans who had migrated to Australia in search of gold and "better rights." Or maybe Daniel wanted to keep them as a reminder that, in his words, "the darkest hours are but the preludes to brighter sunshine."[42] In either case, the request further shows that African Americans understood emancipation and the pursuit of equality as processes that connected black people in Australia to their peers in the United States and their forbearers in Haiti.

Books were just one source available to postemancipation-era African Americans eager to draw conclusions about themselves and their world across Afro-diasporic time and space. Public lectures were another. Following emancipation, speakers of African descent across the United States routinely highlighted Haitian history. For instance, in the winter of 1864, an "octoroon orator" in Colorado delivered several lectures entitled "Toussaint l'Ouvreture; or, the Hero of Hayti." The talks, according to one observer, were well-attended and much "appreciated by the intelligent people of color . . . on account of the prejudice existing in the mountain cities against men of color."[43] He implied that each one offered a powerful refutation of racism, assuring black Coloradans that they shared the same qualities as the Hero of Hayti, who belied every racial stereotype imaginable.

Similar lectures appealed to black Virginians, too. As the Civil War reached its final stages, an African American woman claiming to be Haitian lectured in Alexandria, the northern Virginia city that included a historic middle-class black neighborhood named "Hayti."[44] Her talk recounted her escape from slavery before concluding with a "glowing tribute to the memory of the *Negro hero, statesman, and martyr, Toussaint L'Ouverture.*" One attendee noted that the admission fees for the address went toward the establishment of a school for girls in Gonaïves, the city where Dessalines had proclaimed Haitian independence. Although he did not indicate the amount that the lecture raised, it is quite possible that it achieved not only "great applause" but also financial profit.[45] After all, by linking resistance to slavery in the United States with black independence in Haiti, the lecturer attended to the intellectual needs of black audiences who found encouragement in romanticized albeit historical examples of black self-emancipation *and* the black self-governance that it enabled. She made their postemancipation ideals seem possible.

At the end of the Civil War, such visions of freedom and celebrations of Haiti articulated in emancipation celebrations, newspapers, books, and lectures found additional expression in official political gatherings. In the meetings of colored state conventions, a burgeoning black leadership class consisting of abolitionists, veterans of the Union Army, editors, ministers, businessmen, and skilled artisans pressed for full political and civil rights for African Americans. They frequently did so by alluding to the recognition of Haitian independence. In October 1865, the attendees of North Carolina's Colored State Convention hailed "the event of Emancipation, the establishment of the Freedmen's Bureau . . . [and] the recognition of the independence of Hayti."[46] Leading black male Pennsylvanians and Californians echoed the sentiments of their southern counterparts. While a speaker at Pennsylvania's State Equal Rights Convention welcomed the fact that Haiti was now "placed in the same category with other nations of the earth," participants at the California Colored State Convention called for the extension of the franchise to black men. They insisted that a federal government that abolished slavery in Washington, D.C., employed black troops in the Union Army, and formally recognized Haiti ought to heed their call for voting rights and further its commitment to racial equality.[47]

Despite their geographical separation, the participants in these conventions articulated similar goals and shared a common language. At the same time that the Thirteenth Amendment garnered sufficient support for adoption into the U.S. Constitution, black public figures linked their changing fortunes to the contemporary and historical signs of black progress they saw in Haiti. In particular, they derived inspiration from the triumph of the Haitian Revolution and the diplomatic recognition of the country forged in its aftermath. From the Atlantic seaboard to the Pacific coast, black spokespersons suggested that a federal government willing to acknowledge an independent black country birthed in slave insurrection would also extend

African Americans the rights and protections needed to evolve from an oppressed people into a self-determining community. What had been achieved in Haiti could be made possible in the United States.

Realizing this goal would prove difficult, though. African Americans who desired the same autonomy won by Haitians confronted the stubbornness of President Andrew Johnson, the unprepared successor to the assassinated Abraham Lincoln and a former slaveowner whose third annual message to Congress stressed the danger of extending the vote to African Americans. "Negroes," Johnson told his fellow politicians in that speech, "have shown less capacity for government than any other race of people." Maligning Haiti, he proclaimed that "no independent government of any form has ever been successful in their hands."[48] Most congressmen believed him. His accusations were gospel to countless white Americans. As Reconstruction progressed, numerous predictions of a coming apocalypse, of a South turned into a hellish imitation of Haiti with the onset of black suffrage, would find their way into public discourse. In one representative piece from January 1868, the editors of the *Charleston Courier* insisted that Haiti warns "this republic of the danger of extending the privilege of the ballot to great masses of the blacks without reference to any preliminary qualifications whatever."[49] It presaged "Negro rule."

In short, diminishing the Haitian past and present became a popular way for white supremacists to condemn black political participation following the defeat of the Confederacy.[50] Such discourses received a mixed response from African Americans. As white Democrats alleged that "negro anarchy" in Haiti proved the absurdity of the "atrocious negro supremacy policy of our radical Congress," thousands of black citizens realized the promises of the Thirteenth and Fourteenth Amendments, began voting for public officials, assumed elected office themselves, and laid the groundwork for the first albeit fleeting instance of biracial democracy in U.S. history.[51] To that end, black religious and political leaders in the urban North attempted to strengthen their tenuous position in national life by repurposing the ideas of Haiti. They sometimes claimed superiority over Haitians to assert their cultural progress, advancing anti-Haitian stereotypes in the process. In other moments, they characterized Haiti as a unique proving ground for black diplomats from the United States. Both actions rested on the assumption that Haiti, so central to imaginings of emancipation, was no less important to the eventual outcome of Reconstruction.

As African Americans considered the meaning of Haiti, they also grappled with scientific racism. In fact, the two processes became intertwined. Educated black intellectuals were keenly aware of white-authored scholarship that offered supposedly empirical evidence in support of racism. They sometimes viewed Haiti and Haitians through the lens of that racist pseudoscience. It helped generate their ambivalence about both.

By the late 1860s, some of the foremost white scientists, social scientists, and medical doctors in the United States flatly rejected the theory that black inferiority (which they assumed to be obvious) was a product of the social conditions in which black people lived. Instead, they built on earlier ethnographic work and articulated a more rigid racism that presented apparent racial difference as immutable and biological rather than mutable and environmental. Despite the publication of Charles Darwin's *Origin of Species* and other evidence to the contrary, their books and articles continued to represent people of African descent and people of European descent as members of two distinct species with separate origins and unequal capabilities. Such arguments rested on a thin veneer of objectivity. Men unabashed in their disdain for black people made liberal use of previous forays into the faulty pseudoscience of phrenology. Their examinations of human skulls from across the world often produced suspect data that just happened to match a predetermined conclusion palatable to countless white Americans: in intellectual capacity and physical attributes, African Americans had more in common with apes than with white people.[52]

Such findings would eventually receive the ridicule they deserved—a century later. During Reconstruction, however, they remained fashionable and practical in the eyes of a cohort of leading white supremacists.[53] For instance, John Van Evrie went to great lengths to make sure that northern laypeople knew that the inherent inferiority of African Americans advised against the political and civil rights legislation enacted by Radical Republicans. Eschewing academic jargon, the New York physician, editor, and polygenesis theorist argued that the academic research of his day required that "every man and woman . . . in this broad land *must* accept the simple but stupendous truth of white supremacy and negro subordination." To do otherwise—to allow the same politicians who had delivered African Americans from their "normal condition" to now " 'reconstruct' American society on a Mongrel basis"—was pure idiocy.[54]

His allies speculated that doing so was dangerous, too. Appropriating Darwin's doctrine of natural selection to meet their own ends, a number of white southern intellectuals argued that emancipation had placed African Americans into a competition that they were bound to lose. Positioning himself as the friend of the freedman, one writer in the *Southern Review* lamented the plight of African Americans who had entered "into competition . . . with a race whose numbers surround him, as the sea surrounds the sandbar . . . a race who possess every extrinsic advantage . . . the Anglo-Saxons, the ruling race of the world . . . a race, surpassing in all the elements of domination and success, equaled by none on the globe in energy, intellect, courage, determination, shrewdness, avidity, [and] pride."[55] The writer advised African Americans facing extinction to forego their political and civil rights, distance themselves from northern Republicans, and acquiesce to the dominance of white southerners, who would care for them in return for their service as menial laborers. In short, he cautioned them not to attempt "a Hayti in the United States."[56] African Americans had to see or, more accurately, had to be made to see that "emancipation did not work the miracle of perfecting him." On the contrary, it had "terminated the primary shape of his education [slavery]" and assigned him a task of self-determination already proven impossible by "the failures of African rule in the West Indies."[57]

Black intellectuals of the age knew these racist discourses well.[58] It stands to reason, then, that they would influence how Benjamin Tucker Tanner, a college-educated native of Pittsburgh, Pennsylvania, an AME minister, and the editor of the *Christian Recorder*, tried to vindicate the progress of African Americans and the project of Radical Reconstruction by using the status of Haitians as a foil. In an editorial appearing in the November 1868 edition of the *Recorder*, Tanner insisted that the "negroes of the Spanish West Indies and of Brazilian America" were "the lowest of our race on the American continent" because most "were doubtless born in Africa, and [had] never thrown off its barbaric usages" under their Iberian masters. He afforded the "Negroes of the Danish West Indies" a bit more credit. Tanner claimed that they were "a clever set; measurably intelligent, and well to do; but they are not in harmony with the age. Like Denmark, the mother country, they are not up to the ideas that must prevail throughout the American continent." The "British Negroes of the West Indies" came closer to earning his approval. Although Tanner speculated that West Indians were not fully animated by "the spirit of the 19th century," he conceded that the average Jamaican or Barbadian had not "altogether misapplied their thirty years of freedom."[59]

There is no question that Tanner's article disavowed biological determinism while affirming the racial hierarchies becoming entrenched in U.S. racial science and public consciousness. Tanner ranked Europeans, but he organized them on the basis of their supposed cultural peculiarities rather than on their innate biological traits. He then evaluated black populations throughout the Americas according to the degree of their assimilation and the supposed qualities of the Euro-American culture to which they assimilated. In essence, he embraced an older romantic racialism, conceding a superior cultural status to Anglo-Saxons while insinuating that black people were a malleable race that had improved and proven its capabilities once exposed to modern civilization as it existed in the United States, not Haiti.[60]

Tanner, like numerous other black spokesmen of his day, failed to see assimilationism as a form of racism, though. In fact, he reified supposed hierarchies among black people in his rush to deracialize the idea of culture.[61] Having dismissed biological traits as a determinant of racial progress, Tanner boasted that "the American Negro [was] the best type of his race extant." He, Tanner continued, "unlike his brethren, [had] been the pupil of the cool, aspiring, all-conquering Anglo-Saxon." He had "partaken of all of the greatness of his master." Harkening back to arguments made by antebellum white northerners, Tanner suggested that Anglo-Saxons (and, by extension, their black pupils) honed their best characteristics in the United States. In fact, the prominent black journalist proclaimed, African Americans had "learned the *modus operandi* of Republican government [and] Protestant faith" from white Americans and thus become an example for Africans and the African Diaspora. In Tanner's estimation, African Americans were thus a "candle in the great house of Negro darkness and barbarity," lit by God so "that all the millions of Negroes in all parts of this great house may see." They, not Haitians, were at the vanguard of the black race, and none but the "unbeliever" could doubt such a self-evident truth.[62]

Tanner's editorial was not just another iteration of the Fortunate Fall doctrine. Instead, it was an attempt to assign some meaning to the black experience of slavery and oppression *and* assert that the transcendence of both made a promise of Reconstruction—full racial inclusion—possible. As Tanner searched for a silver lining to an enslavement that, in his words, left African Americans with a "deformed mind" and a "mean soul," he also attempted to manipulate a racial stereotype about the imitative rather than creative capabilities of black people. According to the AME minister, the "American Negro has been close by the side of his white brethren . . . and being the most imitative of men, as saith his enemies, he bids fair to rival his great teacher."[63] He had, Tanner suggested, proven so successful at imitation that he had become a full-fledged U.S. citizen indistinguishable from his white counterparts in every respect save the color of his skin.

At the same moment that Tanner issued his paean to assimilationism and black cultural perfectibility, a possible annexation of Haiti by the United States loomed.[64] Following the Civil War, the U.S. government had adopted a pronounced expansionist agenda. Secretary of State William Seward was particularly adamant that the acquisition of a naval base in the Caribbean would deter European expansion in the Western Hemisphere and secure the U.S. regional dominance implied in the Monroe Doctrine. In early 1868, he agreed to a treaty that allowed the United States to lease part of the Dominican Republic's Samaná Bay in exchange for a payment of money and munitions to the Dominican government. An even greater offer soon materialized. Months later, the Dominican president Buenaventura Báez, who had assumed office after several previous inaugurations went unrecognized by rival political factions, asked the United States to take ownership of Samaná Bay and establish a protectorate over the Dominican Republic. The hopes of some influential U.S. politicians exceeded Báez's expectation that these would be the first steps toward the acquisition of his country by the United States. In his final address to Congress, Andrew Johnson proposed the annexation of the Dominican Republic *and* Haiti by the United States. The same president who vetoed the 1866 Civil Rights Act now insisted that he was capable of lending "some effective aid" to the problems that he perceived in Haiti. Even more outlandish was his claim that Haitians had given him their full "consent" to do so.[65]

Johnson's annexation proposal had neither the backing of Haitians nor the support of U.S. congressmen, who tabled his resolution by a vote of 126 to 36. It did, however, spark Tanner's imagination. Tanner was scarcely more impressed by Haitians than he was by Afro-Cubans or Afro-Brazilians. In fact, he informed readers of the *Christian Recorder* that he felt great sadness when writing about Haiti and its people. Echoing the paternalistic sentiments of the U.S. president even while claiming to reject his racism, Tanner romanticized Haitians as a "noble race" whose dearth of "those elements of order, of cool deliberation, of submission to authority, that are ever demanded in a good government" obscured a "record . . . of which the world will yet be proud." He wished that "the land of Toussaint" could fulfill its promise as "the home of freedom, of government, and of true religion" but concluded that it was "vexed by the demon of civil war." That demon had to be "cast out" before Haiti could progress.[66]

The prognosis of the AME minister showed little regard for the complexities of Haitian social life. Tanner portrayed Haitians as uniformly impoverished and uneducated, a homogenous population wholly inferior to African Americans who possessed all the trappings of civilization. In truth, the social stratification that existed among African Americans due in large part to regional differences and the history of interracial sex and rape during slavery was also apparent in Haiti. Some Haitian intellectuals, military officers, and politicians, including the light-skinned Ernest Roumain, shared Tanner's cultural elitism. They, too, distanced themselves from or criticized black folk culture while attempting to consolidate economic power, political leadership, and social prestige among a privileged class of educated urban elites. Like the northern-born AME members who led missions in the postemancipation South, Haitian leaders often comported themselves as bearers of culture whose fluency in European and Euro-American languages, art, politics, and religion demonstrated the progress of their race and gave them a mandate to lead its less developed members. In some respects, their accomplishments encouraged such self-representation. Haitian artists, writers, historians, and diplomats had no trouble surpassing the standards of refinement recognized in Europe and the Americas. For them, the accusation that all Haitians were backward was ludicrous.[67]

So was the allegation that the Haitian state presented a poor representation of black self-government to the world. To be certain, Haitians sometimes decried the imperfections of their country. But such laments were often more akin to the jeremiads that flourished among African Americans and less like an objective assessment of current affairs. In reality, Haiti was far from a failed state. Although some foreigners were preoccupied with the ongoing political tumult that resulted in few casualties when compared to major European and American wars, more flocked to Haiti. They did so because the rural regions, whose governance remained stable even when Port-au-Prince's did not, contributed a steady stream of exports to thriving port cities including Cap-Haïtien. In general, the Haitians who produced those export crops and sustained their families from their plots of land maintained a sustainable existence and constructed enduring social institutions regardless of the intermittent struggles for power that broke out in the capital.[68]

Of course, Tanner overlooked the complexities of Haitian life, missing important points about his own country in the process. A discussion of political violence that focused on Haitians rather than the "all-conquering Saxon" was misguided. For example, estimates of the freedpeople killed by white vigilantes around Shreveport, Louisiana, in one year of Reconstruction reached as high as two thousand. The Freedman's Bureau recorded equally staggering numbers of casualties from other states, including Texas, where more than one thousand African Americans lost their lives to white terrorists between 1865 and 1868. For black southerners the failure to remove a hat in the presence of a white man or woman became one of many capital crimes, an act (or perceived inaction) that white supremacists saw as a measure of disrespect toward them and of the new forms of racial domination erected in the aftermath of slavery. Their lives—black lives—were far cheaper in the postemancipation South than they were in Haiti.[69]

Accuracy was not Tanner's chief goal, however. As the U.S. government investigated the possibilities of overseas territorial expansion, Tanner found little value in exploring the similarities between elites of African descent in Haiti and the United States, investigating the actual dynamics of the Haitian state and nation, or scrutinizing the "*modus operandi*" of local government in the U.S. South. Instead, he possessed great interest in placing African Americans' claim to full citizenship on what he thought was firmer ground. Influenced by scientific racism, shaped by dominant discourses of U.S. exceptionalism, impressed by the material achievements of his country and the industrialization of his native North, and cognizant of the politics of his day, Tanner thought it prudent to prioritize culture and nationality over race. He hoped that African Americans could establish their Americanness by proving themselves successful imperialists.

He was not alone. A number of black intellectuals expressed similar sentiments. They insisted that slavery had prepared educated African Americans to flaunt their level of acculturation, introduce bourgeois U.S. culture to benighted black people abroad, and encourage the development of African societies through civilization, Christianity, and commerce. Much attention has been given to the ideological complexities of those black nationalists who combined affection for Africa with a commitment to ideals rooted in their American experience. But Tanner's writings reveal that this ambivalence had ramifications for Haiti, too. As imagined by the *Christian Recorder* editor and like-minded African Americans, Haiti emerged as the ideal place for African Americans, the proverbial "candle in the great house of Negro darkness," to illuminate.[70]

Tanner was also forthcoming about his preferred method of illumination. In January 1869, a convention of his peers met in Washington, D.C. Although their principal concern was securing the right to vote for black men, participants in the National Convention of the Colored Men of America could not avoid the issue of annexation. On the third day of the meeting of leading black men, two black newspaper editors offered up the following resolution for adoption: "Whereas we are in sympathy with our kindred and blood, and in view of advancing Republicanism, and the unsettled state of the Spanish Government, *Resolved*, That we ask Congress to institute negotiations for the annexation of Cuba and Hayti, or of their acceptance of the American flag."[71] To Tanner's dismay, the resolution garnered little reaction. He admonished convention attendees for cheering the news of the election of the Missouri Republican Carl Schurz, a vocal opponent of U.S. territorial expansion, to the U.S. Senate while greeting the annexation resolution with a more tepid response. The latter, he insisted, was much more critical than the former. Tanner explained that the sentiment expressed in the proposed resolution was one "that should predominate in the heart of every civilized and Christian Negro of the world." It had, he concluded, "the ring of Negro unity and identity."[72]

Negro unity did not mean ethnic equality, however. Instead, Tanner continued to insist that the best way for African Americans to demonstrate their race pride was to emphasize rather than transcend the national boundaries that separated black people in the Americas. The editor of the most circulated black newspaper in the United States told "Christian Negroes . . . to act the mother to our race, to bring it up to a well developed manhood." They, he continued, possessed a unique burden to redeem their benighted brethren, a mandate to alleviate the "poverty" and "shame" of Haitians because the "strong [had] to bear the infirmities of the weak."[73]

Intentional or not, there was clear irony in Tanner's call to duty. Decades before he assigned educated African Americans the responsibility of performing "the mother's part to our race," thousands of black emigrants from the United States welcomed the appeals of Haitian officials who insisted that Haiti would "become . . . a tender Mother" to their afflicted brethren.[74] The history of African Americans' flight from slavery and oppression in the United States to freedom and citizenship in Haiti survived.[75] The migrants who had moved to Haiti during the antebellum and

Civil War eras and remained Haitian citizens embodied it. Yet Tanner transposed this familial metaphor with ease, claiming what seemed to him a preordained place at the forefront of the black race.

The idea that Haitians might not embrace their infantilization does not seem to have occurred to Tanner. If it did, he assigned it little weight. After a congressman from Indiana introduced a joint resolution for the immediate annexation of the Dominican Republic by the United States, Tanner demurred, wondering why Haiti was not included in the proposed measure. Should "the countrymen of Toussaint," he asked readers of the *Christian Recorder*, also "be taken by the hand and . . . accounted American citizens?" "With all our heart," he replied, "we say, *Yea Lord, and Amen.*" Tanner promised that civil war and the "*spirit* of anarchy" would vanish from annexed Haiti. The "streams of their fair valleys" would flow without the stain of "their children's blood" as lawless elements came to see "that the sword of justice was unsheathed." Haitian economic and social life would improve, too. Tanner predicted that "common schools would be opened" and "trade would revive" following annexation. He boasted that Americans would "ensure protection to invested capital" while guaranteeing that Haitian "children would no longer grow up to ignorant manhood." Finally, Haitians would gain unprecedented exposure to Protestantism. Tanner expected that the "Bible would have free circulation and men would learn to walk in the light of it . . . truth would not be manacled nor tripped." He believed that the "beneficent results" of annexation were clear. Not only would African Americans vindicate their Americanness by augmenting the U.S. imperial project but Haitians would accrue innumerable "blessings" from their subordination to the United States. They would become animated by the "peculiar force" that only "annexation would give."[76]

According to Tanner, annexation presented a unique opportunity for white Americans, too. While propagandizing the annexation measure, the *Christian Recorder* editor provided his readers with a brief history lesson. "We rejoiced at our late war," Tanner remembered, "for we were persuaded that it was of the Lord, and that it meant liberty." Ignoring the fact that Lincoln suppressed both wartime emancipation measures, Tanner recalled that African Americans "rejoiced at [John C.] Frémont's Missouri Proclamation and [David] Hunter's Edict" because both gave "liberty to the oppressed." In a less contestable recollection, Tanner reminded readers that "we hailed the final First of January Proclamation with tears, and prayers and laughter." Why had they done so? "Because," Tanner proclaimed, "we viewed all these as evidences that our long night was passing away, and that the morning approached." Now another sign of that deliverance from misery was available. The AME minister concluded that "the proposition to extend the Stars and Stripes over Hayti" was "akin" to the abolitionist acts proposed and enacted during the Civil War. It was "a continuation of the good work which God has begun to do for the Negro and for the word." The congressmen considering the current annexation proposal could therefore demonstrate their commitment to the continued "uplifting of black humanity" by voting in favor of it.[77] They could earn the respect of Tanner and prove themselves enlightened men by usurping control of the singular example of black self-government in the Western Hemisphere.

Religious fervor was not the only inspiration for Tanner's excitement about U.S. territorial expansion. Instead, his favorable allusion to the Stars and Stripes was a sign of the patriotism then taking hold of countless African Americans. In churches, schools, Union League clubs, and other black social and political institutions that emerged during Reconstruction, black ministers, teachers, students, and former soldiers celebrated the United States. They hung pictures of Abraham Lincoln, U.S. flags, and framed reproductions of the Emancipation Proclamation. They recited the Declaration of Independence and sang "My Country, 'Tis of Thee." Those patriotic actions were a useful means of distinguishing African Americans from treasonous Confederates and strengthening their claims to the rights and benefits of U.S. citizenship. Still, they just as often stemmed from genuine belief in the principles established in the Declaration of Independence and seemingly realized with the Emancipation Proclamation. In the same moment that Tanner expressed his support for the U.S. government, a fellow AME minister prefaced a singing of "Oh! Be True to Our Flag" with the prediction that "The time is fast approaching, when we as citizens of the United States, will be respected as such."[78] He, too, had a new love for *his* country or, at the very least, optimism about what it finally could become.

For a number of black public figures, their hope for a biracial democracy was intertwined with their interest in black diplomatic representation in Haiti. Prior to Reconstruction, African Americans had great interest in but limited formal influence on U.S. foreign policy. Certainly, the U.S. government gave no thought to the appointment of black diplomats who would represent it overseas. Times were changing, though. Following the end of slavery and the U.S. diplomatic recognition of Liberia and, most important,

FIGURE 1. Benjamin Tucker Tanner, 1898. The portrait's inscription, "Your dear Papa, Benjamin Tucker Tanner, Kansas City, Kansas 3–30–98," is addressed to Tanner's son, the prolific artist Henry Ossawa Tanner. Henry Ossawa Tanner Papers, Archives of American Art, Smithsonian Institution.

Haiti, African Americans did not just celebrate the symbolic importance of a black country that was birthed in slave insurrection and now apparently welcomed into the international community. Instead, they identified Haiti as a practical site to confirm their capacities as U.S. citizens. In the estimation of black spokesmen, the U.S. government could reinforce its commitment to racial equality and its faith in black self-governance by appointing a black man as its diplomatic representative to the Black Republic.

Ebenezer Don Carlos Bassett had strong qualifications for and interest in becoming the first black diplomat in U.S. history. Born in Connecticut to parents of African, Euro-American, and Pequot descent, Bassett was an outstanding student who graduated with honors from the Connecticut State Normal School before continuing his education at Yale College. He eventually moved to Philadelphia. In the City of Brotherly Love, Bassett became the principal of Philadelphia's Institute for Colored Youth (ICY), a prestigious school that, even before changing its name to Cheyney University, counted a number of well-known abolitionists, activists, artists, and politicians among its alumni. While Bassett nurtured a generation of black leaders that included one student named Toussaint L'Ouverture Martin, acted as the ICY's librarian, taught mathematics, classics, and natural sciences, *and* oversaw his school's operations, he also held ambitions that stretched far beyond the field of black education.[79] As early as 1867, Bassett put in a request for the position of U.S. minister resident and consul general to Haiti. Having attained a similar stature as his good friend Frederick Douglass, his hope was not unrealistic.[80]

Bassett was not only interested in the diplomatic post in Port-au-Prince but also confident that his application would merit serious consideration. He was, of course, well qualified to hold a position of such prominence. Just as important, he had the backing of influential black and white men. His most vocal supporters included white politicians from Connecticut, Rhode Island, and Pennsylvania; twelve professors from Yale, where Bassett had studied French among other subjects; John Mercer Langston, inspector general for the Freedmen's Bureau; George T. Downing, the president of the National Executive Committee of Colored Men; and Frederick Douglass. Douglass expressed a prevalent sentiment when he congratulated Bassett for trying to ensure that "competent colored citizens" represented their country abroad. In his opinion, Bassett's appointment as U.S. minister resident and consul general to Haiti would bring satisfaction to Haitians and the "millions of colored citizens of the United States" alike.[81]

Bassett's own assurance that he would "uphold the honor of our country" and protect "the glory and dignity of its flag" did not sway Andrew Johnson.[82] Instead, Johnson offered the position to Langston, a dedicated Republican who promptly refused the opportunity. Although circumspect about the rationale for this decision—he would later claim that he simply had "no disposition whatever to accept this foreign place"—it is possible that he based it, at least in part, on his intimate knowledge of Johnson's antagonistic relationship with African Americans.[83]

That Johnson exhibited a remarkable degree of anti-black prejudice even for his era was obvious to his black contemporaries. It had become clear to Frederick Douglass years before. Looking through a driving rain alongside other attendees at the second inauguration of Abraham Lincoln, Douglass had his initial introduction to the white Tennessean then being sworn in as vice president. "The first expression which came to his face, and which I think was the true index of his heart, was one of bitter contempt and aversion," Douglass recalled thinking. Turning to the wife of the most successful black caterer of the day, he acknowledged what the "frown of the man" had made plain: "Whatever Andrew Johnson may be, he is no friend of our race."[84]

Aspirational black men caught between the antagonisms of Andrew Johnson and their desire for federal political appointments would find relief in the election of the Republican Ulysses S. Grant in 1868. The arrival of the famed Union general in the White House brought renewed hope that African Americans would benefit from the patronage politics of the era and gain access to key diplomatic positions, all while serving an administration sympathetic to their visions of racial equality. In May 1869, a committee of black Republicans from Baltimore presented the new president with a list of African Americans deemed suitable for diplomatic service in Africa and Latin America. While the black Baltimoreans looked favorably on the federal posts in Costa Rica, El Salvador, Honduras, Colombia, and other countries, they preferred that black leaders including Bassett, Downing, and Douglass first receive consideration for an appointment to Haiti. In their estimation, sending any of these men there would confirm their capacities as U.S. citizens and the significance of Haiti as an independent black country. It would affirm the new position "occupied by <u>our</u> people" and prove "the competence of the leading men of our race."[85]

The pursuit of the Haitian post was competitive, but Bassett ran a strong campaign. According to the *New York Times*, the "colored people of intelligence" throughout the North "warmly pressed" for the appointment of the accomplished black educator.[86] Black Republicans in Philadelphia, Baltimore, and Washington, D.C., also petitioned Grant on Bassett's behalf, asking him to give the black Philadelphian a job for which a white man was not suited due to the rampant racism of the day. Even his would-be competitors rallied behind him. For instance, Downing informed Grant that African Americans would view Bassett's appointment as an acknowledgement of their enhanced political status.[87] Bassett echoed these sentiments in his own overtures to Grant. In one petition submitted on his own behalf, he assured the president that he was a "representative colored man" whose appointment to the diplomatic post would "be hailed . . . especially by the recently enfranchised colored citizens." It would be, he wrote, "a marked recognition of our new condition in the Republic and an auspicious token of our great future."[88]

Grant was convinced. In April 1869, he selected Bassett as the U.S. minister resident and consul general to Haiti. Bassett achieved his goal in becoming his country's first black diplomat.

In the following weeks, the newest member of the U.S. diplomatic corps received an enthusiastic reception among African Americans, particularly in northern cities. The Philadelphia Bethel AME Church held a banquet for him, AME officials asked Bassett to deliver an address at their annual conference, and the "best class of the colored and white people" held a formal reception in his honor at New York City's historic Shiloh Presbyterian Church.[89] Those New York festivities were especially exuberant. There, following an opening prayer, William P. Powell delivered introductory remarks to his "fellow citizens." In the estimation of the black abolitionist, Bassett's appointment was "one of the most auspicious events within the history of American civilization." Recognizing that fact, the most respectable black people from all across New York City had not assembled to "be tried before a high court of a malignant American negro hate . . . to demand of this nation personal liberty for ourselves and children . . . [or] to prove or to disprove the superiority of one race of men over another." Those days, Powell thundered, were gone. Instead, his people had come together in acknowledgment that they were "now living in an age of political elevation and progressive civilization." From the impending ratification of the

Fifteenth Amendment to the elevation of black men to diplomatic posts, all signs pointed to the dawning of a new era in which "negro slavery and its terrible concomitants" would be relegated to the dustbins of history and cast off into the "dark shades of oblivion."[90]

Powell did not stop there. Changes in African Americans' attitudes toward their country, he continued, should complement their sense of unprecedented historical change. Powell admitted that there was once a time when African Americans "looked upon the United States Constitution, and the Stars and Stripes with loathing and utter contempt; because they gave to the *slave-owners* of the South, and the *slaveholders* of the North . . . the power to enforce the atrocious laws to keep in perpetual slavery four millions of our race." But that time, too, had passed. Powell argued that cause for greater patriotism among African Americans had emerged since the abolition of slavery, the granting of voting and political rights to black men, and the appointment of leading black men to federal office. Now, Powell insisted, "the Stars and Stripes look holier and shine brighter in the glorious sunlight of a righteous civil government." He further linked the cause of black equality and opportunity to vocal patriotism for their country.[91]

After Powell relinquished the stage, the keynote speaker struck a harmonious note. John J. Zuille, cashier of the Freedman's Bank, opened the ensuing reception with an equally glowing paean to the U.S. government and black progress. The black people seated before him were not there to listen "to the dying groans of the institution which dehumanized the black man and degraded the white man." No, Zuille insisted, the sole reason for the gathering was to celebrate Bassett, a man who embodied the incredible transformation in the status of African Americans. Yesterday, that "despised race" was chattel; today, it counted a diplomat. For that, Zuille thanked "our noble President" and praised Bassett. Turning to address the guest of honor, Zuille commended him and spoke to the historical significance that Bassett had achieved already. He noted that Bassett was going to Haiti "as the representative of the United States . . . as one of the colored race . . . [and] as an American citizen." What better captured the changes wrought by the Civil War, a "bloody revolution" that toppled the Slave Power and invalidated *Dred Scott*?[92]

When it was his turn to speak, Bassett built upon that last point. Although he thought that there was "not a colored man in the whole country who [had] not pledged to me his prayers for my success," Bassett was too humble to "believe that this public expression [was] designed to honor me only." He announced that the praise heaped upon him suggested a greater "appreciation of the recognition of our new status, under the new interpretation of our laws, and under a higher civilization." In fact, like Powell, Bassett made the astute observation that receptions held in his honor highlighted a "nobler patriotism." The "colored people of New York had come together to say God bless our noble Ulysses S. Grant for the noble stand he had taken," for taking "hold of the helm of the Ship of State" and "guiding it with a steadiness and integrity of purpose never before known." They had gathered, Bassett knew, because the "appointment of one of our race . . . not of the black man alone, but as the representative of the United States" was the clearest sign that African Americans and the nation writ large had arrived at that "glorious day, for which our fathers had labored for 200 years." His listeners confirmed that they did, in fact, share Bassett's "elevated patriotism."[93] The reception ended with a stirring rendition of "Auld Lang Syne." As African Americans bid farewell to the literal and metaphorical enslavement of yesteryear, even Scottish poetry assumed new meaning.[94]

Still, a paradox complicated this optimism. Even as it acquiesced to black political participation at home, the United States government disregarded black self-determination abroad by considering the annexation of Haiti. That contradiction begged explanation. Zuille attempted to explain the divergent paths of U.S. domestic and foreign policy by assigning Bassett the same role that Tanner envisioned for the "best type" of African Americans. He told the new diplomat that he was going "from this Government to a nation now, unfortunately, in a state of revolution." It was up to Bassett to "contribute to a better state of feeling in that country" and elevate his Haitian pupils in the same way that he uplifted children at the ICY.[95] In essence, a seeming paradox was no paradox at all. At the same time that some white Americans argued that a Haitian state in "a chronic state of revolution" was in need of "the blessings of our government," Zuille insisted that African Americans could play a key role in that civilizing mission.[96] He suggested that Haitians would appreciate their tutelage while leaving unsaid the benefits that would accrue to African Americans in this role: validation of their contributions to U.S. political life and proof of their cultural sophistication and capacity for responsible citizenship.

Zuille could speak without making explicit reference to annexation. The man he envisioned as the vanguard of enlightened U.S. republicanism in

Haiti could not. For Bassett, it was impossible to separate his diplomatic responsibilities from the debates about territorial expansion that swirled about the United States. He revealed as much in one interview with the Washington correspondent of the *New York Herald*. Conducted just before his departure from the United States to Haiti, the interview covered Bassett's final debriefing from Grant. Bassett told the newspaper correspondent that he, the president, and Postmaster General John Creswell smoked cigars as they engaged in a "free and cordial" conversation about "the resources of Hayti, its history, customs of the people, &c." Creswell examined an encyclopedia throughout the conversation while, at one point, Grant stood and opened a giant map of the Caribbean. Eventually the subject turned to annexation. Perhaps being too candid with the Washington journalist, Bassett reported that Grant "was very emphatic, and at the same time very cautious in expressing himself about the policy of annexation." The same might have been said of Bassett. Presaging the stance taken by Frederick Douglass in regard to the Dominican Republic, he admitted that "his own views were in favor of such policy, but he thought in all cases the people of a country to be annexed should first show themselves anxious for union with us." Only then "would it be a subject for the consideration of our Government."[97]

If Bassett meant to assuage concerns about unwelcome incursions into Haitian affairs, he also raised questions about the intentions of the U.S. government in Haiti. Bassett told his interviewer that, after he thanked Grant for honoring his "patriotism, honesty, fidelity, and industry," the president expressed his high hopes for Bassett's diplomatic tenure. Grant, Bassett recalled, said that he "felt there could be some advantage to be derived from my appointment to Hayti; that being accredited to a people of the same race as myself I would be received with more cordiality, and be enabled perhaps to be of more service to the United States."[98] In the political climate of the day, that statement demanded scrutiny. Given the Grant administration's stated interest in territorial acquisitions in the Caribbean, it stood to reason that U.S. officials would assign a practical purpose to the shared histories that bound disparate communities across the African Diaspora. For them, it was logical that an African American acting on behalf of his government and (presumably) in the interests of his race could secure material or territorial concessions from Haitians. After all, one caught more flies with honey than with vinegar.

This first test of "colored diplomacy" began in earnest on June 5, 1869. That afternoon, black people representing several different countries came together on the docks of New York City for the common purpose of wishing Bassett a safe passage to Haiti. The well-wishers included the African American abolitionist William Whipper, the Haitian diplomat Evariste Laroche, and Joseph Jenkins Roberts, the once and future president of Liberia. Once again, though, William P. Powell took charge of the proceedings. Seizing another opportunity to comment on the ascending status of African Americans, he recalled that "in our form of American civilization it has heretofore been the custom . . . to denationalize, dehumanize and chattelize the negro." Now, though, Powell observed that African Americans had "passed through the first terrible, long and tedious night-watch of slavery, and are now simply enjoying the afternoon of its jubilee." Proudly, they were becoming American in a more meaningful sense than ever before. Taking the hyperbole of nineteenth-century rhetoric to dizzying heights, Powell concluded that the "illustrious" Bassett was helping African Americans "adapt ourselves to our new status of equal law and American citizenship." He was proving that a once degraded race was "now sitting, as it were, on the left hand in the new Republican kingdom of political greatness and grandeur."[99]

The extent of this metaphor is unclear: was Grant the Son seated at the right hand of Lincoln the Father in the "Republican kingdom"? The effect, however, is certain. By depicting African Americans as a previously "denationalized" people who had finally gained acceptance in a "Great Republic" founded on the promise of racial egalitarianism, Powell deemphasized a history of migration throughout and identification across the African Diaspora.[100] He glossed over it, eliding it even as black men who embodied it stood beside him looking out across the Atlantic Ocean that summer day. Roberts and at least ten thousand of his fellow African Americans had appointed themselves nation builders in Liberia since the 1820s. Beginning in the same period, even more African Americans had left the United States to become citizens of Laroche's Haiti. Those African Americans who became Haitian or Liberian were clearly nationalized, just not in the way now prioritized by Powell and other black patriots who championed the United States.

For Powell, the effect of the Civil War and Reconstruction should transform how black people thought about U.S. nationality. Stirred by the memories of the Civil War, in which black soldiers had secured the Union victory over treasonous white southerners, and emboldened by the current political and civil rights initiatives of Radical Republicans, Powell now assigned African Americans the task of giving "to this nation, *brain* and intellectual culture, as we have heretofore given iron-strung muscles and loyal hearts." Their principal identification, Powell believed, had to be with their "native country," not that "distracted" Republic of Haiti whose revolutionary glory was diminished by its current "political distraction" and attendant "sanguinary conflict."[101]

To be sure, Powell saw African Americans as the most devoted champions and potential beneficiaries of a federal government that considered the postbellum period a time of territorial expansion as well as domestic reconstruction. In the same moment that Grant prepared to send Bassett to Haiti, the president readied his personal secretary and former aide-de-camp for a trip to the Dominican Republic. There, in September 1869, the representative of the Grant administration and the Dominican foreign minister signed a preliminary annexation agreement. A month later the two sides reached two more accords. The first was a treaty for the annexation of the Dominican Republic by the United States, and the second gave the U.S. government the right to lease Samaná Bay if the first treaty failed in the U.S. Congress. For Grant, the advantages of the latter were obvious. Although he kept his plan to relocate freedpeople to the Dominican Republic private, he made public his conviction that the annexation treaty would give Americans control over the rich mineral resources of that nation and access to a key naval base at Samaná Bay. The risks were minimal, too. With the ink on the Thirteenth Amendment dry, Grant believed that southern territorial expansion no longer augured the extension of slavery. It's sole purpose would be to ease racial tensions in the South and bolster the international might of the reunified nation.

Other Americans were not so certain that was true. More to the point, they were concerned about whether the treaty would involve the United States in the affairs of Haiti. The Republican Charles Sumner, then the chair of the U.S. Senate Committee on Foreign Relations, based his disapproval of the annexation measure on the assumption that it would engender conflict between the United States and Haiti. It might, he feared, even result in the erasure of Haitian sovereignty. Accordingly, the chief proponent for the diplomatic recognition of Haiti among U.S. politicians during the antebellum era implored his colleagues to reject the treaty, demanding that no steps be taken that might diminish hard-fought Haitian independence.[102]

Numerous white Democrats joined Sumner in opposing annexation. Unlike the esteemed abolitionist, however, those politicians were motivated by racism rather than sympathy for Haiti. Many assumed that the treaty between the United States and the Dominican Republic would apply to the entire island of Hispaniola and scorned it on the grounds that it would increase the number of black citizens in "their" country. They took special delight when Sumner's fellow Republicans echoed their racial anxieties. For example, the *Mobile Register* crowed upon learning that the *Cincinnati Daily Gazette*, a paper edited by a leading Ohio Republican, was "opposed to Hayti annexation, because it will necessarily introduce the black element into the councils of the Government." Moreover, the Alabama paper praised its northern counterpart for realizing the dangerous connection between annexation and the constitutional amendment then under consideration in the House of Representatives. By criticizing the annexation treaty and the Fifteenth Amendment, the *Gazette* had ostensibly declared that the "*enfranchisement of the blacks was in itself a mistake.*" White southerners, the *Register* concluded, could not have "put the case any more strongly."[103]

For these anti-imperialist white supremacists, the success of a black diplomat in Haiti was a particular threat. Haitians embraced Bassett—days after his arrival in Port-au-Prince, Bassett wrote to Frederick Douglass that it seemed as if the entire city had greeted him at the docks or paid him a visit.[104] Meanwhile, the State Department gave Bassett a letter of commendation for managing a difficult transition in Haitian governance. Taking note, the black press called Bassett a man of "high intellectual, moral, and diplomatic qualifications" who was proving wrong the "weak-kneed Republicans" who questioned the appropriateness of his appointment.[105] The editors of the Columbus *Crisis* could not stand for such acclaim. The two Ohio Democrats feared that a man who was dismantling the notion that African Americans had no political acumen might cause greater harm. Their paper impugned the "negro named Bassett" for leading the "movement . . . in progress looking to the purchase or annexation of the nigger Pandemonium of Hayti." It assailed the "representative of the mongrel government at Washington to the pure black of Hayti." By (supposedly) bringing the "miserable negro republic" closer to U.S. statehood, the "sooty minister" threatened to further expose the lie of white supremacy. Once made U.S. citizens, Haitian "savages" might prove to be otherwise.[106] In fact, they, like Bassett, might ably fill political offices that were meant for whites only.

To the delight of white journalists who wailed about "negro domination," the United States annexed neither the Dominican Republic nor Haiti.

In March 1870, Sumner's Foreign Relations Committee voted against the agreement reached by Grant's representatives and the Dominican government. Three months later, the U.S. Senate rejected the annexation treaty.

The initial failure of the annexation measure was a real disappointment to Frederick Douglass. During the antebellum era, Douglass had condemned the annexation of Texas as an immoral endeavor motivated by greed and racism. U.S. territorial expansion, he reasoned, was responsible for the continued displacement of Native Americans and the growth of slavery. It meant settler colonialism and racial domination. But by the 1870s, Douglass saw things differently. From his perspective, the ratification of the Thirteenth, Fourteenth, and Fifteenth Amendments to the U.S. Constitution, the federal prosecution of the Ku Klux Klan, and the dispatching of federal troops to protect the political and civil rights of African Americans demonstrated the changing tenor of his times. They showed that the United States was making astounding industrial progress and achieving moral advances, too. For Douglass, black people in the U.S. South and Santo Domingo now had the chance to prosper under the U.S. flag. There was, he believed, a discernible difference between U.S. interventionism born out of benevolence and cooperation and "rapacious" imperialism done "in the name of manifest destiny, which [was] but another name for manifest privacy."[107]

Accordingly, Douglass accepted the offer to become the assistant secretary of the presidential commission that Congress approved for the continued study of Dominican annexation. In January 1871, Douglass landed at Samaná Bay along with the white scientists, journalists, politicians, and businessmen who made up the rest of the commission. He then conducted interviews with African Americans who had emigrated from the United States to the northeastern seaport during the 1820s when it was still under Haitian control. Their favorable responses to the commission, influenced by weariness with ongoing Dominican political conflict, the pro-annexation propaganda of the Báez regime, and, perhaps, their national origins, solidified Douglass's position. "I don't see any reason why the United States should withhold needed help to another country that claims for it," Douglass told audiences upon his return to the United States. He saw annexation as an opportunity, not an imposition; he accepted that Dominicans wanted and needed "to become a part of a large, strong and growing nation—only obey[ing] the grand organizing impulse of the age."[108]

Douglass's words cohered with the thoughts of a number of black political and religious leaders. Along with Douglass, the Mississippi senator

Hiram Revels, the South Carolina congressman Joseph Rainey, and, of course, Benjamin Tucker Tanner all supported U.S. expansion in the Caribbean. In one form or another, they and a host of African Americans of lesser stature argued that annexation to a U.S. government more committed to racial egalitarianism than ever before could uplift black people abroad, aiding them on their path to unprecedented economic development, political stability, and cultural improvement. The presumption that educated African Americans would lead the civilizing mission associated with expansion often followed. The question of whether Dominicans or Haitians would simply become more susceptible to U.S. capitalism and corporatism was not yet asked. Instead, annexation became an accepted means of racial progress for some black intellectuals. It was a vehicle by which they could ensure that supposedly less developed black communities abroad seized the opportunities for material advancement and secured the benefits of bourgeois U.S. culture available in that moment.

Besides postemancipation optimism and ethnic chauvinism, the investment in U.S. expansion also stemmed from the tenuous embrace of U.S. nationalism evident in black institutions across the United States. The pro-annexation statements from black male religious and political elites were near universal in their inclusion of favorable assessments of the United States. Boasts of U.S. industrial and technological development flowed from Tanner's pen. Celebrations of the Radical Republican agenda now codified in U.S. law emerged from Douglass's lips. Both men promoted an idea—Dominicans or Haitians could benefit from U.S. influence and accrue all the benefits of U.S. citizenship—that rested on the belief that African Americans were making a remarkable transition from enslaved people to unquestioned *Americans*. Neither believed that process to be complete or unquestioned, though. Accordingly, their patriotic homages to the United States were just as aspirational as they were assertive. Tanner, Douglass, and their ilk hoped to cement, not just celebrate, African Americans' claims to citizenship, their vital role in the Republican Party, and their quintessential Americanness.

Fantasies of a fully inclusive U.S. democracy were butting up against hard realities, however. While the presidential commission on Dominican annexation failed to shift public opinion, leaving Grant to lament his failure to acquire the Dominican Republic and Haiti, Congress removed restrictions on the voting rights of unreconstructed Confederates, and between 1869 and 1875, Democrats returned to power in several southern states.[109]

White southerners drove black political officials out of office in South Carolina, threatened black voters in Kentucky with whippings, maiming, and hanging, and brought Mississippi and Louisiana to the brink of civil war. They also erected a racialized system of convict leasing. Complicit in the reemergence of racial caste, white northerners grew less committed to the pursuit of racial equality and more willing to give white southerners governance over their politics and black people. By the mid-1870s, white Democrats abetted by their white Republican counterparts could boast that they had restored white supremacy to the South. They had redeemed their region.

The redeemers and their enablers welcomed every chance to disparage Haiti. As economic depression, political corruption, legal injustice, and paramilitary groups devastated the South, even liberal white northerners argued that Haitian cultural backwardness showed that black people were unprepared for political self-governance. For instance, Horace White, a Republican who had supported universal emancipation and helped Lincoln gain office, decried the "sad state of Hayti." Citing the alleged prevalence of infanticide and cannibalism among Vodou practitioners, the editor of the *Chicago Tribune* lamented that the condition of most Haitians was "that of barbarism."[110] The pervasiveness of superstition not only explained the inability of Haitians to maintain a stable republican government but also offered insights into the perceived failure of Reconstruction. For White and others, the ascension of ignorant and childlike African Americans to political power would have the same undesired results as "Negro rule" in Haiti. More tutelage under the Anglo-American was necessary before full citizenship was granted.

Such scrutiny of and attacks on black peoples' capacities for self-government profoundly affected how some African Americans perceived themselves in relation to Haiti. Although remaining confident in the superiority of their U.S. Protestant culture, they found it increasingly difficult to make unequivocal claims that they were at the vanguard of the black race. For them, the discrepancy between their hardships and Haitian independence was increasingly glaring. One black Republican noted that while African Americans struggled to establish a postemancipation independence, Haiti had solidified its "place among the nations."[111] In fact, in order to affirm their right to the ballot and self-determination, it appeared that African Americans now needed to rely on Haitians. If Haitians could somehow convince white Americans of their material and cultural advancement, they would by example invalidate white supremacy in the United States. They would make it impossible to justify the violent backlash to black civil and political rights in the United States by pointing to the failings of black self-government where it existed already.

Therein lay a quandary. The cultural chauvinism and patriotism of outspoken African Americans was colliding with the mounting anxiety caused by the rising tide of scientific racism and the increasing efforts of white southerners to take back a region they assumed was theirs and theirs alone. This conflict resulted in intensified calls for the reform of Haitian society. Black intellectuals believed that Haiti should be, had to be, but was not yet a convincing representation of black self-government. It did not meet their standards of industrialization, expectations of capitalism, or understandings of republicanism. It certainly fell far short of matching their definition of Christian morality. Accordingly, influential black Protestants built upon the notions of perfection, elevation, and respectability that influenced the evangelical reform movements of the antebellum era, presaged the racial uplift doctrines that crystallized in ensuing decades, and committed themselves to missionary work in Haiti.[112] These black men and women hoped to vindicate Haitians, in the process continuing Tanner's self-appointed task of replacing notions of biological racial inferiority with evolutionary views of cultural assimilation. They accomplished neither goal. Instead, in their haste to help themselves by "improving" Haiti, black missionaries and their allies often struggled with an unintended outcome of their words and actions: the replication and reinforcement of the same racial ideologies to which they objected.[113]

Black Protestants had long looked to Haiti as an inviting missionary field but had never established a firm organizational presence there. Although some of the African Americans who flocked to Haiti during the 1820s were AME members, they maintained only loose connections to Haitians as well as to church bodies in the United States.[114] By the early 1860s, James Theodore Holly, an African American born free in Washington, D.C., who led another wave of black refugees from the United States to Haiti, had established Holy Trinity Church in Port-au-Prince, organized missions across Haiti, and secured three native converts to the clergy.[115] Yet his Episcopal denomination lacked a sizeable black membership. AME members who wanted to augment Holly's work because they felt Haiti "demonstrated the truth that colored men are capable of self-government" found little support.[116] Their church, the largest independent black religious organization

FIGURE 2. Bishops of the AME Church, 1876. Richard Allen (1760–1831) sits at the center of the engraving, surrounded by the past and present bishops of the church that he founded. Wilberforce University is in the upper left corner while the scene at the middle of the engraving's right side shows the precedents of AME missionary work in Haiti. Its surrounding caption reads, "First Missionaries to Port-au-Prince, Hayti, Revs. Scipio Beans, Richard Robinson, 1824." Prints & Photographs Division, Library of Congress.

until the National Baptist Convention eclipsed it at the turn of the century, had limited financial resources, and for the time being, it devoted those to domestic missions among freedpeople in the U.S. South.[117]

The priorities of the AME Church began to shift in the late 1860s and early 1870s. As Benjamin Tucker Tanner touted the advantages of annexation for all involved parties, he also suggested that missionary work would provide the perfect complement to U.S. political intervention in Haiti. He insisted that neither the AME Church nor the United States had realized their greatness. In particular, Tanner lamented that just as his country had not fulfilled its manifest destiny of territorial expansion, his church had "never yet risen to the high work imposed upon the Christian Church—even the conquest of the world to Christ." AME congregations now had the opportunity to do just that. Tanner guaranteed that church bishops were ready to "reap our missionary conquest" as the "drum of the Lord" could be "heard beating up volunteers" to go to Haiti. All that remained, he proclaimed, anticipating militant expressions of imperialism and evangelism that intensified in subsequent decades, was for AME church treasurers to respond to the enthusiasm and "send one or more missionaries to Hayti along with the starry flag."[118]

Tanner was not alone in demanding the spiritual renewal of Haiti during a moment of U.S. expansionism. For other AME leaders, promoting the Gospel abroad became more feasible and more essential as their church infrastructure solidified, its financial state improved, and African Americans saw their "new condition" challenged. It became inevitable in 1872. That year, Reverend Theophilus Gould Steward asked the AME General Conference to invigorate the church's missionary work in Haiti with new life. Since entering the ministry a decade earlier, Steward had established missions in Georgia and South Carolina, but he came to the Philadelphia convention with a proposal to aid those whom he considered even more benighted than the southern freedman. He could not have expected a more enthusiastic response. Most AME members endorsed it with great zeal. Tanner reported that "the heart of the whole [Conference] body seemed to throb with renewed life" after Steward introduced his resolution.[119] Like tens of thousands of other U.S. citizens of the era, the black men and women who heard or learned about Steward's appeal felt compelled to take an active role in the foreign missionary movement, save heathen souls abroad, and strengthen their churches at home. They devoted themselves to fundraising, and by the next year, Steward was on his way to Haiti.[120]

The departing missionary, born free in southern New Jersey, had modest formal education. Still, he knew about Haiti or, more accurately, its romanticized history that pervaded the antebellum and Civil War eras. In his autobiography, Steward recalled that one of the first books given to him during his childhood was "a graphic account of the struggles of the blacks of that island for their freedom and independence." That account introduced the young Steward to "the plumes and drums, swords and guns, lace and gilt, fine sayings and thrilling movements" of the Haitian Revolution.

All had "enamored [his] soul." Steward remembered that he then "pictured the island as the theatre upon whose stage those matchless actors, Toussaint, Dessalines, Christophe, Petion, and Boyer enacted their sublime drama." He recalled, too, that he was attracted to Haiti because it was his grandmother's final resting place. In the 1820s, two decades before Steward's birth, she had fled the United States in pursuit of a more meaningful freedom and the promises of citizenship in Haiti. Inspired by the epic stories of emigration and slave insurrection, Steward wrote, travel to Haiti thus became a recurring "dream of my boyhood."[121]

When that dream became reality, Steward yearned for Haiti to be as he had long imagined it. Soon after arriving in Port-au-Prince in June 1873, the AME minister looked upon the "lofty hills" of Haiti, thought of the "toiling people at their base," and "fancied an appealing cry coming from [those] masses." In Haitians, Steward pictured a race pride that could only come from an historic independence. A journal that Steward kept during his time in Haiti contains notes about the "fine country gentlemen" and "ladies dressed in snowy white dash" that he passed while traveling along a road leading up Haiti's western coast. Whether galloping on "beautiful horses with most magnificent saddles and trappings," riding atop the humbler donkey, or even traveling on foot, each one gave the heartiest "*bonjour, monsieur.*"[122] Here were Haitians, filled with confidence regardless of their social status. Here was "poor, poor Haiti . . . the veriest humbug; and yet . . . splendid."[123]

Haiti, however, was not and could never be the idyllic country of Steward's dreams. Instead, it was a very real place with concrete social and political conditions that Steward was ill-prepared to understand. The same journal that contains his sentimental perceptions of a Haiti rooted in history and myth also records Steward's chauvinism. Traveling about Port-au-Prince, Steward sniffed at the "dirty" food found in Haitian markets. He derided the vendors and purchasers of the offensive cooking, calling the Haitians in the capital polite but "very ostentatious, superstitious and overbearing in their manners." In fact, even when Steward attempted to sympathize with Haitians, he ascribed an exoticism to their behaviors. Within a day of arriving in Port-au-Prince, the AME missionary decided that Haitians were capitalistic but not in the same sense as black or white Americans. No, Steward concluded, Haitians were a "nation of traders" whose economic success was the result of a disagreeable thriftiness. In that sense, they were "the only people who [could] beat the Jews."[124]

Disillusionment overtook any lingering romanticism during Steward's time in what he derided as a "military establishment" masquerading as a republic. His journal offers scathing denunciations of the alleged immodesty of Haitian women, condemnations of public sanitation in Port-au-Prince, and shock at the perceived prevalence of interracial marriage. The proliferation of Vodou, the Haitian religion created by enslaved Africans, further infuriated Steward. He argued that other countries might not be able to conquer Haiti but "liquor, licentiousness, and superstition" certainly would. Growing more and more pessimistic about Haitian progress, Steward took refuge in the company of Ebenezer Don Carlos Bassett, James Theodore Holly, and other educated African Americans living in Port-au-Prince. In his view, they were the sole examples of Christian virtue in Haiti and its only hope for national, racial redemption.[125]

Steward's condemnations of Haitian life demonstrate the importance and displaced anxieties that black political and religious leaders thrust upon Haiti. Steward's reaction to supposed cultural pathologies in Haiti cohered with a civilizing impulse that animated many conservative evangelicals and liberal Protestants, black as well as white. AME missionaries' attendant propagation of "respectable" U.S. culture in Haiti was not just ordained by faith, however. Practical considerations and ideas of racial progress informed by nationality and class also contributed to it. As Steward preached the Gospel in Haiti, African Americans faced allegations that they were just as uncivilized as Haitians. Those charges of cultural backwardness, which implied similarities among black people regardless of educational background or socioeconomic status, were used in an attempt to negate emerging claims for black self-determination in the United States. Accordingly, while some of his contemporaries encouraged African Americans to become the agents of civilization in Africa, Steward tried to improve the image of the black race by proposing remedies for perceived Haitian ills.[126]

Ultimately, Steward proved more capable at pinpointing alleged problems than providing meaningful solutions—he abandoned Haiti only six months after his arrival in Port-au-Prince. In a letter published in a February 1874 edition of the *Christian Recorder*, Steward protested that he returned to the United States only because financial "support was not forthcoming." Either the church needed to increase the budget for its work in Haiti or find a missionary who was more willing to "sacrifice time in impracticalities."[127]

Steward was direct in his complaints but not entirely candid. Years later, when he no longer worried about discouraging other AME missionaries from going to Haiti, he was more forthright. Steward wrote in his autobiography that he had "embarked upon a work with insufficient preparation." He did not "know enough of the language" of a "strange land" whose inhabitants were "far away in manner of thinking and in modes of life." Neither his knowledge of Haitian history nor his previous work among black southerners had prepared him for his undertakings in Haiti. In fact, Steward conceded that his "experience among the freedmen of the South was of no value" in Haiti because Haitians were "not freedmen, but citizens of an independent country."[128] What once came as a surprise to Steward now seemed obvious: his Haitian contemporaries had never known anything but freedom. Most had always owned their own labor and land. It was no wonder, then, that foreigners, even black ones, who assumed a right to teach Haitians about the proper foundations of self-government made little progress.

Greater realization of that lesson would come as radical political currents flowed about the African Diaspora of the twentieth century. In the immediate wake of Steward's flight from Port-au-Prince, however, Benjamin Tucker Tanner demanded that African Americans persist in their urgent attempts to civilize Haitians. More specifically, the AME minister called for the creation of a "women's missionary society" that would assume responsibility for Haitian missions.

He would get more than he bargained for as the expectations of churchwomen contradicted his patriarchal goals. Tanner's interest in creating a female missionary body was born out of his belief that women ought to take a greater role in church affairs because they were idle, indolent, and irresponsible parishioners. Moreover, he envisioned a women's missionary organization that would operate as a subsidiary of a larger patriarchal church structure rather than as an autonomous site of female leadership. Ordinary women in the AME Church rejected Tanner's opinions, though. They pointed to their support of temperance and home missions as evidence of their vital contributions to their churches. Upon agreeing to organize foreign missionary work, the wives of leading bishops and clergymen made it clear that they too objected to the editor's paternalism. Their Woman's Parent Mite Missionary Society (WPMMS) would respond to the concerns of black women as well as to the priorities of male church leaders.[129]

Indeed, WPMMS members saw their group not only as a continuation of the work begun by Steward but also as a means of demonstrating that the elevation of black women was critical to the progress of the race. The educated northerners of the WPMMS acknowledged that all African Americans were invested in the fate of Haitians, inhabitants of a "historic island . . . whose blood flowed so freely for the emancipation of our race."[130] Nevertheless, WPMMS president Mary A. Campbell implored black women to embrace a leading role in reforming Haitian society. The mother of four from Philadelphia spoke directly to what she perceived to be the concerns of her peers when she accentuated the plight of her "Haytian sisters," characterized other Haitians as "sable children," and highlighted allegations of rampant infant sacrifice in Haiti.[131] Anticipating later representations of missionary work in Africa, Campbell implied that black churchwomen had a "special mission" to save Haitian children from their terrible fates and redeem the women responsible for raising future generations of Haitian citizens.[132] By improving Haitian domestic life, the women of the WPMMS would thus strengthen the Haitian republic. They would place the concerns of black women on the AME agenda and assert their right to church leadership positions, all while vindicating black self-government in the Caribbean.[133]

Campbell's male counterparts demonstrated less interest in female empowerment but an equal proclivity for stressing the immediate need for reforms in Haitian society. As the WPMMS organized, the AME minister Thomas A. Cuff spoke to his colleagues about the importance of temperance. While decrying the corrosive impact of intemperance on the human soul, he paid particular attention to its tangible effect on black populations. African Americans, Cuff argued, needed to stop spending money on spirits and invest in foreign missions. If not for intemperance in the black community, "the gospel of Christ, religion, science and literature would flourish" in Haiti while "heathenism would disappear as the snow before the sun."[134] The expected benefits for African Americans needed little explanation. As other church leaders called on Haitian political dissidents to "simmer down . . . for the sake of the race," Cuff assumed that white Americans would grant more respect to Haitians if Haitian culture resembled theirs. And higher regard for Haitians would, of course, mean more esteem for their brethren in the United States.[135]

By August 1876, AME leaders like Cuff were moving to strengthen their oversight of the Haitian mission field and the Ladies' Mite Missionary Society in Port-au-Prince.[136] To a certain extent, the AME churchwomen in the Haitian capital welcomed a greater association between their community and the church body in the United States because it might ensure enhanced prestige and funding for their endeavors. This attitude did not, however, mean that they were willing to leave the selection of a lead resident missionary to the men back home. Eventually, negotiations between WPMMS members and AME officials resulted in the selection of Reverend Charles W. Mossell. Before leaving the United States for Haiti, the graduate of Lincoln University asked Jesus Christ to grant him "great success" in his "efforts to assist in making the Haytians a great nation."[137] He, by all indications, was well-aware of the importance of his task.

Indeed, Mossell made no distinction between the spiritual and political dimensions of his work. The new leader of the AME Church's Haitian missions maintained that "every American Negro ought to be deeply interested in the republic of Haiti." In fact, he argued, the AME Church "ought to be willing to make any sacrifice, to bring about a moral reformation among the Haitian people." Writing to the *Christian Recorder* from Port-au-Prince, he lamented the continued reign of "Roman Catholicism, French Infidelity, and Voudouism" in Haiti. The latter, he continued, the "lowest and grossest form of superstition" first introduced to Saint-Domingue by enslaved Africans, remained rampant while the "better society of Hayti" expressed frequent shock at "the sad news of some atrocious act perpetrated" by Vodou worshippers. It was prime evidence that the "painful and present moral status of the Haitian people" was just as irrefutable as its consequences. Mossell informed potential contributors to the AME missions that "the religion of a people . . . determine [*sic*] not only their future destiny; but their present and comparative worth." In his estimation, the absence of Protestantism in Haiti would have damning repercussions for the entire race.[138]

As the new head of AME missions in Haiti began his providential work, Mary Ella Mossell took a trip around Port-au-Prince. The graduate of Baltimore's well-regarded Colored Normal School would soon begin her own job as the principal of the local AME mission school, but, for now, she was preoccupied with absorbing the unfamiliar sights and sounds of the Haitian capital.[139] Mossell left her husband, Charles, to his responsibilities and traveled alongside a member of the WPMMS who introduced her to the central market, a bustling place congested with stalls, abundant produce, ornate architecture, and an endless stream of pedestrians.

EXECUTIVE COMMITTEE W. P. M. MISSIONARY SOCIETY, DETROIT, MICH., 1915.

FIGURE 3. Executive Committee of the WPMMS, 1915. By this date, the AME Women's Home and Foreign Missionary Society (WHFMS) had outgrown the WPMMS. The members and the southern-based leadership of the WHFMS primarily supported missions in South Africa. Prints and Photographs Department, Moorland-Spingarn Research Center, Howard University.

Mossell was overwhelmed by the scene. In a report published in the *Christian Recorder*, she characterized the Haitian modes of transportation—horses and donkeys—as "very inferior to that of our own country." Mossell further decried the lack of men in the marketplace and identified the efforts of the Haitian market women as "amusing" rather than indicative of female social and economic empowerment. To her, the language and decorum of these women and their children was even more alarming. Mossell lamented "the current and peculiar customs, the unintelligible and musical dialect of the natives" and remarked with astonishment that "children are seen running hither and thither; naked." It could not have been any plainer: "the moral condition of Hayti" was "by no means sound."[140]

Mossell was certain that her peers needed to rectify this situation. Apart from James Theodore Holly, black Protestants did not seem to be giving sufficient attention to the cultural improvement of Haitians. The response of some Haitians to these inadequate efforts had, however, convinced Mossell that an increased presence of genteel African Americans in Haiti could bear fruit. By the time she arrived in Port-au-Prince, Holly's Église Orthodoxe Apostolique d'Haïti (Orthodox Apostolic Church of Haiti) had eleven Haitian clergymen, ten parishes across Haiti, and dozens of confirmations and baptisms each year.[141] The burden now rested on other black missionaries to join Holly and provide resources for Haitians who identified Protestantism as an antidote to poverty and political strife.[142] Mossell thus challenged female missionaries in the United States to join the ongoing struggle for racial uplift in Haiti. She reiterated the declarations of other WPMMS leaders, declaring "Women of America, this work of moral elevation concerns you!"[143]

Much had changed in the nearly decade and a half since freedpeople carved out freedom in New Hayti, North Carolina. While African Americans had celebrated the Haitian Revolution, Haiti, and the U.S. recognition of Haitian independence as the precursor, model, and possible fruit of emancipation, Mossell and her peers faced the difficult challenge of realizing the fleeting promises of Reconstruction. Those promises remained connected to the ideas of Haiti and the Haitian Revolution. In the view of numerous black public figures such as Benjamin Tucker Tanner, Charles and Ella Mossell, and the women of the WPMMS, a Haitian state lacking in moral and material progress threatened their now formalized right to freedom *and* self-governance. It was the subject of foreign scorn and fodder for the white supremacist ideologies on which Redemption, the violent overthrow of Reconstruction, rested. So it required improvement. Appropriating the cultural chauvinism that inspired evangelists and imperialists alike, black missionaries accentuated the differences between themselves and Haitians, traveled to Haiti, and took up the mission of "moral elevation." Echoing the patriotic sentiments of other black political and religious leaders, they insisted that they were *Americans* who, by making Haiti the "home of freedom, of government, and of true religion," could prove that very point.

Those ways of imagining Haiti and interacting with Haitians would endure. Those attendant means of thinking about what racial progress meant and on what terms it could be achieved would persist. Over the course of the first decade after Reconstruction, black public figures and intellectuals would, however, work toward new ideas about race and nation even as long-standing traditions in black thought lingered. In doing so, they continued to prioritize Haiti, which had become a canvas upon which to express their hopes and anxieties, new as well as old.

CHAPTER 2

The Reinventions of Haiti After Reconstruction

While the Mossells were on their way to Haiti, the preparations for the Centennial of 1876 were being finalized back home. African Americans were especially invested in the upcoming national birthday celebration.[1] For decades, black abolitionists had declined to participate in Fourth of July ceremonies that whitewashed the sins of their slaveholding country and promised that they would partake in the revelry only "when the Declaration of Independence is finally executed."[2] That day had dawned, cloudier than those black activists anticipated. With chattel slavery abolished but the political and civil rights of African Americans still contested, black spokesmen saw the Centennial as a chance to reaffirm the contributions of African Americans to the construction of the United States. It was, they believed, a powerful moment to reassert that white *and* black men were "created equal . . . [and] endowed by their Creator with certain unalienable Rights."[3]

Yet, on July 4, 1876, George Washington Williams had a different declaration of independence in mind as he stood before a large crowd in Avondale, a predominantly black section of Cincinnati, Ohio.[4] After opening his keynote with platitudes about the "deeds of patriotism . . . [and] heroism of the fathers of '76," the Union veteran, Baptist minister, and budding historian praised the military valor of the black men who those so-called Founding Fathers enslaved. The black soldier, Williams proclaimed, was an "integral part" of the War for U.S. Independence and one of "the defenders of the country" during the War of 1812. In fact, he had since become a liberator just like his Haitian brethren. "It will ever be the glory of the black man's government in Hayti that he built it on the ruins of slavery, and ratified its benign and humane principles with his own blood," Williams boasted. "Neither France nor England can glory in that they freed St. Domingo; but the negro can boast that he threw off his own yoke, drove his oppressors from the island . . . and built his own government upon the rock of human justice and equal rights—a government that has stood during the present century, and will stand through the ages to come!" The 200,000 black veterans who served in the Union Army and United States Navy were foremost among the African Americans who could now say the same. "This," Williams concluded, "is the negro's place in history—his own deliverer, the defender of the Union."[5] The Fourth of July was theirs, the day for African Americans to acknowledge U.S. independence but celebrate black self-determination, too.

"The American Negro, from 1776 to 1876," the foundation of Williams's pioneering *History of the Negro Race from 1619 to 1880: Negroes as Slaves, Soldiers, and as Citizens*, presaged larger trends and tensions in black thought after Reconstruction. As Williams celebrated the Haitian Revolution on the U.S. Centennial and suggested that black soldiers emulated Haitians even as they built the United States, Haiti maintained its practical and symbolic value to African Americans. Black politicians including John Mercer Langston continued to view Haiti as a singular site where African Americans could participate in U.S. politics. AME members joined them in thinking of it as an inspiring albeit imperfect model of black self-determination. So did emigrationists who saw Haiti as a refuge from the backlash to Reconstruction and a black nation-state that was central to their racial destiny or collective fate.

Still, as black intellectuals fought for a place in U.S. public life and continued their attempts to perfect Haiti through U.S. values and institutions, the violent collapse and uncertain aftermath of Reconstruction threw sharp relief onto two pressing questions: who, exactly, were African Americans, and what was their actual relationship to the United States? In a moment when white Americans insisted that African Americans were not fellow citizens but, much like Haitians, a population incapable or undeserving of freedom, it seemed possible that uncritical black patriotism had run its course. Maybe the United States, reunified on the principle of white supremacy, encouraged pessimism, not faith. Perhaps Haiti, built on "the rock of human justice and equal rights," deserved the allegiance of black men, women, and even schoolchildren.[6]

A definitive moment for black ideas about nation and race, Haiti and the United States came in the mid-1880s. Holding on to the hopes that accompanied emancipation, some African Americans, including missionaries in Haiti, continued to celebrate the United States. A number of their peers abstained, though. Following the nearly simultaneous publication of Nathaniel Southgate Shaler's "The Negro Problem" and Spenser St. John's *Hayti; Or, the Black Republic*—two widely circulated works that amplified a transnational debate on the potential of black people in postemancipation societies and identified Haiti and Haitians as irrefutable proof of black inferiority—members of the growing black press and other African Americans became more convinced that rhetorical attacks on and military threats to Haiti paralleled the ongoing efforts to restrict the freedoms of black populations throughout the Americas. Their subsequent vindications of Haiti often articulated a transnational politics of defiance forged in response to an encroaching era of global white supremacy. For numerous black intellectuals, U.S. attempts to undermine Haitian sovereignty, which were made evident during a diplomatic dispute over a U.S. merchant ship that armed Haitian insurgents, seemed all too familiar. They and the parallel loss of Reconstruction's gains encouraged forceful critiques of racism at home, more critical assessments of imperialism abroad, and more precise evaluations of the common causes that linked black people wherever they lived.

A few weeks after delivering "The American Negro, from 1776 to 1876," George Washington Williams joined the executive committee of Cincinnati's Colored Protective Association (CPA). The organization, one of several local precursors to the National Colored Protective Association meant to "secure such laws as will protect the race," was founded in response to intensified opposition to black citizenship.[7] Years after the Ohio legislature rescinded its earlier support for the Fourteenth Amendment and refused to ratify the Fifteenth Amendment, hotel owners in Cincinnati had told a local newspaper reporter that they would ignore the Civil Rights Act of 1875. For black Ohioans, such brazen resistance to the federal law granting African Americans equal access to public accommodations, public transportation, and jury duty foreshadowed more discrimination—or worse. Soon after the formation of the CPA, black Cincinnatians gathered in protest of the summary executions of black militiamen by a white mob in Hamburg, South Carolina. To Williams, the meeting in "protest against the Hamburg massacre" was a natural and worthy outgrowth of the activism on behalf of black legal rights "in this section of the country."[8]

To be sure, the political currents were turning against African Americans wherever they lived or looked. In South Carolina, the Democrat, former slaveholder, and unreformed Confederate Wade Hampton misrepresented the Hamburg Massacre as evidence of "Negro rule" run amuck. His subsequent election as governor marked the end of Reconstruction in South Carolina and the United States. As Hampton stormed into office, northern white Republicans, many of them swayed by stereotypes of black political corruption, insensitive to the demands of organized labor, and weary from the economic depression that began with the Wall Street Panic of 1873, agreed that it was time to return southern governance into the hands of the "[white] wealth and intelligence of the South." They cheered the compromise that delivered the Republican Rutherford B. Hayes into the White House while removing the final U.S. troops from southern state capitals. Finally, the *Nation* sighed in relief, white supremacists might "purify Southern politics."[9]

For one white southerner, named J. R. Ralls, Redemption was preordained by Haitian history. While black South Carolinians insisted that Haiti proved their ability to govern, the obscure author published *The Negro Problem: An Essay on the Industrial, Political and Moral Aspects of the Negro Race in the Southern States as Presented Under the Late Amendments to the Constitution.*[10] The pamphlet's arguments were less complex than its lengthy title. "During the great social and political upheaval that brought in the French revolution," Ralls wrote, "the Jacobin faction, in their mad carnival of 'equality and fraternity,' proclaimed the freedom of the blacks in Hayti, and allowed the people of that province to establish an independent government, giving the negro race political rights under it." Haitians had then failed in their experiment in black self-government, he continued. According to Ralls, Haiti proved that black people had neither "conceived a plan, or attempted . . . their liberation from bondage" nor solved "the problems of civilized life, without the superior intelligence of the white man to aid and direct him." The Black Republic, put simply, identified the "Negro problem" as a question: what should be done with a population of black citizens who clearly had no capacity for freedom?[11]

The silencing of the Haitian Revolution and the slandering of Haiti were not new. But, published in the same moment that Hampton and his ilk returned to power, both were meant to set the white supremacist terms of national reconciliation. If, as Ralls argued, black people had "submitted to the rule of the master, until the restraints of slavery were lifted by the power that imposed it . . . and gave him his freedom" then George Washington Williams was a liar.[12] There was no case for black self-emancipation. There was no reason to recognize the rights of the lone race that had not fought for its own freedom. For white southerners including Ralls, a history in which the Haitian Revolution never happened and Haitians never progressed required that "the rational, considerate mind of the North, viewing the subject of negro politics at the South for the last ten years, in its ruinous acts, and disgusting details, and especially in view of the present political embroglio growing out of the Presidential race, for which universal suffrage must be regarded, by every candid mind in the country, as the sole cause . . . pause, reflect, and in the experience of better reason, demand a removal of this dangerous, disturbing element from the theatre of American politics."[13] It demanded that the United States renounce its own experiment in black self-government or, better yet, forget that "reconstruction, with bayonet rule, and . . . the odious feature of negro suffrage" was ever tried.[14]

African Americans were neither willing to accept that revisionist history nor concede their hard-fought place in U.S. politics. Following the end of Ebenezer Don Carlos Bassett's diplomatic tenure in late 1877, black leaders hoped to receive more prestigious federal appointments, particularly in diplomatic service. Benjamin Tucker Tanner believed that African Americans deserved favorable treatment from the incoming Hayes administration precisely because Bassett had brought "so much credit upon his country and upon the race with which he is especially identified." In the *Christian Recorder*, he suggested that the federal government should reward Bassett and, by extension, African Americans by sending the former U.S. minister resident and consul general to Haiti to a European court such as Belgium or Switzerland.[15] Later, perhaps after realizing the unlikelihood of a diplomatic position in Europe for an African American, Tanner modified his call for Bassett's reappointment. He expressed his hope that John Mercer Langston's selection as the new minister resident and consul general in Port-au-Prince did not mean that the U.S. government believed the substitution of one African American for another was an appropriate way to acknowledge their contributions to the Republican Party. Instead, Tanner maintained that the fairest policy would result in Langston assuming the Haitian post while Bassett received a comparable role in Brazil or elsewhere in South America.[16]

Although the demand for increased and higher-profile diplomatic placements for black leaders would go unfulfilled, the appointment of

Langston, meant to appease black voters who worried about the Republicans' commitment to racial equality as Reconstruction crumbled before them, was an obvious one. The child of a prominent white slaveowner and an emancipated mother of African and Pamunkey descent, Langston was one of the earliest black graduates of Oberlin College, a seasoned abolitionist, and, more recently, dean of Howard University's School of Law. He was also Ohio's first black elected official and a prominent member of the Republican Party. Before the presidential election of 1872, Langston had canvassed the United States on behalf of Ulysses S. Grant. After helping the incumbent Republican president win a second term and gaining a federal appointment to Washington D.C.'s Board of Health, Langston then campaigned for Grant's successor, Hayes. Throughout the fall of 1876, he had delivered dozens of speeches on behalf of the Republican presidential candidate from Ohio. Those efforts made it clear that there was no man more deserving of the diplomatic post in Haiti. Certainly, no one had done more to reinforce the bond between African Americans and the party of Abraham Lincoln.[17]

Langston's long-standing appreciation for the symbolic importance of Haiti was a significant reason for his excitement about the appointment. In his autobiography, Langston recalled that he had "familiarized himself in youth with the history of the people who, emancipating themselves under Toussaint, had under Dessalines declared and established their sovereignty founding for themselves a republican form of government." Those childhood lessons clearly stuck. More than two decades before his diplomatic appointment, Langston named his firstborn son Arthur Dessalines Langston in honor of Haiti's first head of state. Now, as he prepared to leave for Port-au-Prince, he welcomed the chance to realize a boyhood dream and "behold . . . negro nationality in harmonious, honored activity."[18]

His peers were excited, too. On the night of October 24, 1877, a veritable who's who of black America gathered in Washington D.C., to honor Langston before he set sail for Port-au-Prince. Attendees at the banquet included Frederick Douglass and Daniel Alexander Payne Murray, the personal assistant to the Librarian of Congress and the second African American to hold a professional position at the Library of Congress. The evening's toastmaster was John H. Smyth, a former student of Ebenezer Don Carlos Bassett who would become the U.S. minister resident and consul general to Liberia the following year. Richard Theodore Greener presided over the entire affair. It was, ultimately, his responsibility to speak on behalf of the esteemed guests as well as the innumerable young admirers who could not attend but still wished to "show their esteem of one [Langston] who has always delighted to do what he could to lift his race."[19]

Greener is best known as the first black graduate of Harvard University, as a college professor who taught at the University of South Carolina and Howard University, and as a diplomat who served the United States in India and Russia. On that fall night, however, he was a poet who marked the occasion with the following words:

> Across the darksome waves of Carib's gentle sea,
> Proud Hayti lifts her dark-browed, beauteous head,
> Crowned with stately palm and fitting laurel-tree,
> For Liberty's brave defenders wide o'erspread.
>
> There first our brothers proved their val'rous steel
> Then, made they Negro manhood long respected
> By doughty deeds, such as stout Saxons feel
> In tawny bosoms brilliantly reflected . . .
>
> Such, the far-famed island our Langston seeks,
> All radiant still in song, in cheering story;
> Worthy Tell's renown and Switzer's snow clad peaks
> Aglow with civic pride and martial glory . . .
>
> The native shore he leaves, alas, 'tis one where,
> Freedom's fetters still impede the newly free,
> But warmest welcomes wait yet to greet him there,
> Where National Freedom means Equality.
>
> Long may the memory of the sturdy blows,
> Struck quick and sharp and hard for Race and Right,
> Linger like stirring music in hearts of those,
> Who've heard his ringing voice and felt its might.
>
> We, too, are of the race from Afric's burning sun,
> Whose noblest triumphs lie unattained before,
> The trophies of manly arm were long since won,
> On Hayti's plain and on Carolina's shore.
>
> Higher glories still of mind must surely come
> To mark proud entrance into Race-like life,

Science's lofty height and Art and Verse when won,
Conquer the bigot's sneer and Prejudices strife . . .[20]

Greener's ode hints at the complex and sometimes competing ideas that Langston would bring with him to Haiti. African Americans felt a kinship with Haitians, their "brothers" who were also part "of the race from Afric's burning sun." They not only celebrated the Haitian Revolution that "made . . . Negro manhood long respected" but also exalted "Proud Hayti" for being a country "where National Freedom means Equality." Such praise coincided with critiques of the post-Reconstruction United States. As educated black spokesmen contrasted Haiti with their "native shore . . . where freedom's fetters still impeded the newly free," they also revealed the influences that continued to shape expressions of black nationalism. Black men raised in Protestant churches, educated in U.S. colleges and universities, and exposed to the literature, arts, and inventions of the Victorian era did not question the cultural values and institutions of "stout Saxons." Instead, they accepted them as superior albeit inclusive and race neutral. While white elites like Wade Hampton announced that it was time for the best men to rule, Greener joined a chorus of voices insisting that some of those best men had black skin. Whether in Haiti or the United States, they asserted, black people would achieve "Higher glories." Through "Science . . . and Art and Verse," they would "Conquer the bigot's sneer and Prejudices strife."[21]

From the moment he first arrived in Haiti, Langston demonstrated similar support for Haitian self-determination colored by his upbringing in the United States. Upon landing in Cap-Haïtien in November 1877, the black diplomat had his first opportunity to interact with the people he had romanticized for so long. After his ship entered the harbor of the northwestern port city, several Haitian professionals came aboard. The first to arrive was a Haitian doctor who was quickly received by the white captain "as a person of character and authority." A Haitian pilot then joined them and "taking full command, issued his first order, in obedience to which, at once, the vessel was put under way and carried to her place of anchorage within the harbor." Langston marveled that "these officers both were extremely black men; and yet, appearing in uniforms of official character and demeaning themselves with intelligence and propriety, they made a remarkably good impression." Until that point, Langston "had never seen . . . men of their complexion holding such positions and performing such duties." When he voiced his surprise, he received a simple explanation: "You are now, Mr. Minister, in a negro country."[22] For Langston, the most mundane manifestations of Haitian sovereignty—of black nationalism in motion—produced sheer wonder. They reinforced the hope that the current U.S. political climate was passing and African Americans might possess similar rights in the immediate future.

At the conclusion of his brief introduction to Cap-Haïtien, Langston traveled south to Port-au-Prince. His subsequent experiences in the Haitian capital provided further insights into the practice of black self-determination. Although he took note of nearly every new sight and sound in the city where he would live for much of the next eight years, one experience in particular sparked Langston's imagination. While attending his official reception at the National Palace, Langston recognized the portraits of John Brown and Charles Sumner hanging on a wall. He interpreted the artwork as evidence that the "negro patriots" of Haiti "loved John Brown because he stuck, against every odds, for the freedom of the slaves of the United States" and immortalized Sumner because "besides being the bold, fearless, eloquent champion of negro liberty, he opposed the annexation of Santo Domingo to the United States."[23] As Langston finished viewing the palace's décor and bid goodnight to the Haitian president Pierre Boisrond-Canal, the national band played "John Brown's Body," the popular marching song about the martyred abolitionist that had reverberated in Union camps during the Civil War.[24] Langston did not record his response to the musical selection. Still, it is plausible that he felt in that moment that Haitians not only celebrated the demise of slavery in the United States but also embodied the unrestricted independence that African Americans had hoped would accompany emancipation.

In many respects, the fascination and, perhaps, nostalgia that influenced Langston's earliest impressions of Haiti would shape his ensuing diplomatic tenure. James Theodore Holly, by then a Haitian citizen and the first black bishop of the Protestant Episcopal Church, reported that "open and undisguised sympathies" for Haiti and a desire to see it achieve "distinction among the great civilized nations" fashioned friendships between Langston and Haitian leaders.[25] On one representative occasion, after the Haitian president Lysius Salomon called him "bone of his bone and flesh of his flesh," Langston replied that he was honored to represent millions of African Americans "who were proud of him and his people, who sympathized with him and prayed for him."[26] At times, Langston's sympathies influenced

Figure 4. Cap-Haïtien, Haiti, 1937. Although taken well after John Mercer Langston's death in 1897, this photograph captures the type of urban scene that greeted him and other African Americans upon their arrival "in a negro country." Prints & Photographs Division, Library of Congress.

his diplomatic policies, too. In Haiti, Langston would, for instance, refuse asylum in the U.S. embassy to Haitian insurgents. He believed that past assurances of sanctuary had emboldened perpetrators of political violence, encouraged revolutions, and thus hampered the development of strong black self-government.[27]

Langston affirmed that belief in the singular importance of Haitian independence in public speeches. On one visit back to the United States, he told African Americans attending a banquet in Washington, D.C., to take pride in their accomplishments. At the same time, though, he advised them to recognize similar examples of black progress on display across the world. Implying that Haitian self-governance implicated African Americans, Langston assured his audience that while "our advancement has been wonderful . . . in the Island of Hayti *we* are demonstrating *our* capability of self-government."[28] He trusted that African Americans understood their investment in this parallel development—that they would gain inspiration from black people who exercised the types of roles promised during Reconstruction.

Unlike the black people who heard Langston speak, most white Americans valued neither the realization of black freedom in Haiti nor the prospect of racial equality in the United States. Consequently, Langston sought to convince them that Haiti was a civilized nation that proved black potential. He tried to persuade away the "bigot's sneer." In interviews, Langston told reporters from major national newspapers including the *New York Times*, *Chicago Tribune*, *Baltimore Sun*, and *Washington Post* that Haitians had concluded that "constitutional methods" rather than coups were the preferred means of affecting political change. Haitian schools, he continued, were "numerous, fairly attended, and . . . conducted, if not with the greatest efficiency, with commendable success."[29] They proved the capacities of Haitians and African Americans alike. Langston had "Prejudices strife" in mind as he insisted that Haitians were better off than black people in the United States and the British West Indies. He wanted white Americans to rethink the withdrawal of support for black civil and political rights by reconsidering the example of Haiti, a country "capable of great developments" and indicative of "the power of the colored race to govern themselves."[30]

Langston's statements were more critical of the United States than many white contemporaries would have liked. They were certainly more sympathetic to Haitians than most foreign commentaries. Still, Langston hinted at a black nationalism that resembled U.S. nationalism. According to Holly, Langston was "profoundly convinced that the American standpoint of reviewing things . . . is the best adapted to a rising people." He did not hesitate to make that view apparent in his dealings with Haitian politicians. In conversations with them, Langston argued that Haitian political stability would come not only as a result of removing incentives for revolution but also through the establishment of "constitutional self-government" modeled upon U.S. republicanism and the introduction of "Christian civilization" by Protestant missionaries.[31] From his perspective, the means of improving the international reputation of Haiti and helping black people across the African Diaspora was obvious: Haitians had to adhere to a standard of progress identified in the bourgeois institutions and values of his own country.

Indeed, Langston's public interviews indicate a desire to persuade skeptical white audiences that Haitians needed little convincing of the superiority of U.S. civilization. During his diplomatic tenure in Port-au-Prince, Langston assured a reporter from the *Washington Post* that "the form of government in Hayti is republican, and the constitution of the country framed after our own."[32] Furthermore, he noted that Haitians acknowledged the sanctity of religious freedom and welcomed U.S. and European Protestants to their country. Finally, Langston characterized Haitians as enthusiastic trade partners. In the midst of his country's Second Industrial Revolution, in a moment when steel magnate Andrew Carnegie boasted that the United States was thundering past Europe "with the rush of the express," Langston stressed "the value of the carrying trade between the United States and Hayti," including "a very fine line of steamships, running now twice a week, between New York City and Port-au-Prince."[33] Haitians, Langston concluded, "are learning more and more with regard to us and our ability and disposition to supply their wants." They too equated prosperity with mobility and capitalism with progress.[34]

Langston saw no disadvantages to judging Haiti by a bourgeois standard of civilization that he and other black intellectuals thought was the *only* standard of civilization. In fact, he expected great benefits. There was no question in Langston's mind that U.S. political institutions provided the best model for Haitian politicians, that Protestantism offered Haitian peasants unrivaled lessons in piety and industriousness, or that global capitalism was the best structure for organizing Haitian social and economic life. He had no doubt about Haiti's calling, either. As white supremacists argued that Haiti proved the recent mistake of "Negro rule," Langston insisted that Haitians could not only improve their material status but also rehabilitate the image of their entire race. They, he predicted, could become a "negro nationality in harmonious, honored activity."[35] Haiti could be the country of his dreams and African Americans' needs.

Langston was far from alone in his preoccupation with black self-determination. During the late 1870s, countless black southerners dreamed of finding better lives, of fulfilling the lofty promises of emancipation and Reconstruction, in Liberia. Hamstrung by poverty, most never left the United States; however, tens of thousands of them did escape the South for Kansas and Oklahoma. Those refugees fled from the anti-black terrorism that pervaded their native region. They fled toward what they hoped was their Promised Land. Leaders of the migration referred to it as an Exodus and the black refugees as Exodusters. They predicted that the flight out of southern (re)enslavement would bring about a new millennium, the realization that "God says in His Holy Work that he has a place and land for all his people, and our race had better go to it."[36]

The Exodusters frequently invoked racial destiny, too. Forged in the post-Reconstruction era, racial destiny was a malleable and often messianic concept influenced by fierce debates about political reform, race, citizenship, immigration, labor rights, women's suffrage, imperialism, and industrialization. It was intertwined with ideas about national progress. As the United States emerged as a global power, fulfilling a destiny ascribed to it by its white citizens, black intellectuals proclaimed that their race had the potential for similar greatness. It, too, possessed a progressive fate. Whether ecclesiastical or secular, separatist or integrationist, black visions of the future thus shared one common assumption: the race would rise or fall as one.[37]

For Louden S. Langley, recent events made clear the individual consequences of black people's declining collective status. A native of Vermont, Langley and his family joined James Theodore Holly's emigration movement from the United States to Haiti.[38] The Civil War brought them back. Following a Union victory that he helped achieve as a soldier, Langley and his family had settled in a house next door to Robert Smalls, the self-emancipated hero who captured a Confederate ship and surrendered it to the United States Navy. Langley, then an employee of the Freedmen's Bureau, had also joined Smalls on the Beaufort, South Carolina, school

FIGURE 5. John Mercer Langston, c. 1860–1875. Brady-Handy Photograph Collection, Prints & Photographs Division, Library of Congress.

board and at the 1868 South Carolina constitutional convention. He was an active participant in the reconstruction of South Carolina from its promising beginning to its violent end. By 1879, with Wade Hampton in control of his state and the Exodusters on the move, Langley had lost his home. He worked in a lighthouse, not politics. And, barely able to stand due to an injury suffered during the Civil War, he applied for a pension. His request was denied.[39]

In 1880, having experienced betrayal from the same country for which he sacrificed his health, Langley thus took to the pages of the *Christian Recorder* to promote emigration to Haiti once again. In his estimation, Haiti had more "productive force" than any of its Latin American neighbors. Its government, he reasoned, possessed "liberal and advanced views . . . toward their negro brethren throughout the world, and particularly towards the negro of the United States."[40]

Almost two decades since returning to the United States to secure abolition in the Civil War, Langley now had no doubt that emigration was the appropriate course of action for black southerners and no reservations about Haiti as the ideal destination. While many black spokesmen, including Frederick Douglass, encouraged black southerners to weather the storm in the region of their birth, white industrialists and planters complained that the loss of African Americans would shrink the pool of cheap labor and devastate the southern economy. According to Langley, neither party considered the "*welfare of a race.*" Black people, he insisted, had "a destiny to work out on this Western Hemisphere *independent* of and *separate* from the Caucasian." They could not achieve that destiny by an "unfortunate exodus" from the South to Kansas.[41] They could not realize it in a country reunited on the principle of white supremacy.[42] Instead, Langley continued, black self-determination would come through a unified effort "to establish in this Western world a great negro nationality, that will unmistakably demonstrate our equality with the most favored race of men!" It would come in Haiti, the lone country where "the negro, *unaided* and *uncontrolled* by the white man, has demonstrated his military genius, and by the terrible blows of his own arm has won his right to a *separate* and *distinct nationality.*"[43]

Langley cited the invitations of Haitian leaders and the race pride of Haitian citizens as proof that he was correct in placing his black nationalist dreams in their hands. Jean Jacques Dessalines had invited African Americans to "partake of Haytien liberty" at the dawn of Haitian independence.

During the 1820s, the Haitian president Jean-Pierre Boyer had paid the passage of refugees who "desired to expatriate themselves from their ungrateful country." A more recent Haitian president, Fabre Geffrard, had proclaimed that his "ancestors, in taking possession of this marvelous soil, were careful to announce in the Constitution that they formed, that all the negroes scattered through the West Indian Isles and North and South America belonged, of right, to the Haytien family." They had all invoked a spirit of racial unity that endured. Like Langston, Langley was a devoted abolitionist who had traveled to Haiti and found himself entranced. He had observed Haitians in "their martial pageants, their counting rooms and their agricultural labors," received great hospitality "in the houses of some of the best people there," and delighted in "the portraits of Haytien statesmen that adorned the dwellings of Haytian gentlemen." He had become convinced "that a more liberal and race-loving people does not exist on the face of the earth."[44]

These characterizations were strategic, not just romantic. Langley was well aware of the negative portrayals of Haiti—that it was a land of incessant violence, that divisions between mulatto and black people were irreparable, that Haitian culture was worthless. He knew, too, that African Americans "too often re-echoed the charge" that Haitians were "lazy and indolent, bigoted and jealous." His characterizations of Haitians as a people unified around their common African ancestry were therefore meant to counter divisive stereotypes and encourage greater cooperation among people of African descent dispersed throughout the Western Hemisphere. Langley warned that African Americans' "general belief in this slander" directed at Haitians had "worked to our detriment as a people." It had "turned the scales against Hayti whenever we thought of emigrating there" and caused a general aloofness "from our Haytien brethren."[45]

Moreover, that detachment had distracted most but not all African Americans from persistent threats to Haitian sovereignty. Haiti, Langley wrote, was not only a "grand illustration" of black self-determination but also a "glorious nationality" that had "existed for three quarters of a century, notwithstanding the governments of the world have thrown every obstacle in the way of its progress." Those past injustices, including the 150-million-franc indemnity that France levied against Haiti as punishment for the Haitian Revolution and the nonrecognition policy of the United States, remained fresh in Langley's mind. Even more pressing, though, were current efforts to destabilize Haiti. Langley protested that "to-day the extraordinary spectacle is presented of the consulates of the great powers of

Christendom, giving shelter and protection to traitors to the Haytien Government!" He chastised "Republican America," a country that continued to join "hands with monarchical Europe in shielding disturbers of the peace of Hayti" long after "its own Minister there had strongly urged that such protection be discontinued!" To Langley, it was clear that Langston agreed that "but for external influences revolutionary disorders in Hayti would be less frequent and her advancement more rapid and permanent." The fact that the "able minister" served the interests of the U.S. government did not diminish his affinity for a black nationality whose "glory of success [would not] be given by any fair award to the white man."[46]

By calling for a movement of Africans in the Diaspora—a "separate and distinct effort" of "our" people throughout the Americas—Langley sought ways of understanding blackness and racial progress outside of the toxic U.S. political climate. But even as he critiqued the "disjointed and hybridized race effort" of his day, Langley showed that he was not immune to the common tendency to reify distinctions or rankings among black people according to their national origin. During his time in Haiti, Langley later wrote, he could not help but think "that if a colony of colored farmers from the oppressed South could only be induced to settle on these rich lands, what a blessing it would be both to Haiti and themselves." Like the European colonizers of the Americas, the educated emigrationist scrutinized the native use of Haitian land. He found it primitive in its methods and criminal in its inefficiency. "So ancient is the mode of cultivating the soil in Haiti," Langley complained, "that even the old time method of farming practiced here would be an improvement." He concluded that "a settlement of a thousand of our people on these rich lands would revolutionize the system of agriculture for miles around."[47] It would energize Haitians, too. His interpretation of statements made by Charles W. Mossell, Ebenezer Don Carlos Bassett, and Langston led him to believe that most Haitians were able laborers whose manliness and industriousness could benefit from an infusion of a more advanced U.S. culture. He became convinced that "well informed" Haitians agreed, that they, too, looked "upon the American negro as possessing qualities they long to have incorporated in their body politic."[48]

In the winter of 1880, seeking further support for his assessment, Langley wrote to his old acquaintance James Theodore Holly. The quick response of one of Langley's "well known" Haitian confidants was published in a February 1881 edition of the *Christian Recorder*. Holly shared the conviction that Haiti had a unique mission on behalf of all black people, that it was the land of the "free, independent, disenthralled and sovereign [black] citizen" with a commitment to democracy that put the United States to shame. He also agreed with Langley that it required perfecting. Holly insisted that Haitians had yet to develop modern industry, form a stable government, or fund internal improvements. Emigration would solve those problems. To Holly, African Americans could transform themselves from the victims of white terrorism in the U.S. South to the apostles of "industry, religion, and education" in Haiti. They could carry Haitians "onward to their high destiny" and speed its "entrance into the career of the highly civilized nations of the earth."[49]

Holly saw himself and those African Americans who lived and worked alongside him in Haiti as models for future emigrants. Two decades after arriving in Haiti, Holly continued to view his mission there in providential terms. Every conversion to his Orthodox Apostolic Church of Haiti was another step toward the entrenchment of Haitian Protestantism, the creation of a Haitian clergy, and the ultimate eradication of white influence in Haitian Christianity. Each baptism brought Haiti closer to eliminating Catholicism, purging Vodou, recapturing the greatness of ancient Africa, and securing a progressive future for the black race. For Holly, then, the fulfillment of racial destiny demanded the adoption of appropriate aspects of bourgeois U.S. culture even as it required physical separation from white Americans and some of their institutions. It entailed the work of African Americans like John Mercer Langston, who were committed to a civilizing mission that complemented Holly's visions of black nationalism. At the outset of Langston's tenure in Port-au-Prince, Holly noted with unmistakable pride that the U.S. diplomat was "imbued with the spirit of American institutions and the genius of the American people." He observed with clear satisfaction the "salutary effect" that Langston was trying to exert upon Haitians. In his estimation, there was no one more fit to guide Haitians in "the perilous task that they have undertaken to carve out for themselves a high and noble destiny."[50] Certainly, there was no better inspiration for African Americans who hoped to do the same.

Loudon S. Langley, suffering from his war wounds, died in June 1881.[51] He never saw Haiti again. Yet his visions of its "high destiny" endured. The idea of its symbolic meaning persisted.

FIGURE 6. James Theodore Holly, c. 1875. The printmaking firm Currier & Ives published this lithograph after James Theodore Holly became the bishop of what he called the Orthodox Apostolic Church of Haiti. His consecration, coming more than a decade after he emigrated from the United States to Haiti and adopted Haitian citizenship, made him the first black bishop of the Episcopal Church. Prints & Photographs Division, Library of Congress.

As James Theodore Holly sustained his support for emigration, Mary Ella Mossell continued to educate African Americans on the dire state of her mission field. The AME leader informed readers of the *Christian Recorder* that Haitians deserved more immediate attention than black southerners, insisting that

> we are aware that the demands of the home mission are of equal importance with those of the foreign mission; there must be met also. This however is the difference: The Gospel is needed at home to strengthen and perpetuate our free, liberal and republican institutions; the Gospel is needed here to give birth to such institutions. The Gospel is needed in America to prevent the return of ignorance and superstition; it is needed here to break the spell which these twin evils have brought over the people. The Gospel is needed in America to back up the temperance sentiment . . . but it is needed here to create a temperance sentiment.[52]

The rhetoric Mossell used to differentiate between home and foreign missions is telling. She believed that African Americans shared the same concerns and possessed the same needs as Haitians. But she assumed that the moral progress of the lowliest African American still surpassed that of most if not all Haitians. She characterized Haiti as virgin soil in need of cultivation.

The encouragement Mossell received for Haitian missions suggests that her propaganda was well crafted and her characterizations of Haitians and Haiti broadly accepted. From 1880 to 1884, the AME Church gave almost $2,700 to support Mossell and her work.[53] The *Christian Recorder* proudly broadcasted the pledges of financial aid and moral support for Haitian missions that came from rural southern towns, sizeable midwestern cities, and cosmopolitan northeastern communities alike. In a typical year, a minister from Mcintosh, Georgia, and a layman from Cambridge, Massachusetts, found common cause in Haitian missions.[54] So, too, did attendees at AME conferences in Columbia, South Carolina, and Indianapolis, Indiana.[55] Their shared interests and investments show that concern for Haitian souls, for religious missions tied to ideas of racial destiny, knew no geographic or spatial bounds.

Neither did the attendant anxieties about Haitian life and culture. Black Protestants who backed Haitian missions did not just guarantee the extension of religious services to the heart of AME missions in Port-au-Prince, they also enabled a social and cultural program meant to reform individual and collective habits. Throughout the 1880s, Mary Ella Mossell and the members of the WPMMS tried to make Haitian women better housewives as well as devoted Christians. Mossell taught girls needlework, discussed other elements of housework with them, and visited Haitian homes to ensure that impressionable Haitian girls and their mothers were putting their instruction to good use. Such work, she informed AME members, was fundamental to uplifting Haitians and improving the image of all black people. At a time when middle-class white Americans defined civilized women as fragile, spiritual homemakers and identified civilization as a precursor to self-government, Mossell implored her fellow churchwomen to help their Haitian sisters "improve" their lives and vindicate their race by embracing "the art of making home attractive and cheerful."[56]

Her husband, Charles Mossell, tried to affect similar change. On occasional trips back to the United States, the formal leader of the AME Church's Haitian missions treated audiences in rural Georgia, upstate New York, and numerous locations in between to a "picturesque view of the inner and outer life of Hayti." In doing so, he hoped to secure the finances needed to construct new schools and churches in Haiti and achieve the longstanding goal of "conquering . . . the Island for Christ."[57] Moreover, in editorials complementing his lectures, Mossell emphasized and often exaggerated the growth of the Haitian mission field, boasting that the dozens of Mite missionaries, preachers, and teachers who now labored in Port-au-Prince frequently held public meetings that attracted thousands of attendees.[58] That was not all. He expressed, perhaps, the most pride in the innumerable laypersons whose financial contributions were used to send Haitians from what Mossell considered the moral and material depravity of their homeland to the most hallowed grounds of black Protestantism, Wilberforce University.

Indeed, higher education assumed an unparalleled role for black Protestants who assigned providential meaning to Haitian independence. In 1881, Bishop Benjamin F. Lee, the president of Wilberforce and the future father-in-law of the Mossells' daughter, confirmed that the first private university for African Americans had raised scholarships for and enrolled two "active and faithful young gentlemen" from Haiti. Lee expected that Solomon G. Dorce and Adolph H. Mevs would leave Wilberforce after completing the school's liberal arts curriculum and become missionaries in their native country.[59] Charles Mossell shared these expectations. He viewed the Haitian students as key contributors to missionary work that would "preserve Haytian independence and perpetuate the sovereignty of the nation." AME laypersons proved receptive to his idea that Haitians educated in the United States could help "bring about marvelous results in Hayti" and "put beyond question the safety of the people's sovereignty and national independence."[60] By the date of Dorce and Mevs's graduation from Wilberforce, AME members had provided enough scholarship money for three more Haitian students at the Ohio university.

As evidenced by his remarks about the Haitian scholars, Charles Mossell was insistent that African Americans adopt a global consciousness and prioritize the task of black nation-building in Haiti. The leading AME missionary in Port-au-Prince encouraged his peers to realize that they were "bound to this Negro Republic by the ties of race." He insisted that Haiti held "a claim upon us that no other country has" because the Haitian Revolution had altered the "civilization of the new world . . . precipitating a new era and a new condition, particularly in the status of the unrecognized brother in black."[61] Those bonds, he argued, obligated African Americans to either become educators and missionaries in Haiti or, at the very least, support those who did. He implored readers of the *AME Budget* to "let others in their hatred of the African race forget the Haytian nation . . . rejoice at her failures, point the finger of scorn and speak reproachfully of her effort at self government." African Americans would do the opposite. They would, Mossell proclaimed, "hold Hayti and her people in grateful remembrance" and employ their tongues "if not in strains of praise, in prayer and supplication in her behalf."[62]

Those choices—praise, prayer, or supplication—reveal much about the worldview of Mossell and his ilk. It was clear to them that blackness rooted in shared African heritage connected Haitians and African Americans. It was apparent that a mutual history of slavery linked their fortunes and obvious that Haitians deserved praise for their historic role in the abolitionist struggle. Still, assumptions about U.S. and Protestant superiority endured. Feelings that Haitians might require more prayer than praise and more supplication than solidarity persisted.

Both prayer and supplication animated Emily J. Cooper. A WPMMS member, Cooper respected African Americans who emigrated to Haiti during the antebellum era, became Haitian citizens, and might make occasional visits back to the United States but now served as the "lively" albeit "aged" friends of a new generation of African Americans in Haiti. She had little interest in pursuing a similar path, though. For her, the United States was the "land I love best."[63]

Cooper's goal was not to abandon her country forever but to export what she saw as the best parts of it to Haiti. Accordingly, she lauded a pupil at the AME Sabbath School who gave a rousing performance at a school exhibition. Standing beneath the flags of the United States and Haiti, George Harvey, probably the child of parents born in the United States, recited the lyrics of the "Battle Cry of Freedom." After his recitation of the pro-Union song that had been used to celebrate abolitionism, encourage patriotism, and endorse the reelection of Abraham Lincoln during the U.S. Civil War, the boy waved "the good old flag" to the pleasure of Cooper, Charles Mossell, James Theodore Holly, John Mercer Langston, and other attendees who gave it "three hearty cheers." Maybe the Haitian flag received equal applause. Perhaps an ode to Toussaint Louverture stirred similar sentiments. If so, those responses went unrecorded in the account of the event that Cooper gave to the *Christian Recorder*. What was noted, though, was how much the WPMMS organizer and her fellow African Americans loved the sight of the "dear flag of our Union."[64] It was theirs, and its movements across the Haitian skyline seemed to capture an idea reiterated time and time again by Benjamin Tucker Tanner—the "American negro" was a distinct "negro." Because of their national origin African Americans were "the best representative of the negro race on the globe," the most capable architects of sound black self-government even in a foreign land.[65]

In the aftermath of Reconstruction, claiming the United States in this way could be defiant. But rejecting it could be, too. In 1883, the U.S. Supreme Court declared unconstitutional the public accommodations provision of the Civil Rights Act of 1875. It shredded the last major legislation of Reconstruction and confirmed the fears of African Americans like Charles Harris. As the United States abandoned its commitment to biracial democracy, the Union veteran and former Alabama legislator wrote a letter to the secretary of the American Colonization Society, the organization founded in December 1816 to remove free black people from the United States.[66] "We are taxed without representation," Harris lamented. "We obey laws; others make them. We support state educational institutions, whose doors are virtually closed against us. We support asylums and hospitals, and our sick, deaf, dumb, or blind are met at the doors by invidious distinctions and unjust discriminations." "From these and many other oppressions," Harris concluded, "our people long to be *free*."[67]

The ideas of Haiti were inseparable from the anxieties of the moment, from that longing to be *free.* In the post-Reconstruction era, African Americans characterized Haiti as a final bastion of black participation in the U.S. government and as a refuge for embattled black southerners. They described it as a powerful example of black self-government and as a singular site of racial improvement. They understood it as practical and symbolic, as exceptional and perfectible. To African Americans for whom Haiti was real and imagined, an investment in U.S. cultural values and political institutions sometimes paralleled interest in black nationalism. Their strategies for achieving racial destiny were often as complex as the uncertain moment in which they arose. African Americans who assigned Haiti a prominent albeit ambivalent place in their visions of a collective and progressive future were stuck in the limbo between Reconstruction and Jim Crow, between national promise and national failing. Increasingly, they were also struck by the common causes, not the ethnic differences, that faced the entire, embattled black race.

As African Americans reconsidered their ties to nation and race, the Harvard professor Nathaniel Southgate Shaler returned to the topic that J. R. Ralls helped introduce. He, in 1884, wrote the first of several articles on the "Negro problem." For Shaler, uncivilized black people granted a freedom for which they were unprepared posed "a danger to America greater and more insuperable than any of those that menace the other great civilized states of the world." The "armies of the Old World," Shaler explained, "the inheritances of medievalism in its governments, the chance evils of Ireland and Sicily, are all light burdens when compared with this load of African negro blood that an evil past has imposed upon us." He did not blame his peers for this dilemma, however. Instead, Shaler chastised the British colonists and the founding fathers of the United States for being "too stupid to see or too careless to consider anything but immediate gains" when they established a racialized system of chattel slavery. He complained that his forbearers had not foreseen that a black presence would afflict the United States during its current period of increasing immigration, urbanization, and industrialization. For Shaler, it was obvious that African Americans—uniquely criminal, depraved, ignorant, and incapable of assimilating into a more civilized Anglo-American culture—presented a greater challenge than the southern and eastern European immigrants then trying to adjust to the demands of life in the urban North. Calling for more statistical investigations into the causes of black inferiority, Shaler, a self-proclaimed racial liberal, predicted "that for centuries to come the task of weaving these African threads of life into our society will be the greatest of all American problems."[68]

Like Ralls, Shaler asked his readers to cast their gaze abroad when considering his ominous forecast. The native Kentuckian and one-time student of Louis Agassiz, a pioneer of polygenism, insisted that "every experiment of freeing blacks on this continent has in the end resulted in even worse conditions than slavery brought to them." While British rule kept Jamaica from descending into complete barbarism and Spanish and Portuguese blood "served for a little leaven" in otherwise degenerate Cuba and Brazil, Haiti embodied the most abject failures of American societies where slavery was dead or dying. "The trial" of black freedom in Haiti, Shaler argued, "where freemen of the third generation from slaves possess the land to the exclusion of all whites, has been utterly disastrous to the best interests of the negro." Ignoring the fact that mortality rates far exceeded birth rates among the enslaved population of Saint-Domingue, he maintained that his Haitian contemporaries had wasted the efforts of their ancestors, who cultivated "great industries in sugar and coffee culture" under "the relatively mild slavery of resident proprietors." They had, he insisted, retrograded to "a state that is but savagery with a little veneer of European customs." Shaler concluded that modern Haiti was defined by a government that was "but a succession of petty plundering despotisms, a tillage that cannot make headway against the constant encroachments of the tropical forests, [and] a people that is without a single trace of promise except that of extinction through the diseases of sloth and vice."[69]

Shaler was prolific but unoriginal, prominent but unexceptional. In many respects, he was just one of several participants in a transnational dialogue on race, black potential, and the meaning of past and present emancipations across the Americas. He certainly found an intellectual kinship with Spenser St. John, the former British minister-resident and consul general to Haiti and the current British envoy extraordinaire and minister plenipotentiary to Mexico.

In the same year that Shaler wrote his influential article on the "Negro problem," St. John published *Hayti; Or, the Black Republic.* He claimed that the book was a disinterested memoir of his time in Port-au-Prince, even insinuating that it might be too sympathetic to Haitians because he did not look down on his "fellow-creatures" even if they possessed "a difference of complexion." Those claims were pure propaganda. St. John was far from objective and, like Shaler, his racial liberalism was more imagined than real. The career diplomat made it all too apparent that his work was meant to discourage the degree of black self-determination achieved by Haitians after the Haitian Revolution and desired by African Americans in the aftermath of Reconstruction.[70]

In a book that remained the standard text on Haiti long into the twentieth century, St. John condemned the physical characteristics, moral character, political institutions, and culture of Haitians and, by extension, all black people. He lampooned "the awkward figure, the heavy face, the bullet head, the uncouth figure, the cunning blood-shot eyes" of the stereotypical Haitian and informed readers that these features "inherent to the blacks" shattered any illusion of civilization in Haiti.[71] He argued that Haitian professionals simply masked the superstitions, witchcraft, and cannibalism that prevailed among the Haitian masses. They provided nothing more than a veneer of civilization.

Besides reaching that conclusion, St. John admitted that he grew more skeptical of "the capacity of the negro to hold an independent position" during his time in Haiti. He echoed his contemporaries in the United States, insisting that "as long as [the negro] is influenced by contact with the white man, as in the southern portion of the United States, he gets on very well. But place him free from all such influence, as in Hayti, and he shows no signs of improvement." St. John placed himself in direct conversation with northern white social scientists and southern white reactionaries who, in the spirit of Redemption, maintained that Haitians proved the sheer absurdity of black citizenship. Assuring his readers of his agreement "with those who deny that the negro could ever originate a civilization, and that with the best of educations he remains an inferior type of man," St. John argued that black people had proven themselves "totally unfitted for self-government" and "incapable as a people to make any progress whatever." In fact, their only success was in convincing some gullible white liberals otherwise. "To judge the negroes fairly," St. John told his audience, one had to "live a considerable time in their midst." Readers could "not be led away by the theory that all races are capable of equal advance in civilization.[72]

From Mexico City, St. John had a clear view of the battles for national independence and emancipation in Cuba and the move toward the abolition of slavery in Brazil. Still, even as *Hayti; Or, the Black Republic* had advice for planters and government officials across the Americas, it found its greatest appeal in the post-Reconstruction United States. In November 1884, the *Atlanta Constitution*, a paper that boasted a circulation of more than a hundred thousand subscribers, wondered "what might have been the effect upon fair-minded people in our northern states if Sir Spenser St. John's account . . . could have been published simultaneously with 'Uncle Tom's Cabin.'" Although lamenting that the book appeared too late to correct the ills of abolitionism and emancipation in the United States, the paper hoped that it would "arouse the public mind to the gravity of the problem presented by the preponderance and alarmingly disproportionate increase of the black population in several of the southern states."[73] A month later the *Chicago Tribune* reprinted from the London-based *Spectator* a review of St. John's "remarkable, terribly honest, and ruthlessly realistic book." The review, which ran under the headline "Haiti: The Fairest and Richest Island in the World in the Hands of Vaudoux Savages," promised readers that *Hayti; Or, The Black Republic* proved that the country was "sunk in misery, bloodshed, cannibalism, and superstition . . . that, as an experiment in negro self-government, it is a hideous failure."[74] It suggested that the message of this "failure" was clear: African Americans had to remain under white control because Haitians had failed the test of freedom.

The writings of St. John and the enthusiasm of his many admirers would not go unchallenged, though. As *Hayti; Or, the Black Republic* created a "profound sensation" among white Americans who agreed with the *Atlanta Constitution* that the "only safety for the negro is . . . in a great government in which the white man clearly and unmistakably dominates," Herbert S. Fairall made his way to the Colored People's Department at the World's Industrial and Cotton Centennial Exposition being held in New Orleans.[75] There, the white newspaper editor and Iowa State Commissioner to what contemporaries called the New Orleans Exposition saw an interpretation of Haiti far removed from the slanders of St. John. In a book published soon after the end of the exposition, Fairall noted that among the "many specimens of needlework by colored ladies, fire screens, ebony carved wood, window lambrequins, plush panels, wax and hair work" were "very fine portraits of Toussaint l'Ouverture, whose wonderful history in connection with Hayti is so well known." In fact, he continued, one of "the most remarkable exhibits was a history of Hayti" that Sarah H. Shimm, a black school teacher in Washington D.C., "embroidered in silk work" on a sofa.[76]

Remarkable was an apt description for Shimm's creation. The right side panel of the couch displayed "the bars of the bolted iron door" behind which Toussaint Louverture sat "thinking in melancholy lassitude" during the final days before his death in the Fort de Joux. Beneath the scene were words attributed to Louverture: "I am strong in the consciousness of integrity and fidelity." The left side panel contained "a scene in St. Domingo" featuring "palms, tropical plants, castles, high stone walls and towers." Beneath it was another quote ascribed to Louverture: "All France has come to enslave St. Domingo." Three more scenes decorated the sofa's seats. The center picture, contained within "an upright oval of blue silk background and red silk outline," featured several men standing "amid the cane stalks and grasses of a meadow . . . evidently discussing the current topics relating to their dominion." The scene to the right of center had a "placid lake, where stood the date palm or waves the spreading foliage of the tropics, and . . . a party rowing out from shore, no doubt content and in raptures with the marine bit of nature before them." The inscription below the boat gliding over the lake read "I love thee still." To the left of center was a battle between two armies fighting "under the spreading trees." Each side stood above the same words: "L'Ouverture!" "L'Ouverture!" Completing the visual history, situated on the sofa-back, were the flags of Saint-Domingue and Haiti, "between which a hand r[ose] having the flag of the stars and stripes tattooed upon its palm."[77]

Shimm knew her literary history well. The quotes attributed to Toussaint Louverture found on her embroidered couch came from *The Freedmen's Book*, a collection of short stories and poems published in 1866 by the white abolitionist Lydia Maria Child. The quotations were pulled directly from "Toussaint L'Ouverture," one of the book's numerous biographies.[78] It is possible that Shimm, born in Ohio during the mid-1840s, read *The Freedmen's Book* when it was first published, at the same time that she began her teaching career.[79] It is likely that she continued to see its relevance for her students. Dedicated to Robert Smalls and addressed "to the freedmen . . . with the hope that . . . all of you will derive fresh strength and courage from this true record of what colored men have accomplished, under great disadvantages," the book had retained its subversive potential.

It encouraged black readers to disregard the writings of St. John and continue to "take pride in Toussaint l'Ouverture, as the man who made an opening of freedom for their oppressed race."[80]

Shimm's couch was not entirely derivative, however. In addition to the scenes that incorporated Child's homage to Louverture, the educated Shimm included an original poem that clarified her perspective on Haiti. Appearing beneath the scene on the sofa back, it read:

When Albion, from her snowy cliffs,
The air with Hampden rends,
And France with drooping fleur-de-lis,
Bewails the Orleans Maid,
When Austria tells from ramparts high
Of Louis Kossuth's fame,
And Italy wafts through cloudless skies
Her Garibaldi's name:
When Scotia sighs o'er Wallace's grave,
And Freedom weeps the martyred brave:
When patriot hands for country's sake
From Emmet's tomb the shamrocks break,
And o'er the fanes of other lands
The storied radiance shines,
We turn to thee, O sun-kissed isle,
And on thy peaks see Freedom smile—
Ah, Hayti, sea-girt island gem,
'Twas Toussaint won thy diadem.[81]

There is no indication that Shimm crafted those lines in response to St. John or that she was even aware of the publication of his soon-to-be bestseller. Still her "wonderful sofa" was an obvious part of an emerging black public sphere in which African Americans countered discourses about black inferiority.[82] Shimm presented Haiti as a magnificent embodiment of black nationhood, not a shameful representation of black misrule. Her distinctive contribution to the New Orleans Exposition, on display to black and white attendees alike, depicted Toussaint Louverture as a founding father on par with the patriotic heroes of various European countries rather than the instigator of a misbegotten slave insurrection. African Americans, Shimm implied, not only rejected the idea that they required the domineering influence of whites but also embraced Louverture as their William Wallace, their Lajos Kossuth, and their Giuseppe Garibaldi.[83] They turned away from the United States and toward his "sea-girt island gem."

There were clear echoes of antebellum discourses of black nationalism in a poem that affirmed African Americans' ties to an external nationality on par with those claimed by European Americans. Shimm's sofa, however, was also a product of the post-Reconstruction moment. As St. John and his ilk ridiculed Haitian independence rather than denying its existence, an unassuming schoolteacher felt just as compelled as her more famous male contemporaries to defend Haiti and the Haitian Revolution. Her artwork was motivated by an impulse to counter widespread, damaging critiques of postemancipation black progress and show that Haiti was a land where all Americans could—should—look to see black potential and "Freedom smile."

It is no wonder then that Shimm's couch achieved modest fame. In July 1885, seven months after the opening of the New Orleans Exposition, the St. Paul-Minnesota-based *Appeal* reported that Shimm had just died from a "brief illness." It noted that she made a great mark before her premature passing. "Doubtless many who visited the New Orleans Exposition this past winter," the black newspaper predicted, "will call to mind a very remarkable and handsome picture of work in the colored Department, the Toussaint L'Overture sofa." Shimm's couch had "won much praise from the thousands that visit the Exposition," the *Appeal* continued. It had captured the onlookers' attention and admiration through its craftsmanship and content alike.[84]

John Mercer Langston was just as convinced of the need for favorable representations of Haiti in a moment when St. John depicted it as the embodiment of black inferiority. In the same month that the *Appeal* honored Shimm, the Haitian government hosted a reception for Langston. The event marked the end of Langston's tenure in Port-au-Prince and the beginning of a new relationship between the government of President Lysius Salomon and John E. W. Thompson, the incoming U.S. minister resident and consul general to Haiti. When the time for Langston to speak arrived, the guest of honor deviated from standard diplomatic pleasantries and offered a candid assessment of the difficult burden assumed by the Haitian president. Salomon, Langston asserted, was the "chief representative of the black race." The president whose portrait graced the walls of Lincoln University, the first institution of higher education for black people in the United States, had a unique responsibility at a time when the "race must present itself before" and pass the scrutiny of "the most civilized powers." His country, Langston elaborated, was the only one where "the black man can find a place for displaying and perfecting an independent and sovereign nation, his force, his capacity, his wisdom, his virtue, his faith, his patriotism, his courage, his true character." Langston thus had one demand: "guard [Haiti], protect it!"[85]

Salomon and his compatriots found the directive obvious. Like his predecessors, the Haitian president felt that it was his "duty, as head of a Republic composed of descendants of Africa, to spare no effort that Hayti, far from being a blot on the new world, may have a conspicuous place with the great powers which advance rapidly to the summit of civilization."[86] African Americans who had become Haitian embraced a similar burden. They were even more explicit that the slander of St. John needed condemnation. In particular, James Theodore Holly assured foreigners that the British diplomat whom he once considered a friend lacked credibility and presented an unfair, exaggerated, and ultimately inaccurate picture of Haiti. Holly explained that generations of slavery and international neglect born out of anti-black racism had much to do with any shortcomings in Haitian culture or political life. In fact, he posited that the Haitians who bore the brunt of those oppressions were not the main culprits for the cultural backwardness that afflicted their country. Holly suggested that those who wanted to find the roots of Haitian ills needed to look no further than the "profligacy" of foreigners who lived and worked there.[87]

Alonzo P. Holly reiterated that message. The son of James Theodore Holly, and a student at the New York Homeopathic Medical College, Alonzo criticized leading black editor T. Thomas Fortune for an editorial in his *New York Freeman* that gave credence to the lies of St. John. Holly pointed out that the British diplomat had "questionable motives" and relied on "questionable sources," including the outdated work of the slaveholder Moreau de Saint-Méry. How, he implied, could anyone believe a book that impugned all Haitians when it was clear that superstition and heathen practices were confined to the "lowest strata" of Haitian society? Although he disparaged black folk culture to make the point, Holly was correct in noting how white supremacists used broad brushstrokes to paint a picture of universal black depravity. He was accurate, too, in noting the degree to which African Americans had too often acquiesced to the negative portrayals of Haiti in their rush to counter them. Holly advised African Americans to remember Haiti not as the land of St. John's imagination but as the country that "first gave proofs of the ability of the Negro race" at a time when they were "groveling in ignominy."[88]

The public letter, written by the son of one of the thousands of refugees who had fled from slavery and oppression in the United States to freedom and equality in Haiti, had its desired effect. A few months later, when the *New York Evening Post* repeated St. John's allegations of cannibalism in Haiti, Fortune responded with an emphatic rebuttal. "The *Evening Post*," Fortune wrote, "knows that there are no more accomplished gentlemen and statesmen outside of France than the present rulers of Hayti, most of whom were educated at Paris." Certainly, it knew better than to suggest that "had Hayti been annexed to the United States as General Grant desired there might now be a representative in the Federal Congress who was a votary of Voudooism." For Fortune, then, there was now no doubt that the popular *Evening Post* was wrong. It was "not just to the Haytien government when it gives currency to the inventions of Sir Spencer St. John."[89]

Alonzo P. Holly and T. Thomas Fortune were representative of other black intellectuals whose critiques of white supremacy and understandings of black self-determination were strident albeit chauvinistic. They were far from alone in singling out Vodou. During the late nineteenth century, white politicians, diplomats, businessmen, journalists, and travel writers from Europe and the United States continuously cited the creolized religion of the Haitian masses as the principal evidence of Haitian barbarism. Like St. John, they identified it as proof that Haiti was African, premodern, and incapable of self-government. African Americans who joined Haitian politicians in critiquing Vodou understood the material threats those allegations of black backwardness posed in an era of imperialism, while often understanding civilization in the same terms as white imperialists. From their perspective, a civilized Haiti was a Christian Haiti. It was a country achieving industrial and moral progress, one in which Vodou could no longer exist.[90]

AME missionaries including Mary Ella Mossell remained at the forefront of the mission to vindicate Haiti and eradicate the supposed backwardness in their midst. Just before her death in 1886, Mossell wrote "Domestic Life in Hayti," an account that would be published posthumously in the AME's *Church Review*. On the one hand, the article was indicative of the impulse that led her and the members of the WPMMS to heed the initial call for the "work of moral elevation" in Haiti. She, like St. John, claimed intimate knowledge of human sacrifices by Haitian peasants.

Mossell even maintained that she had witnessed a Vodou ceremony that was just as "terrible," "abominable," and "degrading" as the educated readership of the *Church Review* might imagine. It was an event, she wrote, that would "strike all right-minded people with horror, filling their souls with sadness and sorrow."[91]

Still, Mossell departed in significant ways from the anti-Haitian tropes that St. John popularized. She explained that Saint-Domingue was not a colonial paradise but a site of brutal enslavement whose effects had hampered Haitian political and social development. Unlike St. John and his sympathizers, she boasted that the Haitian state was making, and would continue to make, substantial material progress despite decades of international scorn. Any suggestions otherwise were indicative of a lingering bitterness, Mossell concluded. After all, she wrote, Haitians had long ago "*lost the sympathy of the Christian world*" for committing the "*unpardonable sin (?) of cutting the throats of their masters and freeing themselves.*"[92]

At once conservative and subversive, Mossell's final public writings presaged modes of black thought that would become more popular after her death. The assurance of Haitian evolution from an implied African savagery was a long-standing means of depicting African Americans as capable of similar growth during their own transition from slavery to freedom. The assertion of civilized progress contrasted in tone with the statements in support of Haitians who had killed their masters and engaged in the most radical act of self-emancipation in world history. The latter, more militant expressions in celebration of black freedom grew louder in ensuing years. They became a popular refrain within a black press that continued to grow in size, geographical reach, and political scope from its modest ecclesiastical and abolitionist roots in the antebellum North.[93] For black journalists across the United States, voters, and schoolchildren alike, the so-called Christian world was not only misrepresenting black people but also seeking unjust dominance over them. The relentless pursuit of white world supremacy was the obvious cause of the slandering of Haiti, the colonization of Africa, and the lynching of African Americans. It was the reason for black people to affirm their global consciousness and expand the scope of anti-racist resistance.

In March 1886, a group of schoolchildren in Baltimore, Maryland, became part of that resistance. In front of a packed auditorium at the local Samaritan Temple, the boys and girls of the St. John's Sunday School performed

"Homage to Africa." A girl playing the role of Mother Africa sat upon a throne. On one side, she clasped the hand of another student representing the United States. On the other side, she held the hand of a different student embodying Haiti. Classmates cast in the roles of England, Portugal, Spain, France, and Italy circled around them. They prostrated themselves to the Motherland and her African American and Haitian children.

Safe from the gaze of white Baltimoreans and secure within a prominent black institution, the students provided a profound expression of Pan-African unity and black nationalist aspirations. They quite literally joined together Africans, Haitians, and African Americans and placed their countries (or, in the case of African Americans, their nation within a nation) in a superior position relative to their white counterparts. The audience members and a reporting black journalist who cheered the performance must have recognized its implications. The characters on stage reversed an emerging colonial order in which European monarchs and U.S. politicians positioned themselves at the forefront of global affairs and demanded subservience from black people in Africa, the United States, and the Caribbean. They celebrated a rich black cultural heritage that white supremacists insisted was nonexistent and glorified a model of black self-government that their detractors derided as fundamentally flawed. In short, the students expressed a race pride that stood in stark contrast to and represented a clear rejection of the ideas about black inferiority espoused by men like St. John in recent years.[94]

The young black Baltimoreans' celebration of Haiti also diverged from the headlines found in countless U.S. newspapers of the day. Nine months after the St. John's Sunday School performed "Homage to Africa," an absurd yet standard account of black barbarism circulated throughout the United States. A white businessman who claimed to have witnessed a Vodou ceremony in Haiti provided it. How had he gained access to such a sacred ceremony? Simply by donning blackface. The dubious account alleged that the other worshippers, apparently unable to distinguish between a black man and an imposter wearing burnt cork, proceeded to murder a young boy. Perhaps realizing the need to verify his sensational story, the informant cited some corroborating evidence. He noted that he had read St. John.[95]

Subsequent accounts gave new life to the inventions of the British diplomat. In one newspaper correspondence, a white resident of Kingston, Jamaica, wrote that Haitians routinely cooked and ate children. Tellingly, he ignored the conspicuous presence of Protestants and Catholics in Haiti and lamented that not a single church existed there to save Haitians from such a steady lapse into barbarism.[96] An editorial in a March 1888 edition of the *Baltimore Sun* confirmed the irrelevance of any evidence in contradiction to the standard narrative of Haitian backwardness. It informed readers that St. John had already proved the irrationality of the "humanitarian principles" that allowed for the existence of Haiti or any other place where black people possessed too much social independence and political influence.[97] It helped cement his fame. White Americans could not get enough of the salacious stories about Haitian barbarism that reinforced their prejudices toward African Americans. They issued a demand for a second edition of *Hayti; Or, the Black Republic*, with which a New York publishing house soon complied.[98]

The reinventions of St. John occurred at a time of civil unrest in Haiti. In August 1888, an alliance of regional military forces staged a revolt against President Lysius Salomon. The insurgents, accusing Salomon of attempting to make himself president for life, succeeded in overthrowing the Haitian government but failed in establishing a stable replacement as the defeated Salomon regime gave way to a provisional government that included General François Denys Légitime, General Séïde Télémaque, and General Florvil Hyppolite. Soon thereafter, Télémaque was assassinated and Hyppolite's supporters laid the blame for the act on Légitime. When Légitime became president and strengthened his hold on Port-au-Prince in the aftermath of the assassination, Hyppolite launched an insurrection meant to defeat his political rival and establish more economic hegemony for the northern region of Haiti from which he hailed.[99]

U.S. officials and white journalists first identified those events as indicative of black inferiority but inconsequential to U.S. policy. U.S. secretary of state Thomas F. Bayard delegated responsibility for formulating a U.S. response to the early stages of the Haitian revolution to Alvey A. Adee, the second assistant secretary of state. Even after Adee reached the conclusion that the Haitian situation was "becoming intolerable," he still characterized Haiti as a mere "nuisance."[100] At the same time, white journalists throughout the United States depicted the most recent Haitian political upheaval as simply another sign that black people could not govern themselves. One newspaper in South Dakota even speculated that Salomon had been "voodooed . . . unseated by the discontent of the more ignorant blacks who are snake-olaters, or 'voodooists.'" Convinced that the ignorance that delegitimized black political participation was well established—after all, it was an accepted excuse for abandoning Reconstruction—the paper overlooked inconsistencies in its reporting. It gave no indication why Vodou practitioners would revolt against one of their own, a man who the paper claimed was nothing more than a "nominal Christian" and a true practitioner of the "faith which seems natural to the untaught African."[101]

Black journalists refused to back down in the face of such relentless attacks on Haitians. They could not when the dominant public sphere continued to exaggerate reports of political change in the Caribbean while ignoring the mounting violence perpetrated against African Americans in the United States. Mansfield Edward Bryant, managing editor of the AME's *Southern Christian Recorder*, condemned white journalists who embodied the willful ignorance of white Americans. Those hypocrites, the editor opined, "Talk about the rebellion in Hayti but where on earth can there be found worse state of affairs than reigns in parts of Louisiana now. . . . Part of Louisiana is now in the hands of outlaws, murderers, thieves, cutthroats, assassins, and these scourges of humanity are Anglo Saxon white men."[102] For Bryant, the rise in lynching and white terrorism proved that barbarism was endemic to the United States rather than Haiti. It was, he reasoned, white vigilantes, not Haitians, who should feel shame.

Bryant's argument built upon the public testimonies offered by many of his peers. In the post-Reconstruction era, hundreds of African Americans testified about experiencing or witnessing racial violence. Some told Congressional hearings about the terrorist acts that motivated the Exodusters to move. More published descriptions of the painful wounds inflicted on those who stayed behind. By exposing to public view the reign of terror in Louisiana, Bryant corroborated those subversive accounts. By contrasting it with the state of affairs in Haiti, he added another layer to the words that came out of testifiers' mouths. Bryant connected the dots between white journalism and white terrorism, between the epistemic violence or discursive harms inflicted on Haitians and the physical violence endured by African Americans. He extended the well-established politics of defiance. Bearing witness for Haiti, he made it international.[103]

The indignation of men like Bryant would only increase as white Americans began to identify the ongoing Haitian unrest as an opportunity for profit rather than a mere nuisance. Florvil Hyppolite recognized the benefits of gaining the support of the U.S. government through promises of trade concessions and ambiguous discussions of territorial cessions. For their part, U.S. government officials courted Hyppolite. In March 1889, U.S.

secretary of state James G. Blaine and U.S. Navy rear admiral Bancroft Gherardi abetted William P. Clyde, a U.S. steamship proprietor who supplied Hyppolite with large shipments of gun cartridges, powder, rifles, bayonets, and Gatling guns. The realization of an alliance between his rival and U.S. officials who hoped to secure a naval station and increased commercial influence in Haiti created a rational anxiety in François Légitime, and on October 20, 1888, the Haitian president, backed by the French government, ordered the seizure of the *Haytian Republic*, a U.S. merchant ship that he correctly suspected of providing transportation for and selling arms and ammunition to the northern insurgents.[104]

This incident cohered with a recurring theme in Haitian history—the undermining of Haitian governments by outside interference. But it also revealed how foreigners would ignore that fact and focus on what they saw as the illogic of Haitian governments who tried to maintain stability in spite of those external pressures. U.S. newspapers immediately condemned the seizure of the *Haytian Republic*. They argued that Haitians could neither govern themselves nor recognize their innate inferiority. While the *Philadelphia Inquirer* attributed Haiti's wrongdoing to the fact that it was not a "decent republican state," the *New York Times* questioned whether Haiti could even be said to have a government. The paper compared the failed "republic of freedmen" to the Confederates' unsuccessful "oligarchy of slaveholders" and called on the U.S. government to crush Haitians just as it had crushed rebellious white southerners.[105] The *Chicago Tribune* seconded these points. That paper argued that Haitian ignorance had placed the United States in an untenable position. Although civil war was endemic within "a race of people . . . volcanic and unsettled in temperament," the United States had no choice but to issue a robust diplomatic and military response, protect its citizens abroad, and subdue a people "fully as black as the Southern negro."[106] The *Columbus Enquirer-Sun* provided a more succinct expression of white supremacist orthodoxy. As the Haitian government acted in accordance with its rights as a sovereign nation, the Georgia newspaper hoped that the actions of the "savages inhabiting that little island" would result in a "good drubbing at the hands of the United States Government."[107]

African Americans responded not only by creating counternarratives about the seizure of the *Haytian Republic* but also by demanding a more agreeable U.S. policy toward Haiti. In November 1888, the incumbent Democratic president, Grover Cleveland, lost his reelection bid despite winning the majority of the popular vote. Leading black Republicans maintained that the triumph of the Republican Benjamin Harrison in the Electoral College could be attributed to more than the politician's progressive stance on domestic race relations or his promised support for higher tariff levels and the interests of industrial workers. In fact, Calvin Chase contended that the mounting tensions between the United States and Haiti helped swing the election. The sole editor of the *Washington Bee*, born to a free black family in Washington, D.C., and educated at the Howard University School of Law, Chase insisted that black Republicans feared that a Democratic victory would mean a belligerent response to Haiti. They worried, he suggested, that a loss for Harrison would mean the end of Haiti's freedom and the further erosion of their own.[108]

Chase had a point. Still, however effective black Republicans may have been in helping usher Cleveland out of office, they continued to face the challenge of shielding Haiti from conflict with the U.S. government. Even after his defeat, Cleveland heeded incessant calls for action against a Haitian state deemed intolerable and impudent by its U.S. critics. On December 10, 1888, Secretary of State Thomas F. Bayard sent a naval force to Haiti to demand the return of the *Haytian Republic*. Ten days later, threatened with bombardment from the U.S. naval force sent to its coast, the Haitian government restored the vessel to the United States.[109]

Outraged black journalists denounced the act as proof of the international scope and obvious hypocrisies of Democratic racism. Chase, for instance, found a glaring discrepancy between Cleveland's unwillingness to protect black citizens from lynching at home and his eagerness to defend the property rights of white citizens abroad. The *Washington Bee* editor pointed out that the U.S. president "could not find law enough to defend" the thirteen black men recently murdered by white terrorists as they waited for their trial at the courthouse in Carrolton, Mississippi, but had ample time to rush to help "a little old ship that did something that it had no business of doing and was captured by a negro government." Such "aggressive steps to suppress the little negro government of Hayti . . . confirms what we have often said," Chase concluded. Clearly, "when the negro is involved . . . the democratic administration cannot find law to protect him, but it certainly can find law to suppress him."[110]

Although Chase wrote with passion and reason, he unintentionally pinpointed the monumental challenges to his work. Without the ability to exercise their political rights, African Americans could neither stop atrocities like the Carrolton County Courthouse Massacre nor end the military aggressions against Haiti. The increasing frequency of both implied that the prospects for full black citizenship and attendant political influence remained bleak. They suggested that the storm was forthcoming, that the worst had not arrived let alone passed.

The entrenchment of white supremacy across the Americas emboldened rather than stifled many black public figures. In January 1889, Harry C. Smith began an editorial appearing in his *Cleveland Gazette* by lamenting that "a government of Negroes is unable to maintain its equilibrium; that the old story that Negroes are incapable of self-government comes so near being verified in the political life of the little island." He quickly switched tack, though. Despite current events, Smith assured his readers, African Americans were "by no means despairing of the Negroes in Hayti, nor the Negroes in America." Instead, they trusted that "there will be a time, even in demoralized Hayti, when *all will be well* and the Negroes of that island will rise above arms to carry out their plans." They certainly resented any suggestions that Haitians would not vindicate black self-government. Smith, a high-school graduate and longtime resident of Cleveland, insisted that African Americans could not believe that "the picture drawn of the Haytien Negroes" by a correspondent of a local Ohio newspaper was "true to fact." Speaking on behalf of his editorial staff and his race, Smith proclaimed that "we are certain that the references made to the history of Sir Spencer St. John . . . are repudiated by the Haytiens themselves." Rather than accepting the word of the British diplomat, Smith had "inquired of several Haytiens as to the truthfulness of this history." They had confirmed what the black journalist suspected: *Hayti; Or, the Black Republic* was "false and a libel upon the inhabitants of the island."[111]

Smith did not finish with the jab at St. John, however. Continuing, he wrote that the U.S. government "played a foolish part in fitting out a war vessel and in threatening the Haytien authorities with war if there was not an immediate surrender of the 'Haytien Republic.'" Those ridiculous actions on the part of Uncle Sam mystified Smith, as did the conclusions drawn from the dispute between the Haitian and U.S. governments. Smith noted that it was "amusing to read all that is said about this Negro government and the incapacity of the Negro to rule and the application of it to the American Negro in his struggles for equal rights before the law." He was certain that "the enemies of the American Negro" would "take this bit of news [regarding the *Haytien Republic* controversy] as a strong point in their favor to keep the Negro down."[112]

That foregone conclusion did not concern Smith, at least not outwardly. Rather than advising Haitians to reform their ways or refine their habits, he reiterated a point that he had made before: "The colored people of this country will have to work out largely their own destiny, despite opposition and prejudice. Upon them depends the making of their future." For Smith, the "twaddle about the so-called Negro supremacy in America" being a "repetition of the Haytien revolution [was] as meaningless as it can well be." It was senseless. Irrelevant. What mattered was Smith's final point. "The Negro will not down," he proclaimed. "Let that be understood."[113]

Smith's defiant response to the critiques of Haiti, the handling of the *Haytian Republic* controversy, and the restrictions on black civil and political rights in the United States coincided with the beginnings of an ominous period for black people across the world. By the end of the 1880s, the number of black lynching victims rose throughout the United States, Mississippi implemented a plan for disfranchising black voters, and white supremacists solidified their political power in most parts of the South. At the same time, the U.S. government used gunboat diplomacy to force concessions from Haitian officials who they considered innately inferior due to their blackness. The acceleration of European colonialism in Africa made the delineation of a global color line distinguishing subject colored people from white rulers all the more glaring.

Black intellectuals in the United States knew these trends all too well. Although still influenced by ideas of U.S. and Protestant superiority, they voiced a heightened understanding of the common causes for which Haitians and African Americans fought. They appreciated that theirs was an emergent Age of Jim Crow *and* imperialism, a new moment when their liberation was not possible without the assurance that all black people, at home and abroad, could exercise their right to be free.

CHAPTER 3

The Vexing Inspiration of Haiti in the Age of Imperialism and Jim Crow

In 1889, a debate unfolded in St. Louis, Missouri. Under the St. Louis School Board's initial plan for renaming the city's colored schools, Wendell Phillips, the late abolitionist known for his antebellum lecture on Toussaint Louverture, would become the namesake of Colored School No. 5 while a host of other white abolitionists, politicians, and Union officers would receive similar honors.[1] The proposal failed; to the chagrin of the *St. Louis Post-Dispatch*, the names of those "saviors of the colored race" never graced the segregated black schoolhouses in the city. The newspaper, owned and operated by the conservative white Democrat Joseph Pulitzer, complained that the St. Louis School Board revised its recommendation after African Americans protested the renaming of Colored School No. 6 in honor of Winfield Scott Hancock, a deceased Union general, Democratic politician, and avowed segregationist. Bowing to that pressure, the *Post-Dispatch* grumbled, the St. Louis School Board scrapped its first proposal and requested that black principals offer names for their institutions in recognition of black heroes and heroines.[2]

Divided opinions within black St. Louis soon emerged. In a letter to the St. Louis School Board, the principal of Colored School No. 1 argued that "the imputation already rests upon [African Americans] that we are slow to appreciate our real benefactors and friends" and predicted that those "imputations would certainly rest upon stronger grounds" if his school "failed to honor the memory of Wendell Phillips . . . the scholar, the orator, the fearless anti-slavery advocate." Other black principals in St. Louis welcomed the chance to express their race pride even if it meant drawing the ire of their white counterparts. Indeed, some wanted school names that commemorated the most radical expression of black independence in the world.

By 1890, several colored schools in St. Louis paid explicit homage to Haiti.[3] While the principal of Colored School No. 4 told white interviewers that he would have been happy to comply with the original guidelines and rename his school after the Union general and Republican politician John C. Frémont, he ultimately selected Toussaint Louverture as its new namesake. He did so despite the derision of the *Post-Dispatch*, which expected that "many little negro urchin" would "fail to get the proper Haytian twist of the pronunciation" of Louverture. Arthur Dessalines Langston, the principal of Colored School No. 2 and the son of John Mercer Langston, showed similar resolve. At the same time that the *Post-Dispatch* criticized the veneration of the Black Napoleon, Langston celebrated his own namesake. Black boys and girls soon attended the Dessalines School. That development, the *Post-Dispatch* protested, was "not a happy one." It condemned the decision to name a school after an infamous "Haytian leader . . . that became a tyrant and was overthrown by his own race in an attempt to make himself Emperor." It bemoaned the stark departure from the "first and proper aim" of the renaming initiative and chided black St. Louisans for having "thrown away" the chance to thank the white people responsible for "the freeing of their grandfathers from the chains of slavery."[4]

The events in St. Louis, a historical gateway for black migrants moving West and North and a metropolis where racial segregation was more uneven than in the Deep South, highlight the continued salience of the ideas of Haiti among African Americans well after the demise of Reconstruction.[5] As white politicians erected the foundations of Jim Crow across the United States and white imperialists expanded their control in the Caribbean, the Pacific, Asia, and Africa, white journalists in St. Louis claimed credit for black freedom and demanded deference from their black counterparts. They received neither. By demanding a voice in renaming their schools and then honoring Louverture and Dessalines, black St. Louisans reasserted their history of self-emancipation and reclaimed their right to self-determination. They not only celebrated the Haitian Revolution, a historic blow against slavery and colonialism, but also positioned Haitians as protagonists in the enduring fight for black liberation and self-determination at home and abroad.

In many ways, black St. Louisans forecasted important continuities and significant developments in black thought. While black educators rechristened their schools in honor of the Haitian Revolution, black journalists rallied to defend Haitian sovereignty, and black political leaders vied for the Haitian diplomatic post. Both tried and failed to improve the international image of Haiti and dictate more favorable U.S. policies toward it, particularly in the midst of renewed interest in annexation and what became known as the Môle-Saint-Nicolas affair. For Frederick Douglass, the U.S. minister resident and consul general to Haiti at the time, the U.S. effort to seize the coveted port on Haiti's northwestern coast was a devastating blow to his hopes for Pan-American relations established in a spirit of racial egalitarianism and mutual progress. It encouraged a more realistic view of U.S. expansionism, one already adopted and articulated by a number of Douglass's peers.

For black journalists, artists, educators, and activists in the final decade of the nineteenth century, Haiti became not only a rare site where African Americans could still participate in U.S. politics but also the final battleground on which black people could contest global white supremacy—rhetorically and, at times, quite literally. Haiti was the country that had fended off the United States when it tried to compel it to concede a piece of its territory. It, as Douglass proclaimed, was the Star of the North. Although black public figures sometimes infantilized Haitians and still elevated U.S. cultural norms in their nascent anti-imperialist critiques, they came to see Haiti as a real beacon of hope, especially during and after its subversive presentation at the 1893 Chicago World's Fair. In their estimation, in the years before the consolidation of a seemingly more conservative but no less international politics of racial uplift, Haiti came to epitomize virile black manhood and militant resistance to racial oppression. It was an inspiring albeit embattled stronghold of black self-determination in the Age of Imperialism and Jim Crow.

During the first months of 1889, the connection between critiques of and militaristic threats to Haiti grew clearer. White journalists in every region of the United States perpetuated sensational tales of wanton violence, human sacrifice, cannibalism, sexual depravity, and degenerate Vodou rituals in Haiti. Many of them then claimed that U.S. intervention was the only way to civilize Haitians. For example, after complaining that reports about Haitian barbarism were becoming tiresome, one journalist at the *Kansas City Gazette* called on his fellow "white folks and Christians to step in and put an end to [Haiti's] dirty muddle." He encouraged "a regiment or two of Yankee or British soldiers" to descend upon the troublesome "Black Republic," provide Haitians with "a lot of soap and compell them to get clean."

FIGURE 7. Dessalines School, St. Louis, Missouri, c. 1890. The Dessalines School remained open until 1974, nearly two decades after the legal desegregation of public schools in St. Louis. Photographs and Prints Collection, Missouri Historical Society.

The last point was particularly important. "You [could] never civilize" Haitians, the *Gazette* contended, "so long as they are so utterly filthy."[6]

The hypocrisy of such claims stunned black journalists. Jasper Hume Childers, the son of two former slaves and editor of the Topeka, Kansas–based *American Citizen*, wasted little time in building on the defenses of Haiti that emerged during the *Haytian Republic* controversy and responding to the accusations now leveled against Haitians by the *Kansas City Gazette*. His staunchly Republican newspaper pointed out that "white folks and Christians [had] a broad field for missionary operations here at home." In fact, "a more dirty, savage and muddled state of affairs never existed than is to be found in Christian America." From the perspective of the *American Citizen*, white people needed to understand that they would "never civilize the Haytians with a Bible in one hand and a shot gun in the other." Put simply, the "Negros of Hayti" were neither desirous of shipments of soap nor "stuck on Yankee and British religion."[7]

Ongoing developments in the Pacific encouraged similar condemnations of proposed U.S. intervention in Haiti. During the late 1880s, the United States, Great Britain, and Germany all coveted the Samoan Islands for use as a coaling station and naval base. As tensions among them simmered, U.S. and German warships engaged in a tense standoff in a Samoan harbor. It only ended when a storm struck. Dozens of U.S. citizens lost their lives as a result of the natural disaster, and in its wake, Germany, the United States, and Great Britain met in Berlin. There, they agreed to a wide-ranging treaty that ensured the persistence of foreign landholding rights, judicial influence, and political control in Samoa.[8]

Black journalists took note of these international events and saw clearly how the U.S. government negotiated with Europeans at the same time that it strong-armed Pacific Islanders and Haitians. Childers's *American Citizen* asked whether "Cleveland and the American people feel proud of his great and brave act in bullying the feeble republic of Hayti" when the German Empire was brazenly "shaking [its] fists in our face."[9] Charles Hendley, a native of Alabama, a graduate of Rust College in Holly Springs, Mississippi, and a former educator who had become the editor of the pro-Republican *Huntsville Gazette*, insisted that a more consistent foreign policy demanded a swift response to the German affronts. He speculated that such a response was not forthcoming, though. Hendley advised his readers to remember that "Germany is nearer Uncle Sam's equal in strength than little Hayti" and thus would likely suffer no repercussions for its challenges to U.S. interests abroad. In his estimation, the contrast between the U.S. government's cooperation with Germans and its disregard for Samoans and Haitians proved beyond doubt that it was no more than a "cowardly bully."[10]

Partisan interests accounted for some of this criticism. Childers and Hendley were prominent black Republicans whose newspapers offered consistent critiques of the Democratic Party.[11] At times, their readers and those of other black newspapers voiced their own displeasure with Democrats who demonstrated little respect for the rights of black people at home or abroad. On one occasion, a reader of the *Washington Bee* wrote to protest the "striking contrast" evident in the "modus operandi of our government." The United States, he proclaimed, pursued "a bulldozing, intimidating policy" toward Haiti while offering "a weak, vacillating, cowardly course" in its diplomatic relations with Germany. That "palpable difference" between attacks on the "diminutive Haytien Republic" and submission to the "redoubtable Bismark" raised a hypothetical question: "Oh! democrats why were you ever made." Of course, no answer was forthcoming. Left to wonder how long racism would dictate federal policies, the *Washington Bee*'s correspondent mourned the plight of African Americans and Haitians alike. "We are floundering about upon the sea of consternation," he lamented. "We tremble in our boots."[12]

The connections between U.S. imperialism and emerging forms of racial oppression in the United States were all too clear to other black Republicans. In February 1889, Harry C. Smith, the editor of the *Cleveland Gazette*, admitted that he was indifferent to perceived threats to U.S. interests abroad at a time when "our American citizens, colorless, are *insulting* our American citizens, colored, within their very own borders." Smith noted that while white Americans expressed anger over the *Haytien Republic* incident countless "defenceless and offenceless colored people are *shot down* in cold blood . . . driven from their homes regardless of sex or innocence." It was obvious to one of the most ardent black Republicans in Ohio that the righteous indignation over the supposed offenses of Haitians was insincere. Smith insisted that "Hayti and Samoa have offered no grosser insult to America and her citizens than America is inflicting on them every day." He called on white Americans to be "*shamed* that open rapine and fratricide under their very noses haven't been given the effective attention of the proper authorities."[13] From his vantage point, there was no mistaking that U.S. imperialism not only threatened the sovereignty of nonwhite countries but also deflected much-needed attention from the violent efforts to control African Americans and restrict black civil and political rights in the decades after Reconstruction. In fact, that distracting effect did not seem unintentional.

The jockeying over Haiti extended to debates over black representation in U.S. politics as well. Even after Benjamin Harrison supplanted Grover Cleveland in the spring of 1889, it was clear to all but the most unobservant black public figures that there were still very few federal appointments available to African Americans. That scarcity produced intense competition. Some prominent black Republicans attempted to gain the diplomatic post in Port-au-Prince for themselves while black journalists nominated a number of politicians, educators, veterans, journalists, and ministers as potential successors to outgoing diplomat John E. W. Thompson. A diverse range of personal and regional interests made a consensus on the ideal candidate unattainable, but black spokesmen agreed that the Haitian post needed to go to someone capable of serving the United States and concerned for the well-being of Haiti. It had to be filled from their ranks.

In June 1889, Harrison complied with those demands and offered the coveted position to Frederick Douglass. To the Harrison administration, he seemed to be the perfect fit. Almost two decades after serving on Ulysses S. Grant's presidential commission on Dominican annexation, Douglass remained a devoted Republican. He was still an idealistic champion of U.S. exceptionalism and foreign policy, too. In a letter to the Haitian president Florvil Hyppolite following his appointment, Douglass celebrated "the spirit of the age." That spirit, he reasoned, "powerfully assists in establishing a sentiment of universal brotherhood. Art, science, discovery and invention have gone forward with such speed as almost to transcend our ability to keep pace with them. Steam, electricity and enterprise are linking together all the oceans, islands, capes and continents, disclosing more and more the common interests and interdependence of nations."[14] Those nations included Haiti and the United States, Douglass implied. The industrialized latter, he reasoned, could help modernize the underdeveloped former. It could build a Pan-American commercial system predicated on racial egalitarianism and mutual interests, one imbued with a "generous spirit of forbearance and concession, favorable to peace and fraternal relations."[15]

For a number of Haitian elites, that optimistic vision of a nonviolent, noninterventionist U.S. foreign policy was worthy of praise rather than consternation. Hyppolite lauded Douglass as "the incarnation of the idea which Haiti is following—the moral and intellectual development of men of the African race by personal effort and national culture."[16] Stephen Preston, the Haitian minister to the United States, predicted that the U.S. government would now abandon its aggressive attempts to seize control of Haitian territory after making Douglass, perhaps the most famous black abolitionist of his day, its minister resident and consul general to Haiti.[17] Alonzo P. Holly agreed. The son of James Theodore Holly assured the *New York Age* that "Haytians hail the nomination of so lofty-minded and liberal a man as the Hon. Frederick Douglass." In Douglass, he proclaimed, his compatriots "see not an 'annexationist' . . . but a gentleman who, remembering the depths of disgrace and injustice . . . will be better able to appreciate the heroic efforts of a nation whose past history influenced to no mean degree, his own career."[18]

In the United States, concern about the whitewashing of U.S. politics encouraged a less enthusiastic response to Douglass's appointment. As Haitian elites celebrated the decision made by the Harrison administration, African Americans reacted with greater ambivalence. Some black newspapers went so far as to express regret over the selection of Douglass for the desirable diplomatic position. For example, the *Indianapolis Freeman*, a newspaper owned by the conservative publisher Edward Cooper and edited by the future Booker T. Washington disciple Richard W. Thompson, argued that sending Douglass to Haiti was nothing more than a token gesture of goodwill to African Americans. In July 1889, it printed a political cartoon presenting that view. In it, the Republican president, dressed as a Roman emperor, tosses a plum labeled "Haytian Mission" to Douglass. The recipient of Harrison's largesse stands aboard a boat bound to Haiti as less illustrious African Americans strain to catch the fruit. The accompanying caption—"Frederick gets the 'Plum.' (Haytian Mission), While the Score of other Applicants Must Look for Something Else"—clarified any ambiguity readers might have found in the cartoon.[19]

Other black journalists joined in lamenting the scarce options left available to the less known yet equally gifted black men seeking political posts in that moment. Harry C. Smith made clear his regret that Harrison had passed over "the more deserving and more intelligent young men of the race" who were "restless and heartily sick of the appointment to office every four years of the same chronic office seekers and holders of color."[20] The *Leavenworth (Kansas) Advocate*, a paper edited by the leading black Republican and native Alabamian William B. Townsend, was a bit more tactful in voicing its displeasure. Even though a July 1889 editorial admitted that Douglass was an individual who "certainly demands recognition," it expressed disappointment that John L. Waller, another prominent black Republican who joined the Reconstruction-era black migration to Kansas, had been overlooked despite his relative youth, his "valuable services to the Republican Party," and his "unsurpassed qualifications."[21] The *American Citizen* simply suggested that the appointment of Douglass would likely not garner "general approval."[22] Such criticisms of Douglass were unfair albeit predictable. Critics of Harrison's diplomatic appointments saw ever-constricting avenues to black political participation in the United States and thus placed increased importance on their access to the U.S. diplomatic post in Port-au-Prince.

For his part, Douglass knew the significance of the Haitian appointment and the symbolic importance of Haiti. In an interview published in the *Washington Post,* Douglass said that no one could deny that Haiti was "an important element in the question of the possible future of the colored man on that continent." After all, white supremacists often pointed to it, cried out "'Look at Hayti! Torn and rent by division and revolution,'" and asked "what we can expect of the American Negro." To Douglass, those discourses were irritating but inescapable. Like previous black diplomats sent from the United States to Haiti, Douglass felt obliged to defend "the colored man on the continent" at the same time that he served the U.S. government. In fact, he was not ashamed to admit his split allegiances. Douglass informed the *Washington Post* that he was going to Haiti "to represent the interests of the United States, and also with a view to advance the interests of the people likely to be most benefited by the wise, peaceful, and orderly government of what is called 'The Black Republic.'"[23] His contemporaries understood exactly what he meant. As one white journalist acknowledged, Douglass planned to ensure "the peace, well-being, and happiness of Hayti" not only for the sake of Haitians but also for the benefit of African Americans who needed an unassailable "example of [black] self-government."[24]

Perhaps sensing that many of those African Americans were growing more critical of U.S. foreign policy, Douglass also tried to clarify his past and present positions on U.S. territorial expansion. Acknowledging his participation on the presidential commission on Dominican annexation, Douglass complained that the *Washington Post* continued to equate "coercion" with "annexation." He assured that paper that he had "never been a coercionist." While denying that "any American statesmen would counsel any such policy . . . against a friendly nation," Douglass insisted that Haiti did not require the intervention that a number of his most vocal peers feared. The Black Republic, he argued, was simply "going through the experience of the South American republics and of France, which has had twelve revolutions in a single century." It was on the same trajectory as its more powerful neighbor to the north. According to Douglass, the United States, once "a scene of discord, and civil war, as wild, turbulent, and persistent as that which is witnessed to day in the Island of San Domingo" was now home to "a stronger, wiser, happier and more united people than at any other time in our history." It had emerged from a "tempest and whirlwind of war," Douglass concluded. He expected Haiti to do the same.[25]

The romanticized picture of U.S. sectional reconciliation confirms that Douglass targeted a white audience with his words to the *Washington Post*, but even as Douglass glossed over the regressions since the days of Radical Reconstruction, he encouraged white Americans to support a more enlightened foreign policy. Douglass exaggerated the political violence in Haiti—the U.S. Civil War caused far more casualties than every Haitian coup combined—but he suggested, accurately, that the U.S. government was complicit in Haitian political instability. Douglass recalled that white southerners cited Haiti "against the cause of freedom in the United States . . . before we abolished slavery, when our fears created only disaster and ruin in that direction." They had set it up for failure and created the potential of further harm. Haiti, Douglass predicted, would suffer so long as white Americans including U.S. foreign policy makers saw it "as an argument against the ability of the colored race to govern itself."[26] It, like African Americans, would prosper only once accepted as an equal and allowed the conditions to (im)prove itself.

For Douglass, it was critical that his white contemporaries see Haiti as he did: a country capable of replicating a U.S. model of democratic politics and industrial progress, as a potent example of black self-determination. Despite the scorn that it received from the international community, Douglass informed the *Washington Post*, "Hayti [was] still Hayti, sharing the commerce of the world, with representatives in her capital of every great maritime power, and flags of all nations floating in her ports and harbors." He assured critics that Haiti was modern, interdependent yet independent. "No hostile foot has been allowed to tread her soil successfully during three-quarters of a century," Douglass warned. Haiti had a history of armed resistance against racial oppression that paralleled his successful fight with a slave breaker and the exploits of black Union veterans. Its people had clearly shown that "the child may stumble and fall many times and receive many bruises, but the child will become a man for all that."[27]

Despite its paternalistic metaphor, the vindication of black independence in the Caribbean was much needed. In the same moment that Douglass equated Haiti with virile black manhood and expressed support for its sovereignty, rumors of the annexation of Haiti by the United States resurfaced. Although the *Chicago Tribune* acknowledged that there was "no official proof" that U.S. secretary of state James G. Blaine had "matured a plan for the ultimate absorption of Hayti," it still suggested that there were "strong reasons" in favor of such a plan. Those reasons mirrored the justifications for previous annexation proposals. Nearly twenty years after

U.S. politicians boasted of the advantages that U.S. businesses could accrue from the annexation of Hispaniola, the *Tribune* described Haiti as a country rich in "natural advantages" and predicted that it "could be *made* to supply the United States with the greater part of its sugar and molasses, coffee, fine tobaccos, and tropical fruits (emphasis mine)." The implied use of force was no accident. Likely understanding what Douglass knew—that Haitians defended their independence with fierce determination—the *Tribune* offered repeated allusions to the fact that the United States would have to compel Haiti to become its client state. The paper provided consistent evidence that it did not object to that coercion. Haiti "could be greatly enriched if once made a safe field for American labor and capital," the *Tribune* predicted. Any means "which would make it safe and profitable for American labor and capital to go to Hayti" had its full support.[28]

In fact, to white journalists in the Windy City, it seemed obvious that the fruits of U.S. territorial expansion might exceed the material gains to U.S. corporations. As the *Tribune* gushed over the Haitian "sugar cane, coffee, cocoa, and tobacco" ripe for exploitation and export, it also commiserated with "dissatisfied and oppressed Southern blacks" and acknowledged that black sharecroppers desired "better treatment and higher pay." The paper even noted that African Americans who faced the prospects of something comparable to reenslavement in the U.S. South had an understandable "hope of bettering their condition." Those sympathies were far more cunning than sincere. Rather than pressuring white southerners to recognize that black people were now free, the *Tribune* suggested that black southerners were most responsible for deterring the resurgence of white supremacy in their region. In the spirit of the American Colonization Society and its slaveholding members, it advised besieged African Americans to look at colonization outside of the United States as the best answer to their problems. It encouraged them to view Haiti as "an outlet." According to the *Tribune*, colonization could "relieve the pressure of the black population in the Southern States" and offer the easiest possible solution of the so-called "race problem."[29] Black people could free white Americans from a great burden by becoming cogs in the machinery of U.S. imperialism.

To be certain, renewed proposals for colonization were meant to solve the "Negro problem" and serve the interests of white corporations, not those of black southerners. The *Tribune* insisted that the Haitian climate was "well suited to our Southern negroes" while expressing confidence that African Americans would only "migrate in large numbers . . . to some warm

Southern country." The idea that black people were uniquely suited for tropical climates fatal to white people was, of course, one of the rationales for the enslavement of Africans in the Americas. If the *Tribune* knew this, it did not care. Instead, it characterized former slaves and their descendants as "just the kind of laborers suited to Hayti." It positioned them not as the recipients of a more meaningful freedom in Haiti but as the objects of another form of domination. According to the *Tribune*, white businessmen and government officials would "find comfortable and healthy homes" in "the high lands and mountains" of Haiti and oversee the black people who labored in the plains and valleys below. They would ensure that "the power of the United States" was used "to maintain order and insure stable government in Haiti," push "the black people of that country" toward "an era of prosperity such as they have never dreamed of," and open "a new and inviting field . . . for capital and labor, particularly from the Southern States." In short, with "American protection and stable government," Haiti would become "just the place" for African Americans and Haitians alike.[30]

Aside from a few black editors who hoped that annexation would stabilize Haitian politics, most black public figures, even those who acquiesced to anti-Haitian stereotypes, echoed Douglass and demanded respect for Haitian sovereignty.[31] The editors of the Detroit-based *Plaindealer* conceded that "Hayti and San Domingo" were "unquestionably terrible examples of repression carried past the limit of safety and resulting in overwhelming evil." Still, they rejected the "stock arguments of the negrophobic repressionists," who insisted that Haiti and the Haitian Revolution confirmed the barbarism of black people or their "incapacity for self-government." In their opinion, "the history of Negro rule in Hayti, with all its horrors, [had] been no worse than Spanish rule in Cuba; and the massacre of San Domingo was only a feeble imitation of the Reign of Terror in France." Neither were justifiable—"massacre and misrule" never were—but it seemed obvious that misgovernment and revolution knew no color. The editors of the *Plaindealer* concluded with more than a hint of sarcasm that "the Negro [was] not especially blamable" for emulating examples set by Europeans who claimed a superior racial status. They implied that Haitians deserved not only the opportunity to govern their own affairs but also the chance to build a more humane system of governance than those found in the annals of European history.[32]

It was increasingly unclear whether Haitians would have that opportunity. In October 1889, William P. Clyde, the U.S. steamship proprietor whose arms shipments had helped bring Hyppolite to power, lobbied the Haitian government for substantial trade subsidies and exclusive trading rights to seven Haitian ports. He expected Douglass to support him and apply the diplomatic weight needed to turn a private proposal into a national demand. For Clyde, U.S. foreign policy was simply a tool of U.S. capital. It was, he assumed, not cooperation but corporatism that shaped Pan-American relationships and the practice of U.S. diplomacy.[33]

Douglass's introduction to informal imperialism made a distasteful impression but had a transformative effect. Earning the ire of Clyde, white journalists, and U.S. politicians, Douglass rejected a proposition that "shocked" him and "sounded like the words of Satan on the mountain." He did so because he despised an international politics that prioritized only U.S. commercial interests. Believing that he had made clear his respect for Haitian sovereignty and his egalitarian vision of Pan-Americanism, Douglass later wondered what he "had said or done to make it possible for any man to make to me a proposal so plainly dishonest and scandalous." He realized that his unwillingness to undermine Haiti's ability to enter into more favorable multilateral trade agreements "was my first offense." It marked Douglass from the outset of his diplomatic tenure "as an unprofitable servant . . . more a Haïtian than an American."[34]

The Clyde affair was not only an affront to Douglass's idealistic vision of international relations but also a troubling portent of his challenges to come. Upon entering the White House, Benjamin Harrison informed U.S. citizens that the demands of the U.S. Navy required access to convenient coaling stations abroad. Moreover, he promised to build a larger naval fleet, create an international canal zone in Central America conducive to U.S. commercial interests, and support a federally subsidized merchant marine. For Harrison, naval power equaled national might. He agreed with the historian Alfred Thayer Mahan and doubled down upon the aggressive foreign policy that his Republican predecessors embraced.[35]

The repercussions for Haitians soon became apparent. Harrison subscribed to a long-standing belief that Haiti's Môle St. Nicolas was a desirable prize because of its location at the northern entrance to the Windward Passage, its ample harbors, and its defensible geographic features. His administration wasted little time in acting upon that belief. Eight months after Harrison's inauguration, the *Yantic*, an unauthorized U.S. naval warship, arrived at the Môle to measure the distance from the Haitian port to other Caribbean islands where Europeans had established telegraph cables.

By the winter of 1890, Secretary of State Blaine had authorization to use forceful diplomatic tactics to acquire the Môle while Rear Admiral Bancroft Gherardi, commander-in-chief of the North Atlantic Fleet, a squadron of the U.S. Navy, monitored the political situation in Haiti to assess the prospects for U.S. territorial gains there.[36]

As the United States grew bolder, black journalists showed continuing concern for the persistent criticisms of Haiti. For instance, Harry C. Smith used what was becoming a common protest strategy and pointed out the hypocrisy of the exaggerated reports of Haitian disorder found in white newspapers. In February and March 1890, he chastised the Associated Press for producing its "monthly batch of lies about Hayti," advising the influential news source that rising crimes of lynching in the United States proved that "less in proportion transpires in Hayti than in the United States to disgrace the country."[37] The editors of the *Plaindealer* joined their counterparts in defending Haiti, a country that they knew was "pointed to as an example of the failure of the Negro to govern." After imploring Haiti's critics to acknowledge the "prowess and bravery which had made that little island an independent nation," the Detroit-based editors again insisted that civil unrest throughout Europe, South America, and the United States showed that race was not a determinant of political instability. Haiti, they argued, was not an "example of anything save . . . its peculiar disadvantages," namely undeserved scorn from the international community.[38]

These rebuttals of anti-Haitian criticism assumed heightened urgency for African Americans who recognized a link between Jim Crowism at home and imperialism abroad. One contributor to the *Plaindealer* responded to rumors that Frederick Douglass was being tasked with securing the annexation of Haiti by expressing his hope that "such a thing will never be under the present state of affairs." The correspondent surmised that if the U.S. government refused to protect its "loyal citizens" and condoned the abhorrent treatment of black southerners, then there could be no rationale for the annexation of Haiti.[39] Such concerns were neither uncommon nor unfounded. Other black commentators expressed similar fears that the racism abetting racial violence in the United States *was* the motivation for the rumors of annexation and real threats to black independence in Haiti.

Douglass, still convinced that he could help establish a more enlightened U.S. foreign policy, again tried to assuage mounting anxieties by romanticizing the relationship between the United States and Haiti. In the late summer of 1890, Douglass returned to the United States on a leave of absence from his post in Port-au-Prince. His homecoming was of interest to white and black Americans eager to hear his assessment of Haiti. In published correspondence and interviews given during that time, Douglass insisted that Haiti's progress was remarkable given its humble origins and subsequent diplomatic isolation. Moreover, he assured U.S. citizens that the Haitian government was "free from internal strife," supported by the industrious and independent Haitian masses, and on the "most amicable terms" with the U.S. government.[40] The final claim was especially dubious but those willing to take Douglass at his word could rest assured that Haitians faced no internal or external impediments to national prosperity.

A number of black public figures were not convinced that Douglass was striking the right chord, however. For instance, Harry C. Smith chastised the famous U.S. diplomat for telling an interviewer that he had "come to the conclusion that Hayti has a future." The Cleveland-based journalist accused Douglass of being quite late in acknowledging that "any country . . . that has produced such men as Toussaint . . . and has outlived such internal dissensions as Hayti has for eighty or ninety years, 'has a future.' "[41] Of course, Douglass had long advocated for Haiti even if his appraisals of that country betrayed a cultural absolutism that equated progress with the moral, technical, and material advancements achieved by U.S. elites. That fact was lost on Smith, though. As disregard for black self-determination across the world intensified, any commentaries about Haiti that contained even a hint of disparagement were bound to catch his attention.

At times, Douglass invited such scrutiny with statements that were shortsighted and easily misconstrued. During his leave of absence back home, Douglass informed reporters that "Port-au-Prince is a beautiful city, too, and I can hardly imagine the possibilities of that land under the hands of thrifty Americans." The offhand remark was meant to highlight the cosmopolitanism of the Haitian capital, a place where "native black men are often found who speak fluently several languages, and . . . are engaged in every branch of trade." It was not a call for coercion or intervention. Douglass continued to view Haiti through a historical lens, remembering the days when the "slave holding nations, including our own America, refused . . . to recognize [Haiti]." He was slow to recognize the consequences of Haiti's change from an international pariah to an imperial prize.[42] To Douglass, it was still critical to characterize Haiti not only as independent but also as enmeshed in global networks of trade. Haiti's inclusion in the sisterhood of nations, he reasoned, was the antidote to its past ills. It was the best means of reversing the underdevelopment caused by its "most abject slavery" and unequal treatment by "all Christian countries."[43]

For black journalists including T. Thomas Fortune, the means of Haitian progress that Douglass envisioned seemed more deserving of criticism than consideration. After reading and reprinting Douglass's interview, Fortune assured Douglass that the "possibilities" of a Haitian state influenced by "thrifty Americans" were limited at best. Instead, "race prejudice would soon reduce the [Haitians] to the same condition of government and peonage in the industrial system which prevail in Bermuda, Jamaica, Barbados, and . . . to a greater extent in every one of our own Southeastern and Southwestern States." Putting the shared struggle of Haitians and African Americans in biblical terms, Fortune concluded his editorial with the following wish: "Let us hope and pray that the heroic blacks of Hayti will work out a grand and enduring destiny without the selfish and inhuman assistance of 'thrifty Americans,' who believe in and practice this doctrine that God created the black Samson to be kicked and cuffed and robbed and 'kept in his place' by the white Philistines."[44]

Fortune chose an apt biblical metaphor, one that was familiar to many readers of the *New York Age*. God had not created Samson to "be kicked and cuffed and robbed." He had not wished to keep Samson "in his place." Instead, according to the Book of Judges, the Angel of the Lord gave Samson to his parents so that the child would one day deliver the Israelites from the Philistines, a people who used their political and technological strength to dominate the region between the Mediterranean Sea and the Jordan River. From birth, Samson thus had a special relationship with God that was evident in his supernatural strength and the flowing locks which he vowed to never cut. That bond was briefly severed when Delilah, the woman whom Samson loved and the Philistines enticed with promises of silver, cut Samson's hair. It was soon repaired, though. After the Philistines captured and blinded the weakened Samson, they brought him into a temple where a crowd gathered to observe a religious sacrifice and thank their god for delivering Samson into their hands. Leaning against a pillar of the temple, his hair grown long again, Samson prayed. God answered. He gave Samson the strength to bring down the temple. None survived in the rubble.

The suffering of the "black" Samson was the focus of Fortune's editorial. Still, there was a clear message to be found in the ultimate destruction that he wrought upon the "white" Philistines, too. The idea that God favored oppressed black people was not new. During the antebellum era, black leaders had, for instance, argued that militant resistance to slavery was in accordance with divine will.[45] That providential call to struggle remained relevant decades after the U.S. Civil War. It applied to black people in Haiti as well as the United States. As U.S. warships plied Haitian waters, Fortune's editorial not only highlighted the "selfish and inhuman" motives of "thrifty Americans" but also suggested that the allegation that "the heroic blacks of Hayti" were weak was mere myth. It certainly was not congruent with Haitian history or consistent with God's designs for black people. Put simply, Haitians had defeated Napoleon's army. They might flex their muscles again and tear down the pillars of the U.S. empire.

For men like Fortune, the lessons of resistance found in biblical and Haitian history were urgent. During a thirty-year period beginning in 1890, white vigilantes lynched at least two or three black victims every week. Moreover, in March 1890, the U.S. Senate defeated the Blair Education Bill. Black leaders chastised the northern Republicans who joined with southern Democrats in opposing legislation that had come to represent their greatest hope for equal educational opportunities. Months later, the Fifty-First U.S. Congress further diminished the country's commitment to its black citizens when it defeated a Federal Elections Bill that would have deterred the intimidation of black voters by strengthening federal oversight of congressional elections. Afterward, Democrats and their sympathizers claimed they had thwarted the rise of "another Hayti."[46] The apathy of national politicians left African Americans at the mercy of local politicians, including white Mississippians, whose poll taxes, literacy tests, and other disfranchisement measures soon spread to other southern states. African Americans would continue to resist political domination by joining grassroots agrarian organizations and advocating for the Populist Party.[47] Yet, to paraphrase one black Alabamian writing to Douglass in Haiti, the tide seemed to be setting in strongly against black people in whatever direction they looked.[48]

Indeed, black public figures knew that white supremacy was not only a domestic reality but also a transnational menace. After affirming African Americans' "brotherly interest" in Haiti, T. Thomas Fortune admonished a Port-au-Prince correspondent of the New York *Evening Post* who alleged that black people were incapable of self-government. Calling the disparaging remark a "white man's dictum," Fortune asserted that white newspapers and their correspondents were "constitutionally incapable of making an honest estimate of the capacity of the black in Hayti or the United States or Africa." Still, he advised Haitians to unify, because perceptions of Haitian backwardness increased the danger of "some grasping power" seizing control of their country. As other black journalists extolled Haiti as a land of "millions of independent, self-governing Negroes," Fortune warned that the disregard for black political participation showed by white lynch mobs, politicians, and journalists could lead to the "degradation" of Haitians. He was uncertain whether the political climate was making it impossible for black freedom to survive.[49]

In December 1890, Frederick Douglass returned to Port-au-Prince with verbal instructions to begin negotiations for U.S. possession of Môle St. Nicolas. He was ambivalent about the mission. Douglass believed that Haiti would be well served to lease, rent, or sell the Môle to the United States and cement mutually beneficial commercial relations that would erode racial barriers. Still, he worried about how the United States entered into those negotiations. In a letter to Secretary of State Blaine, Douglass warned that "the presence of the 'Yankee' [*Yantic*] and of our naval officers at the Mole" would surely "occasion some comment in Haitian circles." He worried that the show of force violated his ideal spirit of Pan-American relations, racial egalitarianism and cooperation.[50]

Douglass's first opportunity to broach the subject with Haitian officials and test whether it was possible to serve both race and nation in that moment came on January 1, 1891. On New Year's Day, the Haitian minister of foreign affairs, Anténor Firmin, paid Douglass a visit. He made his feelings on the Môle clear from the very start. Firmin, a scholar who favored Pan-American relations that decentered the United States and that unified black people who shared a history of slavery and colonial oppression, complained to Douglass about a U.S. newspaper that repeated the rumor that Hyppolite had promised the Môle to the United States as recompense for its assistance in bringing him to power.[51] Douglass agreed that the claim was baseless, but he told Firmin that the U.S. government was willing to lease, rent, or purchase the Môle according to "proper means . . . consistent with the peace and welfare of Hayti." Firmin, well aware of the U.S. warships waiting off of Haiti's coast, was not convinced. Although the conversation between the two black statesman was cut short, Firmin's icy reaction to Douglass's proposal convinced the U.S. diplomat of one thing: there was "no one point upon which the people of Haiti are more sensitive, superstitious, and united, than upon any question touching the cession of any part of their territory."[52]

Douglass was growing uneasy about the negotiations. His white counterparts were undeterred. On January 25, 1891, the rear admiral Bancroft Gherardi arrived in Port-au-Prince with instructions to supplant Douglass and assume the lead role in direct negotiations for the port. Three days later, he, Douglass, Firmin, Hyppolite, and an interpreter sat around a conference table discussing the U.S. acquisition of territory that contemporaries believed had become "mystically bound" to national sovereignty in the Haitian imagination.[53] Gherardi stressed Haiti's indebtedness to the United States and insisted that the Môle was the U.S. government's rightful possession in return for its services rendered to Hyppolite. Douglass tried to moderate the admiral's awkward candor by appealing to Haitian sensibilities. He insisted that "the concession asked for was in the line of good neighborhood and advanced civilization, and in every way consistent with the autonomy of Haiti." Moreover, while sympathetic to Haitian officials' distrust of the United States, he informed them that isolationism was an antiquated policy no longer necessitated by Haiti's previous standing as a black nation in a world dominated by slaveholding powers.[54]

Hyppolite and Firmin found Douglass unpersuasive and Gherardi combative. Firmin denied that the Môle had ever been promised to the United States, pointing out that U.S. officials did not possess a single piece of original documentation to support their claim to Haitian territory. Incensed, Gherardi shouted that Hyppolite was "morally bound" to concede the Môle. At this point, Douglass interceded. He bristled at the brazen admission that the U.S. government had affected regime change in a sovereign nation, believing that he could "not accept this as a foundation upon which I could base my diplomacy." Firmin subsequently ended the tense meeting and asked that the United States put a coherent request for the Môle in writing.[55]

Douglass watched the ensuing negotiations follow in a similar fashion before grappling with the meaning of their predictable collapse. Gherardi blustered at the unwillingness of Haitian officials to cede a part of their territory and chafed at Firmin's insinuation that he lacked proper diplomatic credentials. For his part, Douglass did nothing to undermine the U.S. government, but he also refused to disregard Haiti's stance that, in the words of Firmin, it could not "compromise . . . our existence as an independent people." In the end, he was not surprised when Firmin declined to lease the Môle and closed negotiations on April 24, 1891. To Douglass, the decision was disheartening albeit understandable. Although he still believed that Pan-American cooperation would modernize Haiti, he now better understood the Haitian position. The United States had a troubling understanding of the "spirit of the age." Instead of cooperation, it favored coercion. Racial domination remained the reason for the "rapacious" foreign policy of the day.[56]

In the United States, the reaction to the collapse of the Môle negotiations was split along racial lines. T. Thomas Fortune spoke for a number of black journalists when he condemned the United States for using "the methods of the bulldozer or the highwayman" in its attempts to secure Haitian territory.[57] White journalists had far fewer problems with the aggressive tactics. Many held Douglass, accused during the Clyde affair of being more Haitian than American, responsible for dashing their hopes of U.S. expansion. Assuming that the black diplomat had sabotaged the negotiations through incompetence, a lack of impartiality, or both, some even demanded that a white diplomat supplant Douglass in Port-au-Prince. In a representative editorial, the *Chicago Tribune* proclaimed that "there is no question . . . that Mr. Douglass's administration of our interests has been a failure and that he is incompetent to hold the position." Although "all other things being equal," the *Tribune* continued, "a colored man would be preferable at the Haytian court, commercial reasons must be paramount." Accordingly, "if a colored man cannot be found who is competent then a white man should be sent."[58]

Douglass recognized the racist assumptions and imperialistic motives that influenced such views. In an interview with Fortune's *New York Age*, he noted that calls for a white diplomat in Haiti were grounded in the belief that "more can be won from the fears of Hayti than can be obtained from [its] reason and good will and on the still further assumption that a white man will command compliance with his demands upon a black man." He admitted that the conditions were ill-suited for his idealistic vision of Pan-American collaboration. To Douglass, the misguided conviction that the United States could bend Haiti to its will was a symptom of the racial caste system that now pervaded the United States. It had no basis in Haitian history or concern for Haitian interests. Douglass boasted that Haitians had "demonstrated by the assertion of independence that they could look a white man squarely in the eye and never lower their chin an inch."[59] He joined a chorus of African Americans singing the same tune. In the opinion of Douglass and his like-minded peers, the failed negotiations for the Môle confirmed the central lesson of the Haitian Revolution: Haitians would never accept white men as their superiors.[60]

For black journalists, Haitian opposition to U.S. demands was a sensible and even admirable response to U.S. racism. As the negotiations for the Môle collapsed, some black journalists concluded that Hyppolite and Firmin feared a public backlash and a potential uprising if they failed to guard Haitian sovereignty.[61] Others noted that Haitian leaders objected to the condescension that U.S. military officers and politicians directed toward Douglass and Ebenezer Don Carlos Bassett, the former diplomat now employed as the secretary to the current U.S. minister resident and consul general to Haiti.[62] Some even cited Port-au-Prince-based correspondents who reported that knowledge of and aversion to U.S. racism was widespread in the Haitian capital.[63] According to the editor of the St. Paul, Minnesota *Appeal*, it was obvious that "color prejudice"—not the failings of Frederick Douglass—"prevented the United States from securing the Mole St. Nicolas." Haitians, he reasoned, had simply done the sensible thing.[64]

As white Americans confirmed their racism by alleging that Douglass had proven that all black men were unfit for diplomatic service, Douglass defended the values that influenced his performance in Haiti. After returning to the United States and resigning his post on July 30, 1891, Douglass shared his perspective on the negotiations for the Môle in a two-part article published in the *North American Review*. He began by insisting that his support for Pan-American relationships that advanced U.S. interests had gone unappreciated. Rather than acknowledging his support for U.S. foreign policy goals, Secretary of State Blaine had given Admiral Gherardi undeserved diplomatic authority based on the assumption that Haitians would defer to the demands of a white man. Douglass pointed out the absurdity of that belief. He reminded readers that Haitians were aware of U.S. racism and prone to reject any hypocrite who discriminated against African Americans while professing to deal equitably with Haitians. Once again, he insisted on racial egalitarianism as a basis of diplomacy. According to Douglass, the United States should cooperate with Haiti even if a white diplomat could coerce it. His country, one that proclaimed that all men are created equal, should "ask nothing of Haïti on grounds less just and reasonable than those upon which they would ask anything of France or England."[65]

To be sure, Douglass believed that the failure of U.S. expansion in Haiti lay with white officials, not black people. In fact, he now wondered whether it was a failure at all. Douglass concluded that Haitians' "well-known, deeply-rooted, and easily-excited" opposition to foreign threats and their knowledge of white Americans' "peculiar and intense prejudice against the colored race" were the principle reasons for the collapse of the Môle negotiations. He was secure in the knowledge that he performed his "honorable duty" to the best of his abilities while not losing sight of his responsibilities to his race. "I am charged with sympathy for Haiti," the former U.S. minister resident and consul general concluded. "I am not ashamed of that charge."[66]

Douglass was not afraid to advocate for Haiti and Haitians with renewed vigor, either. Soon after Douglass returned to Washington, D.C., from Port-au-Prince, Hyppolite quelled an attempted coup before ordering the executions of all conspirators. When the Haitian president became the subject of a new round of condemnations from white Americans, Douglass rallied to his defense. Hyppolite, Douglass told a correspondent of the *New York Age*, was justified in taking those measures. He was working toward securing peace and achieving "wonderful progress." Douglass further maintained that Haiti was welcoming new telegraph and cable technology; building electric plants, bridges, and railroads; and supporting strong schools and churches of all kinds. It was, he implied, racing toward modernity with its sovereignty intact.[67]

For black intellectuals, there remained no contradiction in measuring Haitian progress according to U.S. standards. Such comparisons, they reasoned, could erode racism. They might even encourage race pride. Upon hearing the favorable assessment of Haitian governance from "the lips of the great orator," the correspondent from the *New York Age* "folded [his] copy" and beamed. He predicted that "had the audience been ten thousand instead of one it would have burst involuntarily from profound silence into a joyous acclaim of enthusiasm and applause."[68]

African Americans were not interested only in Douglass's strategic representations of Haiti in that moment. Instead, they searched for and produced other ideas about that country, race, and civilization that undermined the misrepresentations of all three found in white-authored travel narratives, newspapers, and books. Their subversive thoughts took shape in books and

FIGURE 8. Port-au-Prince, Haiti, c. 1901. Detroit Publishing Company Collection, Prints & Photographs Division, Library of Congress.

articles written by Haitian and African American writers, public fairs and festivals, and black newspapers that promoted Afro-diasporic solidarities by advancing the transnational tradition of black print culture.[69]

As Douglass sought to encourage African Americans with tales of Haitian technological advancement, T. Thomas Fortune promoted the work of the Haitian author and statesman Roche Grellier. In the summer of 1891, Fortune's *New York Age* featured substantial reviews of two of Grellier's works: *Haïti: Son Passé, Son Avenir* and *Études Économiques sur Haïti.* The former rejects racist arguments about black self-government by attributing Haitian political instability to partisan squabbles rather than innate racial traits, while the latter emphasizes how Haitians could overcome those disagreements and achieve commercial success. According to Fortune, both books were triumphs of reason over prejudice. After reading them and spending hours in conversation with his "good friend"

Grellier, the prominent black journalist concluded that *Haïti: Son Passé, Son Avenir* and *Études Économiques sur Haïti* provided "the truth about Hayti." He implied that most white-authored "scholarship" did not.[70]

In fact, it was not uncommon for African Americans with firsthand knowledge of Haiti to advance the arguments of Haitians such as Grellier. Even as the AME Church shifted the focus of its missionary work from Haiti to Africa, the AME minister and Port-au-Prince resident Solomon Porter Hood tried to correct "erroneous ideas" about Haitians who the world "looked upon as savages . . . as an illustration of the Negro's incapacity to govern himself."[71] In a two-part article published in the *AME Church Review*, he argued that Haitian political turmoil was a result of the conflict between a Liberal Party that favored mulatto candidates and a National Party that praised the black rulers of the Haitian past while blaming mulattoes for Haiti's ills. Moreover, Hood insisted that those disputes stemmed from the colonial era, when the French created divisions among white people, free men of color, and the enslaved black masses. He chastised those who ignored that history and reveled "in cold criticism of the Negro—whether struggling alone, as in Liberia, Haiti, or San Domingo, in a manly independence . . . or, in the United States battling against desperate odds." According to Hood, white Americans too often forgot that "the faults they now condemn in the race are but the scars of their inhumanity." They ignored the residual effects of slavery and colonialism in their rush to attack black people.[72]

The argument that the social hierarchies of French Saint-Domingue dictated Haitian politics in the late nineteenth century stripped Haitians of some agency, but in a more meaningful sense, it defied crude representations of Haiti and granted the country meaningful historical and sociological analysis. According to Hood, Haitian politics and society were quite rational and comprehensible to any observer willing to look beyond dubious tropes about inherent black inferiority. They were intelligible to anyone prepared to acknowledge that modern Haiti was more influenced by actual white inhumanity than fictional black barbarism.

A number of Hood's peers voiced similar objections to the ahistorical writings of white commentators who ignored anti-black violence in the United States while condemning supposed barbarism in Haiti. In a piece submitted to the *Plaindealer*, one black porter noted that the Haitian government far surpassed the U.S. government in its commitment to maintaining law and order. Surely, he remarked, it was obvious that there was no parallel to the United States' "brutal and fiendish murdering in any civilized and Christian country in the entire world."[73] The editors of the *Plaindealer* were in complete agreement. Although conceding that Hyppolite's suppression of revolutionaries was harsh, they wondered "how often would the civilized world be shocked by equally barbarous crimes in the South if all the facts could be known."[74] Their paper derided Haiti's critics, inquiring whether there was "any more of Christianity, of civilization, of refinement in the almost daily outrages committed by chivalrous (?) bourbons [Democrats] against defenseless Afro-Americans (men, women, and children) than there is in the reported outrages in Hayti?" The answer was obvious. For black journalists, the "fiercer cruelty of those reputed to be civilized" rendered white people incapable of writing intelligently about Haiti.[75]

T. Thomas Fortune knew just as well that the results of true barbarism were the increasing number of beaten and burned black bodies hanging from southern trees. In response to a northern journalist who argued that Haitian political upheaval justified the defeat of the Federal Elections Bill, the editor of the *Age* insisted that the "administration of affairs in Hayti is as orderly as in any one of the Southern States." It was the South after all, not Haiti, where "lynch law, a corrupt administration of the civil law, a universal denial of civil rights and a suppression of . . . legal electors under the Federal Constitution prevail."[76] In fact, Fortune suggested that white southerners needed to look to Haitians for lessons on proper governance. After a white newspaper in Louisville, Kentucky, argued that developments in Haiti justified the suppression of black voters in the United States, Fortune argued that southern governments could learn from Hyppolite's proper use of "the function of every State to maintain its authority against mobocracy and insurrection." In the future, he advised, southern policymakers and journalists should devote more attention to "Southern butcheries" that perpetuated lawlessness and concern themselves less with "Haytian massacres" that upheld law and order.[77]

From the perspective of numerous black intellectuals, including Fortune, more accurate comparative analysis of the United States and Haiti was necessary because anti-Haitian diatribes often buttressed arguments for foreign intervention in Haiti. For example, Fortune was sure "that the menacing tone of U.S. newspapers towards the Haytian Republic . . . emboldened the European cabinets" pondering collective action to "restore order" in Haiti. U.S. officials, he argued, could rectify the situation by treating Haiti as a sovereign country, compelling Europeans to do the same, and allowing Haiti to "work out its own destiny."[78] In no way should the United States contemplate increasing its own influence in Haiti, though. Fortune argued that until "the South is made, forced, compelled, to live up to the Constitutional provision of according equal and exact justice to all citizens . . . we shall have no time to look after the disorders . . . of sister governments." White Americans, he concluded, "have as much as they can manage at home."[79]

Still, Fortune knew that the distinction between home and abroad was growing less and less clear for his contemporaries. In particular, the visual arts that African Americans produced and consumed demonstrated a strong identification with Haitians whose struggles against white supremacy paralleled their own. After the passage of the Separate Coach Law in neighboring Arkansas, a black Texan decided to emigrate to the Dominican Republic. His only concern about the potential move was whether or not Dominicans had any interest in buying the life-sized portraits of Toussaint Louverture that he sold "at sight" in the United States, likely to eager black consumers like Mariah Reddick.[80] Born enslaved in Mississippi during the 1830s, Reddick spent much of her life toiling at the Carnton Plantation in Franklin, Tennessee. The defeat of the Confederacy brought legal freedom—and the chance for a broader range of self-expression. Well into the twentieth century, Reddick's great-granddaughter still recalled that her great-grandmother "had [Louverture's] portrait, on her wall." That portrait possibly revealed ideas about emancipation, black masculinity, racial uplift, or other themes with which Louverture was often linked. It seems to have been part of an enduring and communal clam to self-determination. On January 1, 1884, a group of black Tennesseans calling themselves the Mt. L'Ouverture Association bough four acres of land "for the internment of persons of African descent." The Toussaint L'Ouverture County Cemetery remains Reddick's final resting place.[81]

Emancipation celebrations provided another opportunity for African Americans to declare their sympathies with Haiti. In August 1891, an estimated quarter of the black population in Kansas gathered to celebrate the anniversary of emancipation in the West Indies. Rather than emphasizing the Slavery Abolition Act that ended slavery throughout the British colonies, however, the black revelers, some of them Exodusters, placed Haiti at the forefront of their event. They honored Toussaint Louverture for firing "the first gun that broke the backbone of African slavery" and commemorated the independence of Haiti, "the most advanced negro government on earth."[82] Months later, African Americans in Delaware gathered for the anniversary of the Emancipation Proclamation. Black men, women, and children packed the Bethel AME Church, where they enjoyed songs of jubilee and a reading of the Emancipation Proclamation. Along with these staples of emancipation celebrations, the event featured a speech by Frederick Douglass. The great orator's lecture "Hayti and Its Relations to the Colored People of the United States" helped attendees visualize themselves not as isolated victims of racism but as part of an ongoing struggle for black liberation and self-determination that was occurring in Haiti, too.[83]

It should come as no surprise, then, that the black press tried to take advantage of black interest in and identification with Haiti. Besides living in a moment when African Americans studied a rapidly changing world, black journalists of the 1890s were part of a black publishing tradition that began with *Freedom's Journal*, the first black-owned and black-operated newspaper in the United States. Founded in 1827 by the Jamaican Pan-Africanist John Brown Russwurm and the Delaware-born minister Samuel Cornish, *Freedom's Journal* was distributed throughout the U.S. North, Europe, Canada, and the Caribbean.[84] It was an Afro-diasporic collaboration that established the transnational foundations of the independent black press. During the antebellum era, pioneering black newspapers including the *Christian Recorder* and *Frederick Douglass' Paper* covered events and gained readership across the Atlantic World.[85] They continued a tradition then carried forth by the burgeoning black press of the long postemancipation era.

In the fall of 1891, Edward Cooper, the editor of the Indianapolis-based *Freeman*, hired an agent in Port-au-Prince. Joseph Desce, a Haitian convert of James Theodore Holly's Episcopal Church, reported success in selling the *Freeman* to his countrymen and black immigrants from the United States who felt "proud of a journal" that advertised "the best that the race is and does."[86] He even managed to place copies of the paper into the hands of Florvil Hyppolite, insisting that the Haitian president take note of a publication that reflected African Americans' "fraternal feelings" and "sympathy" for a country whose struggles led them "into the broad, free air of liberty, peace, progress and happiness."[87] In fact, Desce was more than a salesman. At the same time that he secured subscribers for the *Freeman* in Port-au-Prince, Desce also worked as a correspondent for Cooper's paper. With his help, black people in the United States gained access to firsthand accounts of Haitian society. Articles of interest included descriptions of the social gatherings of the Haitian elite, interviews with the U.S. minister resident and consul general John S. Durham, and news of African Americans who made Haiti their temporary or permanent place of residence. Even the most mundane gossip represented something grander. To paraphrase Desce, the lines of communication stretching between Indianapolis and Port-au-Prince suggested that a growing political solidarity between African Americans and Haitians was there to stay.[88]

There is no mistaking the significance of the transnational circulation of the *Freeman*. Yet the linkage of Port-au-Prince to Indianapolis was not the clearest sign of Haiti's centrality to black intellectual life available in that moment. Instead, that proof came at the Chicago World's Fair.

Even before it opened in the summer of 1893, the event known formally as the World's Columbian Exposition possessed multiple meanings and purposes. Officially, it was supposed to commemorate the 400th anniversary of Christopher Columbus's arrival in the Americas. Unofficially, the fair was an attempt to unite a country in which the bloody sectional conflicts of the Civil War and Reconstruction had given way to class tensions resulting from rapid industrialization and mass immigration. It was meant to stir feelings of patriotism among U.S. citizens. Fair organizers envisioned their event as a testament to the transformation of the United States since its rural, agricultural beginnings. Displays of fine art and examples of technological, industrial, and agricultural advancements from across the country would highlight its emergence as an urban, industrial, and imperial power. They would presage a brilliant future for the United States and put its civilization on display for all the world to see.[89]

African Americans, labeled uncivilized, were thus excluded from the fair's planning process. President Benjamin Harrison did not appoint a single African American to either of the two official planning bodies, the all-male United States National Commission and the all-female Board of Lady Managers. He thought it sufficient to give one of the alternate slots on the national commission to Hale Giddings Parker, the former principal of St. Louis's Alexandre Dumas School. The exposition directors followed suit, making ample space for white women and foreign countries at the fair but insisting that African Americans submit proposals for exhibits to all-white state committees. The committees rejected those proposals on sight. At each stage, white men tried to control the black presence at the Chicago World's Fair. They reasoned that black men could work as its janitors, bathroom attendants, or chauffeurs and encouraged the employment of Nancy Green, the formerly enslaved black woman who personified Aunt Jemima while serving thousands of pancakes at the fair. Those forms of black participation did not upset the status quo. Instead, they reinforced the racial hierarchies of Jim Crow.[90]

Educated black professionals objected to their exclusion, rejection, and misrepresentation. For them, the fair was a real chance to show themselves as full-fledged citizens of the United States who helped shape its modern life. It was an opportunity to highlight the progress of African Americans since emancipation and influence the future of the United States, too. Black public figures knew that the fair would host a number of parliaments and congresses on topics ranging from religion to women, and they wanted a seat at the table for discussions on Africa, labor, and education that held particular importance for their race.

Although refused their desired membership among the planners of the fair, African Americans ensured that their participation was neither denied nor circumscribed. Black laborers responded to the first announcements for the fair, approaching the much-needed work opportunities with dignified resolved. One of them guarded the world's first Ferris wheel, a massive structure that impressed the African Americans who came to Chicago determined to enjoy the entertainment of the exposition. Those black fair-goers ranged from domestic servants to graduates of black colleges and universities whose fair exhibits left white visitors convinced "that the Colored people of the South are capable of learning."[91] They included black spokespeople who, heeding the advice of Frederick Douglass, made the most of the event. Prominent black speakers, including Booker T. Washington, gave addresses at the Congress of Labor, the World's Congress of Representative Women, and the Congress on Africa. They voiced their concerns, loudly, outside of the controversial Colored American Day.[92]

To be certain, for African Americans such as Ida B. Wells, the separate day for black attendees was insulting, not all-important. Over the course of the preceding year, the black Mississippian and graduate of Rust College had emerged as the world's foremost anti-lynching activist following the lynching of three friends in her adopted hometown, Memphis. She was a formidable investigative journalist who did not have to strain to see that the "special" day for black people carried more than a hint of subordination. While Wells urged a boycott that ultimately did not come to fruition, she launched a more successful search for other avenues of racial inclusion and black achievement at the exposition. Haiti, she recalled, delivered both when it "accepted the invitation extended to her along with other nations, and erected a building on the World's Fair grounds."[93]

Countless other African Americans came to depend on Haiti to demonstrate black progress to the twenty-seven million people who attended the Chicago World's Fair.[94] It was an excellent decision. Haiti was well prepared to assume that role and represent African Americans as well as Haitians. The clearest evidence of the inclusive ethnic politics of the Haitian government came when it appointed Frederick Douglass as one of its commissioners at the Columbian Exposition. Sol Johnson, the editor of the *Savannah Tribune*, voiced a common gratitude when he remarked that the Haitian government had "come to the aid of the colored people of the United States" with its recognition of Douglass, a man who won even more admiration from Haitians for his role in the Môle affair. Johnson knew all too well that the conspicuous presence of the venerable abolitionist and anti-imperialist in Chicago was "surely a slap in the face" of the organizers of an event that intentionally minimized the progress of African Americans since emancipation. And so, for that subversive action, Johnson gave the Haitian government a hearty "bravo."[95]

The speed with which the Haitian government constructed its national pavilion on the fairgrounds also impressed Johnson's contemporaries.[96] Charles Sumner Dixon, soon on his way to becoming one of the earliest black students at the Massachusetts Institute of Technology, argued that the organizing efforts of "the little republic of Hayti, one of the grandest existing," demonstrated its "energy, patriotism and punctuality." Those were traits that white people frequently denied to people of African descent. Accordingly, as Haiti moved toward becoming the first country among the dozens of participating ones to complete its national structure, Dixon predicted that Haiti's accomplishment would "go down in history to its everlasting credit" and, by extension, to the credit of African Americans as well.[97] Charles Hendley made that connection clear to his readers. The editor of the *Huntsville Gazette* reprinted a report that linked the speedy completion of the Haitian Pavilion to black achievement. To his great satisfaction, the dedication of a structure that would display Haitian "progress in the arts of civilization" to the world even persuaded some white Americans that black self-government could succeed.[98]

The Haitian Pavilion appealed to Hendley and countless other black observers because it undermined the representations of civilization and progress intended by fair organizers. The Columbian Exposition was divided into two sections: the White City and the Midway Plaisance. The former was an immaculate arrangement of neoclassical palaces and Venetian waterways. Upon seeing it, James Weldon Johnson, then a student at Atlanta University, marveled that "no one, who has not seen it, can form any idea of the immensity and grandeur of the exposition. . . . One standing under the Peristyle and looking down the Court of Honor, surrounded by magnificent buildings with their chaste white columns and gilded domes glittering in the sunlight . . . might easily imagine himself in a fairy city."[99] The Midway Plaisance did not elicit the same reaction. On the mile-long avenue running through a less developed part of the fairgrounds, visitors found the Ferris wheel and mock representations of "primitive" people from foreign countries. That section, inspired by the African ethnological villages at the 1889 Paris Universal Exposition, was dedicated to colonial amusements, not white civilization.

For white visitors to the Midway, no exhibit was more alluring or repulsive than the replica of a Dahomey village. Dahomey was a centralized West African kingdom that possessed a reputable standing army and a diverse economy that included a progressive system of taxation. The Fon were one of its principal ethnic groups. When one hundred Fon men, women, and children arrived in Chicago, they expected to present their craftsmanship, religious customs, music, and military valor on a world stage. Their white viewers, however, were encouraged to disregard the "Dahomeans'" display of their humanity. "If you were on the Midway and heard wild thumping of a drum and harsh shouting, and a parting of the people right and left," read a description appended to a picture of the Fon villagers found in a popular souvenir book, "you were sure to see a large white man born on a palanquin by half-dressed Negroes." Those black servants, it continued, "were a detachment from the Dahomeyan village, carrying their master."[100] They were a useful measure and reassurance of white progress. Susan B. Anthony received that message when, having observed the thatched huts of the Dahomey Village, the white suffragist questioned whether "humanity sprang from such as this?" In her eyes, it "seems pretty low down. . . . But I don't think Adam knew much more than this."[101]

The reaction to the Dahomey Village was unsurprising but troubling to Frederick Douglass. There is little question that Douglass's denunciation of an exhibition meant to represent "the Negro as repulsive savage" stemmed from his tendencies to favor the cultural norms of middle-class white and black Americans and discount the cultural practices of non-Western and working-class people.[102] Still, there was much more to his negative appraisal of the Dahomey Village than cultural bias. Although Douglass did not grasp how the Fon saw themselves, he understood well how fairgoers from the United States and Europe were meant to interpret the West Africans. He understandably chafed at the likelihood that many white people would embrace those expectations. To him, the intended distinction between uncivilized black servants and cultured white masters stirred memories of the social hierarchies of the antebellum era. It was a scene born right out of a slaveholder's dream. It should come as no surprise then that Douglass, a man who survived slavery to become the most famous abolitionist in the United States, wanted nothing more than to leave behind what was a nightmare to him.

The Haitian Pavilion allowed him to do just that.[103] Crafted by the Francophone Haitian elite, the building stood in the northwest section of the fairgrounds alongside the pavilions of European and North American countries whose independence anteceded the end of the Haitian Revolution. That situation belied any notion of black subservience. So did the external structure and internal exhibits of the Haitian Pavilion. While the Greco-Colonial architecture of Haiti's building exuded cultural refinement, the central hall contained an elegant marble statue sculpted by a renowned Haitian artist, artifacts of Toussaint Louverture, portraits and busts of prominent black men including Hippolyte and Douglass, examples of fine Haitian mahogany, samples of aromatic and appetizing Haitian coffee, and other arts and goods that showcased the intellectual might, rich history, commercial growth, and future prosperity of Haiti. The contrast with the Dahomey Village could not have been clearer. While Haitian peasants at home incorporated the rites of their Fon ancestors into their current religious practices, Haitian elites in Chicago erected a testament to what they saw as black modernity. In fact, there were no representations of Vodou or any other elements of Haitian popular culture in the Windy City.[104]

Countless black and white fairgoers flocked to the presentation of black civilization at the Haitian Pavilion. It became their chosen location to mingle with black luminaries including Frederick Douglass, listen to the best black musicians of the day, socialize with Haitian political leaders, and meet foreign dignitaries. Some black activists and intellectuals discovered functional uses for the pavilion. The poet Paul Laurence Dunbar found employment as the secretary to Douglass while Ida B. Wells used the Haitian

FIGURE 9. Haitian Pavilion at the 1893 Chicago World's Fair. Located near the national buildings of Germany, Spain, and Canada, the Haitian Pavilion was constructed in a Greco-Colonial style with large Doric columns and a gilded dome that evoked that of the Massachusetts State Capitol. Twelve-foot-wide verandas surrounded three sides of the building, which bore a coat of arms bearing the dates of Christopher Columbus's "discovery" of the Americas, Haiti's declaration of independence, and the present Columbian Exposition. It cost an estimated $20,000 to build. Frederick Douglass Memorial and Historical Association Records, Prints & Photographs Division, Library of Congress.

Pavilion to distribute at least twenty thousand copies of *The Reason Why the Colored American Is Not in The World's Columbian Exposition*, a pamphlet that critiqued lynching and the convict lease system, described the achievements of African Americans since emancipation, and condemned the politics of racial exclusion at the fair. Wells was especially impressed by the meaning that the Haitian Pavilion assumed for African Americans. Decades after the close of the Columbian Exposition, Wells still remembered the Haitian Pavilion as "one of the gems of the World's Fair." It was, she recalled, an important site of diasporic exchange as well as protest; it was a haven where "representative Negroes of the country . . . were to be found along with the Haitians and citizens other foreign countries."[105]

The metaphor chosen by Wells was apt. Increasingly, black intellectuals came to see Haiti, and not just the Haitian Pavilion, as a precious resource whose uniqueness dictated its worth. Frederick Douglass certainly did. On January 2, 1893, one of the official representatives of Haiti at the Chicago World's Fair gave two speeches that indicated as much. First, at midday, Douglass gave the keynote address for the dedication of the Haitian Pavilion to a biracial audience that was quite small on account of poor weather. This initial speech was fitting for a representative of the Haitian government speaking at an official ceremony. While advocating for Haiti's place within the "sisterhood of nations," Douglass characterized the Haitian Revolution as part of a universal struggle for human freedom. He stressed that "the achievement" of Haitian independence was "one of the most remarkable and one of the most wonderful events . . . in the history of mankind." Although rooted in the experiences of enslaved black people and a history of racial oppression, it was a triumph that all who embraced the loftier principles of the Enlightenment could share.[106]

His second speech assumed a more strident tone. In an oration delivered that evening before hundreds of African Americans at Chicago's Quinn Chapel, Douglass detailed the advancement of "the only self-made Black Republic in the world" and emphasized the historical debt that African Americans owed Haiti for striking the most forceful blow against slavery in the history of the world. He proceeded to inform audience members that new manifestations of white supremacy had reinforced long-standing similarities between black life in Haiti and the United States. As white vigilantes, police, and politicians challenged black masculinity through lynching, incarceration, and disfranchisement, Douglass noted that white Americans also refused to acknowledge the "manhood" of Haitian citizens because they had "not yet forgiven Haiti for being black."[107] He assured his audience that neither African Americans nor Haitians would consent to their emasculation. To the great pleasure of his audience, Douglass predicted that just as black men refused to accept political dependency, the Haitian government would protest threats to its sovereignty. The Môle affair proved as much. For speaker and listener alike, Haiti's tenacity in the face of U.S. aggression captured how black people throughout the Americas had overcome improbable odds throughout their long histories of enslavement and oppression.[108]

Douglass concluded his speech in a way that only the great rhetorician could. Haiti, Douglass proclaimed, "still lives and grows" and it "will yet be tall and strong." There was clear support for that thesis. Douglass explained that Haiti's "wealth is greater, her population is larger, her credit is higher, her currency is sounder, her progress is surer, her statesmen are abler, her patriotism is nobler, and her government is steadier and firmer than twenty years ago." There was thus no reason to believe white supremacists who disparaged Haiti. Certainly there was no reason for African Americans to look askance at what Douglass called "the black man's country, now forever." "I will not," Douglass thundered, "I cannot believe that her star is to go out in darkness, but I will rather believe that whatever may happen of peace or war Haiti will remain in the firmament of nations, and, like the star of the north, will shine on and shine on forever."[109]

There was no mistaking Douglass's simile. The audience at Quinn Chapel surely did not as it erupted in sustained applause. Just as fugitive slaves once used the North Star to guide them toward freedom, so too were countless African Americans now willing to look to Haiti as a new "star of the north" that might light the way toward black liberation and self-determination.

Again, a black public figure mustered a comparison for Haiti that was audacious albeit appropriate. The Haitian star was noteworthy for its brightness (its potential) *and* for its distinctiveness (its atypical independence). Black leaders who took part in the weeklong Congress on African Ethnology held at the Chicago fairgrounds would not have missed that point. Nearly a decade after European powers met to partition Africa at the Berlin Congress of 1884–1885, Henry McNeal Turner, Alexander Crummell, Frederick Douglass, John Mercer Langston, and T. Thomas Fortune joined white imperialists and missionaries in discussing how best to transform African culture. Long after the proceedings, some scholars would mistakenly describe the participation of African Americans as a defiant anti-imperialist stance. In reality, the role of those black spokesmen was more complex. For the most part, they condoned an agenda that focused on the growth of civilization, Christianity, and commerce in Africa. Turner, for example, offered a discourse on the African origins of humanity and emphasized the obligation of Westerners to uplift Africans. His goal was to encourage the white reformers in attendance to see Africans as part of global history and a common human experience. Still, Turner's expressed goal of improving Africans according to his preferred cultural standards complemented the worldviews of his white counterparts who praised the "civilizing agencies and influences of Christendom . . . founding lighthouses of civilization amid inland seas of savagery."[110]

The tone struck by black participants at the Congress was not just a product of cultural biases, though. Instead, it reflected a greater anxiety about geopolitical developments. By the time Turner and his peers suggested a more humanitarian albeit still-hierarchical vision of relations between the West and Africa, Europeans controlled most of the latter continent, including the homeland of Chicago's Fon visitors. To a number of black elites, it thus appeared that African colonization was a fait accompli that they might better moderate than defy. Indeed, even the independence of the traditional black nations of Ethiopia and Liberia seemed either precarious or questionable. While the Liberian commissioner to the Columbian Exposition advocated for more trade between Liberia and the United States, the former's so-called parent country, black observers noted that the overbearing role of the United States in Liberian history was evident in the clear similarities between the Liberian and U.S. flags. The obvious signs of enduring U.S. influence in the former colony of the American Colonization Society led one black speaker at the Congress on African Ethnology to lament that Liberia "depended too little on herself."[111] In short, it was not Haiti. It was not an emblem of manly black independence.

In that moment, few ideas caused more concern and conflict than manliness. By the 1890s, anxieties over race, industrialization, immigration, women's rights activism, and organized labor movements caused middle-class white men to reconceptualize manhood. Besides ridiculing women's suffrage, introducing "sissy" into the vernacular, leading the Boy Scouts, participating in boxing, and embracing U.S. imperialism, they emphasized the link between their imagined superiority and white supremacy. From their perspective, the equation was straightforward and undeniable. Anglo-American manliness was the highest form of manhood, and manhood was the foundation of civilization. And civilization was the precursor to sound self-government, a characteristic long denied to Haitians, African Americans, and all people of African descent.[112]

To be sure, the consequences of the attendant assumptions about black people were dire. The defenders of white manhood insisted that black people everywhere possessed none of the qualities associated with proper masculinity. They argued that the black man lacked self-restraint, intelligence, and courage, that he was neither enterprising nor independent, that he was, in essence, not a man at all. Associating whiteness with aggressiveness and sexual prowess, white Americans used stereotypes about black men to justify a host of tactics meant to not only emasculate but also subjugate their counterparts of color at home and abroad. They insisted that African Americans could not possess voting rights, hold public office, make good soldiers, or gain high-status jobs. They castrated then lynched black men in the United States. They celebrated the violent extension of U.S. power in Cuba and the Philippines, deriding anti-imperialists as feminine cowards who should cede their role in the manly field of politics.[113]

Of course, black people were unwilling victims. In response to the physical and discursive violence inflicted upon them, they devised means of asserting their racial manhood. While numerous black men voiced their support for U.S. and European imperialism or became soldiers as a way to affirm their masculinity and patriotism, others were less accommodating of the emerging world order of racial domination. Recognizing that Haiti was long associated with black self-government and could undermine the toxic rhetoric of white masculinity, some black intellectuals reinforced its place at the heart of their incipient anti-imperialist politics. In fact, they frequently pointed to Haitians for proof that blackness and manliness were compatible.[114]

These subversive ideas about Haiti and black masculinity took center stage in Chicago. While debates about the future of emasculated Africa took place on the grounds of the Columbian Exposition, William Edgar Easton's *Dessalines* debuted at a popular Chicago opera house.[115] The play, which the black actress and future leader of the Universal Negro Improvement Association Henrietta Vinton Davis produced and staged, centers on the romance between the protagonist and Clarisse, the Christian sister of André Rigaud, a mulatto military leader during the Haitian Revolution now depicted as the rival of Dessalines. When Clarisse falls prey to a malicious Vodou priestess, Dessalines rescues her and the two fall in love. Clarisse then converts Dessalines to Christianity. There are no hints of Dessalines's turn to despotism, only his mercy, redemption, and national pride. After his conversion, Dessalines proclaims that "the religion which fostered in the slave the love of liberty and gave him the courage to contest the power of might—with the weapons of right, shall be hereafter—the proud heritage of every Haitien!" When his soldiers reply with cries of "Vive la liberté," Dessalines responds with an approving shout of "Fraternité et egalité!" The curtains close as Dessalines and his men belt out *Le Marseillaise*, the stirring anthem of Republican France.[116]

For modern readers, *Dessalines* shows how black intellectuals tended to disparage Vodou, elevate Victorian womanhood, and favor ideas about human equality identified with the Enlightenment, the French Revolution, and the American Revolution.[117] Those themes were not the most salient at the time, however; at least not to the writer of *Dessalines*. In the opinion of Easton, the most pressing lesson of his play lay in its treatment of black masculinity. The novice black playwright and active member of the Texas Republican Party thought that the "Caucasian boy [who] at his mother's feet learns, with pride, of the deeds of his race" held a clear advantage over the black boy who did not learn about the male heroes of his race. His play tried to rectify that. In *Dessalines*, the protagonist boasts that he is "as black as the shadows of night, with muscles of iron and a will that never was enslaved!"[118] He proclaims, in short, that he is a man; that he was, in the words of Easton, "the Negro, we need in the future."[119]

Advertisements for and reviews of *Dessalines* made that clear, too. For example, promotions for *Dessalines* appearing in the *Freeman* implored readers to see the play, attend public readings of it, or purchase copies of the printed version because it "enobles Negro manhood and is a glowing tribute to the Black man's Heroism."[120] Black reviewers corroborated that assessment. Dessalines, they pointed out, proclaimed that a man who accepted slavery was not worthy of life. In their estimation, the play captured that spirit while sanitizing some of the more controversial elements of the historical Dessalines.[121]

Although Easton appropriated Dessalines, few figures were as important to the vindication of black manhood and militant resistance to Jim Crow as Toussaint Louverture. In the same month that the Supreme Court reached a decision in *Plessy v. Ferguson* and upheld the legality of racial segregation in public facilities, a correspondent of the *Freeman* implored African Americans to emulate Louverture. The writer called on his peers to refute racist arguments with facts, devote their energies to correcting "prejudice and wrong," and drive "Negro haters from the field" just as "Toussaint beat down the strongest arms of Europe and made Hayti free."[122] A year later, the *Broad Ax*, a Salt Lake City–based paper edited by the "sharp-tongued, Democratic, atheistic" Julius F. Taylor, published a serialized biography of "the greatest negro that the world has ever produced."[123] The final installment of the weekly series echoed the enduring sentiment of Wendell Phillips by arguing that the greatness of Louverture surpassed that of Napoleon Bonaparte, Oliver Cromwell, and George Washington.[124] The favorable comparison of the hero of the Haitian Revolution to the most exalted names in European and Anglo-American history resonated with black professionals. Throughout the 1890s, the *Freeman* offered readers the chance to decorate their homes, businesses, or educational institutions with pictures of prominent Haitian men including Louverture and Hyppolite.[125] Although the number of African Americans who did so is uncertain, the presence of Haitian iconography among the Portraits of Distinguished Afro-Americans confirms that African Americans looked beyond their national boundaries for useful models of black manhood.

Black educators and journalists were especially keen on accentuating the link between black manliness and Haitian leaders. In August 1896, the principal of a black high school delivered an address titled "Will the Negro Be a Man?" before a crowd in Palestine, Texas. Undaunted by the attempts to deny African Americans the political, social, and economic privileges afforded to white men, he answered the question in the affirmative. After all, the speaker thundered, had not Toussaint Louverture "caused the proud Napoleon to bow low his haughty head."[126] Calvin Chase noted that the descendants of Louverture still possessed the vigor that middle-class white men claimed as their unique possession. Three years after U.S. military forces helped overthrow Queen Liliuokalani of the Hawaiian kingdom, the editor of the *Washington Bee* reflected on that imperial conquest. He challenged white politicians and military officials who created the opportunity for the annexation of Hawaii to "attempt to depose the President of Hayti and see what would be the result."[127] The insinuation was that the results would have been quite different. By juxtaposing the actual overthrow of the Hawaiian queen with the theoretical resistance of Hyppolite's successor, Tirésias Simon Sam, Chase not only vindicated black manhood but also questioned the manliness of white men who were fit only to conquer members of what was widely presumed to be the weaker sex.

Similar claims came from black ministers including John Hurst, a Haitian AME minister whose parents were among the black refugees who fled from the United States to Haiti during the antebellum era. In an essay for the *AME Church Review*, Hurst analyzed the American and Haitian Revolutions and concluded that comparisons between the two republics that emerged from these events were misleading. Whereas an "army of citizen-soldiers" commanded by George Washington rallied against "unjust taxation" and fought for "political freedom," the "horde of slaves" led by Toussaint Louverture took up arms for "human liberty" and "manhood." Hurst acknowledged the success of the U.S. Founding Fathers in forming a government based on their experiences as free colonists, but he also lauded Haitians who had made "themselves citizens by means of brute force" and become "self instructors in the art and duties" of government. The descendants of those architects of Haitian independence, the AME minister argued, continued to demonstrate the manly trait of self-reliance. In fact, Hurst boasted that his compatriots disproved the claim that only Anglo-Saxons possessed the ability to self-govern. He urged African Americans—specifically, black men—to use Haiti to their advantage. The "American Negro," Hurst concluded, just had to point to Haiti "to prove just what he is and what he has done."[128]

In the opinion of some black public figures, African Americans also needed to emulate Haitians. Charles Remond Douglass, the youngest son of Frederick Douglass, insisted that black men in the United States had to follow the militant example of their brethren in Haiti. In a letter written to the *Colored American*, Douglass argued that Haitians were superior to African Americans. He noted that the Haitian had "the manhood to assert his freedom and the power to protect it" and "was especially proud . . . of his country and his manhood rights." According to Douglass, "long years of servitude" made African Americans "humble and lacking in manhood," but a Haitian "fears no man" and would assert his manliness "as quickly in Georgia as he would in Port-au-Prince." Consequently, the solution to the problems facing African Americans was simple: they needed to become more like Haitians. In the estimation of Douglass, black men terrorized by lynch mobs could learn from Haitians who would never accept a practice meant to reinforce white masculinity and suppress black citizenship.[129]

Calvin Chase was even more emphatic about using Haiti as a model of black manliness. Years earlier, the *Washington Bee* editor printed a letter from an African American in Minnesota who lectured black southerners about the need to study "the lessons of Toussant Le Overture" and make a "good manly stand" against lynching.[130] Now Chase used his position as the lead orator at the annual celebration of emancipation in Washington, D.C., to again address African Americans facing the full brunt of racial oppression. The estimated ten thousand attendees of the festive occasion might have expected to hear encouraging words about their communal progress or strong condemnations of the wave of white supremacy that threatened to curtail it. Chase assumed a different tone, though. He told the crowd that there was "something in the American negro that not only makes him a political but a physical coward." Haiti, Chase thundered, "never obtained her independence by cowardice." He therefore demanded that African Americans take heed of the example set by Haitians, reclaim their manliness, and achieve their "manhood rights" by whatever means necessary.[131]

This was more than mere bluster. African Americans did not accept the onslaught of anti-black violence that attended the entrenchment of Jim Crow. Instead, many continued to embrace a politics of defiance.[132] Black resistance to white oppression encompassed armed self-defense just as often as it entailed public testimonials about white vigilantism. Indeed, in the same moment that Chase called on African Americans to mimic the militancy of Haitians, black newspapers carried countless stories of black southerners who asserted their dignity by fighting back against white supremacy despite the likelihood of death. Not even the fiercest backlash could squelch their commitment to an existence free of white domination.

Of course, Chase and a number of his contemporaries did not just implore African Americans to take an aggressive stand for their rights. By exalting Haiti's enduring struggle for self-determination, a host of black journalists, church leaders, artists, and educators embraced a nascent anti-imperial politics in addition to a transnational politics of defiance. They responded to current events in Haiti that seemed to encourage both.

In October 1897, a dispute emerged between the Haitian and German governments after a Haitian court sentenced Emile Lüders, a German national, to one year's imprisonment for assault and battery and resisting arrest. The German chargé d'affaires in Port-au-Prince reacted swiftly. He demanded the immediate release of Lüders, the removal of the presiding judge in the case, and the dismissal of the arresting officers. Although displeased with this affront to the integrity of their justice system, Haitian officials under the leadership of President Tirésias Simon Sam relented to international pressure and pardoned Lüders before deporting him to Germany. That capitulation did not appease German officials. A month later, two German warships entered the harbor of Port-au-Prince. One of the captains gave the Haitian government four hours to consider the following ultimatum: Germany would not bombard Port-au-Prince if Haitian officials produced a $20,000 indemnity, granted Lüders permission to return to Haiti, issued a formal apology to the German government and a twenty-one-gun salute to the German flag, and hosted a state reception for the German chargé d'affaires. Faced with potential devastation, the Haitian government proceeded to raise a white flag of surrender above the presidential palace. It had little choice but to submit to the outrageous demands.[133]

Black journalists were outraged by the insult to Haiti's national honor and sovereignty. Complicating his celebrations of Haitian manliness in order to condemn the abuses of German militarism, Calvin Chase lamented that "Germany, with her great and powerful navy, was anxious to attack poor, little Hayti," whose "people would have rather died than submitted to the tyranny of a German monarchy."[134] Agreeing that European technological advancements had unfairly outweighed Haitian resistance, Sol Johnson proclaimed that the actions of Germany "reminded us of the large boy and small boy." Even the *Freeman*, by then under the ownership of the conservative black businessman George L. Knox, chastised Germany for taking "exasperating extremities" when it could "be lenient to this vastly weaker power without suffering in dignity."[135] It found that the connections between global anti-blackness and German imperialism were clear. While the *Freeman* noted that African Americans were "a unit in protesting against the insult Germany has offered Hayti" because the German emperor Wilhelm II was alleged to have called Haitians "impudent niggers with a smattering of French civilization," Calvin Chase went even further in promoting Afro-diasporic political solidarities.[136] As the nineteenth century came to an end, he still recalled the German abuses of Haiti. He pledged that African Americans would always "remember Hayti" and assert their own manliness by avenging the "outrageous treatment of our [Haitian] brothers" should the United States ever go to war with Germany.[137]

In the same moment that Chase championed armed black resistance, George L. Knox expressed admiration for a different expression of black manhood. In December 1898, the *Freeman* informed readers that it had found a rare occasion to celebrate a man "of worth." That "genuine article" was Aaron M. Middlebrooks, a formerly enslaved man who had become a Baptist minister and one of the leading black Republicans in Arkansas.[138] According to the *Freeman*, Middlebrooks was the embodiment of "true leadership," an "honest and worthy exemplar" of black progress capable of "telling his race what next they must do." The paper felt that it had strong evidence to support those assertions. Readers had written to it about a recent outbreak of violence at a lumber mill in Cleveland County, Arkansas. Black millworkers were said to have killed a white man who had interrupted their picnic, propositioned a black woman in attendance, and drawn a pistol when she rebuffed him. Information received from Arkansas indicated that a white lynch mob delivered its version of justice to one of the black picnickers, but the *Freeman* presented evidence that Middlebrooks had saved two other black men from similar fates. While vengeful white Arkansans threatened their would-be victims, Middlebrooks was said to have hired a lawyer, secured a writ of habeas corpus for the two men, and helped them flee Arkansas after paying their bond. He had, in his own words, "defended these Negro men and saved their lives because they defended the character and virtue of a young Negro girl."[139]

To the *Freeman*, the heroic Middlebrooks was a model of racial progress. In its estimation, he was a former slave who had become a "distinguished race man and great leader." He was an exemplar of "race patriotism." The *Freeman* pointed to the correspondence from readers who also lauded the "brainy, smart and up-to-date man . . . minister, philanthropist, orator, Republican, Odd-fellow and Mason of highstanding" to prove that point. In addition, it recounted times when Middlebrooks encouraged African Americans to not only "build up churches and schools" but also "open stores and enter all avenues of trade and commerce where an honest dollar can be made." That was sound advice according to the *Freeman*, a paper that Knox proudly proclaimed to be the most conservative black newspaper in the United States.[140] From its perspective, Middlebrooks seemed "in tune to all the progress of the age." He defended black womanhood, promoted black capitalism, highlighted the importance of industrial education for black youth, and placed great value on Protestantism. He was by all appearances a new negro for a new century.

Still, Middlebrooks was not incomparable. The *Freeman* boasted that Middlebrooks exhibited the best traits of prominent black men across time and place. He was, in short, "the Booker T. Washington, the W. H. Councill and the Maceo and Dessalines type all concentrated in one Negro." Two of those comparisons were not like the others. While the *Freeman* recalled times when Middlebrooks praised Washington and William Hooper Councill, two men who had survived enslavement to become the leading black educators in Alabama, its linkage of a Baptist minister from Arkansas with the Afro-Cuban general Antonio Maceo and the Haitian emperor Jean-Jacques Dessalines was much less obvious. The *Freeman* implied, however, that the latter connections were perhaps more accurate than the former. To the Indianapolis newspaper, there was no reason for black playwrights to search afar for characters worthy of dramatization when such a man as Middlebrooks stood right before them. In fact, the *Freeman* imagined Middlebrooks in the lead role of *Dessalines*. Quoting from William Edgar Easton's play, it implied that Middlebrooks and Dessalines both proved that "high minded men with purpose firm, and not afraid to die" made true leaders. "Well may Dessalines say, 'Then to the Franks I shall be a worthy and apt pupil, for out of the fertility of my brain shall spring a thousand cruel torture, and every torture shall be as a hundred deaths,'" the paper concluded. Middlebrooks could say the same as he stalked "the stage after running the gamut of trial and metal test."[141]

Decades after the christening of the Dessalines School stirred controversy in St. Louis, a different black institution thus presaged a key development in black intellectual history through its invocation of Dessalines. In the opinion of the *Freeman*, Middlebrooks made himself accountable for the well-being of the black masses. He promoted a doctrine of black self-help and understood the need to combat virulent anti-black stereotypes. He was, in essence, an apostle of the politics of racial uplift. By imagining such a figure in the leading role of *Dessalines*, the *Freeman* attributed a heroic and radical quality to a seemingly conservative strain of black thought. It not only romanticized advocates of racial uplift but also foreshadowed how black intellectuals would reimagine Haiti in the ensuing decades. As black public figures including Knox and Middlebrooks suggested that the material and moral improvement of the black masses might strengthen their claims to political and civil rights in the United States, they would attempt to shoehorn Haiti and Haitians into their understandings of uplift and respectability. Such efforts would reveal very little about the actual political conditions in Haiti or the real lives of its citizens. Instead, they would demonstrate a great deal about how black intellectuals struggled to balance their claims to national belonging with their diasporic identifications in an era when the United States reinforced its commitment to racism and empire.

CHAPTER 4

Haiti, the Negro Problem, and the Transnational Politics of Racial Uplift

In May 1899, Booker T. Washington was on the brink of a physical breakdown. Four years after the death of Frederick Douglass, Washington was now the preeminent black spokesman in the United States. Most of his days were spent traveling throughout the country raising funds for the Tuskegee Institute and promoting his vision of black progress before white and black audiences. Although Washington loved his work, its physical toll exacerbated the emotional stress of being a black public figure in the Jim Crow era. Some of his friends, a group of white philanthropists in Boston, even worried that Washington's wearied face and noticeable weight gain were signs of an eminent collapse. They encouraged Washington to leave at once for a European holiday.[1]

One month into his "vacation," Washington arrived in Paris. Although he took the time to critique what he saw as the Parisian obsession with fashion, Washington paid greater attention to the Haitians he met in the French capital. At first, he thought that some of them might help him make a pilgrimage to the grave of Toussaint Louverture. When his Haitian acquaintances revealed that the French had not given Louverture a proper burial after his death in the Fort de Joux, Washington protested. It seemed to him that it had "been in the minds of the Haytians for some time to remove the body to Hayti," but for unknown reasons the task had "thus far . . . been neglected."[2] Washington thought the fault for Louverture's insufficient commemoration and delayed repatriation could lie only with Haitians. Reflecting on his thwarted attempts to pay homage to Louverture, Washington concluded that the "Haytian government and people owe it to themselves . . . to see to it that the resting place of the great hero is given a proper memorial."[3]

Washington admonished Haitians on other subjects, too. In Paris, he observed the presence of a "good many well educated and cultured Haytians" who took "high rank in scholarship" at the finest colleges in the city. He did not mean that as a compliment. In an article published in the *New York Age*, the paper edited by his close confidant T. Thomas Fortune, Washington regretted that Haitians did "not take advantage of the excellent training" available at Parisian "colleges of physical sciences, agriculture, mechanics, and domestic sciences." He argued that their preference for the humanities and social sciences left them ill-equipped to "return home and assist in developing the agricultural and mineral resources of their native land." In fact, it crippled Haitian self-government. "Hayti," Washington predicted, "will never be what it should until a large number of the natives receive that education which will fit them to develop agriculture, public roads, start manufactories, build bridges, [and] railroads."[4]

Washington's Parisian musings were indicative of broader intellectual transformations. At the outset of the twentieth century, sites of black intellectual life—including newspapers, colleges, civil rights organizations, and even international congresses—flourished in the United States and abroad. Opportunities for meaningful black freedom or full black citizenship did not. Instead, African Americans confronted not only the consolidation of Jim Crow but also the persistent complaints that black people were criminal, degenerate, and unfit for citizenship in modern U.S. society.[5] Many turned to racial uplift, an optimistic ideology that prioritized black self-help while reinforcing intraracial class differences, as a response to the ongoing investigations of the "Negro problem" and a means of fighting pernicious anti-black stereotypes.

As Washington's writings confirm, racial uplift had international applications and implications.[6] At the same time that Washington counseled Haitians on the need for race pride and industrial education, he also welcomed them to his Tuskegee Institute. Some of his contemporaries tried to revive an emigration movement meant to bring educated African Americans to the aid of Haitian peasants. While a mass emigration movement did not materialize, the idea that Haiti required perfecting proliferated in the writings of black intellectuals. In fact, it motivated William Pickens, then a college student and an admirer of Washington, to demand the annexation of Haiti on the eve of its centennial anniversary. Some black activists rebuked Pickens, in the process espousing cultural relativism and articulating anti-imperial politics, but subsequent expressions of support for the U.S. occupation of Haiti that began in 1915 illustrate how racial uplift ideology could and did function as a civilizing mission.

Ultimately, the anxieties about racism that preceded scrutiny of Haitian sovereignty reveal the shortcomings of dividing black intellectuals of the Jim Crow era into integrationist or internationalist camps. A few scholars of Washington have challenged that dichotomy and shown how he embraced elements of black nationalism and Pan-Africanism, the belief that people of African descent have a common history and destiny.[7] While their works have focused on Washington's interest in Africa, his concern with Haitians in Paris confirms that Haiti and its citizens had a parallel position in his diasporic consciousness. For Washington and numerous other black intellectuals, Haitians *had* to embrace an ethos of self-help and adopt practical modes of education or Haiti would never be what it should: an unassailable model of black self-determination in an era when segregationists and imperialists in the United States and Western Europe drew a global color line. For the time being, U.S.-based black intellectuals, outside of a few exceptions, struggled to reconcile their imagined connection to Haiti with their claims to national citizenship. Still, their consistent attempts to link domestic and global issues—their implicit understanding that U.S. birth did not negate Afro-diasporic belonging—provided the foundations for yet another idea of Haiti, one for a new era of black internationalist politics.

At the turn of the twentieth century, Booker T. Washington, born enslaved in Virginia and educated at Hampton Institute, was the most influential black man in the United States. He had held that position since September 1895. That month, the wealthy white organizers of the Cotton States and International Exposition in Atlanta, Georgia, invited Washington to speak at the ambitious event meant to showcase the rise of the modern and industrial "New South." They hoped that the invitation to a black speaker would convince outsiders of the racial progress of their region. They expected, too, that Washington was the right type of black spokesman, one who would not upset the racial hierarchies that his divisive appearance was meant to obscure.[8]

An enthusiastic participant, Washington proceeded to announce his blueprint for racial and sectional progress. At a speech given on the opening day of the exposition, Washington implored southerners, black and white, to "cast down your bucket where you are." For "his race" that meant ignoring the lure of emigration, courting friendships with their white

FIGURE 10. Booker T. Washington, c. 1895. Frances Benjamin Johnston Collection, Prints & Photographs Division, Library of Congress.

counterparts, and accepting that "we shall prosper in proportion as we learn to dignify and glorify common labour." For the "white race" that meant hiring black workers instead of "those of foreign birth and strange tongue and habits." According to Washington, the proposed rapprochement between black and white southerners need not raise delicate "questions of social equality," a concept that white southerners came to associate with the specter of interracial sex. Instead, he assured an audience seated in racially segregated sections that "in all things purely social we can be as separate as the fingers, yet one as the hand in all things essential to mutual progress."[9]

What black activists came to condemn as the Atlanta Compromise that accepted the status quo of Jim Crow was then applauded by some black intellectuals, including W. E. B. Du Bois. Days after the momentous speech at the Cotton States and International Exposition, Du Bois, the first black PhD from Harvard University and a faculty member at Wilberforce University, wrote to "heartily congratulate" Washington for his "phenomenal success at Atlanta."[10] As Du Bois explained in his autobiography, he then thought that Washington had offered "the basis of a real settlement between whites and blacks in the South, if the South opened to the Negroes the doors of economic opportunity and the Negroes cooperated with the white South in political sympathy."[11] He saw in Washington a man who understood the real challenges of advocating for African Americans amid the rise of racial segregation. He heard some compromise in Washington's words but also found promise in the prospect of racial uplift.

Racial uplift ideology was a popular response of middle-class African Americans to the assaults on black rights and black bodies in the decades preceding World War I.[12] While the federal government refused to protect its black citizens from racial violence and sanctioned racial segregation in the landmark case of *Plessy v. Ferguson*, Washington and other black spokespeople promoted the idea that they were responsible for the well-being of the black masses. They hoped to maintain some measure of influence on the material realities of black lives. In an era when African Americans had little formal presence in local, state, or national governance, some of the most vocal advocates of racial uplift assigned great importance to self-help, interracial cooperation, race pride, thrift, temperance, industrial education, capitalism, and patriarchal gender mores. They assured black domestics and sharecroppers, laundresses and porters that their low socioeconomic position was fleeting, that the collective status of African Americans could be elevated through a focus on realistic internal improvement rather than futile civil rights protest. After all, Washington proclaimed in his exposition address, "no race that has anything to contribute to the markets of the world is long in any degree ostracized."[13]

For proponents of racial uplift, representation was key. Knowing that most white Americans viewed African Americans as a homogenous community more fit for enslavement than citizenship, educated black leaders tried to improve the image of black people. They reified intraracial class differences in doing so. Referring to themselves as the "better class" of African Americans, spokespersons including Du Bois not only demanded recognition of their own educational achievements but also encouraged poor and working-class black people to adopt the behaviors that would ostensibly best serve their anti-racist arguments. Those behaviors included abstaining from alcohol, dressing in a modest, professional fashion, and showing female deference to male authority. They reflected a continued belief in the superiority of bourgeois Western culture and some internalization of mainstream ideas about black cultural backwardness.

In short, the idea of racial uplift was intertwined with the redefinition of who African Americans were and who they were becoming. It was inseparable from the concept of the New Negro. For Booker T. Washington, New Negroes were feminine black clubwomen striving to elevate the race with educational and philanthropic work, masculine black soldiers showing their valor and patriotism in the Spanish-American War, and brilliant black scholars struggling to end racial discrimination through their intelligence and dedication to liberal democratic reform. They were, above all, educated, progressive, race conscious, respectable, and self-improving. The latter trait was a theme of *A New Negro for A New Century: An Accurate and Up-to-Date Record of the Upward Struggles of the Negro Race*, a book that Washington coauthored in 1900. "The Negro of today is in every phase of life far advanced over the Negro of thirty years ago," its introduction begins.[14] It suggested that fin de siècle African Americans could not be mistaken for the caricatures of enslaved and free black people—the subservient "Mammy," the idle "Sambo," or the clownish "Zip Coon"—who had stood at the forefront of racist minds since the antebellum era.[15]

The New Negro was disassociated from Haitians, too. In *The Future of the American Negro*, a book first published in 1899 and then republished one year later, Washington stressed that black progress depended on African Americans' willingness to embrace industrial education, schooling that focused on training for manual labor, and shun "the temptation to live mainly by their wits, without producing anything that is of real value to the world."[16] In his opinion, the consequences of miseducation were obvious. While positioning Tuskegee as the mecca of industrial education and thus the heart of racial uplift and black modernity, Washington identified Haiti as evidence of "what must happen to any people who lack industrial or technical training."[17] Put simply, it was the seat of racial stagnation rather than racial elevation, the opposite of Tuskegee. Drawing from earlier writings and talks, Washington proceeded to argue that Haitians had "not yet learned the lesson of turning their education toward the cultivation of the soil and the making of the simplest implements for agricultural and other forms of labour."[18] To the detriment of their national sovereignty, he continued, Haitians had emphasized "belles lettres" and avoided "industrial and scientific education." There were lessons in those mistakes, however. Washington concluded that the struggles of a Haitian state forced "to send abroad even to secure engineers for her men-of-war, for plans for her bridges and other work requiring technical knowledge and skill" predicted the future of African Americans "if industrial education is much longer neglected." It was a fate that he would "very much regret to see."[19] As put to use by Washington, this idea of Haiti thus became the foil in yet another parable meant to reinforce the importance of black self-help. Haiti was symbolic, as always. It was also allegorical.

Washington's use of the trope of premodern Haiti cohered with ideas about that country and its citizens gaining traction among other black intellectuals such as George L. Knox. At the turn of the twentieth century, one of the most prominent black journalists in the Midwest made the alleged shortcomings of the Haitian educational system a frequent target of critique. His Indianapolis-based *Freeman*, then one of the most widely circulated black newspapers in the United States in part because of its consistent support for the influential Booker T. Washington, suggested that if "Haytian sons are educated in Paris to better learn how to break up their governments they had better stay at home and saw wood." It used a dismissive tone of derision that belied deeper apprehensions. For black spokesmen including Knox, industrial education was the most effective means of racial uplift. It was the best way for the race to improve itself and, "as the best representative of governments by colored men," Haiti simply had to "get better."[20]

What distinguished Washington from friends such as Knox was one simple fact: he had a world-renowned school, a hub of black self-help *and* intellectual production, from which he could develop those widespread ideas about Haiti and the African Diaspora. By 1900, Tuskegee had begun to attract students of African descent from Africa, the Caribbean, Central America, and South America in addition to African Americans from across the United States.[21] From the perspective of its principal, U.S. and European imperialism had provided the conditions to bring those disparate communities together. It had, in his opinion, placed educated African Americans including himself in a unique position to regenerate their race not only at home but also abroad. Besides recruiting black international students to

Tuskegee, Washington provided the foundations for industrial education in U.S.-occupied Cuba and the German colony of Togo.

In exporting the Tuskegee model overseas, Washington sought to challenge the guiding rationale of European colonial and U.S. imperial regimes. Under the tutelage of Tuskegee advisers, Afro-Cuban sugar cultivators or Togolese cotton growers would become indispensable parts of their colonial and national economies. Eventually, they would demonstrate the qualities needed for self-rule. Romanticizing the independent black institutions that became essential tools of black survival during the Jim Crow era, Washington predicted that the Tuskegee gospel would accomplish for Afro-Cubans and West Africans what it was doing for black southerners. It would help the race stand on its own two feet in Cuba and Togo as well as in the United States.[22]

Washington believed that industrial training would have a similar effect on black self-government where it already existed—in Haiti. In 1901, Knox's *Freeman* eagerly reported an emerging collaboration between Washington and William F. Powell, the U.S. envoy extraordinary and minister plenipotentiary to Haiti. Before assuming his current position, Powell introduced industrial training to black schoolchildren during his tenure as the district superintendent of black schools in Camden, New Jersey. Now he hoped to help Washington spread their shared beliefs about racial uplift and black education even further. Besides donating money to Tuskegee, Powell became the liaison between Booker T. Washington and the Haitian government. According to the *Freeman*, the native of New York and lifelong educator submitted a proposal whereby Washington would admit to Tuskegee two students of the Haitian government's choosing. Those students, after completing their coursework in agriculture and mechanics, would then return to Haiti "so as to be of some practical assistance to their people."[23]

Washington thought that such "practical assistance" was of special importance in Haiti because he believed it to be exceptional. In later years, Washington would publish a review praising one of the leading British colonial administrators in Africa for writing a book that "indicated what Haiti should do in order to become a progressive nation." The Tuskegee principal found that the author was correct in recommending "that the blighting military despotism should be done away with . . . that there should be great efficiency and justness in the administration of the customs and . . . that education should be put on a practical basis." Those recommendations, he concluded, would allow Haiti to fulfill its great destiny. Washington anticipated that if Haitians carried out the suggestions of the British imperialist, they "would take their rightful place as the leaders of all the black people of the New World." After all, Haiti had "it in her to become a wealthy and respected Negro community."[24]

Washington was not alone in thinking that "the problem in Haiti is for an independent Black people to develop themselves and the great resources of their rich island."[25] In the same moment that he presented the education of Haitians at Tuskegee as the solution to that problem, some Haitian elites considered whether industrial education would help improve their country.[26] In fact, some of them established ties with Washington. For instance, Jean Price-Mars, then an aspiring politician who had just completed his medical studies in Paris, braved what he called "the ignominies of color prejudice" in the U.S. South just to observe the operations at Tuskegee. After two weeks at the famous school, he became convinced that an educational system oriented toward technical training in trade and agriculture would improve the lives of Haitian peasants, lead to the establishment of more productive labor communes, and help democratize the Haitian social and political system. Later, once elected to the Haitian Chamber of Deputies, Price-Mars even made educational reform in accordance with the Tuskegee model a central part of his political agenda.[27]

Given the influence of prominent Haitian reformers like Price-Mars and the global fame of Booker T. Washington, it is unsurprising that the *Tuskegee Student* soon boasted that a "little colony of students have come to us from Haiti."[28] By the 1903–4 academic year, there were twelve students from Port-au-Prince, Gonaïves, Les Cayes, and Jérémie, Haiti, enrolled at Tuskegee. Most were postgraduate students extending the education that they had already received in Haiti. All came with lofty expectations of what more Tuskegee could provide.[29]

One of the first Haitians to enroll at Tuskegee explained some of the aspirations that brought him and his compatriots from their Haitian towns to rural Alabama. In a letter sent to a Tuskegee instructor before its publication in *Technical World Magazine*, the male student from Port-au-Prince proclaimed that he had long "desired to come to America to study practical science and learn a trade." Accordingly, after completing his education at a Haitian lycée, he decided to enroll at Tuskegee because it was known for the "excellent opportunities" it afforded "to the negro for acquiring practical knowledge." In Alabama, the student decided to study electrical engineering, "one of the branches of scientific knowledge least in vogue in Haiti."

Apparently, he chose wisely. Soon after entering Tuskegee, the Haitian student could "install electric bells and annunciators, trim arc lamps, wire buildings, and assist in running the dynamo." Those skills, he implied, would be of great use in Haiti. To that end, he planned on honing his talents at another U.S. college after his graduation from Tuskegee and then return to Haiti, "my home, for work at my trade."[30]

Those goals cohered with the motivations of the dozens of other African, Caribbean, and Central American students at Tuskegee. Like their colleagues from Barbados, the Bahamas, Cuba, Jamaica, Nicaragua, Puerto Rico, South Africa, Trinidad, and Zanzibar, young men and women from Haiti drew inspiration from Washington's life and works, including translations of his famous autobiography, *Up from Slavery*. To them, Washington embodied black upward mobility. Accordingly, their plan was to make use of the most attractive parts of his message of racial uplift, return to their native country with the skills gained at Tuskegee, and become successful professionals, entrepreneurs, and leaders in their own right. Rather than becoming better farmers, bricklayers, or domestic workers, the Haitian students hoped to pave new paths to black economic, political, and social power in an era of rampant U.S. and European imperialism.[31]

At the same time, some educated Haitians proclaimed that their nationality inspired a unique interest in Tuskegee. In a letter to Booker T. Washington, Athanase M. Auguste, a prospective student from Port de Paix, Haiti, explained that he had enjoyed *The Story of My Life and Work*, Washington's autobiography published in 1901. That "brilliant work," Auguste proclaimed, proved that Washington had an unmatched "devotion to the elevation of the black man." It persuaded him that the Tuskegee principal was "the defender of my race and lover of my country." Announcing his desire to study under Washington, Auguste predicted that Tuskegee would instill in him the "civic education" needed to uplift himself and achieve the "material and moral elevation of my poor country . . . this corner of the earth where God has permitted the black man to conduct his destiny." He assured Washington that he, too, appreciated the need to fulfill "our duty . . . to prove to the white race this truth that the races are equal."[32]

Although consistent with how other Haitian elites imagined their country, Auguste's rhetoric also suggests the transnational circulation and salience of U.S. ideas of racial uplift. Auguste expressed his desire to help "the Haytien Republic, cradle of the black race" in an era when Haitian intellectuals including Anténor Firmin, Louis Joseph Janvier, and Jean

Price-Mars understood the defense of Haitian sovereignty as synonymous with the vindication of the black race.[33] He also wrote out of a need for money. Admitting in his letter to Washington that he was unable to pay tuition at Tuskegee and implying that other sources of funding were unavailable, Auguste tried to show that he possessed the same ideals as the Tuskegee principal even though an "ocean comes between us." His appeals to racial pride and uplift and his simultaneous regret about the "errors" and misfortunes of his country were not just critical expressions of Haitian nationalism.[34] They were also an attempt to win Washington's support by echoing the widespread ideas about black progress and education that he famously promoted.

Whether accurately or not, Tuskegee officials and their sympathizers accepted the Haitian expressions of personal ambition, pragmatism, and racial pride at face value. They saw them as proof of a long-awaited Haitian awakening. As the *Technical World Magazine* glorified the search of one Haitian student for "practical knowledge" under the tutelage of Washington and Auguste petitioned for a place at Tuskegee, George L. Knox's *Freeman* juxtaposed the historical shortcomings and current enlightenment of Haitian leaders. According to the paper, the Haitian elite had long possessed "great opportunities for instituting and promoting such work" as that conducted at Tuskegee, but it had wasted "its energies and geniuses, whatever they may be, in the art of government snatching." Times were changing, though. As the "little colony" of Haitian students in Alabama immersed themselves in "fields more consonant with the progress of progressive countries," the *Freeman* praised the Haitian government for funding some of those students and encouraging a model of education that augured "better things for the future." Haiti, Knox's paper concluded, was "waking up to her necessities." And although her slumber was far too prolonged, it was "better late than never."[35]

The patronizing praise afforded to Haiti suggests why it was so central to the international politics of racial uplift. As the United States plunged into what one historian called the "nadir of American race relations," black male leaders including Washington, Knox, and Powell advised African Americans removed from the political arena to focus on internal improvement and the rehabilitation of their racial image as paths toward racial progress.[36] They found it obvious that Haiti and Haitians were implicated in both processes. Convinced of the long-standing idea that Haiti was a singular representation of black self-government, advocates of racial uplift encouraged Haitians to adopt industrial educational practices associated with black improvement and to appreciate the value of manual labor. They implored it to disprove racist stereotypes used to justify racial segregation. In the same moment that black educators, journalists, and diplomats assured African Americans that economic success was a means of achieving respect, they counted on Haiti to become a "wealthy and respected Negro community."[37] Its standing, they concluded, would foretell the future for African Americans.

Most white Americans did not believe that African Americans were capable of achieving a progressive and civilized future. They were more worried than ever about the enduring "Negro problem." White social scientists, statisticians, politicians, and novelists promoted the social Darwinist doctrine that African Americans were not just incapable of assimilating into U.S. society but also were the inevitable losers of a racial contest in which there could only be "survival of the fittest." Many of those intellectuals excused lynching as a practice needed to control black brutes and encouraged mass incarceration as a solution to black criminality. Some refused to write life insurance policies for African Americans, believed to be dying at disproportionate rates, while others demanded the expulsion of black people from the United States. For all of them, it was clear that African Americans were "gradually parting with the virtues . . . developed under the regime of slavery." Having failed the test of freedom, "gradual extinction [was] only a question of time.[38]

Exclusionary ideas of civilization were the foundation of the bleak forecasts of the collective black future. To white intellectuals seeking to solve the so-called Negro problem, civilization was whiteness and whiteness was civilization. It was elevated in the political institutions and cultural values of Europe and the United States. And it was absent in Haiti, the litmus test of black self-determination. For writers who brought the inventions of Spenser St. John into the new century, Haitians showed how black people degenerated once free from racial subordination. Haiti proved the righteousness of imperial, colonial, and Jim Crow regimes that, through proximity to whiteness, dragged black people out of African barbarism "into the light of . . . serene civilization."[39]

Influenced by racial uplift ideology and eager to disprove the racist discourses that buttressed white world supremacy, black activists and intellectuals from the United States forged new international networks in defense

FIGURE 11. International Students in Tuskegee's 1908 Class. Moving from left to right and back to front the students are: Sierra Feijoo Saturnino of San Juan, Puerto Rico; Edward Andreas Anthony of Lomé, Togo; Bethuel Aldrick Pusey of San Andrés, Colombia; Alvin Joseph Neely of Newberry, South Carolina; Malcolm Iwane Kawahara of Saga-shi, Japan; Alexandre Lavaud of Port-au-Prince, Haiti; and Luis Delfín Valdés of Havana, Cuba. Tuskegee University Archives, Tuskegee University.

of black progress. In July 1900, delegates from the United States, Canada, Haiti, Liberia, Sierra Leone, the Gold Coast, and the British West Indies met in London for the first Pan-African Conference, which was organized by the Trinidadian barrister Henry Sylvester Williams. The "very important movement," as Booker T. Washington called the pioneering event, challenged the prevailing logic of European colonialism and U.S. empire and Jim Crow. Over the course of three days, delegates including the U.S. scholar W. E. B. Du Bois and the Haitian diplomat Benito Sylvain resolved that Great Britain should grant self-government to its African and West Indian colonies, the United States should recognize the constitutional rights of African Americans, and the Congo Free State should become the "great central Negro State of the world." Together, they called on the world to "respect the integrity and independence of the first Negro States of Abyssinia, Liberia, Haiti" and announced that black people deserved the same rights as white people in light of their similar attainments of civilized progress.[40]

To be sure, the conference that ended with Du Bois's prescient prediction that the "problem of the twentieth century is the problem of the color line" demanded inclusion within rather than refutation of dominant ideas of civilization. Participants at the Pan-African Conference called on the United States and Europe to allow black people "the opportunities and privileges of modern civilization." They argued that the crimes of colonialism and Jim Crow were antithetical to Western "ideals of civilization." To black intellectuals like Du Bois, it was not then apparent that racial domination was inherent to, rather than a departure from, modern Western civilization. Instead, it seemed critical to refute the scientific racism that motivated investigations into the "Negro problem" and minimize racial difference. The most persuasive claim to black self-government, they believed, was the assimilative capacities of black people who were not dying but rising to Western standards of culture, education, and modernity.[41]

Unlike most white thinkers, however, black intellectuals knew that the majority of white people were ill-suited to be agents of racial uplift in the United States or civilization in Haiti. In an editorial circulated by the black press in April 1901, William F. Powell lamented that Haiti "stands today, as she stood from the day she achieved her Independence, like our people in the states, isolated, with no helping hand stretched forth to assist, to advise or to help her."[42] The claims of friendlessness were mostly accurate, the allegations of isolation less so. While statesmen and businessmen from the

United States, Germany, England, and France battled to secure economic dominance in Haiti, a host of foreign elites, including Syrio-Lebanese merchants, gained prominence in the Haitian import-export business. Powell was well aware of those attempts to exploit Haiti. Foreigners, he wrote, "not of our race, have come [to Haiti] and are daily coming to enrich themselves at her expense, leaving her poor when they leave." Even worse, those non-black outsiders who made their fortunes in Haiti had "no good word to utter in her behalf, but desire to bleed her again and again."[43]

For the time being, the Haitian government managed to stave off the worst threats to its sovereignty through the practice of multilateral diplomacy. Still, Powell wondered how long Haitian nationalists could play off the foreign powers against each other. He was not entirely optimistic that, in the face of imperialism, Haiti could maintain what he characterized as a "progressive and independent government of its own."[44]

In the midst of that uncertainty, Powell suggested that black farmers and manufacturers from the United States could be the friends that Haiti needed. Echoing mainstream imperialist discourses, Powell informed black readers that opportunities for "large results and quick returns" awaited African Americans willing to leave the United States and join him in Haiti. From his perspective, the conditions for a renewed emigration movement were ideal. Haiti's climate was "delightful," its soil was "fertile," and its natural resources were "abundant." All that was missing was a "class of agriculturists who will take the initiative to cultivate the soil on a different principle than has been done heretofore and introduce therein such farming utensils as are common on any farm or plantation, in the states." To that end, Powell cautioned that he was not interested in "that class which is naturally tired." Instead, his intended audience was the segment of African Americans who were "willing to work . . . suffer some privation . . . bring with them improved farming utensils and . . . labor-saving machines" and use their own funds "to sustain them in their new land until the ground yields to them its fruits." Put simply, Powell wanted aspirational emigrants who possessed the motivations and means to not only benefit themselves but also help Haiti compete on the global stage.[45]

In appealing to prospective emigrants, Powell did not just invoke an emerging ideology of racial uplift that linked manual labor and the Protestant work ethic to black progress, he also appealed to an older black nationalist tradition. Powell, like Washington, assigned great meaning to Haitian independence. In his published writings he chastised African Americans for failing to remember that if Haiti "should lose the independence that it has won, and the government it has maintained for . . . nearly 100 years, we in the States add to ourselves another load to the many we are now bearing of the failure of the Negro to maintain a system of government." In fact, Powell felt that more than remembrance was required of his peers. He insisted that the "leading men of the race," including AME clergy, "owe it to the race, to direct the attention of our people to this island, and to assist this people in the great struggle of life." Black leaders had to make the black masses in the United States see the Haitian struggle as their own. Refashioning arguments made by nineteenth-century emigrationists, Powell proclaimed that Haiti had "room for all that are willing to cast their destiny with this people, in a land where . . . each will prosper as the republic increases in its resources and in wealth, and this wealth will be controlled by our race." It was prepared to welcome all African Americans who understood the significance of an independent black republic, who knew that "the influence [Haiti] will exert in the world at large" would "redound to the credit of those of our race."[46]

The ideological coherence between this current emigration proposal and earlier ones was no coincidence. Anticipating opposition from anti-emigrationists, Powell told the black press that African Americans who sought sanctuary in Haiti during the presidency of Fabre Geffrard were at fault for their ensuing disappointment. They had arrived "without money or farming implements" and thus "were of little benefit to the country in an agricultural sense." Powell drew his intimate knowledge of and claims about that preceding movement from its most famous participant. In Haiti, Powell, a practicing Episcopalian, became acquainted with James Theodore Holly, the former emigrant who had since become the Episcopal bishop of the Orthodox Apostolic Church of Haiti. In fact, the two would become colleagues of sorts. As Powell advised Haitian president Tirésias Simon Sam and black newspapers on the benefits of his plan, the white press treated Holly as a subject of interest. Leading white newspapers, including the *Los Angeles Times*, *Louisville Courier-Journal*, and *Chicago Tribune*, claimed that during a recent return to the United States, one of the few that he made during his lifetime, Holly declared "it the duty and destiny of the American negro to help the black republic fully develop its resources." According to those papers, he also articulated his hopes for "the development and evangelization of the black republic" and argued that both went hand in hand as "part of divine design." Those paraphrased statements cohered with the arguments for emigration that Holly first articulated during the antebellum era. Regardless of their precision, they captured an undeniable truth: four decades after Holly fled his native country to make a new home in Haiti, he was an "enthusiastic advocate" of a new movement promising to regenerate Haiti.[47]

Of course, a good deal had changed since the 1860s. As the United States and Western Europe continued to extend their overseas empires, numerous black intellectuals scrutinized the relationship between imperialism and racial destiny. Although some came to oppose imperialism in all of its forms, others argued that African Americans should simply displace white imperialists. Subsequent appeals to a "black man's burden" most often recommended the conquering of Africa for black civilization, commerce, and Christianity, but they implicated Haiti, too.[48]

For instance, at the same time that T. Thomas Fortune predicted that European imperialists could sooth the savage impulses of African tribes and endorsed U.S. colonization of the Philippines, the outspoken journalist advised African Americans to move to Haiti. His reasons for supporting the renewed emigration movement matched his rationales for black colonization elsewhere. Fortune insisted that Haitians would welcome African Americans who brought their habits of thrift and enterprise to Haiti. Of equal importance, he contended, African Americans could ensure the rise of a great Christian civilization in their new country.[49] Both claims revised ecclesiastical notions of racial destiny and collective black identity that emerged decades before. For Fortune and black men of his ilk, the reclamation of Haiti required a demonstration of material as well as spiritual strength. It encouraged imperialism, a practice that was often associated with black modernization, political power, and economic might.

As imagined by black intellectuals including Monroe Work, the work of civilizing Haiti was becoming more and more intertwined with the domestic project of racial uplift. When black diplomats, journalists, and religious leaders began promoting emigration from the United States to Haiti, Work was one of the most promising students in the Department of Sociology at the University of Chicago. Although his studies there would focus on cultural practices in Africa and crime among African Americans, the up-and-coming black scholar-activist also found the growing debates about Haiti of great relevance. In an article published in a May 1901 edition of the *Chicago Tribune*, Work asked a simple question: "Could there not be an emigration to Africa and to Hayti as there has been of foreign peoples to this country?" The obvious answer, he continued, was no. Work insisted that whereas "foreigners who come to this country find themselves in a better environment from which they came," the "American negro . . . would, in Hayti or in Africa, be in a civilization inferior to that from which he came." Rather than "being in the midst of culture which could be inspiring to himself he would have to furnish civilization and culture for a more ignorant people." Work did not think that was a situation for which "the general mass of the negroes of this country" was suited. He proceeded to inform readers of the *Tribune* that most African Americans had not "yet sufficiently developed themselves so as to be able to furnish the means of uplifting others." That fact, Work concluded, "in connection with their poverty and the lack of inducements does not make emigration attractive to them."[50]

Assumptions about the superiority of bourgeois U.S. culture, the inferiority of working-class black culture, and the hierarchies of the African Diaspora filled Work's article. The central idea, however, pertained to the abilities of educated black men like himself. Work, who would later join the faculty at Tuskegee despite being a member of W. E. B. Du Bois's Niagara Movement, did not doubt the capabilities of those he considered to be the best of his race. In fact, he felt that a vanguard of refined black leaders bore the burden of uplifting the ignorant black masses in the United States *and* civilizing the underdeveloped peasants of Haiti. Work believed that African Americans who had taken advantage of their access to a "high degree of civilization" and their abundant opportunities "for acquiring knowledge and culture" were obligated "to bring this knowledge and culture to [their] less favored brethren." In fact, it was their destiny. While insisting that "the general mass" of African Americans remained in need of their own development, Work called on "the select few" to move to Haiti or other "countries where there are a great number of their benighted brethren." In Haiti, armed with "training and education," the most talented members of the race would "develop the resources of that republic" and "enlighten and evangelize the people."[51] They would, in short, lead the civilizing mission abroad in the same moment that they directed the project of racial uplift at home.

To be certain, the appeal of a limited emigration movement rested in its consistency with well-established theories of racial leadership. Years before forming the Niagara Movement, the black civil rights organization that would challenge the racial leadership of Booker T. Washington, Du Bois argued that the salvation of the black race or any other race must come through the efforts of its exceptional men. Accordingly, he called for the cultivation of a Talented Tenth, a cohort of educated black men (women were deemed marginal) who would become "leaders of thought and missionaries of culture among their people."[52] For numerous black intellectuals, the call to become "missionaries of culture" was not just a rhetorical flourish. Rather than limiting their ambitions to domestic leadership as teachers, clergymen, doctors, journalists, and businessmen, some black male elites found it fitting to embrace imperial roles for themselves. They not only conceptualized Africa as a site for redeeming the race and reclaiming black manhood but also construed Haiti as a place where black people could challenge racist principles of social Darwinism that were more entrenched than ever. From the perspective of black men including Monroe Work, a Haitian state under the influence of the Talented Tenth would show that the black race was fit to compete with the mighty Anglo-American. It would prove that black men were no less capable than white men of making technological and industrial advances, demonstrating cultural progress, or asserting their right to self-government.

Still, opposition to emigration was bound to outpace support for it. The reasons for anti-emigrationist sentiment were obvious to Charles Spencer Smith. In June 1901, the AME bishop who had served in the Alabama House of Representatives during Reconstruction returned from Haiti. One of the initial objectives of the trip, he explained in a speech delivered in Detroit, was to observe the conditions in that country and determine whether he should advise emigration from the United States to it. Although promising that he would refrain from making a final judgement on the subject since his visit to Haiti was cut short, Smith did, in fact, reveal his thoughts on the matter. According to a correspondent of the *Detroit Journal*, they were quite pessimistic. Referring to William F. Powell, Smith informed his audience that the "American ambassador to Hayti has already discussed that question with the president and the cabinet, and prominent Haitians, and that they said; while they would be glad enough to welcome immigration from the United States it must be immigration of a certain kind." Haitian president Simon Sam and members of his government, Smith continued, had made it clear that "colored men who were tired of the United States did not need to come to Hayti." In his estimation, the implications of that preference were apparent. Smith concluded that the "only people who would be welcomed there are the ones who are too loyal Americans to leave, for the colored man is loyal."[53] Patriotism, Smith implied, stifled an interest in Afro-diasporic initiatives. It required black elites to remain in the United States even as they considered their obligations to Haiti.

A sense of American identity, investment in lives built in the United States, and financial constraints certainly discouraged many African Americans from leaving the country of their birth. Still, the strongest deterrent to emigration was political instability within Haiti. By 1902, Simon Sam, the Haitian president whom Powell and other emigrationists relied on for support, was under siege. Haitians desired a democratic government that would protect their desires for true national sovereignty, but recent developments, including the Lüders affair, had revealed the increasing vulnerability of the Haitian state in the face of U.S. and European aggression. For critics of Sam, the opportunity to create a state more receptive to the needs of its people seemed to present itself in May, when the embattled president agreed to leave office. Concerned that a constitutional provision allowing the National Assembly to name the next president would once again produce a leader unresponsive to the people, Haitians quickly demanded a direct vote to appoint the successor to Sam. Their protests would lead to political change. As calls for a more democratic election mounted, the National Assembly dispersed and commissions gathered in towns throughout Haiti. Delegates from across the country soon converged on Port-au-Prince to debate how the presidential election would proceed. In the end, they settled on a system in which Haitians would select electors, who would then pledge their votes for certain candidates.[54]

Anténor Firmin emerged as the frontrunner for the presidency due in large part to his defiant stance during the Môle St. Nicolas negotiations and his demands for political reform. Lawyers and teachers threw their support behind the celebrated statesman and intellectual as did the Société des Coeurs Unis, an association of artisans. Young reformers flocked to his camp. Although constitutional provisions still restricted the vote to Haitian men who owned or rented land, practiced a profession, or could prove employment, Firmin had achieved mass support as it was defined in his era. That was evident when, arriving in Port-au-Prince weeks after Sam left office, a crowd of several thousand supporters serenaded him with cries of "Long live Firmin!"[55]

The imperialist forces that Firmin and his supporters had long opposed would, however, also be his downfall. As support for Firmin solidified,

General Nord Alexis launched his own presidential bid. He mobilized the military against Firmin, claiming that his adversary was an academic elitist who planned on surrendering control of Haiti to white foreigners. His efforts to manipulate public perception of Firmin as well as the selection of electors and the registration of voters ensured that the presidential election would be decided through violence, not via a democratic process. It was a battle that Alexis was well equipped to win. In the ensuing civil conflict between the forces of Alexis and Firmin, the German government supplied the former with weapons and ammunition. In fact, the Germans would deliver the final blow to Firmin. After a German warship forced the evacuation and self-destruction of Firmin's most important warship, the lifelong Haitian nationalist fled to St. Thomas. He would live the rest of his life in exile.[56]

For black public figures in the United States, there was no glory in Firmin's struggle for Haitian self-determination and political reform. The only lessons were in his defeat. While Alexis used his superior military expertise and greater foreign support to bolster his claims to power, black journalists looked askance at Haiti. From their perspective, recurring political violence in that country did a great disservice to their race at a time when white reactionaries characterized black men as savages and brutes. It seemed to make a mockery of the claims that black leaders made for racial advancement in the new century. These broader anxieties certainly shaped the descriptions of Haiti found in the pages of Julius F. Taylor's *Broad Ax*. According to that popular black newspaper, the current "reign of terror" was an unfortunate confirmation of the "normal condition down that way.[57] It was an indefensible embarrassment. Whether unaware of or unconcerned with the external pressures that weighed upon the Haitian state or the internal forces that were struggling to reform it, the *Broad Ax* painted Haiti with broad brushstrokes and found all its citizens complicit in "frequent revolutions" that tended "decidedly toward opéra bouffe."[58]

John Stephens Durham found Haiti just as troubling, but he imagined it as an object of reform rather than ridicule. Following his graduation from the University of Pennsylvania, Durham served the United States as its minister resident and consul general to Haiti from 1891 to 1893. That experience would impact him long after he left Port-au-Prince. By the turn of the twentieth century, Durham was a prominent educator and a successful lawyer. He was also an ardent supporter of Booker T. Washington, and Durham's exposure to Washington and his ideas about Haiti informed how he thought about racial uplift. In the same moment that Durham advised graduates of the Tuskegee Institute to teach the next generation to "learn a trade and . . . hate fine clothing," he also spoke of the need for educated African Americans to uplift rural black southerners whose "mode of worship still bears the traces which mark their close relationship to the voudou of the French colonies."[59] For Durham, then, the practice of serving the spirits was much more than evidence that Haitians were the lowest standard of blackness. Instead, it was confirmation that Haiti could become the greatest testament to racial improvement even without the aid of a mass influx of African Americans.

Durham made that belief clear in *Diane, Priestess of* Haïti, a novella that appeared in the April 1902 edition of the popular *Lippincott's Monthly Magazine.* The story, which Durham presented as "a complete study of the social and political life in Haïti," centers on two star-crossed Haitian lovers who find themselves implicated in an international conspiracy not unlike those routinely described in press dispatches from Port-au-Prince.[60] Alcide is an intelligent polyglot who hopes that his employment as the servant of the German minister will help him become a scholar in Europe rather than a soldier in Haiti. In contrast, Diane is the illiterate daughter of the most influential Vodou priest in Haiti. She loves Alcide but struggles to reconcile his disdain for her religion with her desire to become a Vodou priestess. While the two youths attempt to resolve their differences, they become separated as the result of a planned insurrection in which the Haitian minister of war, a German coconspirator, and two Vodou priests, including Diane's father, are implicated. All ends well, however. Along with the German minister, Alcide helps the Haitian president crush the attempted coup before reuniting with Diane. The two then anticipate a bright future as husband and wife, he having relinquished his plans to leave what had become a more republican Haiti and she having renounced her ties to Vodou.[61]

Durham presented Alcide and Diane as embodiments of a rehabilitated race; their reunion and redemption represented the culmination of racial uplift. Alcide, the hero of *Diane,* is intelligent and courageous. Most important, he is civilized. Although Diane's father derides Alcide as a "black imitator of white men, a dog," the mentee of the benevolent German minister comes to see his tutelage in the arts of Western civilization as a weapon that he can wield to the advantage of his country and Diane.[62] As a defender of republican governance, he helps thwart a coup that would have placed Haiti in the hands of Haitian militants, German nationals, and Vodou priests. As a crusader for Victorian gender norms and Protestant values, he delivers Diane from the superstition and licentiousness of the "Vodou deception" into the institution of marriage and the security of a patriarchal household.[63] Her salvation is then linked to the redemption of Haiti. By the end of the novella, Durham positions Alcide and Diane as the proper models of racial advancement and imitable representations of black male leadership and respectable black womanhood. It is under their influence that Haiti will become safe from despotism, ignorance, and foreign rule. Their country will be a true realization of black potential.

At a time when the German government helped affect regime change in Haiti, it was impossible for black intellectuals including Durham to divorce these theories about racial progress or longings for black self-determination from the realities of imperialism.[64] In *Diane*, the namesake of the novella and Alcide become the bedrocks of a stronger black nation, but their redemption occurs under the shadow of a European power. Although the fictional adversaries of Alcide and Diane include ill-intentioned German insurrectionists bent on usurping Haitian autonomy, their friends include well-meaning German diplomats who exert a positive and powerful cultural influence on the young impressionable Haitians. Such a diverse cast of characters and the final salvation of Haiti in the aftermath of an attempted coup offered mixed messages of anti-imperialism and pacifism. Still, the greatest truth in *Diane*'s Haiti was that its progress came under the guidance of educated foreigners and the inspiration of bourgeois Western culture. For Durham, racial advancement in Haiti was, in short, reliant upon a civilizing mission in which black elites and white officials could work as allies rather than adversaries.

There were troubling implications to those suggestions. As Haiti approached its centennial anniversary, a number of black intellectuals took the ideas that Durham articulated in *Diane* to their logical conclusion. Perhaps, they suggested, neither emigrationist schemes nor fictional dreams were enough to redeem Haiti. Maybe it was annexation that Haiti truly required.

In February 1903, William Pickens entered the annual Ten Eyck Prize oratorical competition at Yale University. He was, as he had been for much of his life, determined to succeed in spite of his underdog status. Pickens was born in post-Reconstruction South Carolina, the child of two former slaves turned sharecroppers. During his early childhood, his family moved to central Arkansas, where he picked cotton alongside his parents before heading off to Talladega College. Four years after entering the oldest private black college in Alabama, Pickens left with a bachelor's degree and a firm belief that he could rise even higher. Accordingly, in the fall of 1902, Pickens enrolled at Yale University. That he belonged to a different world than his white classmates who came to Yale from prestigious New England prep schools and affluent households did not bother Pickens. Instead, it fueled him. He was, to his own understanding, the embodiment of Washington's New Negro, a part of an emerging generation of educated African Americans who could improve the image of the entire race through their singular talents. In his own words, the Ten Eyck Prize competition was his chance to do just that. "I decided to win first prize," Pickens would later write, "my ambition to win . . . stimulated by a desire to further the acquaintance of other peoples with my race."[65]

Pickens and the other thirty-five competitors from Yale's junior class had ten topics from which they could choose. One caught Pickens's attention: Haiti. He selected it at once. Pickens began his oration, first given as a written piece to a preliminary panel of judges and later published in the *Yale Literary Review*, with an introduction to his chosen subject. "To the average American," he contended, "the word *Hayti* vaguely suggests a far-off island home of semi-civilized black men." Such ignorance of Haiti had profound implications for race relations in the United States, he believed. Pickens argued that Haiti deserved more thoughtful consideration because "the history of the negro in one hundred years of political freedom and supremacy" shed "light upon the much-mooted questions which involve the welfare of the whole southern section of our country, and vitally concern the status of a tenth of our entire population."[66] In short, Haiti provided answers to the "Negro problem."

To emphasize that the story of African Americans was one of substantial progress since emancipation, Pickens proceeded to characterize Haitian history as one of decline. The island of Hispaniola, Pickens argued, was once a "paradise." No language could capture its beauty. Unfortunately, the island and its native people fell victim to the Spaniards, who, after decimating those indigenous people, began importing enslaved Africans by the thousands. That practice, Pickens explained, accelerated once the French gained power over the western half of the island. In the territory that the French christened Saint-Domingue, a "tricolored" society developed

FIGURE 12. Reunion of Yale College's Class of 1904. William Pickens is pictured standing in the top row, fifth from the right-hand side. James Weldon Johnson Collection of Negro Arts and Letters, Beinecke Rare Book and Manuscript Library, Yale University.

consisting of whites, mulattoes, and enslaved black people. While Pickens insisted that many of the mulattoes were intelligent and inspired by "the intractable spirit of liberty" from the French Revolution, he characterized the enslaved people as a brutalized and ignorant mass. It was their savagery that made the Haitian Revolution a low point in Western civilization rather than the greatest blow in defense of human rights. According to Pickens, whites and mulattoes struggling over political rights inaugurated the "most bloody, cruel and vindictive struggle of history," but "the black slave, with his savage nature untamed by two hundred and fifty years of subjection to French and Spanish scourge" aggravated it. In his opinion, the historic revolt was unconscionable. It was nothing more than a gory record of white infants impaled on spears and wanton massacres of "every accessible community of Europeans."[67]

Pickens clearly accepted popular caricatures of the Haitian Revolution. Yet, like a preceding generation of black historians, he refashioned tropes of Haiti and the Haitian Revolution according to his ideas about black progress. After describing mobs of marauding slaves in Saint-Domingue, Pickens introduced his audience to Toussaint Louverture. He praised the former "black slave" for "securing the escape of his master's family" before joining the "negro army." That act, Pickens proclaimed, demonstrated "such fidelity as showed the American slave who lay like a watchful mastiff on the doorsteps of the absent confederate soldier." Moreover, it foreshadowed the policies that Louverture enacted once he became governor-general of Saint-Domingue. Pickens proclaimed that "the black general . . . having none of that suicidal race-hatred which is at present the bane of Hayti . . . abolished slavery but restored the whites to their estates, and appointed to his council of nine, eight white planters."[68] Such high-mindedness did not disprove that vengeful black people contributed to what Pickens called the undeniable "horrors" of the Haitian Revolution. Instead, it provided a counterpart to that trope. While contemporaries including Booker T. Washington also conjured the image of the faithful plantation slave to counter the specter of the bestial black rapist, Pickens presented the mythical Louverture as the opposite of the savage freedman.[69] In his telling, Louverture was loyal and forgiving. His life was a refutation of racial warfare and a confirmation of the possibilities of black self-improvement, racial reconciliation, and interracial cooperation.

Pickens insisted that there were also lessons in the premature death of Louverture. Following his praise of the "negro general-in-chief," Pickens lamented the seizure, imprisonment, and death of Louverture at the order of Napoleon Bonaparte. He argued that the "act which history brands 'the blackest treachery'" was a key moment in the declension narrative of Haitian history. With the death of the respectable Louverture, the "Haytian negroes were enraged and the brand of savage warfare was relit." They succeeded in ousting the French—and ensuring their own demise. Pickens argued that "with the gain of absolute independence the uncivilized horde gained the most efficient weapon of self-destruction." The black masses made it "their first savage duty to butcher indiscriminately mulattoes and Europeans, who were the only possible hope of the island." They "destroyed every trace and hope of internal civilization," leaving no other option but for "the imbruted ex-slaves . . . to relapse into a savagery and cannibalism comparable to any state of their African ancestry."[70]

Such incendiary claims demonstrated the extent to which racist polemics such as Spenser St. John's were regarded as objective scholarship. But they also reinforced Pickens's message about postemancipation societies. When the French killed Louverture, they left the "imbruted ex-slaves" of Haiti adrift. Because they regarded Louverture as a "revolted slave," not an equal, they eroded the foundations of a progressive multiracial nation and consigned themselves to death.[71]

In fact, Pickens argued that the retrogression of Haiti was the inevitable result of an absence of sound racial leadership. To Pickens, Dessalines was a "feeble imitation of Napoleon Bonaparte . . . summarily shot by his own creatures" while Faustin Soulouque "was a king 'voodoo'" who "surpassed all precedent of excess and tyranny." He contended that, with the exception of Jean-Pierre Boyer, who established "prosperous rule" for more than two decades, most Haitian presidents were no better. From his perspective, there had "been nothing constant and uniform in Hayti save revolution and decline." Pickens charged the Haitian state with despotism and the abetting of the "fetish-worship" that flourished under its nose. He characterized Haitian agriculture as "primitive" and insisted that Haitian commerce was "hampered by dishonesty." In essence, Pickens proclaimed, the Haitian government "is a failure—financially and instrumentally."[72]

Once again, Pickens used the alleged failings of Haitians as a foil for the progress of African Americans. Haiti, he charged, was not a "demonstration of the incapacity of the *negro* race for self-government." Instead, it was "complete historical proof of the inability of any *uncivilized* race for maintaining a civil community with no outside constraining force . . . a miniature picture of the fate that threatened the Southern United States in the Period of Reconstruction."[73] Like Washington, Pickens, addressing a white audience, cast Reconstruction as a period in which African Americans tried to run before they could walk.[74] Doing so not only flattered white elites who were skeptical about black political rights but also cohered with Pickens's strategic narrative of black progress. Pickens argued that U.S. history proved that "the savage and the child to rise to higher things must feel the power of a stronger hand." And African Americans had, in fact, risen. Tutelage under the Anglo-American was "the special blessing of the American negro," who had, in less than four decades of freedom, surpassed "his Haytian brother, who has been "self-governing" for one hundred years."[75] Once enslaved, Pickens insisted, the American Negro was now a New Negro, fully capable of full citizenship.

As the writings of Washington and other black intellectuals make clear, such assumptions about Afro-diasporic hierarchies were quite common. Unlike his peers, however, Pickens did not assign African Americans the leading role in uplifting Haitians. Instead, he placed that burden on the U.S. government.

Coming to the end of his oration, Pickens declared that there were four reasons why the U.S. government should undertake that "act of kindness." First, the Monroe Doctrine gave "this country a measure of responsibility for the political and diplomatic conduct of the lesser American states." Second, it was in the self-interest of the United States "to prevent in the best possible way the interruptions of trade and commerce and the demoralizing influence from a constant state of warfare in a vicinal power." Third, U.S. politicians were "schooled as no other in the problems of the negro race." Despite misguided "remonstrances against injustice and oppression," African Americans had "reached the highest plane of civilization of which the negro's history has record." Fourth, the United States could not allow the untapped resources of Haiti "to be subjected to ceaseless fire and rapine by an unindustrious and revolutionary few." Annexation, Pickens concluded, "would not only destroy that discrimination which renders foreign enterprise impracticable, and invite the more self-dependent and industrious American negroes to a new field, but would discover clamorous and unsuspected opportunities for the Christian missionary."[76] It would, in short, profit Americans and civilize Haitians.

Black intellectuals had already blurred the line between racial uplift and the civilizing mission. Now erasing it, Pickens earned an unusual amount of respect for a black orator. The first sign of acclaim came from the five judges, who made Pickens the first black winner of the prestigious Ten Eyck prize. More adulation soon followed. For weeks after his victory, Pickens received dozens of letters of commendation each day. One of his admirers was Grover Cleveland, the Tuskegee benefactor and former U.S. president credited with reviving the Monroe Doctrine and making U.S. hegemony in the Western Hemisphere the central tenet of U.S. foreign policy. Another was Corinne Roosevelt Robinson, the younger sister of Theodore Roosevelt, the current U.S. president, who would provide the Roosevelt Corollary to the Monroe Doctrine and make interventionism the new guiding principle of U.S. foreign policy. Along with those luminaries, one socialite from Rhode Island gave Pickens a diamond pin, an unknown fan from New York mailed him three fifty-dollar gold certificates, and a group of Yale student clubs gave Pickens fifty dollars. Additional invitations for speaking engagements came from white religious organizations, trade associations, and colleges. A famous lecture bureau even offered Pickens a lucrative contract.[77]

Pickens owed much of his newfound celebrity and earnings to the conservative aspects of his politics. Besides confirming popular representations of Haiti, Pickens showed an appreciation for the material and moral motivations for the pursuit of U.S. empire. He represented the United States as his elite supporters knew it, as an industrial, progressive and exceptional imperial power.

Once in the spotlight, Pickens clarified his ideas about imperialism and black progress by claiming objectivity about Haitian history. In his first public interviews following his victory, Pickens said that he "knew no more about Hayti than the average citizen when I started to study my subject." Perhaps that was true. It is more likely, though, that he claimed ignorance in order to exaggerate his impartiality. To that end, he stated that while his "first notion was a plea for the Haytian nation," empirical research changed his thesis. Pickens declared that "as I read and studied I became convinced that the country needed the influence of some great restraining power, so that civilization might be permitted to extend itself and develop in the island." In his estimation, that fact was borne out by the progressive history of African Americans. "The American Negro," Pickens argued, "has been lauded for his rapid strides toward civilization. But where was there ever a race so surrounded by the advantages of a civilizing influence?" Pickens, suggesting that the most educated African Americans had become indistinguishable from their white counterparts, then proposed that their refinement was not only the grounds for their leadership of the race but also a testament to the potential fruits of imperialism. Connecting those two lines of thought, he pronounced that it was "just this opinion"—his enlightened prescription of U.S. annexation—"that Hayti needs."[78]

Haitians believed otherwise. In April 1903, a copy of Pickens's speech reached Emmanuel Guilbaud, a Haitian man living in Brooklyn.[79] It shocked him. In a letter published in an April 1903 edition of the *New York Sun*, Guilbaud explained that being "a Haytian and having a true love for my country, it is impossible for me to keep silent after reading such uncalled for and unreasonable remarks." His issues with Pickens were numerous. Guilbaud pointed out that Pickens, who had never traveled outside of the United States, was "so ignorant" of Haiti and had simply ascribed to it "the vilest corruption and the most degrading condition" that he could imagine. In that sense, he was no better than St. John. Maybe he was worse. Guilbaud could not fathom how an African American could slander Haiti since the "negroes of this country . . . have so much of their own trouble to mind." How, he wondered, could Pickens so misunderstand the racist mind? Surely, it should have been obvious that "in putting down our people he has equally spoken against the people of his own race in this country." Since it clearly was not, Guilbaud concluded his letter with a historical rejoinder to Pickens's claims about Afro-diasporic hierarchies and the civilizing mission. The "would-be orator," Guilbaud wrote, "in wishing the annexation of Hayti, seems to have forgotten our kind offer some years back, when we, for the good of his people here, invited them to emigrate to our country, where they would find a home." Maybe, he chafed, "it was a good thing that they did not accept our offer."[80]

The idea that an emigration movement never materialized came from hurt not honesty. Guilbaud, who seems well aware of his history, probably knew that thousands of black people *had* left the United States to forge new lives in Haiti. More important, though, he despised a key development in black thought at that moment. Whereas a sense of racial kinship once motivated Haitian leaders to reach out to embattled African Americans, Guilbaud now realized that some educated African Americans looked down on Haitians. In a sense, his erasure of African American immigrants from Haitian history was a response to that offense. If Pickens felt superior to Haitians, then Guilbaud had no need for Pickens, a "would-be orator" whose "efforts would be better directed in an endeavor to aid his own race in this country."[81]

For Guilbaud, it was apparent that Pickens had imbibed racist ideas about Haiti. Yet, in pointing that out, the Haitian writer unwittingly reinforced the nationalism, misinformation, and chauvinism that divided people of African descent. In his letter to the *Sun*, Guilbaud referred to Pickens and his black compatriots with a series of impersonal pronouns: "They." "His own people." "Their own trouble." "His own race in this country." "Them in their migration." That language stood in stark contrast to the way in which Guilbaud referenced Haiti and its citizens in phrases that included "my country" and "our people." It also showed that Guilbaud, like countless other immigrants in the United States, absorbed prevailing stereotypes about African Americans. In rebuking Pickens for not realizing the common struggle against racism that bound African Americans and Haitians, Guilbaud charged that Haitians who visited the United States and saw the "conduct" of African Americans thought "they would be an utter disgrace among us."[82]

Published in a white newspaper, that insult was a detriment to Guilbaud's cause. And he knew it. As the Haitian Brooklynite had already pointed out, white Americans were neither conditioned nor willing to draw distinctions among black people regardless of their national origins. Racism respected no boundaries. So long as caricatures of black criminality persisted in the age of the "Negro problem," stereotypes of Haiti as the seat of "vilest corruption and the most degrading condition" would abound.[83] The two were inseparable, even dependent.

Guilbaud raised his objections to Pickens at the same time that black activists including W. E. B. Du Bois became more critical of Pickens's idol, Booker T. Washington. In the spring of 1903, Du Bois, then a professor of history and economics at Atlanta University, published the *Souls of Black Folk*. In the chapter titled "Of Mr. Booker T. Washington and Others," Du Bois accuses Washington of having asked African Americans to relinquish their claims to political empowerment, civil rights, and higher education. He also condemns Washington's preoccupation with economic advancement and industrial education. To Du Bois, having retained his belief in the burden of black elites to represent the black masses but having grown skeptical of the degree to which self-help and racial solidarity alone could aid African Americans, Washington had advanced positions that led to black disfranchisement, racial segregation, and the withdrawal of financial support for nonindustrial black education. The Wizard of Tuskegee, Du Bois believed, had accepted Jim Crow and voiced "the old attitude of adjustment and submission."[84]

Du Bois was not alone in his criticisms of Washington. In July 1903, William Monroe Trotter, the recipient of two degrees from Harvard University and the founding editor of the *Guardian*, confronted Washington during his speech at a meeting of the National Negro Business League held in Boston. Trotter, one of the earliest critics of Washington's politics and his grip on the black press, was arrested for disorderly conduct in the chaos that followed. What became known as the Boston Riot captured the broader conflict between black activists, primarily but not exclusively educated black businessmen, teachers, and ministers living in the Northeast, and what they condemned as the Tuskegee Machine. It presaged the formation of the Niagara Movement, a civil rights organization that Du Bois and Trotter founded to secure black civil rights and the ultimate "abolition of all caste distinctions based simply on race and color."[85]

For black activists including John Edward Bruce, Pickens did the growing black civil rights struggle wrong by repeating stereotypes about Haiti that reinforced Jim Crow. Born into slavery, Bruce had become a leading black journalist and an officer of the Afro-American League, the first national black civil rights organization in the United States.[86] He, a few years before joining forces with Du Bois, Trotter, and the Niagara Movement, took Pickens to task. Writing under the pen name of Bruce Grit, he reminded readers of the Washington, D.C.–based *Colored American* that "whenever the critics of the negro in America want to make an alleged point to show that the Negro is not fitted for self government they point to Hayti and cite that English slanderer of the Haytians, Sir Spencer St. John." Those claims were hypocritical, Bruce continued. At a time when white supremacists used the rope, torch, and shotgun to reinforce the racial hierarchies of the antebellum era, Bruce pointed out that the criticisms of "the morals and customs of the Haytians" from the supposedly " 'superior races' of the Western Hemisphere" amounted to nothing more than "a case of the pot calling the kettle black."[87]

Pickens should have known that, Bruce argued. Admitting that he had read all of Guilbaud's letter but only fragments of Pickens's speech, Bruce charged the Yale orator with taking the "popular" side in critiquing Haiti. In this case, it was the wrong side. Haiti, Bruce declared, was no different than any other country during its infant stage. It was the same as Germany, "which has been four hundred years attaining to its present high state of civilization as 'we superior races['] use and understand these terms," or England, where the "early Britons . . . lived on the raw flesh of wild animals and in caves and were not as far advanced in civilization when their country was as old as Hayti now is as Haytians now are." Certainly, Bruce continued, Haiti was not worse than the United States, where newspapers in major metropolitan areas still carried "columns of advertisements of voodoo doctors spirit mediums, conjurors, clairvoyants, test mediums, etc." Accordingly, Bruce concluded that it would not "do for Americans, black or white, to make faces at Hayti, for the Haytians" had every reason to recite an old Irish toast:

> Here's to you as good as you are,
> And here's to me as bad as I am,
> But as good as you are, and as bad as I am,
> I'm as good as you are as bad as I am.[88]

Bruce's editorial was not just a rebuke of Pickens or his accomodationist politics. It was also a repudiation of the ideas that so clearly influenced the Yale student and motivated his call for annexation. Bruce placed "the superior races" in scare quotes throughout his column to cast doubt on whether such a category even existed. Moreover, he qualified the term "civilization," noting that he only used it as those who defined themselves as part of the "superior races" understood that term. In doing both, Bruce articulated cultural relativism, the emerging idea that civilization was neither absolute nor synonymous with whiteness. While the Jewish anthropologist Franz Boas would become most famous for distinguishing race from culture and arguing that cultures had to be understood on their own terms, black intellectuals including Bruce offered equally forceful challenges to the longstanding evolutionary view of human races and development. Indeed, they saw the most profound implications of their revisionist interpretations of global history. If, as Bruce argued, the concept of a superior race or races was a historical fiction, then there could be no contemporary justification for imperialism. In the absence of an unassailable and universal standard of civilization, the civilizing mission was an impossibility.[89]

It took time for cultural relativism to gain mass appeal, but Bruce had several allies, including William Monroe Trotter, who were even more passionate in their criticism of Pickens. In April 1903, the outspoken civil rights activist and managing editor of the Boston-based *Guardian* launched a crusade against the Yale student. The first *Guardian* article about Pickens charged that he "seems to have been unable to write except in a destructive way about his own race and . . . seems to have been well rewarded for his pains." He seemed to embody a broader problem. The article argued that the Yale student showed that "the Negro, either as an individual, race, or nation" had not "gained sufficient respect for his own race to affect a philosophic and critical analysis of them without cause." He demonstrated, the *Guardian* continued, that accomodationist black leaders were willing to sell their soul for a mere mess of pottage.[90]

Trotter published additional critiques a month later. As Pickens continued to gain fame, the *Guardian* credited him with having "the unique honor of being the first Negro ever to have won literary oratorical honors at Yale by surrendering his self-respect, sacrificing his pride, emasculating his manhood, and throwing down his race." The "uncouth and provincial" orator, it continued, was "the first Negro at Yale who blindly accepted the white man's estimate of the Negro and proclaimed from the house-top that the Negro is an inferior being and not fit to govern himself." His triumph was no victory for the race. Instead, Trotter's paper insisted that Pickens had shown himself to be "unique, not because he distinguished himself at Yale, but because he is the first Negro at Yale who evinced a slavish, servile and sycophantic spirit." He had, in short, played to his crowd. Clarifying that point, the *Guardian* noted that the "present policy of the Anglo-Saxon [was] to single out and honor as a genius a Negro who wallows in the mud and mire of American prejudice and sacrifices his race to gain the good opinion of white men." Pickens, in his pursuit of that misbegotten honor, had demonstrated that he, too, was "afflicted with this malady," the "curse of the Negro that he has not faith in his own race."[91]

At times, Trotter had difficulty restraining himself when expressing his righteous discontent. That was true in the case of his dispute with Pickens. In a third article published two weeks after his denunciation of the "present policy of the Anglo-Saxon," the *Guardian* complained that the Citizens Trade Association of Cambridge, Massachusetts, had invited "the little black freak student at Yale to come out to talk on the 'Misrule in Hayti.'" It wondered why the association did not ask Pickens to speak about misrule in a place that he knew about—Jim Crow Arkansas would have sufficed—instead of speculating about Haiti, a country about which he knew "absolutely nothing beyond a few hours' reading to write a sophomoric essay." The answer seemed obvious: the white businessmen in Cambridge and the black student from Yale both relished the chance to disparage black people. Descending into racial caricature to prove that point, Trotter's paper suggested that a "mere glance at this Negro freak with his enormous lips, huge mouth, and a monkey grin" explained Pickens's desire "to abuse his own race, in these days of . . . Negro baiting." In fact, it surprised the *Guardian* that Pickens did "not go further in his race attacks." Replicating the same behavior of which it accused Pickens, the leading black newspaper in Boston concluded that a steady "literary diet of Uncle Remus" had encouraged Pickens to "play the monkey." Pickens, the *Guardian* suggested, was no New Negro but simply a relic of a bygone era "whose early training and surroundings, were naturally slavish."[92]

Historians would come to see the ugly dispute between Pickens and the *Guardian* as a by-product of Trotter's battle with Washington. That assessment has its merits. After all, Trotter associated Pickens with Washington, whom he called Benedict Arnold, and Pickens, with the support of Washington, had plans to sue the *Guardian* for libel until Trotter apologized.[93]

Still, the *Guardian's* rebuke of the Ten Eyck champion owed just as much to Trotter's internationalist politics as his disagreement with other black leaders. Like Guilbaud, the *Guardian* accused Pickens of imbibing racist ideas even as it recycled other anti-black stereotypes. But, unlike the Haitian Brooklynite, Trotter and his newspaper offered a definition of blackness that transcended national boundaries and bound Haitians to African Americans. In the words of the *Guardian*, Pickens was at fault for "throwing down his race" by representing Haiti, a nation in which African Americans should take interest and pride, as a failed experiment in the masculine art of self-government.[94]

Taken together, those criticisms of Pickens provided an anti-imperialist complement to John Edward Bruce's challenges to the logic of the civilizing mission. Whereas numerous black intellectuals, including Booker T. Washington, called on black ministers, entrepreneurs, and soldiers to prove their manliness and patriotism through the colonization of Africa or service to U.S. imperialism, the *Guardian* accused Pickens of unmanning the race by recommending the annexation of Haiti. Put simply, it suggested that anti-imperialism was a manlier pursuit than imperialism. Just as Trotter demanded that his peers fight for their rights and stop accommodating racial segregation, his newspaper insisted that African Americans recognize their commonalities with Haitians. In his estimation, it was necessary to renounce chauvinistic ideas that weakened black self-determination at home and across the African Diaspora.

Yet, African Americans were being pulled in the opposite direction. As some black activists defended Haiti through articulations of cultural relativism and anti-imperialism, newspapers across the United States reported on a curious development. One admirer of Pickens was not only heaping praise on the Yale student but also encouraging African Americans to carry out the annexation that Pickens proposed.

The reports focused on the plans of a man named either N. L. or H. L. Musgrove. While uncertain about his first initial, the U.S. press was more consistent in reporting that Musgrove was a black man who migrated from Alabama to Sturgis, Kentucky. Those claims about his racial identity and geographic origins were probably false, though. Census records show that a white man named Herbert L. Musgrove (or Mosgrove) was born in Kentucky during the middle of Reconstruction, lived in Sturgis by 1900, and, a decade later, remained employed by a "country paper" in the small town located in the far northwestern corner of the Bluegrass State.[95]

Quotations attributed to Musgrove further suggest that he was white. One oft-repeated passage reported that Musgrove, claiming to have formed a Sturgis-based lodge called the Sons of Freedom, was certain that "As far as the United States is concerned, the colored man might as well get his grip and go, for the days of his political power are over. The mawkish sentiment of the north and the demagogic politicians south, which were wont to raise him to a standard for which neither fate, nature, circumstances nor education ever fitted him, are about to let him drop as a failure and a nuisance to civilization. The colored man is now looking for a safe place to fall when the inevitable storm breaks."[96] Of course, numerous black intellectuals expressed misgivings about their future in the United States. Some considered the merits of leaving it. Still, the words credited to Musgrove voiced biological racism, not black separatism. They suggested that black citizenship was a mistake of Reconstruction-era reformers and politicians who gave African Americans rights to which nature had not equipped them. They gave African Americans two options: leave a country where they were a problem or face extinction in competition with the more civilized Anglo-Saxon.

Voicing concern with the "Negro problem" rather than care for the well-being of black people, Musgrove implicated Pickens in his scheme to find African Americans their "safe place to fall." In interviews given in the spring of 1903, Pickens revealed that Musgrove sent him a letter claiming that the Sons of Freedom had at least a hundred branches in the South and planned on spreading their operations into the North. It also proposed that Pickens take a leading role in the organization. In speeches given throughout the North, Pickens would build the membership of the Sons of Freedom and help the "junta" purchase a warship and munitions needed for an imminent invasion of Port-au-Prince. Pickens would then displace the current Haitian president and form a republican government. Under Pickens, the new Haitian state would expel its criminals, promote public education, agriculture, and manufacturing, administer land titles and businesses, and operate as a giant corporation in which all Haitian citizens held stock.[97] Of course, the new Haitian state would not be autonomous. Pickens noted that the Sons of Freedom planned on placing Haiti under the "protection" of the U.S. government and making Port-au-Prince a commercial mecca for U.S. investors.[98] They would realize Pickens's dream. The Yale student turned would-be president of Haiti disclosed that U.S. imperialism was at the heart of a scheme that otherwise rested on an incoherent amalgamation of utopian, socialist, and capitalist principles. In fact, Pickens proclaimed, Musgrove had ultimately assured him that he was the black leader to whom "the people should look to carry out the noble dream of empire."[99]

The revelations from Pickens about his courting by Musgrove confirm the connections between U.S. empire and Jim Crow. For Musgrove, black people were a problem—a "nuisance to civilization"—whether in Haiti or the United States. They had to be returned to an inferior state either by expulsion, annexation, or a form of racial domination that combined the two.

Given the transparent motivations of the outlandish scheme, Pickens gave it a surprising amount of thought. The most common press reports that swept the United States noted that Pickens assured reporters that he "has the matter under consideration and will seek advice before enlisting his services in the movement."[100] Others suggested that he saw some appeal in the scheme. Pickens, believing that Musgrove and the Sons of Freedom were African American, told reporters that it was "not surprising to me that my countrymen of my own race are planning to intervene themselves [in Haiti] and attempt to bring order out of chaos." Of course, he continued, it would "take some time to perfect the plans of this junta which the colored people, led by most of the strongest headed and most intellectual colored men of the country, are forming down South, but they are taking up the matter coolly and logically."[101] That ambivalence endured. Later, in his autobiography, Pickens would remember that an "organization in Kentucky, which seemed . . . to have had some designs on Hayti for some time" offered him the presidency of Haiti. His stated reasons for finally disavowing the scheme did not stress an improved faith in Haitian independence. Instead, Pickens explained that he distanced himself from the "filibustering expedition" because it was unclear whether it was the most appropriate means of intervention. "Shades of Dessalines and Toussaint L'Overture," he recalled. "I had no desire to add to the volcanic little government's already too numerous chief executives."[102]

Pickens's peers, even those who shared his politics, were much less generous about the proposed invasion of Haiti. As newspapers rushed to implicate Booker T. Washington in the scheme, the Tuskegee principal dismissed it. When one reporter showed him a dispatch regarding Pickens and the plans for "an Afro-American republic in Hayti," Washington said that he was "quite surprised that the press handled it at all. It usually uses pretty good judgment."[103]

Some black journalists argued that the inane plot detracted attention from the atrocities occurring in the Jim Crow South. The Wichita, Kansas–based *Colored Citizen* advised Pickens and Musgrove that it would be "more fitting and far more profitable" to "equip an army South and help to free our people from the murderous hands of the Southern American and restore quiet THERE and stay away from Hayti." A belief in the justice of black self-defense motivated that response. The paper proclaimed that it had "often been apprised of the fact that a negro will fight a negro but it is hard for him to get up courage enough to fight a white man." Nothing supported that allegation more than the "childish dream" of the Sons of Freedom. "The idea," it marveled; an invasion force of black men who did not even have "guns to . . . protect their own families from a local mob." Clearly, the would-be conquerors had misplaced priorities. In conclusion, the *Colored Citizen* advised that "all who wish to go to Hayti had better learn to swim, for those Haytians will drive any man, be he black or white, into the Caribbean Sea that ever attempts to trample upon their God-given rights." "Buy a gun," it implored. "Take care of the negroes of America and let the sons of Toussaint L'Ouverture alone!"[104]

That demand, which echoed past equations of Haitians with black manhood, was urgent. Although countless details about Musgrove and the Sons of Freedom remained uncertain, one thing was clear: Pickens attracted so much attention and became the center of a national controversy because his call for the U.S. annexation of Haiti resonated with countless Americans, some of whom had the power to turn imperialist dreams into realities.

At the same time that Pickens entertained half-baked proposals to become the head of Haiti, Weldon B. Heyburn, a U.S. senator from Idaho, introduced to Congress a resolution for the annexation of Haiti and the Dominican Republic.[105] His reasoning was wholly unoriginal. The resolution declared that the United States should annex the island of Hispaniola because of its proximity to the United States and its potential use for U.S. ships headed to the Panama Canal. Drawing on long-standing stereotypes about black self-government, it also endorsed U.S. territorial expansion because "the governments heretofore existing in the island [of Hispaniola] are unstable in character and at times a menace to the best interests of civilization."[106] In the parlance of the day, submission to U.S. authority was their only hope for civilized progress.

For the time being, Heyburn failed. Once again, southern segregationists expressed particular disdain for another proposal for the annexation of

Haiti. The *Atlanta Constitution*, which had become a leading voice of the Jim Crow South under the editorship of Clark Howell, predicted that when "we shall have thoroughly Americanized Porto Rico, subdued and made good our 'benevolent assimilation' of the Filipinos, converted the Hawaiians into 'good Americans' in costume and customs, we may then listen with more open minds to a proposition to take in the 'turn about, whirl-about, jump Jim Crow' revolutionaries of the island of San Domingo."[107] The sardonic tone, scare quotes, and references to Dominican and Haitian temperaments made the stance of the Atlanta-based paper obvious. In its estimation, it would be suicidal to introduce another unassimilable population into the United States. The *Constitution* had no more confidence in Haitians than it did in Jim Crow, the outlandish black character who stalked the minstrel stage and embodied the worst stereotypes attributed to black people.

Still, a question lingered: how long would beliefs about black inferiority deter rather than encourage the usurpation of Haitian sovereignty? Not long, if the opinions offered in the *Constitution* were any indication. The same editorial that opposed the annexation of the "African" state of Haiti encouraged the United States to assume a protectorate over it. "In this fashion," the paper reasoned, "while benefiting ourselves, we may also guide them into higher and better forms of government, good order and prosperity."[108] The proposed protectorate would help the United States accrue all the benefits of imperialism—the extraction of natural resources, the strengthening of its naval power, the increase of commercial and trade opportunities—while avoiding the pitfalls of annexation. It could, in the reasoning of white supremacists, solve Haitian ills without exacerbating its own "Negro problem."

The Pickens controversy and attendant debates about U.S. territorial expansion came at a pivotal moment in Haitian history. Throughout 1903, the Haitian government made plans for a nationwide celebration. The preparations were for the centennial anniversary of Haitian independence.

Not all Haitians were in a festive mood, however. In a speech delivered in anticipation of the centennial, Rosalvo Bobo, a Haitian politician and staunch nationalist, chided his compatriots for what he regarded as their failures. "Centennial of our freedom? No." he began. Demanding reflection rather than revelry, Bobo proceeded to grieve for the

> Centennial of blacks enslaving blacks. Centennial of our follies, of our depravities . . . of our systemic retrocession.
> Centennial of our fraternal hatreds and of our moral, social and political impotence. Centennial amidst assassinations in our cities and towns.
> Centennial of our vices, our political crimes.
> Centennial of everything that can be the more odious with the breast of men.
> Centennial of the ruin of a country by misery and filth.
> Centennial of humiliation and perhaps the final degradation of the black race, by its Haitian representatives.

For Bobo, those sins had gone unspoken; so had a need for penance. Accordingly, Bobo resolved that "on January 1, 1904, if anything must be done, instead of placing laurels on the elusive spirit of our forbearers, after having forgotten about them for a century, after soiling their memory, making outrageous mockery of their heroism . . . we will ask forgiveness from Dessalines, from Toussaint . . . and from all the immortal combatants of our history."[109]

Bobo, speaking in French, addressed his "dear fellow compatriots," not an international audience. In that sense, his speech was a close relative of the American jeremiad, a rhetorical practice rooted in biblical tradition and used to express indignation and dissatisfaction with the nation while urging it to reform.[110] Whereas black orators in the United States often issued jeremiads to call attention to how their country had perpetuated racism and failed to live up to its founding principles of human equality, Bobo encouraged Haitians, especially elites, to fulfill the lofty potential of the first black republic in global history. His speech was not a resignation of Haitian independence. Instead, it was an urgent call for Haiti to become a model of black self-determination, a black "city upon a hill" for all of the world to see. For Bobo, 1904 could be "the first year of existence of a gathering of brave black people working modestly and with dignity to be a people." It could become the beginning of a new "centennial of the great freedom of the Haitian people."[111]

The true meaning of Bobo's speech was lost in translation. Indeed, it, like countless other expressions of nationalism from Haitian intellectuals, was not translated at all. Left to assign their own meanings to the Haitian centennial, black intellectuals in the United States offered similar criticisms of Haiti as those that Bobo expressed. But their writings lacked his spirit. They were calls for an external civilizing mission in the absence of a capacity for Haitian self-improvement.

The most scathing—and revealing—critiques of Haiti came in the *Voice of the Negro*, a new black literary journal that became the voice of the Niagara Movement under the managing editorship of J. Max Barber. In March 1904, the journal publicized its plans to devote its next issue to Hispaniola. "The time has come," the *Voice* explained, "for a halt to be called to the reign of anarchy which now exists in the island." Doing away with any pretense to humanitarianism or altruism, the *Voice* admitted that African Americans, who were "struggling in this country . . . to be allowed to participate in the affairs of the Government," desired "order down there for our own sakes." Accusations of black misrule in Haiti hurt their cause. In fact, the *Voice* continued, "confusion . . . in Haiti and San Domingo where Negroes have full control of the government" threatened to "further prejudice the world against our cause." It concluded that if African Americans wanted "to count on the moral support of civilization in our efforts to secure even-handed justice, we must not have the bad example of this little Negro Republic flaunted before the face of the world." There was just one question: "What must be done?"[112]

In asking that question, the *Voice* reiterated the long-standing idea that rehabilitating the image of Haitians would erode white racism in the United States. Given that international application of racial uplift ideology, it was fitting that its subsequent issue on Haiti featured answers from T. Thomas Fortune, John Stephens Durham, and William Pickens, three "very able men who [had] been studying the situation and searching for the right thing to recommend to civilization."[113] In many respects, the articles that those men published in the *Voice* simply rehashed well-established ideas about Haiti's supposed failures. Fortune, for instance, wrote that the death of Louverture in the Fort de Joux "removed from Hayti the only man who had the ability to shape the destinies of the people in the ways of self-reliance and government." While he offered no solutions as to how Haitians would move forward from "the fearful conditions which have dragged the country down to degradation in the past one hundred years," Pickens repeated his call for annexation.[114] In fact, his contribution to the *Voice* was a copy of the Ten Eyck oration in which he argued that "the intervention of some outside power" in Haiti "is imperative."[115]

A more original offering came from Durham. Two years after publishing *Diane* in *Lippincott's*, a Philadelphia-based publication with a predominantly white readership, Durham gave African Americans a more polemical answer to the so-called Haitian question. He began his article, entitled "The Hidden Wealth of Hayti," with his recollection of a lecture about that country delivered by a famous orator some years ago. Durham remembered it as a "thrilling oration" typical of its time, a "gorgeous panorama of military achievement" that presented Haitian leaders from Toussaint Louverture to Lysius Salmon in glowing terms. Still, it was devoid of real substance. Durham suggested that the panegyric was no better than a recent magazine article that characterized Haiti as a land of "petty thieving, continued insurrection, promiscuous poisoning and counterfeit finance." In his opinion, neither the prejudiced writer nor the sympathetic orator had offered a fair assessment of Haiti because each focused on Haitian elites rather than "the people of Hayti, the people who live next to the soil, the class to whom we must go in order to judge fairly the promise of any nation." Addressing their error, Durham insisted that Haitian peasants were "the real wealth of Hayti, the untouched resources of the little republic, out of which . . . the statesmanship of the new century will develop the future of the nation."[116] They were, in short, true diamonds in the rough.

Durham believed that it was a blessing that Haitian peasants had remained unpolished. After ruminating on the "untouched resources of Hayti," Durham noted that its leaders had long "insisted that Hayti shall be the black republic." While ambivalent about the merits of what he considered a departure from the universalist republicanism of Louverture, he did express some pleasure in the pride that Haitians took in being "the measure of the Negro in the possibilities of self government." Since the end of the Haitian Revolution, Durham suggested, the Haitian masses had clung tenaciously to the right of black self-determination and managed to avoid "those contacts with the Teutonic civilization which unman the Negro while they refine him." That distance from Western racism had made men out of Haitians. Durham boasted that a Haitian man would never "be bullied because of his color . . . insulted . . . [or] set apart in public places" because he possessed "that elementary self respect and that barbaric self confidence which mark the primitive man whether he be Sepoy, Mahdist, Boxer or Ashantee." In fact, Durham found the Haitian singular in his primitive manliness.[117] Durham feared that a rising tide of imperialism might make Haiti "the only place on the face of the earth where the Negro will have the chance to develop." He did not, however, worry that the Haitian man would suffer a similar emasculation. Instead, he predicted that the "Haytian man of to-day would not have to be told what to do with the . . . jim crow car of the colored American of to-day—any more than a good, strong self respecting bull has to be told his first business with a red rag."[118]

Of course, such savage manliness had to be tamed. It had to be civilized. Uplifted. Revisiting his ideas about black womanhood introduced in *Diane*, Durham now assured readers of the *Voice* that the Haitian woman was "a devoted mother . . . a loyal wife . . . [and] the conservative force of the republic; for it is she who inspires the traditions of the republic." In short, she was the embodiment of [black] republican motherhood, the virtuous woman who would inspire and instill the gendered values of republicanism in a younger generation of Haitians.[119] To that point, Durham insisted that Haitian women handed down the domestic arts to their sons and daughters. Indeed, they "kept strong and full of life the roots of a fine national growth." Accordingly, Durham concluded, a foreigner had to experience the "kindly welcome of the [Haitian] family" and immerse themselves in the female domain of the Haitian home in order "to know the wealth of Hayti."[120]

Without question, there were subversive elements to those claims. Durham wrote in an era when the most common stereotypes of black women in mainstream U.S. popular culture and academic discourse were the lewd and lascivious Jezebel, who solicited sex from white and black men; the domineering and masculine Sapphire, who emasculated black men; and the overweight and nurturing Mammy, who cared for her white employers as if they were her own family. One assumption shaped all three: black women lacked and did not warrant respect. In turn, advocates of racial uplift including Durham and, most notably, black clubwomen pioneered what would become known as the politics of respectability. Their shared idea that black women, whether in Haiti or the United States, were virtuous housewives, pious Christians, and nurturing mothers regardless of their social status contradicted the most demeaning representations of black womanhood. It assigned worth to black women bombarded with accusations of worthlessness, associating them with respectable Victorian womanhood rather than disreputable behavior.[121]

Still, there were conservative aspects to those racial politics and attendant notions of black progress. That became quite clear when black intellectuals in the United States engaged black people abroad. In the conclusion to "The Hidden Wealth of Hayti," Durham declared that the "real hope" of

Haiti rested "in the hearts and minds and bodies of her people who live close to the soil and whose good traits simply baffle analysis in view of the way in which that class has been exploited by the fortunate few." His condemnation of Haitian elites was crucial. Even as Durham characterized Haitian women as civilizing agents, he identified a vacuum of racial leadership in Haiti and assigned African Americans a leading role in uplifting its citizens. The longtime admirer of Booker T. Washington predicted that a "national system of agriculture" in Haiti "would be helped by the introduction of the best agricultural implements and the employment of capable, sympathetic, directors, such as Tuskegee could readily furnish." Tuskegee officials would rehabilitate Haiti's international image as they revitalized its economy. For Durham, a writer who routinely used the word "development" while imploring Haitian peasants to use "modern methods and . . . modern machinery," it was especially critical that Haitians adhere to Western cultural standards. Just as a number of his peers demanded of African Americans behaviors that were "respectable" but had no bearing on the attainment of black civil rights, Durham prescribed to Haitians dubious models of "progress" that looked civilized but ignored Haitians' historical resistance to plantation-based and export-oriented agriculture.[122]

Increasingly, few black intellectuals saw or felt compelled to challenge the shortsightedness of development models that cohered with imperialism, the civilizing mission, and recent proposals for the U.S. annexation of Haiti. In fact, the most vocal dissent did not come from the civil rights activists whose formative years came in the age of Jim Crow. Instead, it was offered by Ebenezer Don Carlos Bassett, the former U.S. diplomat who, after returning to the United States, spent ten years representing Haiti as its consul general in New York City.[123]

In the May 1904 edition of the *Voice of the Negro*, Bassett, a man whom Ida B. Wells admired as one of the "old war horses" of the fight against slavery and ensuing struggle for black civil and political rights, published an article entitled "Should Haiti Be Annexed to the United States." The answer was no. More than three decades after becoming the first black diplomat in U.S. history, Bassett gave four reasons why the United States should not pursue the annexation of Haiti. First, Bassett argued that, excepting the recent annexation of Hawaii, the United States had never acquired noncontiguous territories. Second, he noted that the current U.S. assistant secretary of state had acknowledged that old policy and objected to proposed annexations of Cuba, Haiti, and the Dominican Republic. Third,

Basset suggested that the United States should not annex territories unless it planned on granting full citizenship to their residents. Finally, Bassett argued that these discussions about annexation should omit Haiti. Recalling his participation in the contentious Môle St. Nicolas negotiations, he asserted that "on the subject of the absolute autonomy of their country, the government and the people of Haiti are one solid, indivisible and extremely sensitive unit." Given "such firmly fixed patriotic sentiments as these," Bassett concluded, "ought any one to advise or say that Haiti should be annexed to the United States?"[124]

To be sure, Bassett felt that the sovereignty of Haiti was sacrosanct.[125] Offering African Americans a far more optimistic view of the Haitian centennial than many of his peers, Bassett boasted that Haiti, which had staved off "every possible scheme . . . for the alienation of any part of their territory and independence," would never "consent to share her sovereignty with any other power whatsoever." In fact, he continued, Haiti was "by far the most advanced, the most important and the best established of the only three Republics in the world, where alone the Negro race has full and untrammeled liberty to develop its faculties and its possibilities." Bassett knew that such claims defied popular caricatures of Haiti. His resolve was strong, though. Chastising U.S. newspapers that wrote "only evil of Haiti," Bassett implored his audience to ignore "wholly unfair" representations of Haiti and consider "the gigantic difficulties" that it had "overcome to maintain her independence." In light of that resilience, Bassett asked a rhetorical question: "should Haiti then be annexed to the United States?" His answer was unambiguous. "Why, no, no!" he proclaimed. "Let Haiti alone; let her alone to work out her mission for the children of Africa in the New World and to fulfill her destiny among the Nations of the Earth."[126]

Bassett's declaration provided a profound albeit fleeting glimpse into past developments in black thought and political activism. As Haiti marked one hundred years of independence, Bassett rearticulated long-standing ideas about its exceptionalism. His proclamation that Haiti had a singular mission to the world and a special obligation to black people echoed the sentiments of nineteenth-century black activists including his late friend Frederick Douglass. It also married a passionate defense of Haitian independence to the enduring convictions that people of African descent had a common heritage and a shared representative nation in Haiti.

In doing so, the article responded to present concerns while presaging future directions of black political thought. Bassett had served the United

States and Haiti. He had experienced power on each side of the global color line and decided with which side he was aligned. Generations after representing U.S. administrations determined to annex Haiti, Bassett expressed unequivocal support for Haitian sovereignty. He, since employed by Haiti, tried to protect it from a country that had long abandoned the racial egalitarianism promised during Reconstruction. As other black intellectuals, even an activist journal like the *Voice of the Negro*, suggested that foreign intervention would benefit Haitians, Bassett rejected the logic of the civilizing mission and defended Haitian self-determination. He foretold the construction of transnational black political solidarities on the basis of anti-imperialism and anti-capitalism rather than racial uplift.

John Hurst was one of the few voices echoing Bassett in that moment. In 1863, Hurst was born in Port-au-Prince to an African American father and a Haitian mother whose own parents were part of the antebellum emigration movement from the United States to Haiti. With the support of Charles and Mary Ella Mossell, he had joined the AME Church during the final year of Reconstruction and earned a bachelor of divinity degree from Wilberforce a decade later. Since then, Hurst had married a black woman from South Carolina, settled in Maryland, and held prominent positions in the AME Church and the Haitian government, including superintendent of AME missions in Haiti, attaché to the United States legation in Port-au-Prince, first secretary of the Haitian Legation in Washington, D.C., and financial secretary of the AME Church. Later, he would become the national director of the NAACP. In many respects, then, Hurst embodied the established institutional and cultural ties that bound African Americans and Haitians. Certainly, there was no one better equipped to evaluate how African Americans and Haitians thought about one another decades after his U.S.-born kin imagined Haiti as a potential haven and home.[127]

On the evening of September 21, 1909, an estimated crowd of more than one hundred black residents of the Washington-Baltimore metropolitan area gathered in the Metropolitan AME Church to hear Hurst deliver his evaluation of the relationships among the "children of Africa in the New World." The mood in the church, the same one where African Americans had once gathered to see Frederick Douglass off to Haiti, was festive. Hurst was making a much-anticipated return to his Baltimore home after spending two months visiting his ailing mother in Port-au-Prince. While his admirers in attendance that night enjoyed a fancy banquet prepared by one of the best caterers in the capital, a host of prominent black ministers, professors, and journalists from across the United States delivered toasts to Hurst in celebration of his many accomplishments. Some of the more excited speakers even predicted that the guest of honor would soon become a bishop of the AME Church, one of the most visible leadership positions available to black men. Those predictions came true when the AME Church elected Hurst as the bishop of its Eleventh Episcopal District.[128]

For the time being, though, Hurst did not revel in his past or potential achievements. Instead, he gave a sober assessment of tensions between African Americans and Haitians. Standing before the audience at the Metropolitan AME, he noted that educated Haitians were taking an unprecedented amount of interest in current events in the United States thanks to the increased availability of French editions of mainstream U.S. newspapers. Hurst lamented that development. Haitians, he pointed out, were now bombarded with images of brutal lynchings and exaggerated accounts of black crime. They were shocked by the declining status of African Americans since Reconstruction and baffled that "a policy of negation and acquiescence" seemed to have supplanted the "great pronouncement[s] upon moral and political issues" once heard from black leaders "in protest against attempts towards infringing upon the rights of his race." Where was the heir of Frederick Douglass, they asked? Was it true that the "American Negro was retrograding" and accepting his subjugation? Hurst promised that when his Haitian friends asked those questions, he reminded them that African Americans "were under the impression that [Haitians] were Voudou worshippers and Cannibals, and that the American press was responsible for it." He often stressed that "to the people of America, Negroes, whether speaking English or French, were all alike, lacking in the elements that make for a strong character."[129]

To Hurst, that fact was essential. It demanded that black people, whether Haitian or American, build political solidarities, not intraracial hierarchies. Hurst told the African Americans gathered before him that the "common interest of both the Haitian and the American Negro . . . is to get together and study each other more closely, and endeavor to share the view-point of each other in facing the great questions affecting the race as a whole." One means of building those lines of communication and understanding, he continued, was through the black press. Reiterating that white journalists too often dictated what the "American Negro" and the "foreign Negro" learned about each other, Hurst argued that black editors in the United States "should see to it that their papers reach the newspapers in Haiti, Cuba and South America and Central America and at both ends such matters of interest affecting the race should be translated." At the very least, he proclaimed, Jamaicans and Anglophone West Indians should have easy access to well-established black newspapers including the *New York Age*, the *Guardian*, the *Cleveland Gazette*, and the *Freeman*. To Hurst, such an exchange would guarantee that "an era of approachment" would soon "dawn upon my race in America."[130]

In fact, Hurst characterized the international black press as a catalyst for an "era of co-operation and of sound understanding" among all of "the various branches of the Negro race." Building to the conclusion of his talk, Hurst recalled a recent conversation with the headmaster of Saint-Louis de Gonzague, a prestigious secondary school in Port-au-Prince. The priest had worked in Senegal, a colonial territory of France, before coming to Haiti, and he informed Hurst that French West Africa had become "self-supporting." Moreover, he credited what Hurst called that "splendid result" to the influence of colored colonial administrators from Guadeloupe and Martinique.[131] Those claims were exaggerated. France did send an educated class of nonwhite administrators from its departments in the Caribbean to its colonies in Africa, but those men then reinforced rather than alleviated colonial regimes that lasted another half-century.[132] Still, it was rational and useful for Hurst to believe the romanticized depiction of black self-rule in Africa. Years before Senegalese intellectuals collaborated with Martiniquan writers to critique French colonialism, Hurst imagined colonized people from the black Francophone world in a shared struggle for black self-determination. To him, the "revelation" about Senegal proved that the black race was strong. It just did "not know its strength because it [did] not know itself."[133]

Hurst, the son of black migrants who then spent his life moving between the United States and Haiti, saw the rich possibilities of a black world not beholden to linguistic, geographic, or cultural boundaries. He envisioned the disillusionment of Afro-diasporic hierarchies through a transnational black print culture. He saw the winning of a common struggle through networks of communication predicated on shared interests and mutual respect.

Many of his peers did not see the possibilities of what scholars would later theorize as the "practice of diaspora."[134] Not yet. In the same moment that Hurst called for a greater international circulation of the *Freeman*,

George L. Knox's newspaper chided (and exaggerated the number of) black apologists of Haiti. It noted that too many "race men of the United States, noting the attitude of the white press relative to the little republic . . . have expressed some fear as to what our country may do in event Haiti continues restless." Those Pollyannas, the *Freeman* continued, "hope to see the island yet dominated by Negroes, maintained for Negroes." Their priorities were misplaced. According to the popular black newspaper, the concern should not be when or if the United States would consume Haiti. Instead, the problem was whether or not Haiti would "conform to the agreements of its own society—that of nations—or else pay the awful penalty." Applying the politics of racial uplift to international relations, the *Freeman* argued that Haiti could avoid being "gobbled up by any nation" simply by subscribing "to the tenets of to-day's civilization" and rehabilitating its image. Haiti, it concluded, "knows how it is regarded by other nations. It should not fail to take a hint."[135]

Indeed, the *Freeman* became sterner in its dismissals of those who still tried to explain how U.S. imperialism weighed upon the Haitian state. In August 1914, the newspaper rebuked an African American who lived in Haiti and believed that his adopted country was "suffering from a campaign of misrepresentation." Implying that the defender of Haiti was ignorant, it disregarded his well-reasoned argument that Haiti had never defaulted on the payment of its foreign debt even as foreign governments pressured it. The *Freeman* neither cared that the U.S. navy routinely dispatched warships into Haitian waters nor worried that the U.S. government continued to consider the annexation of Haiti. Again it insisted that Haitians alone would decide their fate. "Haytians," the newspaper argued, "should read between the lines." If Haiti truly did suffer from a "campaign of misrepresentation," then "it should see to it that it comes up to the level of men's expectations."[136]

There were several inconsistencies in that logic. Perhaps the most glaring was that the expectations placed upon Haiti were unique, unfair, and ever changing. Knox's *Freeman* argued that Haiti could evade the imperial grasp of the United States by shipping more of its goods overseas, "inviting attention to its fields and shops," sending the United States "its brilliantly learned men and women to talk of the fair prospects of their land," and inviting black immigrants from the United States. The fact that the Haitian government had done all of those things was lost upon Knox. Decade after decade, the Haitian government participated in international commerce, showcased its valuable agricultural products at international expositions and fairs, supported and sometimes financed the trips of Haitian spokespersons and students to the United States, and encouraged African Americans to leave their homeland for Haiti. None of those efforts staved off imperialist threats. In fact, some had the unintended effect of reinforcing foreign interest in Haiti. Whereas Knox predicted that Haitians could "destroy the thought of annexation" with "more activity" along so-called civilized lines, U.S. politicians became increasingly interested in dictating the fate of a country that had displayed its rich resources to the world. To them, Haitian progress was a canard. Nothing could dissuade them from exerting their authority over a smaller nation that was black and therefore subject to their domination.[137]

In fact, U.S. attempts to subordinate Haitians soon escalated. While Knox mocked the idea that Haiti suffered from unfair representations, a detachment of U.S. Marines disembarked at Port-au-Prince. They entered the Banque Nationale d'Haïti, a financial institution already controlled by two U.S. banks operating under the influence of the U.S. State Department.[138] The Marines proceeded to remove half a million dollars' worth of gold belonging to the Haitian government from the vaults, load it back onto their ship, and sail back to New York City. The U.S. government claimed that the heist was necessary to cover Haitian debts to U.S. bankers. Haitians knew otherwise. To them, the criminal act was further proof that the United States, in the hands of white supremacists and corporate interests, considered them incapable of self-government or progressive civilization.[139]

The heightened aggressiveness of the United States made effective governance in Haiti a near impossibility. It helped secure the fate of Vilbrun Guillaume Sam. On the one hand, the former general who became president of Haiti in March 1915 needed to accommodate the United States because it controlled the coffers of his bankrupt state. On the other hand, though, members of the Haitian parliament, urban elites, and rebels in the countryside all made it clear that they would not tolerate any submission to their racist neighbors to the north. Sam's attempts to navigate this treacherous political terrain failed to appease his critics, including Rosalvo Bobo. A decade after the centennial, Bobo had become one of the strongest voices of Haitian nationalism and appeared to be on the verge of overthrowing a president who he thought was willing to surrender control of Haiti to the United States.

By July 1915, Bobo's increasing popularity and the looming shadow of the United States caused the collapse of the Sam administration. After a military officer operating with orders from Sam executed 167 political prisoners thought to be loyal to Bobo, Port-au-Prince erupted. A crowd seized Sam from his refuge in the French legation, dragged him into the streets, and killed him. Dissidents then paraded his corpse throughout the city, cheering the death of the man responsible for the deaths of their family members and, possibly, their national sovereignty.[140]

The United States looked upon the scene with glee. On July 28, 1915, under the authorization of President Woodrow Wilson, the USS *Washington* entered the harbor of Port-au-Prince. Hundreds of Marines landed just south of the city, quickly assessed their surroundings, and then moved toward the central part of the Haitian capital. It was not long before they subdued the city. In doing so, the Marines acted as agents of civilization; as the military arm of a country whose secretary of state, Robert Lansing, insisted that black people were "devoid of any capacity for political organization . . . [or] genius for government." Their efforts to stem what Lansing further called the "tendency" of black people "to revert to savagery"—to exhibit the traits that "makes the negro problem practically unsolvable"—and assume control of Haiti's future were quickly processed by Haitians who watched the initial throng of Marines multiply into a force of two thousand by late August. In the words of one eyewitness, "[we] understood then that a new phase of our history was beginning."[141]

Booker T. Washington had to respond to the unfolding events in the Caribbean. In an article published in the *New York Age* one month before his death, the most influential black man of his time contended that "Haitians themselves are largely at fault for their present unhappy conditions." He identified various links in a brittle chain of evidence to prove that point. Haitian leaders, Washington pointed out, were enamored with French culture. Consequently, they eschewed industrial training, instead devoting "themselves to politics, little knowing, it seems, that political independence disappears without economic independence, that economic independence is the foundation of political independence." He claimed that this folly left the country underdeveloped, reliant on the financial largesse of foreigners, and ultimately responsible for the actions of the U.S. Marines. Washington concluded that the U.S. government had to take control of Haiti or else some European nation, in violation of the Monroe

Doctrine, would have taken action to obtain the money owed to them by the Haitian government.[142]

Without question, Washington saw promise in the inevitable intervention by the United States in Haiti. The Tuskegee principal suggested that the United States would seize "the opportunity to do a big piece of fine work for Haiti" and act with "unselfish benevolence" in Haiti. In particular, he identified education as a fruitful area of potential development. Washington expressed his hope that the United States would give Haitians "a thorough up-to-date system of common school, agricultural and industrial education." Moreover, he identified the military invasion as a providential chance for African Americans "educated in the best methods of education . . . to go to Haiti and help their fellows." Perhaps, Washington anticipated, black educators might build upon his own initiatives, bring more Haitian students to the United States, and give them "something they have never had . . . education, real education."[143]

Still, despite this optimism, Washington had some misgivings. He advised the U.S. government to be careful "in the class of white men sent to Haiti" because the "average American white man" was ill-suited to work among black people. Indeed, he cautioned that "there are only a few white men in the United States who understand, or even undertake to understand, the American Negro, and there are still fewer white men in this country who can go into Haiti and get the sympathy, the co-operation and the confidence of the Haitians." Great care was needed in selecting the civilian and military officers who would help Haitians "establish a republican form of government on the basic principles of liberty, fraternity and equality."[144]

Ultimately, Washington implied that the success or failure of the U.S. invasion of Haiti would provide a referendum on race relations in the United States. Developing that point, he argued that the U.S. government had the chance to prove "that in spite of the many wrongs inflicted upon their fellows in the United States that in all the real things of civilization [African Americans] are further ahead of any similar number of black people anywhere in the world." Washington's meaning was difficult to miss. After witnessing the continued assaults on black citizenship during his lifetime, the preeminent black leader called on the United States to recognize the advancement of its own black population while proving its commitment to racial egalitarianism through the uplift of Haitians. Accordingly, Washington ended his article with a guarantee or, perhaps, a warning: "The ten million black people in the United States are watching this government prayerfully, watching to see if it will exercise the same patience with Haiti that it has exercised with larger and more important countries that have been as disorderly as Haiti." African Americans, he assured his readers, would be monitoring events in Haiti, hoping to see portents of a brighter future for African Americans as well as signs of Haitian progress.[145]

Washington would not live to see the results of the U.S. invasion of Haiti. But, in one of the final public writings of his illustrious career, he laid out the foundations on which black intellectuals in the United States would build new understandings of themselves and their world. The persistence of long-standing and entangled ideas about racial uplift and civilization would encourage a number of black public figures to first applaud the usurpation of Haitian independence. Their enchantment with the emerging principles of U.S. foreign policy, including interventionism, would have a similar effect. Still, even as a number of outspoken black intellectuals reified the supposed hierarchies of the African Diaspora, most were convinced that developments in Haiti were intimately linked to those in the United States. They assumed a connection to Haitians even while prioritizing their struggle for political and civil rights.

That Afro-diasporic consciousness would come to matter a great deal as an invasion promoted as a civilizing mission turned into a decades-long military occupation that devastated Haiti. It would, in fact, help reshape the contours of black thought as it became clear that the intertwined forces of racism, imperialism, capitalism, and militarism rather than benevolence motivated the U.S. occupation of Haiti. For many of the "ten million black people" who watched the injustices that followed the invasion of Haiti, protest became far more attractive than prayer. To them, the fight for black self-determination required the liberation rather than the salvation of Haiti. It demanded the strengthening of a black internationalism more radical than before.

CHAPTER 5

W. E. B. Du Bois, the Occupation, and Radical Black Internationalism

On the morning of July 29, 1915, George Foster Peabody sat down to breakfast at Yaddo, the luxurious four-hundred-acre estate and artists' community that he helped finance in Saratoga Springs, New York. Between sips of coffee, the prominent white philanthropist and former trustee of Tuskegee scanned the pages of the New York–based *World*. Coming to the editorial section, Peabody took note of a lurid headline: "A Red-Stained 'Republic.'" He paused. Then he took the bait. Peabody quickly consumed the opening revelation that "amid scenes of bloodshed . . . the Haytian revolutionists yesterday dragged President Guillaume from the French Legation and killed him in the street." He then moved past that macabre scene, partaking of the ensuing descriptions of Haiti as a "rich land cursed by appalling ignorance and savagery" and populated by "descendants of the African slaves . . . [who] have advanced little under nominal self-government." Finally, Peabody took in the prediction that "Hayti's tragedy"—"that she is unfit for self-rule"—would soon become the burden of the United States. More unsettled than satiated, only then did he begin to digest the looming reality that the "thankless responsibility" of "helping [Haiti] toward civilization" could no longer "be avoided." Occupation was inevitable.[1]

In fact, Peabody was bothered enough to turn his attention away from his relaxing morning routines and the immaculate gardens and marble statues that dotted Yaddo's grounds. One day after learning of the occupation, he wrote to Oswald Garrison Villard. He first asked the leading white journalist, grandson of the abolitionist William Lloyd Garrison and member of the National Association for the Advancement of Colored People (NAACP) board of directors, whether it was "time for the Negroes of mind and heart, with power and vision to plan somewhat for a right way to help Haiti?" Had Villard, he continued, thought that "anything would help the progress of the Negro to a recovery of his political standing in this country as much as a real turn over of the politics of Haiti?" Certainly African Americans must suffer "harm beyond measure to have such an instance as this last outbreak in Haiti for the haters of the Negro to refer to?" To Peabody, Haitian backwardness was obvious, but the prejudices of the "haters of the Negro" were just as vexing. And so, while he was uncertain about what role the U.S. government or African Americans should take in Haiti, Peabody was sure that like-minded white reformers and their black collaborators had to take immediate action. So he concluded his letter by asking Villard whether his "organization and Doctor [had] given any special study to the situation in Haiti and the way to best help those poor benighted people."[2]

The doctor to whom Peabody referred was giving "special study" to Haiti. Indeed, W. E. B. Du Bois gave careful consideration to the U.S. occupation of Haiti from its outset to its conclusion two decades later. As the editor of the *Crisis*, he made sure that the principal organ of the NAACP, the successor to the Niagara Movement, maintained extensive coverage of the occupation. Articles and editorials about it filled its pages. Photographs from occupied Haiti did, too. Moreover, Du Bois corresponded with the U.S. politicians who enforced the occupation as well as with the white reformers, black activists, and Haitians who opposed it. Those private dialogues influenced his public performances, including speeches and debates on Haiti. For Du Bois, the importance of the occupation rivaled the significance of World War I, the European colonization of Africa, and the entrenchment of Jim Crow in the United States. It was an event whose global consequences weighed heavily upon the most prolific black intellectual of his era.

There is no question that Du Bois had a persistent interest in the occupation. He did not, however, articulate a consistent opinion on it or its consequences. At first, he, like Peabody, saw great promise in an intervention that might "help those poor benighted people" of Haiti. The chief proponent of the Talented Tenth theory on black leadership viewed interventionism as a means by which black and white politicians, academics, and businessmen from the United States could save Haiti from itself, pay a form of reparations to black people, and affirm U.S. leadership throughout the Americas. As he received more information about the occupation and expanded his circle of informants on it, Du Bois saw clear parallels between the abuse of Haitians by the U.S. Marines and the oppression of African Americans by white southerners. He also reached the conclusion that the U.S. occupation of Haiti was a symptom of a much larger problem: the exploitation of the working people of the global South by elites in the global North. Accordingly, by the 1920s, Du Bois joined a growing cohort of African Americans and Haitians in an anti-occupation movement that would play a key role in the restoration of Haitian independence.

Unrecognized by historians, this changing view of the occupation illustrates a key moment of transition in black thought.[3] In the earliest days of the occupation, a faith in liberal activism and integrationism still animated Du Bois. He was adamant that African Americans could improve their political and social status by aligning themselves with and investing in U.S. foreign policy initiatives. Du Bois also believed that the benefits of U.S. liberalism could extend across the Americas. Like black intellectuals before him, Du Bois assumed that the introduction of bourgeois values and political institutions from the United States complemented the aims of nationalists in Haiti and throughout Latin America. When the occupation proved him wrong, Du Bois admitted his errors and reached different conclusions about race and culture, and nation and black liberation. Although he sometimes reverted to the rhetoric of racial uplift to articulate his hopes for an independent Haiti, he assigned diminishing importance to the geographical and cultural boundaries that divided Africa and the African Diaspora. In fact, he called for a new understanding of blackness. To Du Bois—operating within a vibrant black public sphere that expanded as a result of migration, took root in places such as Harlem, and included a radical print culture and an organized Left—blackness became a political condition rooted in a common struggle for cultural, economic, and political self-determination and a shared fight against the intertwined forces of capitalism, colonialism, and racism. It was, in short, the basis of an international movement—the foundation of a radical black internationalism—that shattered Afro-diasporic hierarchies and reshaped the contours of global black thought and politics.

And Haiti was at the heart of it all. The occupation of a country long regarded as *the* "experiment in black self-government" animated black Marxists, Garveyites, NAACP activists, and black clubwomen. It encouraged many, including Du Bois, to scrutinize the link between colonialism and racism and connect the issue of class to that of racial oppression. In essence, to Du Bois and his fellow black intellectuals, Haiti's second war for

FIGURE 13. W. E. B. Du Bois, c. 1919. Prints & Photographs Division, Library of Congress.

independence became emblematic of the crisis facing the colored world—and the clarion call for its liberation.

The histories of Haiti and the Du Bois family were intertwined. At the outset of the American Revolution, James Du Bois practiced medicine in Poughkeepsie, New York. By its end, the physician of French Huguenot descent parlayed his loyalty to King George III into a rich reward of Bahamian land from the British crown. James proceeded to extend his plantation holdings from the Bahamas into neighboring Saint-Domingue and fathered at least four children with one (or more) of his enslaved black women. He brought two of them, one being Alexander Du Bois, with him when he returned to New York around 1812.

There the fortunes of the mixed-race child soon deteriorated. His father died, his white family disowned him, and the funds for his education at an elite private school disappeared. Of course, Alexander had no mother to whom he could turn, and so, effectively orphaned and alone, he became a merchant in New Haven, Connecticut, married, and then left for Haiti. The promises of land and freedom offered by Haitian president Jean-Pierre Boyer must have appealed to Alexander just as they did to thousands of other free black northerners. It is likely that the recovery of his patrimony did, too. But the sojourn of the biracial son of a Saint-Dominguan planter produced an unwanted child rather than the complete recovery of a long-lost inheritance.

Alexander's second Haitian experience would not last long, either. Soon after leaving for Haiti in June 1861, he returned to the U.S. North, having had enough of Haiti's "Jackasses, Negroes, mud, water, soldiers, universal filth."[4] Back in more familiar terrain, his unwanted son waited. Decades after Alexander Du Bois abandoned Alfred Du Bois's Haitian mother, Alfred had also left Haiti for the United States. It is unclear whether he did so with the help of his father, Alexander, who had since remarried following the death of his first wife. Regardless, Alfred did marry an attractive, bright, younger single mother named Mary Silvina. Before the demise of their marriage—before yet another Du Bois man dissolved a romantic relationship in favor of an itinerant life—the two settled in Great Barrington, Massachusetts, and had a son. His birth certificate read "William E. Duboise."[5]

The familial connection between W. E. B. Du Bois and Haiti would prove indelible. It would spur his growing interest in the singular example of black self-determination in the Americas. In 1895, some years after he began reconstructing his ancestry from the diaries bequeathed to him by his late grandfather, Du Bois defended his Harvard doctoral dissertation, "The Suppression of the African Slave Trade to the United States of America, 1638–1870." Like much of his scholarship, the dissertation was pioneering. It not only provided the first scholarly analysis of the federal ban on the importation of slaves but also pointed out that the Haitian Revolution "rendered more certain the final prohibition of the slave-trade by the United States in 1807." As he waited for other professional historians to appreciate the significant role "which the great Negro Toussaint, called L'Ouverture, played in the history of the United States," Du Bois continued to educate himself about Haitian history and concern himself with developments in contemporary Haiti.[6] Besides finding common ground with the

Haitian diplomat Benito Sylvain at the Pan-African Conference held in London during the summer of 1900, Du Bois read the well-researched account *Haiti: Her History and Her Detractors*, authored by the Haitian statesmen Jacques Léger.[7] His Haitian acquaintances also included extended family. In the year before the U.S. occupation of Haiti, Du Bois communicated with his cousin Alfred Dubois about the possibilities of creating new commercial ties between African American and Haitian merchants.[8]

In short, Du Bois developed a strong personal and professional attraction to Haiti long before its occupation. It is no surprise, then, that he was prompt in responding to George Foster Peabody. Five days after U.S. Marines swarmed Port-au-Prince, the cofounder of the NAACP informed his longtime acquaintance that Villard had shown him the letter requesting his recommendation for the best way to aid the helpless Haitians. In his brief reply to Peabody, Du Bois wrote that there was "another side to the Haytian matter" that the white philanthropist was overlooking. He pointed out that Lindon Bates, Jr., an affluent white New Yorker traveling on the RMS *Lusitania* when a German U-boat sunk the British ocean liner, "said in one of his last speeches" before his death "that Hayti had succeeded in putting on their own individual farms the happiest peasant proprietors in the world."[9]

Although passing and ambiguous in meaning, the allusion was indicative of Du Bois's tendency to appoint U.S. elites as the most reliable experts on Haiti. Bates was an aspiring Republican politician, the vice president of the Bates Engineering Company, and a consultant for major international oil corporations. His travels throughout Russia and Latin America had been in the interest of capitalist development projects, not academic study. Still, Du Bois appointed him an authority on Haiti.[10] Even after Bates drowned in the North Atlantic, he remained the type of man that Du Bois thought should shape public opinion and exert a positive influence on what he referred to as the "Haytian matter."

In fact, Du Bois was proud to have already implored Woodrow Wilson, the leading white progressive of the day, to "take some wise and generous move in this matter."[11] In his correspondence with Peabody, Du Bois included a copy of the letter in which he informed Wilson that he was "so deeply disturbed over the situation in Hayti and the action of the United States" that he felt compelled to address the Democratic president. The initial tone of the letter and the eagerness with which Du Bois shared it belied the substance of the appeal. Du Bois followed his brazen opening with the more restrained opinion that "in this case, even more than in the case of Mexico," the United States seemed to owe "it to herself and humanity to make her position absolutely clear." After all, Du Bois proposed to Wilson, Haiti was "not all bad." Having "contributed something to human uplift," all it needed was the chance to "do more."[12]

The main purpose of the letter in which Du Bois requested sympathy not independence for Haiti was to influence how Wilson carried out its occupation. To that end, Du Bois begged Wilson "to consider the appointment of a Haytian Commission" for the chief purpose of making "our attitude perfectly clear to Hayti, the world and our own citizens." Demonstrating his elitist tendencies, he also recommended that Wilson appoint only "men of high standing" to "the proposed Commission." Du Bois predicted that well-educated "representatives of the white North and the white South, citizens of Negro descent and representatives of [U.S.] business interests" would ensure the commission "proper weight and influence." They would accomplish what Haitians could not. While Du Bois conceded that "possibly South America might also co-operate" with the commission, he assigned the prospective group of representative men from the United States a privileged role in deciding the future of Haiti. He insisted that a "frank, high-minded move like [the formation of the Haitian commission] following upon a policy of honesty in Cuba and patience in Mexico would have incalculable effect." Put simply, it would further establish "the moral hegemony of the United States in the Western Hemisphere."[13]

Honesty and patience were absent from U.S. relations with Cuba and Mexico in that moment. In 1906, President Theodore Roosevelt used the terms of the Platt Amendment, which stipulated the conditions of the U.S. withdrawal from Cuba after the Spanish-American War, to justify an invasion of Cuba. U.S. Marines stayed for almost four years, leaving only after they crushed a nationalist movement formed in response to the fraudulent election of a puppet president beholden to powerful U.S. economic interests on the island. The United States again used civil unrest in Cuba as a pretense for intervention a decade later. By then, Woodrow Wilson had invaded Mexico.[14] Like the ensuing use of military occupation to protect U.S. investments in Cuban sugar, capitalism motivated the landing of thousands of U.S. Marines at Veracruz in April 1914. While Wilson claimed that his motivation was to keep Germany from shipping arms to Mexico, it was no accident that the U.S. military expedition landed in an area with rich oil wells. Veracruzans certainly saw the invasion for what it was. In a period when Cubans expressed deep resentment over the melding of U.S. foreign policy and U.S. private investment, residents of the Mexican port city mounted an armed resistance to the occupying force.[15] To them, Wilson was dishonest for promising to teach Mexicans about democracy at the point of the bayonet and impatient for his rash reaction to a dictatorship that would fall a few months later. He exposed U.S. moral hegemony as a lie.[16]

To think that the United States could act as a benevolent international power without radical change to its foreign policy thus required either a great deal of jingoism or a significant amount of naiveté. That Du Bois possessed neither raises several questions. How could a man who complained that the United States had "Cuba by the industrial throat and the Philippines on its knees" reiterate the same tropes of U.S. exceptionalism used to justify U.S. imperialism? How could an editor who worried that the United States might "blunder into murder and shame and call it a Mexican war" also simply request clarification of its position toward that country?[17] Perhaps most puzzling, how could Du Bois, an intellectual already attracted to socialism, assign Wilson the task of overseeing a Pan-American system predicated on capitalism, egalitarianism, and an appreciation for the political sovereignty of *all* nations in the Western Hemisphere? Surely Du Bois knew better. After all, in the same year that he advised Wilson on the best way to oversee Haiti, Du Bois distanced himself from his past support of the president. He had no other choice after Wilson, the son of a slaveholding Virginian, had the gall to tell William Monroe Trotter and a delegation of concerned black citizens that the extension of segregation into the federal civil service was "not humiliating but a benefit, and ought to be so regarded by you."[18]

One possible reason for Du Bois's tepid response to Wilson's aggression is that he then felt that his best course of action was to act as an architect of the U.S. occupation of Haiti rather than an opponent of it. Besides asking the U.S. president to explain recent developments in U.S. foreign policy and encouraging him to strengthen a paternalistic relationship between Uncle Sam and Latin Americans, Du Bois told Wilson that the proposed Haitian commission should have three objects. First, it would assure Haitians that "the United States does not wish to infringe in any way upon their integrity as a nation." Second, the Haytian Commission would discuss "plans for the establishment of permanent peace, and for hastening the industrial development" of Haiti with a separate committee of Haitian leaders. Finally, it would "establish closer and more cordial relation and understanding between the United States and Hayti."[19] Reassure Haitians. Discuss plans for peace and industrial development. Build greater understanding between the United States and Haiti. These were vague suggestions in tacit support of U.S. supervision of Haitian governance, not meaningful recommendations for the restoration and future respect of Haitian sovereignty. At the very least, the recommendations that mirror the preoccupations of countless Progressive Era reformers contradict the long-standing assumption that the invasion of Haiti by U.S. Marines provoked immediate "howls" from the editor of the *Crisis*.[20]

Indeed, Du Bois first argued that the U.S. government could pay reparations to people of African descent *through* its occupation of Haiti. In *The Souls of Black Folk*, Du Bois had expressed his frustrations with white Americans' unwillingness to acknowledge the legacies of slavery, and he would further condemn their historical amnesia in *Black Reconstruction in America*.[21] But one of his most direct calls for the United States to not only recognize but also rectify its crimes committed against black people came in response to the U.S. occupation of Haiti. In his letter to Wilson, Du Bois reminded the U.S. president that Haiti was "almost the sole modern representative of a great race of men among the nations." It was thus "not only our privilege as a nation to rescue her from her worst self, but this would be in a sense a solemn set of reparation on our part for the great wrongs inflicted by this land on the Negro race."[22]

For Du Bois, this payment of reparations would assume special meaning if initiated by a Democratic regime. Besides noting that the "United States has throughout the world a reputation for studied unfairness toward black folk," he reminded Wilson that "the political party whose nominee you are is historically the party of Negro slavery." Harkening back to the unfulfilled promises that the Democratic politician made to African Americans during his successful presidential campaign, he asked Wilson a simple question: was it "not a peculiarly opportune occasion" to mend the wrongs of his party "by doing, in the words of your letter . . . to [AME] Bishop Alexander Walters, 'not mere grudging justice, but justice executed with liberality and cordial good feeling,' to the only independent Negro government in the New World?"[23]

Du Bois knew the right answer and he thought that other African Americans did, too. Echoing Booker T. Washington, he told Wilson that the United States could not "help [Haiti] most effectively unless we have the cordial support of the Haytian people, nor unless ten million American citizens of Negro descent" felt comfortable with U.S.–Haitian relations.

African Americans, Du Bois concluded, had to "feel that we have no designs on the political independence of the island and no desire to exploit it ruthlessly for the sake of selfish business interests here."[24]

In a moment when the U.S. government indicted black activists who sought reparations for formerly enslaved people, Du Bois's insistence that the United States owed its black citizens was bold.[25] His suggestion that the U.S. government could compensate for black suffering by rescuing Haiti from her "worst self" was not. In fact, it had echoes of earlier eras. Du Bois's consistent use of first-person pronouns to refer to the United States and third-person pronouns to refer to Haiti implied a greater identification with nation than race. It resonated with the patriotic rhetoric of predecessors who called for the U.S. annexation of Haiti. It could have come from Benjamin Tucker Tanner.

Unlike would-be annexationists during Reconstruction, Du Bois was under no illusion that the United States was on an inexorable path to racial equality. He did, however, cling to the hope that a vote for Woodrow Wilson had not been a vote for white supremacy. Du Bois believed that Wilson could be convinced to renew his "sense of fairness and broad cosmopolitanism." If he did, then his administration could not only recognize the full citizenship of African Americans but also aid Haitians lacking in cultural sophistication and education.[26]

Du Bois did worry that foreign intervention could lead to economic exploitation and political subjugation. Still, he thought those were risks, not inevitable outcomes, that did not outweigh the possible rewards for African Americans or Haitians. Despite the pride with which the latter protected their sovereignty, Du Bois assigned the U.S. government the task of civilizing Haitians and appointed African Americans as the supervisors of U.S. relations with Haiti.

That desired role for African Americans cohered with his integrationist leanings.[27] More precisely, his demand for the full involvement of African Americans in U.S. foreign policy toward Haiti complemented his calls for the full inclusion of African Americans in U.S. democracy. It was in complete harmony with the NAACP campaign to secure civil and political rights for black citizens. By insinuating that "ten million *American citizens of Negro descent*" (emphasis added) would maintain a loyalty to their federal government even as they expressed critical interest in its policies, Du Bois diminished the racial distinctiveness of African Americans in the same moment that he acknowledged it. His people, he insinuated, were black but no less American and they would prove it through their involvement in the occupation.

To Du Bois, it was obvious that his initial thoughts on the U.S. occupation of Haiti deserved a hearing beyond the White House. So, naturally, he published them in the *Crisis*. Du Bois began his editorial in the September 1915 edition of the magazine by reiterating that Haiti possessed positive attributes. Echoing the abolitionists of the antebellum era and alluding to arguments made in his own Harvard dissertation, he noted that Haiti was "a noble nation . . . that [gave] the world one of its greatest names—Toussaint L'Ouverture" and "made slaves free." Moreover, Du Bois boasted that Haiti was "a nation that dared and dares to fight for freedom." Taking a sly dig at Booker T. Washington, Du Bois insisted that "American Negroes who seldom have had courage to fight" had to appreciate that militancy. They certainly could not "point scornful fingers at our brothers" or forget that "in one respect Hayti leads the world." Once again deferring to the late Lindon Bates, Jr., while also building toward a more critical analysis of the relationship among land redistribution, proletarian struggle, and democratic change, Du Bois contended that "out of a hell of slavery [Haiti] has succeeded in placing on their own little farms the happiest peasants in the world." It had, he argued, achieved what "France, Germany, England [and] Russia" could not and succeeded where the United States failed.[28]

Yet Haiti was not all right to Du Bois. He suggested that "Hayti has lagged because she lacks capital and capital is the present day monopoly of white nations." It suffered because the economic strains placed upon Haitian politicians led them down an inadvisable path. Du Bois argued that Haitian leaders "stung by poverty and lured by European luxury" had "robbed [Haiti] shamefully." They, not the United States, presented Haiti with her most pressing challenge.[29]

But it was up to Americans rather than Haitians to meet it. Reaching the main point of his editorial, Du Bois announced that "the time calls for a Haytian Commission of white and colored men appointed by the President." The proposed commission would "co-operate with Hayti in establishing permanent peace and in assuring our stricken sister that the United States respects and will always respect her political integrity." It would help democratize Haiti. Du Bois was adamant that Haiti was "struggling to rid herself of these grafters," the Haitian elite. He was just as certain that Haitians could not do so alone. Suggesting that white and black Americans were the most qualified agents of change in Haiti, he issued a simple directive to his readers: "Let us save Hayti." By helping Haiti "rid herself of thieves" without fastening "American thieves on her," the United States could rescue a country that could not rescue itself.[30]

A shift in audience from a white supremacist president to a sympathetic black readership allowed Du Bois the chance to adopt a more strident tone. Still, even as he characterized Haiti as a model of black resistance, applauded its postemancipation social organization, and referenced the global economic forces that weighed upon it, Du Bois remained committed to a moderate solution to an assumed Haitian problem. He still presented a foreign commission as the remedy to Haitian ills. Du Bois proposed that educated men from the United States work together to eliminate corruption in Haitian government, modernize a Haitian state lacking industrial development, and allow average Haitians fairer governance. In essence, he asked them to validate the central tenets of U.S. progressivism and interventionism, the twin pillars of Wilsonian foreign policy.

That reaction was all too typical. For the most part, black intellectuals in the United States were ambivalent about the occupation at its outset.[31] Their reluctance to condemn U.S. military intervention in Haiti did not just stem from the instability of Haitian politics in an era when popular thinking held that government reflected racial capacity.[32] It also emerged from the intersections of diasporic belonging and national identity. Rather than swinging between the poles of pride and despair or expectation and embarrassment, black intellectuals occupied both positions on Haiti simultaneously.[33] To Du Bois and his ilk, Haiti remained exceptional. Its incomparable revolution and unique standing in the world seemed to justify the extraordinary hopes *and* the extensive grievances heaped upon it. Black responses to the outset of the occupation captured those beliefs, signaling the evolution of well-established ideas about the link between African Americans and Haiti. Indeed, they illustrate the perceived implications of those transnational connections. For "American citizens of Negro descent," the occupation was an opportunity to affirm their own standing in the United States by helping Haiti, a historic albeit flawed nation that would, as always, determine their prospects for a more meaningful freedom.

But what did the struggle for black freedom entail? As Du Bois continued to contemplate that question, the United States solidified its control over Haiti. Within one week of the initial invasion, Admiral William Caperton, commander of the U.S. Marines in Haiti, identified Philippe Sudre Dartiguenave as the preferred candidate for the Haitian presidency. Enticed by promises of support from the U.S. military in exchange for compliance, the Haitian National Assembly elected a man who understood his chief responsibility to be the acceptance of all terms that the United States set. More change soon followed. With Dartiguenave in power, the U.S. government began drafting a convention between it and its puppet government in Haiti. The document was meant to accomplish four main tasks: give the United States control over Haitian customs houses and the Haitian treasury, ensure that Haiti would not cede or rent any part of its territory to another country, displace the Haitian army in favor of a new military under U.S. command, and guarantee that the U.S. president controlled all nominations and appointments to Haitian government positions. Knowing that the proposed convention would incite strident opposition from Haitians, Caperton took extreme measures to assure its passage. He declared martial law in Port-au-Prince, censored the press, and arrested Haitian journalists, all the while assuring Haitians that a spirit of goodwill inspired every act of suppression.[34]

These developments disheartened Ernest Chauvet. The editor of *Le Nouvelliste*, a popular newspaper published in Port-au-Prince, once studied journalism in the offices of the *Brooklyn Daily Eagle*. More recently, he had served Haiti as a consular official in New York City. He remembered both experiences fondly. His time in New York convinced Chauvet that the "United States stood supreme as a respecter of nations' rights" and led him to the conclusion that "Haiti should proceed hand in hand with the United States." In fact, it encouraged him to spend much of his early professional life fighting "for the noble ideas of Pan-Americanism"—and against armed intervention in Haiti. Now, with the latter realized, Chauvet wondered whether his strivings for more enlightened diplomacy had been for naught. As the U.S. government tried to force a convention upon Haiti that reflected the interests of Americans rather than the needs of Haitians, the journalist and former diplomat considered the worth of a career "devoted to cultivating the friendship and business relations between" his country and the United States.[35]

Chauvet hoped that hemispheric cooperation remained possible, though. He still wanted to appeal to the better sensibilities of U.S. citizens and policy makers. In September 1915, Chauvet returned to New York with a letter directed to Woodrow Wilson and the U.S. Congress. It centered on a pointed question: "If part of the convention could be changed . . . in order not to hurt Haitian feeling and sensitiveness and not bruise national dignity, would it not be to the advantage of everybody that that be done?" In particular, Chauvet objected to the provisions made for a receiver general and a financial adviser in the occupation government. He thought it made little sense that the former would take "charge of all Haitian custom houses," the latter would exercise "considerable more power than the President of Haiti," and both would receive their appointments from and answer only to Wilson. After all, Haiti had never defaulted on the payment of its debts to foreign governments, and it did not need to give foreigners more power than its own president. Thus, while appealing to the paternalism of U.S. officials by stressing that "we look to you—and you only—for salvation and prosperity and peace," Chauvet reminded his U.S. counterparts of the national pride of the people they sought to conquer. Haiti, he declared, "is very proud of its freedom," a freedom that it "obtained at the cost of great sacrifice."[36]

In interviews given during his time in the United States that fall, Chauvet repeated his reminder about the historical depths of Haitian resistance to colonialism. He told reporter after reporter that the conditions of the proposed convention were "unfair in the extreme." Although agreeing that the political situation preceding the arrival of U.S. Marines in Haiti was untenable, he was adamant that "the conditions do not warrant the United States in forcing upon Haiti a treaty which so seriously involves its sovereignty as an independent republic."[37] He had trouble envisioning any situation that would justify such utter disregard for Haitian independence. Chauvet knew and pointed out that "with Americans in control of our customs and finances there will be no necessity for a secretary of finance; with the [U.S.] constabulary there will be no need for secretaries of war and public security; with American engineers, no necessity for a secretary of public works." The Haitian government, in short, would "be left powerless, our officials will become superfluous, our laws will be of no avail." While Chauvet maintained a vocal commitment to Pan-Americanism, he nevertheless used his interviews to affirm the unrivalled importance and sanctity of Haitian independence. Haitians, he asserted, were "a small people, but we love liberty and freedom." They wanted "co-operation, not subjection" and knew their "right to ask that the essentials of our liberties be left to us."[38]

Chauvet expected that W. E. B. Du Bois would find those points reasonable. To an extent, he was right. When Chauvet called upon Du Bois after arriving in New York, the *Crisis* editor said that African Americans could do little about an occupation that might benefit Haitians.[39] That rebuff was fleeting, though. Du Bois had heard Chauvet. In an editorial in the October 1915 edition of the *Crisis*, Du Bois accused the United States of violating "the independence of a sister state" and making "a white American Admiral sole and irresponsible dictator" of Haiti. Moreover, he denounced the United States for not only acting "with absolutely no adequate excuse" but also for exaggerating the problems afflicting Haitians. Du Bois further noted that "the anarchy in Hayti is no worse than the anarchy in the United States at the time of our Civil War . . . [and] the lynching and murder in Port-au-Prince is no worse than, if as bad as, the lynching in Georgia." Clearly, he reasoned, Haiti was "more civilized today than Texas."[40]

In the same month that the Haitian Chamber of Deputies ratified the convention that Chauvet condemned, Du Bois had come to recognize "the outrage of uninvited American intervention" in Haiti. He decried "the shooting and disarming of peaceful Haytian citizens, the seizure of public funds, the veiled, but deliberate design to alienate Haytian territory at the Môle St. Nicholas, and the pushing of the monopoly claims of an American corporation which holds a filched, if not a fraudulent railway character." He achieved an anger that emanated from the pages of the *Crisis*. "SHAME ON AMERICA," Du Bois thundered. Shame on the United States for its attack on Haiti, a country that could and would "work out her destiny."[41]

Despite such forceful critiques Du Bois was not yet the anti-occupation activist or the radical black internationalist that he would become. His recommended course of action still did not match his indignant tone. After chiding the United States, Du Bois concluded his October 1915 editorial by asking, "What are we ten million Negroes going to do about [the occupation]?" The question was rhetorical. Du Bois told readers to write letters "to President Wilson and protest; ask for a distinct, honest statement of our purposes in Hayti and an American Commission of white and colored men to point the way of Honor instead of Graft." "WRITE NOW," he demanded, "and let the editor of The Crisis have a copy" of a letter calling, once again, for a biracial commission or perhaps a bit of clarification.[42]

Some readers of the *Crisis* were more than willing to follow the lead of its respected editor. One white pacifist, and Unitarian minister, sent Du Bois a copy of a letter in which he asked U.S. secretary of state Robert Lansing for an explanation about "the action of our government in Hayti, already unfortunately attended with bloodshed." In his estimation, the

United States was "not welcome to the Haytian people" and was "actually engaged in war with them compelling our soldiers to lose their lives in subduing those who doubtless seem to themselves to be defending their liberties."[43]

The letter, which predicted the degeneration from benevolent protectorate to imperial conquest, pleased Du Bois. He ran it in the November 1915 edition of the *Crisis* alongside a guest editorial on the occupation. According to the author of that editorial, the "thousands of Haitians at home and abroad who are not grafting politicians, who know nothing about the Vaudoux, and who would welcome any effort looking towards a solution" to their country's difficulties outnumbered the savages "as primitive as their African forebears" living "in the bushes of Haiti." The burden was on the United States to help those enlightened Haitians—to recognize that the potential agents of uplift among the Haitian elite sought foreign assistance but would "not give their support to a government which even thinks of selling the Haitian's birthright of liberty . . . for the promise of a mess of American pottage." This point should have been obvious to anyone who saw "the Black Republic with eyes other than those of Spenser St. John." Echoing Du Bois, the writer sought recognition that "foreign assistance in financial and other governmental problems could best be assured by the formation of a commission comprising nationals of the European powers having interests in Haiti." If the U.S. government "could call into being such a commission and appoint a qualified representative to that body, some arrangement might be reached for the security of an orderly development of the Haitian people."[44]

Although Du Bois reveled in the support for his ideas, not everyone who looked to him for guidance or read the *Crisis* was as enamored with his modest challenge to the occupation.[45] Alonzo P. Holly certainly was not. In January 1916, the son of the late James Theodore Holly wrote to his peer. After assuring Du Bois that he was a European-educated medical doctor now practicing in Miami, a coveted public speaker, a former consul from Haiti to the Bahamas, and thus an equal of Du Bois, Holly came to his point. Would Du Bois, Holly asked, "help me save Haiti?" In particular, Holly asked Du Bois to fund his prospective lecture tour across the United States. He identified two main advantages to the proposed series of public speeches about the occupation of his homeland. First, the denial of speaking opportunities to Haitians in the United States had "sorely handicapped the fraternal relations that would have inevitably grown up between us and our brethren in the U.S." Greater interaction between the two groups would lead African Americans to express more sympathy with the current troubles afflicting Haitians. Second, Haitian lecturers were best positioned to expose "details which if revealed would arouse public indignation" in the United States and contribute to the "defeat of the Convention" that the U.S. government had "literally wrung from Haiti." The U.S. public, Holly suggested, supported the occupation only because it had yet to receive firsthand evidence of its wrongs.[46]

Holly promised Du Bois that he had ample amounts of that proof. Appropriating the words used by Woodrow Wilson and Robert Lansing to denounce recent German and Austro-Hungarian attacks on passenger ships, Holly assured Du Bois that he had "incontrovertible facts that prove beyond the shadow of a doubt" that Haitians were the victims of "deliberately unfriendly acts" and U.S. Marines were responsible for the "wanton slaughter of defenceless non-combatants."[47] To validate his assertion, Holly sent Du Bois advance copies of a series of articles that he hoped to publish or sell in order to finance his lecture tour. Based on information from Haitian newspapers sent to him by immediate family and friends in Haiti, the articles showed that Caperton and his men were "arresting, fining and imprisoning Haitian editors" for not complying with the new regime. They were, it proved, forcing journalists, including the editor of Port-au-Prince-based newspaper *Haïti Intégrale*, to pay steep fines and serve lengthy prison sentences for not acknowledging that there was neither freedom of speech nor freedom of the press under the "American usurpation and annexation."[48]

A lecture tour exposing those truths might have made a profit. Still, personal benefit from a national tragedy was not Holly's principal motivation. Besides expressing his willingness to share any money received from the lectures with Du Bois in exchange for his help in arranging them, Holly suggested that he felt compelled to act as the voice of besieged Haiti because its leaders were neglecting their duties. Rather than speaking on behalf of their compatriots, Haitian diplomats in the United States "created the belief that they [had] been won over to the plans of the [U.S.] administration" in Haiti. They were "handicapped" but Holly was not. He therefore wanted a hearing before the U.S. Senate Foreign Relations Committee in addition to a U.S. Congressional investigation into the occupation. And while Holly did not have the "means of meeting the expenses incidental to such a project," he was optimistic that a better-connected man than himself did. In fact, Holly was hopeful that an editor who was "striking the right key-note" in the *Crisis* would help him "to do anything to save my country." He was convinced that the challenge issued by Du Bois—"Let Us Save Hayti"—"should be our slogan."[49]

Such flattery was more strategic than sincere. In the same moment that Holly praised Du Bois, he also hinted at the limitations of the current stance on the occupation articulated in the *Crisis*. Suggesting that a Haitian commission appointed by Woodrow Wilson would still be an affront to Haitian sovereignty and insinuating that explanations for the occupation offered by the U.S. government would not make it less egregious, Holly concluded his letter by asking Du Bois for "some definite plans that will tend to save Haiti" and an acknowledgment of his correspondence.[50]

Neither were forthcoming. Two months after he asked Du Bois to help him sell his articles about the occupation or identify an alternative source of funding for his lecture tour, Holly wrote to Du Bois to ask why he had not received an answer to his previous letter. He was baffled. How could Du Bois not see the urgency of a communication designed to enlist his "support and influence in a campaign that would help enlighten the American public" about an occupation of which Haiti "had been the victim at the hands" of the Wilson administration? Indeed, the silence stunned Holly. Hurt and confused, he asked for the return of his articles and some justification for the lack of communication and the cool attitude expressed toward him.[51]

Holly's impatience was understandable—his country was occupied, his friends and family were suffering, and help was not forthcoming. But Du Bois's neglect was unintentional. On March 10, 1916, Du Bois wrote to Holly and confirmed that he received his letters from the preceding months and possibly another from the previous year. He assured Holly that his unresponsiveness was no personal slight. In fact, it was the result of having "received a large amount of matter concerning Haiti." Du Bois misunderstood the intentions of Holly (he wrote that he might be able to use some of Holly's articles "from time to time"), but he tried to reassure his Haitian counterpart. The attitude of the NAACP and the *Crisis*, Du Bois insisted, was "the same now as ever." Both were doing "everything" in their power to secure Haiti's liberation.[52]

The claim to an unmitigated commitment to the restoration of Haitian independence was exaggerated. It was, however, becoming truer due in no small part to the information about Haiti that flooded the offices of the

Crisis. As the United States entered its first full year in control of Haitian economic, political, and social life, Du Bois learned that the leading organization of lawyers in Port-au-Prince boycotted a ceremonial hymn and a reception held to celebrate the inauguration of the U.S. puppet Dartiguenave.[53] He received and reprinted articles from *Le Nouvelliste*, one of the most popular newspapers in Port-au-Prince, including one piece calling the occupation "not only an annexation, not even a protectorate, but rather a frank attempt at colonization."[54] Of course, Du Bois listened to Chauvet and Holly. Such protests from Haitians at home and abroad augmented what Du Bois learned from black newspapers. Some of them, including the Baltimore *Afro-American Ledger*, departed from the mainstream U.S. press and objected to the occupation instead of endorsing it. They cheered Republican candidates in the presidential election of 1916 who scolded Woodrow Wilson for his mistreatment of Haiti and encouraged African Americans including Du Bois to adopt a similar opposition to the occupation.[55] He would. As Du Bois paid more attention to those voices of black protest and less deference to white progressives and politicians, he developed more perceptive ideas about the occupation, its implications for African Americans, and its relationship to international events.

By 1917, World War I had accelerated dramatic changes in black intellectual life. During the global conflict that stemmed from rivalries among the European colonial powers, almost half a million African Americans fled the South for the urban North and Midwest. Many sought work in steel mills, railroad companies, foundries, and munitions factories experiencing labor shortages as immigration dried up in the midst of war. All sought to escape the racial caste system of their native region. For refugees who formed what became known as the Great Migration, cities such as Detroit, Chicago, Philadelphia, and New York were potential havens. They were refuges where black people might finally achieve meaningful freedom and self-determination.[56]

At the same time, Woodrow Wilson, having extended U.S. empire in the Caribbean, appropriated the language of self-determination. On the evening of April 2, 1917, the U.S. president went before a joint session of the U.S. Congress and declared that the "world must be made safe for democracy." Two days later, he got his wish when the United States declared war on Germany. For Wilson, the war, which resulted in tens of millions of casualties, was an opportunity to translate the progressive ideal

FIGURE 14. Anti-Occupation Protest in Haiti. Alaska and Polar Regions Collections, Elmer E. Rasmuson Library, University of Alaska Fairbanks.

of democratic political reform into foreign policy. His "Fourteen Points," a statement of principles outlining his vision for the postwar world, included the establishment of the League of Nations to guarantee the political independence and territorial integrity of small nation-states. It assured self-determination to ethnic minorities in Russia's Baltic territories, the Austro-Hungarian Empire, and the Ottoman Empire while saying nothing of Haiti, a nation that African Americans had long associated with the right to black self-government or self-determination.[57]

For African Americans, U.S. participation in World War I offered the opportunity to make the United States live up to its founding principles and Wilson's democratic ambitions. It presented another chance for the practice of martial citizenship.[58] The idea that African Americans could affirm their rights as citizens of the United States by serving its military had inspired black soldiers since the American Revolution. Now nearly four hundred thousand black men possessing those same hopes joined the United States in its fight against the Central Powers.[59] One black Virginian who enlisted in October 1917 and fought at the Battle of the Argonne Forest the following year felt "that it was my patriotic duty to serve my country at the most critical hour in the Nation's history though my Race had not been given the proper rights."[60] Left unsaid but implied was the attendant understanding that the United States had a duty, too. African Americans demanded that their government give them their "proper rights" in return for the sacrifices of the black servicemen who had embraced their "patriotic duty." In the words of one correspondent of Du Bois, they expected that black military valor and patriotism would not only "make the world safe for democracy and America" but also compel "a reluctant recognition from friend and foe." Both would prove that the United States was "*our* country right or wrong."[61]

Du Bois was just as certain that African Americans had to fight to ensure their inclusion in the Wilsonian idea of self-determination. In July 1918, he informed readers of the *Crisis* that "the colored race [had] no ordinary interest in the outcome" of "the crisis of the world." According to Du Bois, a German victory would mean the perpetuation of its colonial rule and "death to the aspirations of Negroes and all darker races for equality, freedom, and democracy" while an Allied victory over the "menace of German militarism" would help "inaugurate the United States of the World." To Du Bois, the obligations of African Americans were obvious. Coming to the main point of his editorial, he encouraged African Americans to "forget our special grievances and close our ranks shoulder to shoulder without our own white fellow citizens and the allied nations that are fighting for democracy." "We make no ordinary sacrifice," Du Bois concluded, "but we make it gladly and willingly with our eyes lifted to the hills."[62]

The reaction to the editorial, entitled "Close Ranks," was as immediate as it was fierce. Within days of its publication, Hubert Harrison, a West Indian journalist and socialist working in Harlem, pointed out that Du Bois crafted the conciliatory editorial in the hopes of securing a military intelligence post for himself. According to Harrison, Du Bois was akin to the "knight in the middle ages who had his armor stripped from him, his arms reversed and his spurs hacked off" and thus ruined "as an influential person among Negroes at this time."[63] Harrison's view was hardly uncommon. A. Philip Randolph and Chandler Owen, two black southerners who migrated separately to Harlem before becoming co-editors of the socialist newspaper named the *Messenger*, were some of the most outspoken critics of what became known as the "Surrender Editorial." Even members of the

NAACP joined in demanding an explanation from Du Bois, a longtime crusader for black political and civil rights who now asked African Americans to set aside their racial protests in the name of national unity.[64]

Some of Du Bois's critics were instrumental in giving black internationalism more coordination and organizational structure than ever before. Harrison was the founder of the Liberty League, a socialist and anti-imperialist protest organization born out of the belief that the NAACP was too moderate. When he condemned "Close Ranks," he was in the process of revitalizing the *Voice*, a paper that advanced internationalism, labor organizing, and armed black self-defense.[65] Randolph and Owen, although then at odds with Harrison due to different approaches to electoral politics, promoted similar class- and race-based causes. Besides endorsing trade unionism in the *Messenger*, the two southern migrants condemned "the ultra-patriotism of the old-line, old-type Negro leaders" who did not see the danger of "conscripting the Negro into the military and industrial establishment to achieve this end for white democracy."[66] They attracted a following among black radicals unwilling to link the global black freedom struggle to an investment in U.S. militarism.

Those voices of what became known as the Harlem or New Negro Renaissance knew the folly of closing ranks with white Americans. The end of World War I proved them right. There were eighty-three lynchings in 1919, an increase of more than 8 percent from the previous year. Some of the black victims were veterans who died in their uniforms. Countless more faced abuses and assaults that illustrated the fundamental truth that black military participation had fueled white rage, not dampened it. Throughout the United States, black servicemen returning from Europe received neither support nor gratitude from their white counterparts. Instead, they stood at the eye of a storm that swept across the country, touching down in a number of cities, including Chicago, Washington, D.C., and Elaine, Arkansas. The outbreak of anti-black violence directed at black veterans resulted in hundreds of deaths, thousands of injuries, and hundreds of thousands of dollars in property loss. It corresponded with the revitalization of the Ku Klux Klan and led James Weldon Johnson, now the NAACP's field secretary, to give the bloody months following the end of World War I an appropriate and enduring label: the Red Summer.[67]

Still, a number of the black intellectuals who surveyed the burning and bleeding world before them saw not only devastation but also opportunity. Du Bois surely did when, on the morning of December 9, 1918, he stepped off of his ocean liner onto the dock at Brest, a port city in northwestern France. Still smarting from the criticism of "Close Ranks," he had but one reason for enduring the long transatlantic journey from the United States and the subsequent sixteen-hour train ride into Paris. Along with Blaise Diagne, a Senegalese deputy to the French Parliament, Du Bois had organized the Pan-African Congress, a gathering of dozens of delegates from more than fifteen countries and colonies throughout Africa and the African Diaspora.

The timing seemed ideal. Du Bois planned his congress, modeled after the Pan-African Conference of 1900, to coincide with the Paris Peace Conference, which concluded World War I. He imagined that his gathering would ensure that the Allied powers not only set the peace terms for the Central powers but also placed their former African colonies under a system of international governance. The righteousness of that cause was self-evident to Du Bois. He was well aware of Woodrow Wilson's famous guarantees of self-determination and territorial integrity. Indeed, as both of those visions for a more democratic postwar world started to come to fruition—as participants in the Paris Peace Conference began dismantling decaying empires and organizing the League of Nations—Du Bois took note. Clearly, he reasoned, an international protectorate was a means to African home rule, the first step in assuring that Africans would one day enjoy the same self-determination now extended to Lithuanians and Poles.[68]

As historians and Du Bois's colleagues would later note, the uncertain fate of colonized Africa was at the forefront of his mind during the three days in which the Pan-African Congress convened at Paris's Grand Hotel.[69] Less acknowledged is the fact that occupied Haiti was, too. In the French capital, Du Bois became well acquainted with Tertulien Guilbaud, Haiti's minister plenipotentiary to the Paris Peace Conference, an honorary president of the Pan-African Congress, and a well-regarded intellectual and poet.[70] Du Bois also struck up a friendship with Isaac Beton, a Martiniquan educator who assured Du Bois that the "American intervention in Haiti [was] in flagrant contradiction" of Wilsonian democracy. It was Beton who introduced Du Bois to a Haitian doctor who "had taken refuge in France in order not to become an American."[71]

Conversations with those Afro-diasporic intellectuals highlighted the depths of Haitian resistance to the occupation. They also strengthened Du Bois's increasing misgivings about it. In the same moment that the delegates at the Pan-African Congress resolved that "wherever persons of African descent are civilized and able to meet the tests of surrounding culture, they shall be accorded the same rights as their fellow citizens," Du Bois recognized the occupation as an egregious affront to the "Civilized Negroes" of Haiti.[72] The occupation stifled Guilbaud, a man whom the Haitian politician and writer Anténor Firmin once praised for refuting "the doctrine of the inequality of the human races" through his "unquestionable talent, refined mind, and charming wit."[73] It constricted the opportunities of the well-educated Haitian doctor who had chosen "exile" over submission to the United States.[74] Convinced that the occupation was a strong deterrent to rather than an accomplice of Haitian uplift and its agents, Du Bois now felt more certain than ever that, as he had written to Diagne, "the future development of the Negro race" demanded "full recognition of the independent governments of Abyssinia, Liberia, and Hayti."[75]

Eliézer Cadet was part of a growing cohort of black intellectuals who agreed with that message but not its messenger. Cadet was born in Port-de-Paix, an arrondissement on Haiti's Atlantic Coast. His father was a successful dyewood merchant who enrolled Cadet at L'Institution St. Louis de Gonzague. After graduating in July 1916, Cadet left Haiti to pursue further education and employment in the United States. He found work at a federal munitions factory in West Virginia but also made frequent trips to Brooklyn, a city then becoming home to more and more Haitians fleeing the occupation. In the midst of the embryonic Haitian diaspora, Cadet discovered a new publication: the *Negro World*. He was awestruck. Cadet learned that the newspaper was the official voice of the Universal Negro Improvement Association (UNIA), the Harlem-based organization that the Jamaican Pan-Africanists Marcus Garvey and Amy Ashwood cofounded on the principles of black pride, black political and economic self-determination, anti-colonialism, and black self-help. Captivated by a newspaper soon found in the more than four hundred UNIA divisions in the Caribbean, Central and South America, Africa, and the United States, Cadet became a dedicated reader of it and a regular attendee at UNIA meetings.[76]

In fact, for a brief period, Cadet stood at the vanguard of the UNIA, the largest black mass movement in global history. In 1918, he published an article in the *Negro World* "with the sole aim to justifying my country in the eyes of foreigners."[77] Its impact was immediate. The U.S. government censored Cadet's mail, the Bureau of Investigation (BOI) tracked his movements, and key members of the Haitian political elite regarded him as persona non grata, as a dangerous dissident who threatened their attempts to placate the U.S. occupiers. Marcus Garvey also took note. While his rival Du Bois planned the Pan-African Congress, Garvey held a mass meeting at which the attendees elected A. Philip Randolph and Ida B. Wells as delegates to the Paris Peace Conference and selected Cadet as their secretary and interpreter. It was an obvious match. Although just twenty-one years old, Cadet had proven his opposition to white imperialism, demonstrated strong writing abilities, and confirmed his fluency in English and French. He had, most importantly, become articulate in a new "global metalanguage" of black liberation.[78] After his appointment, Cadet wrote to a friend and former classmate that he was studying "the administration and the history of the black race" and preparing "to contribute to the administration of the German colonies which are to be returned to the blacks." Moreover, predicting that the "next world war will be a war of races," he forecasted an imminent reunion of victorious black people the world over. "We," Cadet assured his friend, "are not going to fight and die for the white man Liberty any more, but for the good and welfare of the negro race."[79]

It was not long before Cadet tried to broadcast that same message to a much larger audience. As the Pan-African Congress unfolded in Paris, Cadet arrived in London with his passport, copies of the *Negro World*, two addresses from Marcus Garvey to the citizens of Great Britain and France, credentials introducing him to the European press, and a copy of "Peace Aims," which had been drafted at an earlier UNIA meeting and intended for the delegates at the Paris Peace Conference. He was without Randolph and Wells, though. After the U.S. government refused to issue passports to either of them, Cadet became the UNIA's high commissioner to the Paris Peace Conference and assumed the task of, in the words of Marcus Garvey, "representing the interest of 12,000,000 American, 10,000,000 West Indian Negroes, and 280,000,000 Africans."[80]

It was a daunting challenge due to the racism of the Allies. During his four days in London, the white press rebuffed Cadet—his only success was meeting Dusé Mohamed Ali, a prominent UNIA member from Alexandria, Egypt, and publisher of the London-based *African Times and Orient Review*. Those frustrations mounted after he arrived in Paris on March 1. Cadet immediately rushed about the French capital, attempting to speak with influential French editors and calling upon delegates to the peace conference. Few listened. Cadet could neither gain an audience with French prime minister Georges Clemenceau nor get French newspapers to publish his statements condemning anti-black lynching in the U.S. South, European colonialism in Africa, and U.S. imperialism in the Caribbean. Instead, his primary contacts were with delegates from Brazil, Cuba, Liberia, and other smaller nations whom the so-called Big Five—the United States, France, Great Britain, Japan, and Italy—relegated to minor roles at the conference.

Cadet could not miss the racist writing on the wall. Soon after his arrival, the discouraged commissioner felt obligated to inform his "dear comrades" back in Harlem that "*the 'liberal' French newspapers work under the whip of the Peace Conference which is itself under the whip of Wilson.*"[81] The postwar world, he suggested, was in grave danger of reverting to its prewar status quo, and the U.S. president, belying his promises of democratic inclusion, was to blame.

For UNIA leaders, Du Bois was another culprit for the sham that was unfolding in Paris. From France, Cadet alleged that the *Crisis* editor had undermined his efforts to solicit support from the French press, delegates to the Paris Peace Conference, and "our men from all parts of Africa, the Antilles, Central, North, and South America, at Liverpool, Havre and Paris . . . animated with the same spirit."[82] His colleagues believed him. In April 1919, Chandler Owen began a mass meeting at Harlem's Mother Zion AME Church with the announcement that only "good niggers" who would ignore lynching, peonage, disfranchisement, and discrimination had been given passports to attend the Pan-African Congress.[83] He then introduced Garvey, who eagerly upheld those claims. The UNIA cofounder declared that Du Bois was the representative of the "capitalistic class" and the culprit behind Cadet's failure to publicize "the sufferings of our people and the outrages committed in America."[84] He was, Wilfred A. Domingo next agreed, the worst of the "good niggers." Launching the final salvo against Du Bois, the editor of the *Negro World* concluded the meeting with a resolution denouncing "this person . . . [who] changed his face and wrote a certain editorial called "Clothed Faces." To Domingo and the attendees who carried the motion unanimously, there was nothing to do but "dishonor and disfavor him."[85]

The scathing allegations were baseless. In a subsequent issue of the *Crisis*, Du Bois insisted that he "never denied . . . [Cadet's] statements of the wretched American condition, did everything possible to arouse rather than quiet the French press and would have been delighted to welcome and cooperate with any colored fellow-worker." In fact, Du Bois maintained, he neither heard of nor met Cadet while in Paris![86] That response struck at what was most obvious to Du Bois—that the criticism of him was groundless, the unfortunate result of black political rivalries that would soon include a bitter divide between Garvey's black nationalists and black leftists who included Owen, A. Philip Randolph, and Hubert Harrison.

Still, the criticism of Du Bois did raise important questions about the value of his liberal politics. As Du Bois considered the merits of international administration and gradual self-rule in Africa, Cadet, who remained in France through December 1919 and published extensively in the *Negro World* and the Port-au-Prince-based *L'Essor*, rejected "the policy of the Caucasians which consists in effecting the disunion of the 400,000,000 black[s] of the world by leading those of one country to believe that they are better than those of another."[87] Put simply, he announced that his ideal world was one in which Haiti was free not only from the domineering Wilson—"this man . . . Jupiter"—but also from the assumed Afro-diasporic hierarchies and moderation that continued to hamper the Pan-African movement.[88] Was that Du Bois's ideal world, too? Concealed within the hyperbolic accusations that Du Bois was nothing more than a puppet or "the mouthpiece of the [U.S.] government" was the more incisive albeit less explicit critique that the NAACP activist still prioritized reform when only true renewal and revolution would do.[89]

Indeed, in that very moment, Cadet's compatriots were revolting against the United States. When the U.S. Marines first landed in Haiti, a Haitian military commander named Charlemagne Péralte refused to surrender his post in the port city of Léogâne. Although President Dartiguenave swiftly removed Péralte from his post, he could not squelch the spirit that the intractable commander embodied. Throughout 1915, *cacos*, insurgents from the Haitian countryside who traditionally led revolts against anti-democratic governments in Port-au-Prince, attacked the U.S. Marines. Their will persisted long after the United States claimed victory over them in the so-called Caco War. In fact, armed Haitian resistance reemerged three years later under the leadership of Péralte and Benoît Batraville. Having escaped the corvée, a colonial system of forced labor reintroduced under the U.S. occupation, Péralte mobilized Haiti's Department du Nord against the occupation. His efforts, along with those of Batraville in the Artibonite region, quickly bore fruit. By October 1919, thousands of Haitians, particularly those who had also survived the corvée, took up arms against the U.S. Marines. For his defiance, the United States assassinated Péralte then distributed a picture of the slain "bandit" nearly naked with his slumped body tied to a board and leaning against a wall. Again, though, resistance continued. The *cacos* fought on for another year, dispersing only after an unprecedented wave of aerial bombardments, civilian causalities, and the eventual killing of Batraville in 1920.[90]

The grassroots Haitian fight against the occupation moved African Americans. Throughout the United States, black newspapers that previously had raised few words in defense of Haiti now compared the *cacos* to Gabriel, Denmark Vesey, Nat Turner, and other U.S. slave insurrectionists who had been inspired by the Haitian Revolution.[91] They insinuated that this second war for Haitian independence had similar emancipatory meaning as the first. To black journalists, the repression of the *cacos* exposed the violence of slavery, colonialism, and white imperialism while their persistence provided an inspiring, imitable model of militancy in defense of black freedom and self-determination.

Du Bois applied similar meaning to a Haitian uprising that stimulated the international anti-occupation movement. As Haitians struggled for their freedom, the *Crisis* published a photograph of a U.S. Marine summarily executing an unarmed and injured *caco.*[92] The message was clear. With such evidence of imperial violence in Haiti, Du Bois had enlisted in the fight for Haitian independence. He had returned from Europe fighting. Embodying the militant spirit captured in the words of his famous "Returning Soldiers" editorial, Du Bois proceeded to look "America squarely in the face" and call it a "shameful land" for having struck a peace with the Central Powers while remaining "at war with Haiti."[93] In his estimation, U.S. secretary of the navy Josephus Daniels had "illegally unjustly occupied a free foreign land and murdered its inhabitants by the thousands." He had "deposed its officials and dispersed its legally elected representatives" before conducting "a reign of terror, brow-beating, and cruelty, at the hands of southern white naval officers and marines."[94]

Du Bois traced the roots of this "cruelty" back to the resurgence of the Haitian liberation movement in 1919. In the wake of that Haitian uprising, the relentless white vigilantism across the United States during the Red Summer, and the disappointments and debates that arose in Paris, Du Bois ridiculed long-standing ideas about [white] civilization and [black] savagery. He inverted them, proclaiming that "for more than a year this red-handed deviltry has proceeded [in Haiti], and today the Island is in open rebellion." Just as real "red-handed deviltry"—U.S. imperial policy rather than Vodou rituals—required swift condemnation, Haitian freedom fighters deserved sympathy from U.S. citizens and their elected officials. "The greatest single question before the parties at the next election," Du Bois concluded, "is the Freedom of Haiti."[95]

To be sure, the seeds of a more radical program of anti-occupation activism blossomed in 1920. In the June 1920 edition of the *Crisis*, Du Bois informed his readers that the NAACP had pressed the presidential candidates about their attitude on the following issues: lynching, "Jim Crow" cars, disfranchisement, Haiti, national aid to Negro common schools, colored army officers, and segregation in the civil service.[96] The list, ordered from one to seven in the sequence above, illustrated the evolution of Du Bois's ideas about Haiti, the occupation, and its meaning for black people the world over. To Du Bois, it was obvious that the U.S. occupation of Haiti was an issue at least as important as the funding of black schools, the appointment of black army officers, or the hiring of black civil servants. Moreover, he now called on rank-and-file members of the NAACP to reserve their support for politicians who would fight for the independence of Haiti and withhold their votes from any candidate who vacillated on the issue of the occupation. Requests for biracial commissions and international oversight of Haiti disappeared. Now Du Bois linked growing black political power in the urban North to black self-determination in Haiti, marking 1920 as the start of the "campaign for the freedom of Haiti."[97]

Some Republicans were listening and enabled a transformative investigation into the conditions of occupied Haiti. Eager to solidify its standing among the thousands of black northerners who had fled the South in recent years and to strike a blow at Democrats, the Republican Party financed James Weldon Johnson's investigative mission to Haiti during the summer of 1920. The result of the ensuing visit was a searing indictment of the U.S. occupation. In "Self-Determining Haiti," a series of four articles published in Oswald Garrison Villard's the *Nation*, Johnson pointed out that the United States had constructed a brutal and exploitative military regime under the guise of humanitarianism. Rather than delivering "civilization" to Haitians, the occupation had served the interests of the National City Bank of New York, which controlled the Banque Nationale de la République d'Haïti (National Bank of the Republic of Haiti) and major development projects in occupied Haiti.[98] Even worse, Johnson wrote, the United States had exported its pernicious brand of anti-blackness to Haiti. In interview after interview, Johnson listened as U.S. Marines boasted of raping Haitian women and bragged about shooting Haitian freedom fighters. Their accounts corroborated what he witnessed. Johnson had noticed that military "families that could not keep a hired girl in the United States [possessed] a half-dozen servants" in Haiti.[99] He had already observed their attempts to reconstruct the antebellum South in Port-au-Prince. To Johnson, everything about the occupation, including the corvée, proved that the United States was attempting to keep another population of black people "enslaved." He left Haiti convinced that "Americans [had] carried American hatred to Haiti."[100]

"Self-Determining Haiti" was more than a revelation. It was a clarion call. Prominent Haitian intellectuals and politicians praised Johnson's articles and credited him with inspiring L'Union Patriotique d'Haïti (the Patriotic Union of Haiti), an organization modeled after the NAACP. With a leadership that included Alonzo P. Holly, it quickly ascended to the forefront of the growing international campaign for the independence of Haiti.[101]

African Americans responded in a similar fashion while thinking of new foundations on which to build black economic self-determination. In July 1920, Du Bois wrote a letter to Herbert Stone, the editor of *Yachting*, the founder of a commercial shipping company, and a lifelong friend of Oswald Garrison Villard. After following up on a previous conversation concerning Marcus Garvey's Black Star Line and reiterating his opinion that his rival was "financially more or less a fraud," Du Bois informed Stone that Johnson had just returned from Haiti "very much disgusted with the American occupation and at the same time certain of the business opportunities." In particular, Du Bois continued, the "American invaders" and "banking interests" were trying to drive the "Black Haytian merchants who still control most of the trade" out of business. Something had to be done. To that end, Du Bois concluded his letter by asking Stone "what investment of capital it would involve to establish a line of two steamers carrying freight and a small number of passengers between here and Haiti."[102]

That word—capital—was taking on new meaning to Du Bois in light of the occupation. In the wake of Johnson's exposure of the devastation that U.S. banks were inflicting on Haiti, Du Bois considered how to not only supplant U.S. capitalism with black capitalism but to also build a different economic order. When an NAACP member wrote to Du Bois to share her idea about a proposed store, Du Bois responded with great enthusiasm and suggested that she form it in accordance with the Rochdale principles, a set of ideals for economic cooperatives established in England during the 1840s.[103] That advice was unsurprising—Du Bois had shown increasing interest in the European cooperative movement for several years. On this occasion, though, he linked that interest to his changing thoughts about Haiti and black self-determination. Du Bois suggested that the store "begin with some simple commodities like Haitian coffee, anti-lynching buttons and candy, that the profits . . . be divided equally between the N.A.A.C.P. and between a dividend which shall be paid back to the share holders." This action, he predicted, would connect "the Negroes of New York" to "the great cooperative movement which is the greatest modern movement throughout Europe for saving the money of the poor."[104]

Du Bois's proposal contains a number of limitations and raises several concerns. What would the peasants who produced Haitian coffee receive for their contribution to this cooperative? How would "the Negroes of New York" relate to them, not just the well-to-do Haitian merchants who would hold a stake in the steamships and freight that Du Bois mentioned to Stone? To that end, why were black New Yorkers presented as the sole beneficiaries of the proposed "N.A.A.C.P. Cooperative Store #1?" Answers were not yet forthcoming. In fact, it is not at all apparent that Du Bois saw that there were even questions that needed answering.

Still, it is certain that he had identified U.S. finance capital as a problem that afflicted Haiti and demanded redress in addition to the attention of African Americans. In October 1920, Du Bois announced in the *Crisis* that Johnson, who had just returned from Haiti, had intended "to investigate . . . rumors of oppression and brutalities there" but had "found conditions worse than were suspected."[105] More precisely, Du Bois proclaimed that Johnson's report, published in the previous issue of the NAACP organ, had completely exposed "the seizure of a nation by the National City Bank of Wall Street" and implicated Democratic vice presidential nominee Franklin D. Roosevelt in the erosion of Haitian democracy. To Du Bois, Roosevelt's "impudent assertion" that he had written the new Haitian constitution while serving as the assistant secretary of the Navy proved that "this great government has been made the catspaw of thieves."[106]

For Du Bois, the occupation had clarified the connections among U.S. capitalism, militarism, and imperialism, exposing the unstable foundations of the world that white supremacy had made. Accordingly, he further distanced himself from his previous suggestions that U.S. imperialism might improve Haiti or bring about a romanticized Pan-American union. He now expressed one wish: "May the League of Nations be delivered from its fool friends, and may Haiti find New Freedom when the impossible Wilson and his lackeys disappear."[107]

As Du Bois sharpened his critique of the U.S. occupation of Haiti, black intellectuals were, in fact, contemplating how black people across the world could best achieve that new freedom. A. Philip Randolph and Chandler Owen best captured this development in two political cartoons published in the *Messenger*. The first depicts two black men, one the target of a violent mob composed of white soldiers and sailors and the other slumped against the Statue of Liberty. Three black leaders stand above the fray: a minister advising African Americans to turn the other cheek, W. E. B. Du Bois directing them to "close ranks" and "forget our grievances," and Booker T. Washington reminding them to "be modest and unassuming" even in the midst of assault. The caption reads "Following the Advice of the " 'Old Crowd' Negro."[108] In sharp contrast to the first cartoon, the second one depicts a black man driving a car emblazoned with the slogan "The New Negro" and adorned with a banner bearing the names of Chicago, Longview, Texas, and Washington, D.C. All three were sites of anti-black violence and armed black self-defense during the Red Summer. Embodying that spirit of resistance, the black driver, declaring that "since the government won't stop mob violence I'll take a hand," shoots and strikes at least one member of a fleeing mob of white men. "Giving the 'Hun' a dose of his own medicine" hovers above the militant black man; "The 'New Crowd Negro' Making America Safe for Himself" appears below him.[109]

The Department of Justice, keeping a close watch on the "insolently offensive" *Messenger*, identified the cartoons as further proof "of the Negro's pride in fighting back."[110] That interpretation was incomplete—the new New Negro was not only militant and masculinized but a radical internationalist, too. As the occupation continued, the crowded tenement houses of Harlem continued to welcome thousands of black migrants from the Caribbean including Eliézer Cadet and Hubert Harrison, black refugees from the South such as Randolph and Owen, and black New Yorkers displaced from Manhattan. The melding of those distinct black populations produced tension, no doubt, but it also created synergy. Haitians, African Americans, Jamaicans, and Trinidadians came together in barbershops and beauty parlors, social clubs and restaurants. They listened to the same street preachers, gossiped about the latest news, and discussed editorials from the *Messenger*, the *Crisis*, and other publications within a burgeoning radical black print culture.[111] They forged new bonds. While many black New Yorkers became members of the NAACP and joined the UNIA, a smaller number embraced leftist organizations that included the African Blood Brotherhood for African Liberation and Redemption (ABB). Founded by Grace Campbell, a black Georgian and a member of the Socialist Party, and Cyril Briggs, a native of Nevis and a former journalist at the *New York Amsterdam News*, the ABB promoted socialism, armed black self-defense, and anti-colonialism while becoming the nesting ground for black Communists. Indeed, despite its modest size, it epitomized the radical changes afoot in Harlem, the incubator of the remarkable New Negro renaissance in black culture, politics, and thought.[112]

Briggs had opposed the occupation—"this last insult to the colored race, this last straw added to the immeasurable burden of the black man"—from its outset.[113] However, after the release of "Self-Determining Haiti," he saw its impact as something far more troubling than the emasculation of black men. In the same month that Du Bois decried the "impossible Wilson and his lackeys," Briggs published "American Kultur in the Island of Hayti" in the *Crusader*, a Pan-African and Communist newspaper he founded in support of Africa's right to self-determination. Briggs began by praising James Weldon Johnson for helping put "the Wilson administration . . . upon the defensive in its Haitian policy—a policy of the wanton destruction of the independence of a sister republic and the cold-blooded murder by American marines of unarmed Haitians." That imperial violence, Briggs continued, was linked to the greed and corruption of Wall Street. Quoting Johnson at length, the Harlem-based editor wrote that "to understand why . . . some three thousand Haitian men, women and children have been shot down by American rifles and machine guns, it is necessary . . . to know that the National City Bank of New York is very much interested in Haiti." He suggested that it was to know the lie of U.S. interventionism, too. "James Weldon Johnson," Briggs concluded, "shatters the argument that the United States embarked on the murder of Haitians and the wrecking of the Haitian Constitution and Government merely for altruistic purpose." U.S. democracy was clearly no more effective in Haiti than it was at home.[114]

For Briggs, the need for a complete abolition of Western economic and political structures was clear. So, too, was the means through which the revolution would be realized. Throughout 1921, Briggs pointed out that

Republican president Warren G. Harding, the man who succeeded Wilson "partly upon the pledge to put a stop to the private war . . . upon the unoffending peoples of the Haitian and Dominican Republics," was just as beholden to corporate interests as his Democratic predecessor. There was, Briggs argued, no justice for black people in either political party, not when both ruled Haiti with "uncivilized American marines, acting under Cracker instructions" and "American citizens [were] . . . murdered daily in the Southern States." Briggs thus advised "the American Negro [to] . . . forthwith recognize his duty toward the Negro republics of Haiti and Santo Domingo and the extent to which his destinies are bound up with those of the Negro peoples of these two republics." He implored him to embrace an insurgent politics predicated on militant anti-imperial struggle and shared opposition to "The Big Imperial thieves [who] prate a great deal about national and international morality, fair play and Christian ethics, etc."[115]

In the same moment that Briggs explained the interplay of race, class, and imperialism, Margaret Murray Washington, the widow of Booker T. Washington and an accomplished educator in her own right, organized the International Council of Women of the Darker Races (ICWDR). The organization's mission was just as clear as it was ambitious: to bring about "definite cooperation among the women of all the darker races for the purpose of studying the conditions under which each subgroup lived and progressed, of disseminating knowledge of their handicaps and of their achievements, and of stimulating by closer fellowship and understanding to higher endeavor."[116] There were, no doubt, countless "subgroups" for ICWDR members to consider. Still, none seemed more deserving of attention in that moment than Haitians. For that reason, the pioneering group of black women internationalists made its top priority during its inaugural year the complete assessment of the "conditions of the women and children of Haiti."[117]

The initial attempt at firsthand study of the "conditions under which" Haitians found themselves during the occupation came in December 1922. That month, Emily Williams arrived in Port-au-Prince. While her husband, a dean at the Tuskegee Institute, had been commissioned to study the Haitian educational system, Williams, a graduate of the University of Michigan and a fellow educator at Tuskegee, had come to Haiti at the behest of the ICWDR. Her earliest report shows that she found more "handicaps" than "achievements" among the Haitian women and children she observed. In a letter to Margaret Murry Washington, Williams lamented that Haitian "peasants live as in darkest Africa." Echoing previous appeals from Washington's late husband and other black advocates of industrial education, she urged her colleague to consider the ample "opportunities for our students to really serve" Haiti. In particular, she encouraged Washington to "talk to the Haitians now in school about returning to their country as teachers." To Williams, it was apparent that Haitians trained at Tuskegee remained best positioned to plant the seeds of knowledge, industry, and civilization in the "virgin soil" of their native land. In her estimation, it was all too obvious that "darkest" Haiti required "help" not unequivocal independence.[118]

That ambivalence was common among black activists who, unlike Briggs, felt that "fair play and Christian ethics" could be the basis of racial uplift at home and abroad. As the occupation entered into its second decade, Addie Hunton, the ICWDR president and NAACP spokeswoman, traveled to Haiti as part of an investigative team assembled by the Women's International League for Peace and Freedom (WILPF). There she found Jim Crow. In a chapter coauthored with the white peace activist Emily Green Balch and published in a subsequent report entitled *Occupied Haiti*, Hunton wrote that the "race situation in Haiti is what one would expect under existing conditions: a black people and white Americans . . . the white American of the group particularly noted for its caste system—the military—and of the division of that group that prides itself on absolute exclusion of the black American." To Hunton, exclusion rather than intervention was the problem. Even as she critiqued the occupation, she insisted that "the Americans needed in Haiti are men broad in interracial understanding, able not only to meet the upper-class Haitian in his social environment but to help him to a fuller recognition of his responsibility toward the great peasant mass of the island." Haitians, Hunton surmised, still required guidance from above and abroad even if they did not deserve the violent oppression of the occupation.[119]

For Hunton and other black clubwomen, the occupation confirmed entrenched ideas about the value of self-help, education, and sound elite leadership in black communities. It did not, however, affirm the paternalistic practices that traditionally stemmed from racial uplift ideology. In 1927, the same year that Hunton called for "men broad in interracial understanding" to help the "upper-class Haitian . . . to a fuller recognition of his responsibility," she chaired the Women's International Circle for Peace and

Foreign Relations (WICPFR). That New York–based black women's political organization reinvigorated the Pan-African movement.[120]

While Du Bois criticized white reformers who blocked the assembly of a Fourth Pan-African Congress because they wanted to "take personal charge of all efforts toward African uplift and unity," WICPFR activists including his wife Nina Du Bois and the writer Jessie Fauset raised more than three thousand dollars and arranged for Harlem churches to host the event.[121] With their work, the congress convened. In August 1927, an estimated five thousand participants joined the more than two hundred delegates from the Gold Coast, Haiti, Germany, and seemingly everywhere else that black people lived. To Du Bois, the chair of the proceedings, the Fourth Pan-African Congress was a necessary means of "drawing the negro's problems and interests in all parts of the world into a common cause so that they may be faced with a united front." He might have also added that it was a testament to the role of black women in the building of the insurgent black international, the vanguard who knew that the "question of the status of the negro" was not a "domestic . . . parochial . . . or a colonial policy problem" but a "great world-wide problem."[122]

In fact, the event funded by black clubwomen was part of a broader revolutionary program of black liberation that was challenging older ideas about black progress. Months before the Fourth Pan-African Congress, the black Communists and former ABB members Otto Huiswood and Richard B. Moore joined nearly two hundred delegates from more than twenty countries at the International Congress Against Colonial Oppression and Imperialism in Brussels, Belgium. The event led to the creation of the League Against Imperialism, an organization that undermined the colonial agenda of the League of Nations. Thanks to Moore, a black delegate representing the UNIA and the Marxist American Negro Labor Congress (ANLC), it also condemned U.S. empire. By the end of the Brussels conference, attendees including representatives from the Indian National Congress and African National Congress had adopted unanimously "The Common Resolution on the Negro Question." The document that Moore drafted demanded "support of the Patriotic Union and Haiti in a powerful campaign to expose to the world the terrible suppression of the Haitian people."[123]

The Fourth Pan-African Congress embraced the same spirit as the International Congress Against Colonial Oppression and Imperialism in part because it welcomed the same intellectuals. At its outset, Du Bois warned Hunton against potential delegates, including Blaise Diagne, who were "conservative and reactionary and afraid of American Negro radicalism."[124] That warning set the event's ensuing tone. While some resolutions simply calling for African participation in African colonial governments resonated with the moderate proposals of the previous Pan-African congresses, Otto Huiswood offered a more strident demand for the end to white colonial and imperial exploitation.[125] His resolution supported black laborers and called on white workers to make common cause with them, demanded national independence for Egypt, China, and India, praised the Soviet Union for its "liberal attitude toward the colored races," and advised West Indians to not only fight for national liberation but also forge a regional federation.[126] It also cohered with the contributions of Richard Moore and William Pickens. While Moore submitted a resolution praising the International Congress Against Colonial Oppression and Imperialism, Pickens, who had planned to attend the Brussels event before its unexpected delay, railed against the "devouring of Africa, the spoliation of Hayti and the bullying of Nicaragua." He warned, too, that such exploitation had no natural end—it would stop only when the proletariat recognized their "common interest and make common cause with the other oppressed and exploited peoples of the world."[127]

Haiti was fundamental to Pickens's transformation from aspiring imperialist to Communist sympathizer, and it was central to Du Bois's ideological evolution, too. As his fellow NAACP spokesman decried the "spoliation" of a country he once wanted annexed, Du Bois listened intently to the Haitians who accepted their invitations to the congress.[128] Those Haitian statesmen, activists, and intellectuals included Dantès Bellegarde, Jean Price-Mars, Sténio Vincent, Ernest Chauvet, and Alonzo P. Holly. Most were leaders in the Patriotic Union; all were outspoken opponents of the occupation. Du Bois found great appeal in their protests, including Bellegarde's "moving" speech revealing "that more Haitians were killed in one year under the American Corvee System than had been killed previously in all the revolutions that had taken place in Haiti!"[129] That violence, Du Bois understood, was the most noticeable consequence of white imperialism. It was certainly not the only one, though. Drawing from the information that Haitian nationalists continued to offer, Du Bois and the congress delegates resolved that "the attempt of American capital to dominate the industry and monopolize the land of Haiti be decisively checked and turned into such channels as will encourage industry and agriculture for the benefit of the Haitian people."[130] It was time to let black workers determine their own fates.

Du Bois still believed in some key tenets of racial uplift. He told any who asked that he loved *Occupied Haiti* for showing the need for sound racial leadership. To him, it was a strong argument to end the occupation but "restore to their rightful leadership the educated class of Haiti . . . to lead a movement for the uplift of the masses."[131]

Yet he was more cognizant of the actual challenges confronting and the real needs of those masses. In December 1929, two months after the crash of the stock market sent Wall Street into a panic and initiated what would soon become a worldwide economic depression, Du Bois joined James Weldon Johnson, the historian Rayford Logan, the former occupation administrator W. W. Cumberland, and the anti-occupation activist Napoleon Bonaparte Marshall as speakers at a luncheon hosted by the Foreign Policy Association at New York's Hotel Astor.[132] When it was his turn to speak, Du Bois declared that Haiti differed from the United States, a land of peons where a "handful of people" established "outward peace and quiet" by exerting "absolute control of the great mass of labor." Instead, he continued, Haiti was a nation where black people derived "a growing sense of democracy" from independent landownership and control of their labor.[133]

The United States had disregarded that fact in its obsession with finance capital and racial hierarchy, Du Bois continued. It had rushed into an illegal and immoral occupation of Haiti. To Du Bois, the potential of Haitians made that erosion of Haitian autonomy all the more galling. Without the interference of Wall Street and the U.S. Marines, he now knew, Haitians surely would have "pounded out by turmoil and uprising a free, popular and modern government."[134]

Continuing, Du Bois lamented the extent to which external pressures had thwarted the growth of true democracy in Haiti. He noted that as Haitians forged an enlightened political and social consciousness, the "white peoples of the world had made up their mind that the liquidation of self-government so far as colored people was concerned was finally to be accomplished." China would be partitioned among Europeans. Neither Liberia nor Ethiopia would survive. "The final adjustment of European ownership in Africa was to take place" through "the obtaining of raw material from these colored countries at the lowest prices, the manufacture of it and selling at high prices," and the final amassing of "huge profit out of the exploitation of colored labor." That was motivation for the drawing of the color line, the problem that Du Bois had long identified as *the* problem of the twentieth century. It was the reason why "there was in everybody's mind the conclusion that Haiti must disappear as an independent government."[135]

This was more than propaganda meant to buttress a budding critique of the interrelated forces of global capitalism, imperialism, and white supremacy. It was an astute and prescient observation. The mob that killed Guillaume Sam did not act as they did because Sam was an inherently inept leader. Their violence was a direct result of Sam's military commander executing dozens of political prisoners. And those political prisoners had mounted opposition against Sam after the National Bank of the Republic of Haiti, which was under the control of U.S. bankers, refused to finance the Haitian government. To borrow the words of a modern historian, Sam was in an untenable situation.[136] He could make a deal with the United States and risk the ire of Haitian nationalists or he could rebuke the United States and face its wrath. Put simply, the attempts made by the U.S. government to obtain control of Haitian finances and territory were, in Du Bois's analysis, "one of the chief causes of [Haitian] turmoil," instability that in turn became an "excuse and not cause" of the "high-handed act of aggression" of 1915.[137]

For Du Bois, the ensuing conduct of the occupation was unsurprising while the appropriate response to it was no longer vexing. He told attendees at the Foreign Policy Association luncheon and those listening to its radio broadcast that the United States had entered Haiti "ostensibly because there was not enough democracy, and thereupon we took away what little democracy there was there." It had dispersed the Haitian legislature. It had built "military roads so the marines can get from one end of Haiti quickly to kill peasants who ask questions." It had done "nothing about illiteracy at all," choosing instead to make plantation workers out of Haitian peasants. And why had it done so? Du Bois asked. "Because if you can establish in Haiti the same kind of peonage you have in Cuba, you can have the same tremendous profits which you have out of Cuban sugar." You could extend the material practices and benefits of Jim Crow, too. Du Bois noted that the U.S. government gave control of Haiti to white southerners who "could not meet colored people as equals or treat Negroes as men." Those agents of white supremacy helped bring "the Haitian people for the first time face to face with that domestic institution of the United States" and rendered Haitians as defenseless as the lynching victims in Louisiana.

Indeed, they inadvertently laid bare the common cause of African Americans and Haitians. As black Marxists posited that black southerners constituted an oppressed "nation within a nation," Du Bois insinuated that only internationalism could liberate black people who, even in the independent Republic of Haiti, could expect nothing from "the sense of fairness of the people of the United States or the people of the civilized world."[138]

Of course, Du Bois knew that insurgent black political solidarities were forming across national boundaries. He had helped forge them. Accordingly, it was appropriate that Du Bois finished his speech not with a redundant message to black internationalists but with a warning aimed at white listeners. As his time at the luncheon came to an end, Du Bois insisted that the occupation of Haiti showed that elites in the global North were attempting to exploit working-class people in the global South "by making the result of their labor give them bare support while it adds tremendous profits to the exploiting country." Those white imperialists, he continued, were trying "to use those profits as a fund by which democracy is nullified in so many of the so-called republican governments throughout the world." Ultimately, they had to fail. Revising the prediction of Garveyites including Eliézer Cadet, Du Bois proclaimed that "if you are going to keep the colored world in the position of exploitation in which it is today, then you are going to have war; and not necessarily war between colored and white people, but war between those white people who are fighting for the spoils that come from the exploitation of the colored folk." There was only one solution. "If you want to keep war out of the world," Du Bois concluded, "if you want democracy to expand not simply in Haiti but here in the United States . . . you should see that [Haiti] has back the freedom which it so clearly won" in the Haitian Revolution.[139]

In August 1934, the United States finally removed its Marines from Haiti. Thanks to the militant resistance of Haitians and the invaluable assistance of the international anti-occupation movement, Haiti won back its historic freedom. Black people throughout the world rejoiced.

One month later, Sténio Vincent, a founding member of the Patriotic Union who had since become president of Haiti, thanked the multiracial coalition of activists, politicians, and intellectuals who had helped Haitians in the fight for their second independence. He gave special recognition to the NAACP. In a letter published in the *Crisis*, Vincent expressed his "personal gratitude . . . to all those American friends, colored or white, who, so

FIGURE 15: W. E. B. Du Bois in Haiti, 1944. Taken in the small town of Fermathe during Du Bois's first visit to Haiti in the late fall and winter of 1944, the photograph shows him with Émile Saint-Lot, a Haitian lawyer who would soon become a prominent politician, and Laura Trouillot, an intellectual best known as the wife of the Haitian writer and poet Roussan Camille. Department of Special Collections and University Archives, W. E. B. Du Bois Library, University of Massachusetts Amherst.

willingly and so courageously have taken part, on our side, in the long and hard struggle" for Haitian liberation. He acknowledged the men and women "who, by their prayers, by their efforts, and by their great publicity campaign have in such a large measure contributed to the freedom of my country."[140]

Although Du Bois had become one of the most prominent African Americans in the international anti-occupation movement, Vincent addressed the published letter to Roy Wilkins, the reason being that Du Bois had ceded his editorship of the *Crisis* to Wilkins, a man who he thought embodied the bourgeois pretensions and conservative shortcomings of the NAACP. In fact, Du Bois had left the organization due to long-standing disagreements with Walter White, the head of the NAACP and a staunch critic of Du Bois's recent defenses of black separatism.

Neither action was surprising to those following Du Bois's unambiguous turn to the Left. For the past two decades, the period in which Haiti fought for its freedom, Du Bois had voiced more and more trenchant critiques of racism while pinpointing capitalism as a problem facing colored people oppressed by colonialism, white imperialism, and Jim Crow. He had come to view the liberation of Haiti as a step toward stopping militarism, an obstacle to global black freedom that stemmed from the self-destructive tendencies of the so-called civilized world.

Those great expectations soon turned into even greater disappointment, however. Following the U.S. occupation of Haiti, black businessmen such as Charles Clinton Spaulding invested in the business of black internationalism. Situating black investors and capitalists from the United States at the center of Haitian development, they courted partnerships with Vincent and the small cohort of Haitian elites who controlled the operations and profits of their country's tourism and trade. They often did so by appropriating the language of President Franklin D. Roosevelt's U.S.-centric Good Neighbor Policy, couching black capitalism in the promise of mutual progress, the language of racial unity, and the rhetoric of neighborly goodwill.[141]

Despite the efforts of nonstate black actors, the U.S. government and white elites maintained control of Haitian customs, tax collection, and tariffs in an era when it forged new forms of anti-black repression. The end of World War II, the global conflict among imperial and colonial powers that Du Bois had predicted, led to another battle between the United States and the Soviet Union for global domination. During the Cold War, the United States conceded to more moderate demands for integration but suppressed real or perceived threats of black radicalism.[142] While offering unprecedented openings for black civil and political rights gains, it also presented daunting challenges for radical black activists and intellectuals who saw the folly of tearing down racial segregation without dismantling the supporting structures of empire, war, and class.

For Du Bois, whose passport the United States revoked then reinstated before refusing to renew, the problems of the postwar world were no more apparent than in postoccupation Haiti. When Du Bois visited Haiti in the spring of 1955, the country was in the midst of a tourism boom and achieving relative economic prosperity under Colonel Paul Magloire.[143] It was also, as Du Bois wrote, still "under the complete economic and ideological control of the United States." As President Magloire consolidated military rule and courted U.S. investment and financial assistance by repressing leftist activism and union organizing, Du Bois lamented that the Haitian government had succumbed to the destructive idea that "private profit [w]as the best path to public welfare, and . . . Communism is a crime." Haiti, Du Bois continued, "needed . . . social restoration and guidance led by Haitians." Instead, it "got . . . American Big Business, led by men whose aim it was to secure Haitian business allies to share the loot of exploiting Haiti."[144]

If Haiti forged Du Bois's radical black internationalism, then it also illuminated the difficulties of maintaining that necessary work. Du Bois's final public reflections on Haiti's continued plight under "American Big Business" came during the era of desegregation and decolonization. They occurred at a time when black intellectuals achieved civil rights victories and national independence but had far less success in securing global black liberation. To Du Bois, reaching the end of his life, Haiti thus embodied the "great world problems of war and peace, Communism and free enterprise." It showed the need for another wave of radical black internationalism fighting to abolish the "new American slavery" of the postwar liberal order.[145]

EPILOGUE

Just after the centennial of the U.S. occupation of Haiti, I sat in the Miami International Airport, waiting, watching. It was impossible not to notice the difference between the passengers on my previous trip to Cap-Haïtien and those who would soon join me on American Airlines Flight 949 to Port-au-Prince. Instead of Haitians returning home after seeing family in the United States or Haitian Americans leaving home to see family back in Haiti, there were missionaries. Lots and lots of missionaries. All of them were white evangelical Protestants, most of them southern. While I was headed to the Caribbean Studies Association (CSA) annual conference, the international academic association's first-ever meeting in the world's first black republic, they had a grander, godlier mission. At least that's what they announced on matching T-shirts bearing their church names, state outlines, and brazen promises to "Rebuild Haiti."[1]

While I watched, a number of emotions bubbled to the surface. Resentment. Pity. Anger. Alienation. I knew these white missionaries—better yet, I knew the distance between them and me. They live in suburbs where the city buses don't go, attend segregation academies where textbooks teach that the War of Northern Aggression was about the tariff, and spend Sunday morning learning about a white Jesus who sides with the rich rather than the poor. These missionaries neither have nor want contact with African Americans. Yet here they were preparing to descend upon Haitians. They would stay in Haiti for a few days, maybe a week. Hell, some might even go back. All would purport to care about black people in Haiti, just not at home.

Of course, I also knew these white missionaries were not the first of their kind. Their forebears had exaggerated Haitian political instability, deemphasized the United States' role in creating that discord, and begged "for white folks and Christians to step in and put an end to the dirty muddle" created by Haitians. Indeed, they had called for a "regiment or two of

Yankee . . . soldiers" to swoop into Haiti and "then ship in a lot of soap" because "you can never civilize [Haitians] so long as they are so utterly filthy."[2]

The missionaries had simply taken up that mandate. Following an aging script, reproducing old ideas about Haiti, they had wrung their hands over the latest disaster in that country while continuing to ignore racial inequality in the United States. Next, these humanitarians had attributed Haiti's misfortune to fate or God or anything other than historical causes and geopolitical realities. They then responded with self-righteousness, making sure to emphasize the inherent, racial flaws of Haitians. Finally, these self-interested saviors had set out to provide aid that abetted white supremacy and U.S. exceptionalism while sacrificing the needs of Haitians to the wants of U.S. business and foreign policy.[3]

It was easy to judge those who had their minds set on saving their imagined Haiti. Distracting, even. African Americans have long scrutinized their white counterparts for looking down upon Haiti without caring that "a more dirty, savage and muddled state of affairs never existed than is to be found in Christian America." Still, even as we observed that "white folks and Christians have a broad field for missionary operations here at home," anti-black discourses adapted, persisting into a current moment when the vanguard of right wing U.S. politics began lining up to board our flight to Haiti.[4]

There is still great allure in shaming the willful (and willfully ignorant) perpetrators of racism and neocolonialism and drawing attention to their own "savage and muddled state of affairs."[5] I know. After all, I furiously jotted down notes on my flightmates, some laced with expletives.

Still, confronting white supremacy on its own terms is neither effective nor wise. Instead, it is exhausting and ineffective. As Du Bois concluded by the end of the occupation, the defensive intellectual work of vindicating black humanity reinforces the same binaries—civilized and savage, modern and premodern, cultured and uncultured—used to condemn Haitians and distracts from building transnational dialogues and identifying common causes that might produce policies more favorable to Haiti. It recycles old storylines when we need revolutionary narratives.[6]

I can't claim that this realization dawned on me at that moment. It's true, however, that the power of radical black internationalism as a better method of historical narration and change was palpable as soon as we touched down in Port-au-Prince's Toussaint Louverture International

Airport. How could it not have been? Before this most recent trip to Haiti, I had taken a job in middle Tennessee, the region where, since the nineteenth century, African Americans have buried their dead in the Toussaint L'Overture County Cemetery. According to one woman whose relatives rest in the oldest black burial grounds in Davidson County, Tennessee, her ancestors named their cemetery after Toussaint Louverture because "they looked at him as signifying independence and dignity."[7]

Those black Tennesseans were not alone, neither in life nor in death. Their ideas about the Haitian Revolution persist in the origins stories that their descendants continue to tell. Their connections to Haitian and Afro-diasporic burial practices endure in the yucca plants that still sprout alongside their graves. And the revolutionary namesake shared by the Toussaint L'Overture County Cemetery and the Toussaint Louverture International Airport remains a durable guidepost for black people who dream of freedom, independence, and dignity, whether in Nashville or Port-au-Prince.

At the baggage claim, I joined the friend and colleague with whom I was rooming at the CSA and headed toward the waiting area for conference shuttles. Soon we were off on a journey through the black internationalist geographies of Port-au-Prince. Our car, filled with CSA participants from the United States, Europe, Canada, and the Caribbean, sped down Boulevard Toussaint Louverture and passed Rue Patrice Lumumba a few minutes later. In 1960, Lumumba became the first prime minister of the Republic of the Congo after it won independence from Belgium. During his short time in office, before the Central Intelligence Agency authorized his overthrow and assassination, Lumumba positioned his country at the forefront of the global anti-colonial struggle and used Pan-African rhetoric to recruit Haitian and African American professionals to his fledgling country.[8]

Many Haitians found those appeals attractive. Lifesaving, even. In 1957, François Duvalier, a black nationalist who seized the Haitian presidency through electoral fraud, violent suppression of political opposition, and support from the United States due to his anti-Communist posturing.[9] As he solidified his brutal regime, hundreds of Haitians reversed sail, returning to the region of West/Central Africa, where most of their enslaved ancestors lived before being sent to their deaths in the sugar plantations of Saint-Domingue. These refugees included the family of Raoul Peck, the Oscar-nominated filmmaker who has since retold the story—and thus revived the internationalism—of Lumumba in an award-winning documentary and a subsequent movie that debuted at the prestigious Cannes Film Festival.[10]

Continuing down Boulevard Toussaint Louverture, toward the heart of the city in which Peck was born, we next passed Avenue Haile Selassie. In 1935, in the same moment that the U.S. Marines relinquished control of Port-au-Prince, Italian soldiers under orders from Prime Minister Benito Mussolini launched their assault on Addis Ababa. African Americans and West Indians turned their collective attention from Haiti to Ethiopia, the lone independent state in Africa, and pledged allegiance to Selassie, its emperor.[11] Three decades later, following the reclamation of Ethiopia from Italian rule, Selassie made the shortlist for the Nobel Peace Prize due to his establishment of the Organization of African Unity (OAU), a continental body committed to the final eradication of European colonialism and the success of independence movements in Africa. Today, his internationalist legacy remains in the African Union, the successor to the OAU. It is reinforced in rituals profound and mundane—in the weekly prayers at the Brooklyn church and the daily commute down the Port-au-Prince street that both bear Haile Selassie's name.[12]

Veering left and then right down the latter, we entered a roundabout that, after exiting, took us onto Avenue Martin Luther King. Despite the ongoing attempts to nationalize and sanitize his image, there is no question that King was committed to Pan-Africanism. He celebrated Ghanaian independence alongside Prime Minister Kwame Nkrumah and preached to black Alabamians that "Ghana has something to say to us . . . that the oppressor never voluntarily gives freedom to the oppressed. You have to work for it."[13] In fact, he met with anti-colonial leaders in Northern Rhodesia, condemned apartheid South Africa, called for sanctions against Portugal for its colonial abuses in Africa, and attended the inauguration of Nnamdi Azikiwe, Nigeria's first president.[14] That commitment to African liberation, muted in posthumous celebrations of his life and work, did not escape the attention of his contemporaries. In July 1969, five years after losing the Nobel Peace Prize, Haile Selassie traveled to Atlanta. There he laid a wreath at the grave of the man who had won that prize, the civil rights activist, Pan-Africanist, and black internationalist martyred at Memphis's Lorraine Motel one year earlier.

If King demonstrated an underappreciated commitment to black internationalism, his life and the public memorialization of it also revealed the challenges to that intellectual and political project. Like too many leaders of the mainstream civil rights movement, King was silent on Haiti, hesitant to say much of anything about a black republic that had fallen into the hands of Duvalier and his paramilitary force, the Tonton Macoutes.[15] While he weighed the potential costs of defending the democratic rights of Haitians by criticizing the misgovernment of an independent black state, Duvalier manipulated black internationalism to suit his dictatorial ends.

The landscape of Port-au-Prince is a testament to Duvalier's appropriation of black internationalism. Duvalier reinforced his brand of *noirisme*, a political and cultural ideology rooted in black pride, by naming streets after Lumumba, Selassie, and King. In fact, he hosted Selassie on an official state visit and published a posthumous tribute to King after giving his condolences to the widowed Coretta Scott, sending a message to the AME annual conference eulogizing King, proclaiming a national period of mourning on King's behalf, and holding funeral services in his memory. Of course, the tribute to the "Illustrious Negro Leader . . . cut down . . . by the murderous bullets of racism" made no mention of those Haitians cut down by the bullets of the Tonton Macoutes. That was the point of a work that reenvisioned Duvalier as the heir to the "Martyred Leader of Non-Violence" rather than the perpetrator of mass murder.[16]

The silence and cynicism of the Cold War era, of the time when the U.S. black ambassador to Haiti lobbied so successfully for Duvalier that Haitians called him an "honorary" Macoute, soon gave way to dialogue and hope in the present.[17] After a few more minutes of travel on Avenue Martin Luther King, we turned left onto Avenue Jean Paul II and then into the parking lot of the Marriott Port-au-Prince. Over the next few days, the main CSA conference venue hosted local conference organizers and hotel staff, vendors selling everything from books to clothing to artwork, and hundreds of conference participants from seemingly every corner of the African Diaspora. There were also several volunteers—Haitian students from local universities who provided much of the labor that helped make the massive event run.

Over the course of the conference, I spent the scarce downtime between sessions talking to these volunteers. Those conversations, taking place at the linguistic intersections of my subpar Kreyòl and French and their superior English, were often more meaningful than the exceptional panels. My main confidants were a group of friends that included Samuel, a brilliant student studying classical music who told me about his love for African American jazz and Malcolm X, the organic black intellectual and black internationalist whom Duvalier once accused of lacking the "solid academic background" that he and King possessed.[18]

Those parts of our conversations were fun. Easy, perhaps. Words were much harder to find after Samuel and his friends asked, "What is happening with the police and black people in America?" Searching for an answer in Kreyòl or French or English or any language for that matter, I came up empty. There were already too many hashtags, too many names on a list that included Philando Castile, Alton Sterling, and Keith Lamont Scott by the end of that summer. I would continue to march and rally, write and teach on their behalf, but I was tired. My new Haitian friends understood, probably before I shared those feelings. After all, they were tired too and understandably so. The cry of Black Lives Matter first sounded at Bwa Kayiman, in the Vodou ceremony that began the Haitian Revolution. Now its denial—the routine assumption that black lives are literally expendable—is evident in the U.S. government's termination of Temporary Protected Status (TPS) for Haitians *and* in the state-sponsored violence inflicted on African Americans. It is clarified by a U.S. presidential administration that calls Haiti a "shithole" in the same breath that it slanders majority-black congressional districts as being "in horrible shape."[19]

Before Donald Trump wondered "Why do we need more Haitians?" and asked black voters "What do you have to lose?" Angela Davis brought these commonalities and differences—the shared causes emerging from dissimilar positions within the African Diaspora—together like no one else could.[20] At the conference keynote talk, which began with Samuel's powerful rendition of *La Dessalinienne*—Haiti's national anthem named after its first head of state—Davis, the former Black Panther, intellectual, and professor emeritus at the University of California, Santa Cruz, gave the talk "Revolutions and Representation." It connected the black freedom struggle in the United States to the ongoing fight for Haitian liberation, tracing both back to their roots in the Haitian Revolution and the historical fight against slavery, colonialism, and global capitalism. Its most striking moment was a simple albeit uncompromising demand: "Return the $21 billion!"

Most obviously, the figure that Davis named represents the current value of the money that the French extorted from Haiti in return for diplomatic recognition following the Haitian Revolution. But more important, the call for reparations coheres with the ideas of justice that continue to animate black intellectuals ranging from the famous writer Ta-Nehisi Coates to the anonymous vendor on the streets of Haiti. Just as the former argues that reparations are needed to address the wrongs of slavery and the anti-black policies that persist in a supposedly post-racial United States, the latter insists that "Haitians know that a big reason why we are suffering today is because we were forced to pay France for our freedom."[21] Both possess a radical vision of black liberation rooted in economic justice, unmoored from rigid notions of time and place. Together, their dream is of a world unshackled from the same racial oppressions that made it.

The same night that Davis spoke, I ate the final dinner of my trip at a local restaurant in Port-au-Prince. Between sips of cold Prestige and bites of warm griot, I talked with my friend and soon-to-be former roommate about everything from sports to politics to history. We shared our unique histories and our shared understandings of Haiti, a country that had captured the imaginations of a Brit by way of Egypt and an African American from the U.S. South. All the while, Nicki Minaj, Drake, and Lil' Wayne blared out of a speaker hidden from view. It felt like home.

I flew back to Nashville the next day. After reversing the previous journey through the black internationalist streets of Port-au-Prince and making it through security at Toussaint Louverture International Airport, I took a seat at the far end of one of the rows of stiff blue seats that lined the back of the gate. I looked up—and watched. There again, in numbers roughly equal to those of the CSA conference attendees returning to the United States as well as the Haitians and Haitian-Americans leaving Port-au-Prince, were groups of missionaries. Lots and lots of missionaries. All of them were white evangelicals and most of them were southern. Their T-shirts still promised to "Re-Build Haiti," but into what still remained ambiguous.

I know that their ideas stand at odds with Du Bois's, though. During his trip to Haiti two decades after the end of the occupation, Du Bois visited the Citadelle, the great mountaintop fortress that King Henri I built to defend Haiti from what seemed like the inevitable French invasion to reclaim—or perhaps "rebuild"—their former colony.[22] Du Bois sat, reflected and wrote. While observing the shortcomings of the Magloire administration and foreshadowing the conditions that led to the Duvalier regime, Du Bois wrote that while "sitting at Cap-Haïtien this March 10, 1955, looking at Christophe's citadel rising stern on yonder mountain peak . . . I think of what this beautiful island may mean to its people and to the world." To him, a rebuilt Haiti was a Haiti free from "the complete economic and ideological control of the United States." It was a Haiti that, once truly free from the grip of "American Big Business, would recapture the spirit of the "Maroons led by Toussaint," restore the example of

"Haitian peasant agriculture," and prove that socialism or "united social action" was the key to black "political independence and economic survival" in the modern world. It was the Haiti of the Haitian Revolution, a land that had far more to teach than learn.[23]

For Du Bois, there was no better place to capture the impact of Haiti's past fight against slavery and colonialism or to envision the means of future victory in the ongoing struggle against their legacies than at the Citadelle, the largest fortress in the Western Hemisphere. Lucky for us, those who stand however unsteadily on Du Bois's shoulders, it still stands. Proud. Jutting up through the clouds, it towers over the immense valleys of the Plain du Nord, reminding thousands of visitors each year of the possibilities of black liberation even in a world hell-bent on denying black humanity. Without question, it remains as Du Bois once saw it: an impregnable monument—an enduring testament—to the significance of Haiti, the Black Republic that has provided inspiration to the black thinkers and their ideas that might one day rebuild our world.

NOTES

Prologue

1. Jean Bradley Anderson, *Durham County: A History of Durham County, North Carolina* (Durham, NC: Duke University Press, 1990), 155.

2. Booker T. Washington, "Durham, North Carolina: A City of Negro Enterprises," *Independent* 70 (1911): 642–670; W. E. B. Du Bois, "The Upbuilding of Black Durham: The Success of the Negroes and Their Value to a Tolerant and Helpful Southern City," *World's Work* 23 (January 1912): 334–338; E. Franklin Frazier, "Durham: Capital of the Black Middle Class," in Alain Locke, ed., *The New Negro: Voices of the Harlem Renaissance* (Simon & Schuster, 1992), 333–340.

3. Leslie Brown, *Upbuilding Black Durham: Gender, Class, and Black Community Development in the Jim Crow South* (Chapel Hill: University of North Carolina Press, 2008).

4. Christina Greene, *Women and the Black Freedom Movement in Durham, North Carolina* (Chapel Hill: University of North Carolina Press, 2005).

5. The Southern Oral History Program (https://sohp.org) at the University of North Carolina at Chapel Hill's Center for the Study of the American South has a number of interviews with Hayti residents who testify to the impact of urban renewal.

6. Matthew J. Cressler provides an excellent analysis of black Catholic identity in *Authentically Black and Truly Catholic: The Rise of Black Catholicism in the Great Migration* (New York: New York University Press, 2017).

7. William J. Kennedy, *The North Carolina Mutual Story: A Symbol of Progress, 1898–1970* (Durham: North Carolina Mutual Life Insurance Co., 1970); and Walter B. Weare, *Black Business in the New South: A Social History of the North Carolina Mutual Insurance Company* (Durham, NC: Duke University Press, 1993).

8. Anderson, *Durham County*, 372–374, 429–430, 432–434.

9. "F. D. Entertains Goodwill Body," *Baltimore Afro-American*, April 13, 1937.

10. C. C. Spaulding, "My Trip to the Republic of Haiti," *Atlanta Daily World*, May 18, 1937. For context on Spaulding and the business of black internationalism in postoccupation Haiti, see Millery Polyné, *From Douglass to Duvalier: U.S. African Americans, Haiti, and Pan Americanism, 1870–1964* (Gainesville: University Press of Florida, 2010), 89–130.

Introduction

1. George Washington to Jean Baptiste de Ternant, September 24, 1791, quoted in Dorothy Twohig, "'That Species of Property': Washington's Role in the Controversy over Slavery," in Don Higginbotham, ed., *George Washington Reconsidered* (Charlottesville: University of

Virginia Press, 2001), 114–140. See also Timothy M. Matthewson, "George Washington's Policy Toward the Haitian Revolution," *Diplomatic History* 3, no. 3 (July 1979): 321–336.

2. The idea of the Haitian Revolution as an unthinkable event comes from Michel-Rolph Trouillot, *Silencing the Past: Power and the Production of History* (Boston: Beacon Press, 1995), 70–107.

3. On the Haitian Revolution, see especially C. L. R. James, *The Black Jacobins: Toussaint L'Ouverture and the San Domingo Revolution* (New York: Vintage Books, 1989); David Patrick Geggus, *Haitian Revolutionary Studies* (Bloomington: Indiana University Press, 2002); and Laurent Dubois, *Avengers of the New World: The Story of the Haitian Revolution* (Cambridge, MA: Harvard University Press, 2005). The best treatment of representations of the Haitian Revolution is Marlene Daut, *Tropics of Haiti: Race and the Literary History of the Haitian Revolution in the Atlantic World, 1789–1865* (Liverpool, UK: Liverpool University Press, 2015).

4. On early U.S. responses to the Haitian Revolution, see especially Rayford Logan, *The Diplomatic Relations of the United States with Haiti, 1776–1891* (Chapel Hill: University of North Carolina Press, 1941); Alfred Hunt, *Haiti's Influence on Antebellum America: Slumbering Volcano in the Caribbean* (Baton Rouge: Louisiana State University Press, 1988); Brenda Gayle Plummer, *Haiti and the United States: The Psychological Moment* (Athens: University of Georgia Press, 1992), 34–50; Matthew J. Clavin, *Toussaint Louverture and the American Civil War: The Promise and Peril of a Second Haitian Revolution* (Philadelphia: University of Pennsylvania Press, 2010); and Ronald Johnson, *Diplomacy in Black and White: John Adams, Toussaint Louverture, and Their Atlantic World Alliance* (Athens: University of Georgia Press, 2014).

5. *Speech of Mr. Benton, of Missouri, to the Senate of the United States, (In Secret Session), on the Mission to Panama, March 13, 1826* (Washington: Columbian Star Office, 1826), 34–35.

6. Matthew Karp, *The Vast Southern Empire: Slaveholders at the Helm of American Foreign Policy* (Cambridge, MA: Harvard University Press, 2016).

7. Ashli White, *Encountering Revolution: Haiti and the Making of the Early Republic* (Baltimore: Johns Hopkins University Press, 2010).

8. The various networks of information that supplied African Americans with information about the Haitian Revolution are highlighted in Julius S. Scott, *The Common Wind: Afro-American Currents in the Age of the Haitian Revolution* (New York: Verso, 2018) and Scott, "Afro-American Sailors and the International Communication Network: The Case of Newport Bowers," in Colin Howell and Richard J. Twomey, eds., *Jack Tar in History: Essays in the History of Maritime Life and Labour* (Fredericton, NB: Acadiensis Press, 1991), 37–52.

9. Booker T. Washington, *Frederick Douglass* (Philadelphia: G. W. Jacobs & Company, 1907), 144.

10. Michael O. West and William G. Martin, "Haiti, I'm Sorry: The Haitian Revolution and the Forging of the Black International," in Michael O. West, William G. Martin, and Fanon Che Wilkins, eds., *From Toussaint to Tupac: The Black International since the Age of Revolution* (Chapel Hill: University of North Carolina Press, 2009), 72–106; Charlton W. Yingling, "No One Who Reads the History of Hayti Can Doubt the Capacity of Colored Men: Racial Formation and Atlantic Rehabilitation in New York City's Early Black Press, 1827–1841," *Early American Studies* 11 (Spring 2013): 314–348.

11. Maurice Jackson and Jacqueline Bacon, eds., *African Americans and the Haitian Revolution: Selected Essays and Historical Documents* (New York: Routledge, 2009).

12. Sara Fanning, "The Roots of Early Black Nationalism: Northern African Americans' Invocations of Haiti in the Early Nineteenth Century," *Slavery & Abolition* 28, no. 1 (April 2007): 61–85; and Leslie M. Alexander, "'The Black Republic': The Influence of the Haitian Revolution on Northern Black Political Consciousness, 1816–1862," in Jackson and Bacon, *African Americans and the Haitian Revolution*, 57–80.

13. Floyd J. Miller, *The Search for a Black Nationality: Black Emigration and Colonization, 1787–1863* (Urbana: University of Illinois Press, 1975); Chris Dixon, *African America and Haiti: Emigration and Black Nationalism in the Nineteenth-Century* (Westport, CT: Greenwood Press, 2000; Sara Fanning, *Caribbean Crossing: African Americans and the Haitian Emigration Movement* (New York: New York University Press, 2015); and Claire Bourhis-Mariotti, *L'Union fait la force: Les Noirs américains et Haïti, 1804–1893* (Rennes: Presses Universitaires de Rennes, 2016).

14. "Hayti, No. II," *Genius of Universal Emancipation*, June 24, 1826.

15. Laurie Maffly-Kipp, *Setting Down the Sacred Past: African-American Race Histories* (Cambridge, MA: Belknap Press of Harvard University Press, 2010), 109–153.

16. Stephen G. Hall, "Envisioning an Antislavery War: African American Historical Constructions of the Haitian Revolution in the 1850s," in Dawne Y. Curry, Eric D. Duke, and Marshanda A. Smith, eds., *Extending the Diaspora: New Histories of Black People* (Urbana: University of Illinois Press, 2009), 77–99.

17. Charles B. Dew, *Apostles of Disunion: Southern Secession Commissioners and the Causes of the Civil War* (Charlottesville: University Press of Virginia, 2001).

18. "Will the Contrabands Fight," *Washington National Republican*, in *Weekly Anglo-African*, February 15, 1862.

19. Clavin, *Toussaint Louverture*.

20. Clavin, *Toussaint Louverture*; White, *Encountering Revolution*; Hunt, *Haiti's Influence*; James Alexander Dun, *Dangerous Neighbors: Making the Haitian Revolution in Early America* (Philadelphia: University of Pennsylvania Press, 2016).

21. My definition of "black internationalism" draws especially from Robin D. G. Kelley, "'But a Local Phase of a World Problem': Black History's Global Vision, 1883–1950," *Journal of American History* 86 (1999): 1045–1077; Tiffany Ruby Patterson and Robin D. G. Kelley, "Unfinished Migrations: Reflections on the African Diaspora and the Making of the Modern World," *African Studies Review* 43, no. 1 (2000): 11–45; Brent Hayes Edwards, *The Practice of Diaspora: Literature, Translation, and the Rise of Black Internationalism* (Cambridge, MA: Harvard University Press, 2003); West, Martin, and Wilkins, *From Toussaint to Tupac*; and Minkah Makalani, *In the Cause of Freedom: Radical Black Internationalism from Harlem to London, 1917–1939* (Chapel Hill: University of North Carolina Press, 2011).

22. Michael O. West and William G. Martin, "Contours of the Black International," in West, Martin, and Wilkins, *From Toussaint to Tupac*, 1–44.

23. My definition of "black self-determination" and "black self-government" draws primarily from how black intellectuals and activists of the era used those interchangeable terms. It is also shaped by foundational scholarship on the struggle for black self-determination in my period and beyond. Those works include V. P. Franklin, *Black Self-Determination: A Cultural History of African-American Resistance*, 2nd ed. (New York: Lawrence Hill Books, 1992); and Steven Hahn, *A Nation Under Our Feet: Black Political Struggles in the Rural South from Slavery to the Great Migration* (Cambridge, MA: Harvard University Press, 2003).

24. Frederick Douglass, "Lecture on Haiti," January 2, 1893 in the Frederick Douglass Papers, Manuscript Division, Library of Congress (hereafter cited as FDP, LOC).

25. Frederick Douglass, "A Trip to Hayti," *Douglass' Monthly*, May 1861.

26. Francis J. Bremer, *John Winthrop: America's Forgotten Founding Father* (New York: Oxford University Press, 2003).

27. The lie that black political participation during Reconstruction introduced a terrible period of ignorant "Negro rule" to the South was meant to undermine Reconstruction. It then became a central tenet of the historiography of Reconstruction. See Eric Foner, *Reconstruction: America's Unfinished Revolution, 1863–1877* (New York: Harper & Row, 1988); David Levering Lewis, introduction to W. E. B. Du Bois, *Black Reconstruction in America, 1860–1880* (New York: Free Press, 1998); and John David Smith and J. Vincent Lowery, eds., *The Dunning School: Historians, Race, and the Meaning of Reconstruction* (Lexington: University Press of Kentucky, 2013).

28. On testimonies of racial violence in the post-Reconstruction era, see Kidada E. Williams, *They Left Great Marks on Me: African American Testimonies of Racial Violence from Emancipation to World War I* (New York: New York University Press, 2012), 55–100.

29. For the best treatment of race, manhood, and imperialism in black discourse, see Michele Mitchell, *Righteous Propagation: African Americans and the Politics of Racial Destiny after Reconstruction* (Chapel Hill: University of North Carolina Press, 2004), 51–75.

30. Kevin K. Gaines, "Black Americans' Racial Uplift Ideology as 'Civilizing Mission': Pauline E. Hopkins on Race and Imperialism," in Amy Kaplan and Donald E. Pease, eds., *Cultures of United States Imperialism* (Durham, NC: Duke University Press, 1993), 433–455; and Gaines, *Uplifting the Race: Black Leadership, Politics, and Culture During the Twentieth Century* (Chapel Hill: University of North Carolina Press, 2006).

31. Raphael Dalleo has recently demonstrated the impact of the occupation on Caribbean political thought in *American Imperialism's Undead: The Occupation of Haiti and the Rise of Caribbean Anticolonialism* (Charlottesville: University of Virginia Press, 2016).

32. Millery Polyné, "To Make Visible the Invisible Epistemological Order: Haiti, Singularity, and Newness," in Polyné, ed., *The Idea of Haiti: Rethinking Crisis and Development* (Minneapolis: University of Minnesota Press, 2013), xiii. In addition to Polyné, my emphasis on the multiple ideas of Haiti draws inspiration from Gina Athena Ulysse, *Why Haiti Needs New Narratives: A Post-Quake Chronicle* (Middletown, CT: Wesleyan University Press, 2015).

33. Polyné, "To Make Visible," xiii.

34. Michel-Rolph Trouillot, "The Odd and the Ordinary: Haiti, the Caribbean and the World," *Cimarrón: New Perspectives on the Caribbean* 2, no. 3 (Winter 1990): 6.

Chapter 1

1. David Williams, *I Freed Myself: African American Self-Emancipation in the Civil War Era* (New York: Cambridge University Press, 2014).

2. "The Government and the Negroes," *New York Herald*, January 6, 1863.

3. Kemp Plummer Battle, *History of the University of North Carolina from Its Beginning to the Death of President Swain, 1789–1868*, vol. 1 (Raleigh, NC: Edwards & Broughton Printing Co., 1907), 103.

4. Letter from George Nelson Williams, *Christian Recorder*, May 30, 1863. Williams also wrote that the "idol" of his company was a "black boy from Hayti." It is unclear whether he meant the country or the community outside of New Bern. A map of New Bern from 1867

still identifies the black settlement just outside of the town limits as "Hayti." "U.S. Coast Survey, Benjamin Pierce, Superintendent. Part of New Berne, North Carolina," (1867), map collection, North Carolina State Archives, cited in Joe A. Mobley, *James City, A Black Community in North Carolina 1863–1900* (Raleigh: North Carolina Office of Archives and History, 1981), 44.

5. Gerald Horne finds similar evidence of this trend in Horne, *Confronting Black Jacobins: The United States, the Haitian Revolution, and the Origins of the Dominican Republic* (New York: Monthly Review Press, 2015).

6. *Iowa State Register*, March 18, 1863, quoted in Caroline Eliot Kasson, "An Iowa Woman in Washington, D.C., 1861–1865," *Iowa Journal of History* 52 (January 1954): 77. The congressman who hosted the dinner party was probably Samuel Hooper.

7. Kasson, "*An Iowa Woman*," 77–78.

8. See Stephen M. Kantrowitz, *More Than Freedom: Fighting for Black Citizenship in a White Republic, 1829–1889* (New York: Penguin Press, 2012).

9. Jacques Nicolas Léger, *Haiti, Her History and Her Detractors* (New York: Neale, 1907), 204–205.

10. "The Minister from Hayti," *Times-Picayune*, April 10, 1863.

11. *Evening Star*, March 18, 1863; and "The Minister of Hayti and the African Upper Ten," *Times-Picayune*, March 31, 1863.

12. "The Colored Diplomatists," *Detroit Free Press*, March 25, 1863.

13. Henry McNeal Turner, "Washington Correspondence," *Christian Recorder*, March 28, 1863.

14. "Colored Diplomatists."

15. Turner, "Washington Correspondence."

16. "The Minister from Hayti," *Daily Southern Crisis* (Jackson, MS), March 28, 1863.

17. "Colored Diplomatists."

18. On African Americans' ideas about and recollections of Abraham Lincoln, see Leon F. Litwack, *Been in the Storm So Long: The Aftermath of Slavery* (New York: Vintage Books, 1980), 167–220; and John E. Washington, *They Knew Lincoln*, ed. Kate Masur (New York: Oxford University Press, [1942] 2018).

19. Turner, "Washington Correspondence."

20. "The Haytien Minister," *Christian Recorder*, March 28, 1863.

21. "Haytien Minister"; and Turner, "Washington Correspondence."

22. On the Fifteenth Street Presbyterian's place in black Washington, D.C., see especially Jacqueline M. Moore: *Leading the Race: The Transformation of the Black Elite in the Nation's Capital, 1880–1920* (Charlottesville: University Press of Virginia, 1999); Willard B. Gatewood, *Aristocrats of Color: The Black Elite, 1880–1920* (Fayetteville: University of Arkansas Press, 2000); and Audrey Elisa Kerr, *The Paper Bag Principle: Class, Colorism, and Rumor and the Case of Black Washington, D.C.* (Knoxville: University of Tennessee Press, 2006). The best work on wartime Washington is Kate Masur, *An Example for All the Land: Emancipation and the Struggle over Equality in Washington, D.C.* (Chapel Hill: University of North Carolina Press, 2010).

23. "The Emancipation Jubilee Last Night," *Evening Star*, April 17, 1863.

24. *Douglass' Monthly*, March 1863.

25. Patrick Rael, *Black Identity and Black Progress in the Antebellum North* (Chapel Hill: University of North Carolina Press, 2002), 209–237. On nineteenth-century black rhetoric, see

Nan Johnson, *Nineteenth-Century Rhetoric in North America* (Carbondale: Southern Illinois University Press, 1991); and Shirley Wilson Logan, *Liberating Language: Sites of Rhetorical Education in Nineteenth-Century Black America* (Carbondale: Southern Illinois University Press, 2008).

26. Jeffrey R. Kerr-Ritchie, *Rites of August: Emancipation Day in the Black Atlantic World* (Baton Rouge: Louisiana State University Press, 2007), 82–117.

27. "Annual Excursion and Picnic to Forest Bay Grove, August 3rd," *Chicago Tribune*, August 3, 1863; "The Emancipation Celebration," *Chicago Tribune*, August 4, 1863. On African American emancipation celebrations, see Mitch Kachun, *Festivals of Freedom: Memory and Meaning in African American Emancipation Celebrations, 1808–1915* (Amherst: University of Massachusetts Press, 2003).

28. W. J. Davis, "Bloomington Correspondence," *Christian Recorder*, March 21, 1863.

29. King James Version, 2018; Roy Kay, *The Ethiopian Prophecy in Black American Letters* (Gainesville: University of Florida Press, 2011).

30. Wilson Jeremiah Moses, *The Wings of Ethiopia: Studies in African American Life and Letters* (Ames: Iowa State University Press, 1990), 141–158; and Patrick Rael, "Black Theodicy: African Americans and Nationalism in the Antebellum North," *The North Star: A Journal of African American Religious History* 3, no. 2 (Spring 2000).

31. "The War for Freedom," *Douglass' Monthly*, February, 1863.

32. William Wells Brown, *The Black Man: His Antecedents, His Genius, and His Achievements* (New York: Thomas Hamilton, 1863), 5–6. In the words of Stephen G. Hall, Brown attempted to "normalize African Americans as fit subjects for emancipation." See Stephen G. Hall, *A Faithful Account of the Race: African American Historical Writing in Nineteenth-Century America* (Chapel Hill: University of North Carolina Press, 2009), 125–129. Scholarship on Brown includes William L. Andrews, ed., *From Fugitive Slave to Free Man: The Autobiographies of William Wells Brown*, 2nd ed. (Columbia: University of Missouri Press, 2003); and William Edward Farrison, *William Wells Brown: Author and Reformer* (Chicago: University of Chicago Press, 1969).

33. Brown, *Black Man*, 99, 105.

34. Brown, *Black Man*, 111, 116–117.

35. John R. McKivigan, *Forgotten Firebrand: James Redpath and the Making of Nineteenth-Century America* (Ithaca, NY: Cornell University Press, 2008).

36. "Books for Our Times," *Christian Recorder*, January 2, 1864; and "The Black Man, His Antecedents, His Genius, and His Achievements," *Douglass' Monthly*, January 1863. In 1865, James Meriles Simms, a former slave and Union soldier, published an edition of *The Black Man* in Charleston, South Carolina.

37. "Books for Our Times"; "Prize," *Christian Recorder*, January 30, 1864. The unnamed biography advertised was probably John Relly Beard's *The Life of Toussaint L'Ouverture: The Negro Patriot of Hayti*, a book that James Redpath published in 1863.

38. "Get Subscribers," *Christian Recorder*, January 16, 1864.

39. "Rev. Page Tyler, on the Mississippi, Takes the Premium," *Christian Recorder*, April 16, 1864.

40. Daniel R. Biddle, *Tasting Freedom: Octavius Catto and the Battle for Equality in Civil War America* (Philadelphia: Temple University Press, 2010), 101, 185, 201–202.

41. Daniel P. Adger, "Letter from Australia," *Christian Recorder*, May 7, 1864.

42. Adger, "Letter from Australia."

43. *Daily Miners' Register* (Colorado), October 21, 1864; Rover, "Letter from Denver City, Col.," *Christian Recorder*, December 10, 1864.

44. Mary Katherine Gastner, "Valuing 'Others': Free African American Neighborhoods in Antebellum Alexandria" (M.A. thesis, University of Maryland, 2011). On the history of this remarkable lecturer, see Brandon R. Byrd, "'We Are Negroes!' The Haitian Zambo, Racial Spectacle, and the Performance of Black Women's Internationalism, 1863–1877," in Keisha N. Blain and Tiffany M. Gill, eds., *To Turn the Whole World Over: Black Women's Internationalism in Historical Perspective* (Urbana: University of Illinois Press, 2019): 15–37.

45. J. H. H., "Alexandria Correspondent," *Christian Recorder*, April 25, 1863.

46. "Colored Convention in North Carolina," *Christian Recorder*, October 28, 1865.

47. *Proceedings of the State Equal Rights Convention of the Colored People of Pennsylvania* (Philadelphia: Printed for and by the order of the Convention, 1865), 22, in From Slavery to Freedom: The African American Pamphlet Collection, 1822–1909, Rare Book and Special Collections Division, Library of Congress, https://www.loc.gov/item/92838830/.; "Colored State Convention," *Christian Recorder*, November 25, 1865.

48. Andrew Johnson, "Third Annual Message," December 3, 1867, published online by Gerhard Peters and John T. Woolley, the American Presidency Project, https://www.presidency.ucsb.edu/documents/third-annual-message-10.

49. "The Warning from Account," *Charleston Courier*, September 3, 1868.

50. See Clavin, *Toussaint Louverture*.

51. "Serious Troubles in Hayti—The Negro a Disturbing Element Everywhere," *New York Herald*, January 27, 1868.

52. On the foundations of racial science in America, see George Frederickson, *The Black Image in the White Mind: The Debate on Afro-American Character and Destiny, 1817–1914* (New York: Harper & Row, 1971), 71–96, 228–255. In his *Mismeasure of Man* (2nd ed., New York: W. W. Norton, 1996), Stephen Jay Gould identified flaws in the cranial measurements used by Samuel George Morton and other leaders of the American school of ethnology to evaluate racial difference. More recently, the anthropologist C. Loring Brace has argued that Morton's findings are objectionable but his methodologies sound. See Brace, *"Race" Is a Four-Letter Word: The Genesis of the Concept* (New York: Oxford University Press, 2005).

53. In her sweeping history of whiteness, Nell Irvin Painter notes that "the American school of anthropology faded after the publication of its masterworks in the 1850s. . . . But its racist notions served the needs of American culture too well to disappear entirely." Painter, *The History of White People* (New York: W. W. Norton, 2010), 200.

54. John H. Van Evrie, *White Supremacy and Negro Subordination; or, Negroes a Subordinate Race and (So-Called) Slavery Its Normal Condition* (New York: Van Evrie, Horton, 1868), vi–vii.

55. "The African in the United States," *Southern Review*, vol. 15, no. 29 (January 1874): 137–138.

56. "The African in the United States," 147.

57. "The African in the United States," 157, 152.

58. Frederick Douglass wrote in his second autobiography that he read *The Natural History of Man*, a work by the English ethnologist James Cowles Prichard. Although the book suggested that humans shared a common origin, it influenced later writings from the American school of ethnology, including *Types of Mankind*, a book written by the pro-slavery physician Josiah Nott and the ethnologist George R. Gliddon. It is probable that Douglass also

read that work. Likewise, the abolitionist Charlotte Forten praised *English Traits*, a historical ethnography by Ralph Waldo Emerson, which extols the virtues of Anglo-Saxons in exasperating detail.

59. "The American Negro," *Christian Recorder*, November 21, 1868.

60. On antebellum romantic racialism, see especially Frederickson, *Black Image*, 97–129.

61. This is what Ibram X. Kendi calls "ethnic racism" in Kendi, *Stamped from the Beginning: The Definitive History of Racist Ideas* (New York: Nation Books, 2016).

62. "American Negro."

63. "American Negro."

64. On U.S. foreign policy toward Haiti during Reconstruction, see especially Horne, *Confronting Black Jacobins*; and Logan, *Diplomatic Relations*, 315–352.

65. Andrew Johnson, "Fourth Annual Message to Congress," December 9, 1868, published online by Gerhard Peters and John T. Woolley, American Presidency Project, https://www.presidency.ucsb.edu/documents/fourth-annual-message-9. For a succinct treatment on the relations between the United States and the Dominican Republic in the 1860s, see G. Pope Atkins and Larman C. Wilson, *The Dominican Republic and the United States: From Imperialism to Transnationalism* (Athens: University of Georgia Press, 1998); and Christopher Teal, *Hero of Hispaniola: America's First Black Diplomat, Ebenezer D. Bassett* (Westport, CT: Praeger, 2008), 65–76.

66. "The American Negro."

67. The extensive literature on Haitian politics and class conflict includes foundational works by David Nicholls, *From Dessalines to Duvalier: Race, Colour and National Independence in Haiti* (Cambridge: Cambridge University Press, 1979); Michel-Rolph Trouillot, *Haiti: State Against Nation: The Origins & Legacy of Duvalierism* (New York: Monthly Review Press, 1990); and Jean Casimir, *Haïti et ses elites: l'interminable dialogue de sourds* (Port-au-Prince: Éditions de l'Université d'État d'Haïti, 2009).

68. Laurent Dubois, *Haiti: The Aftershocks of History* (Metropolitan Books: Henry Holt and Company, 2012) provides an excellent synopsis of nineteenth-century Haitian economic and political life.

69. General statistics on the violence that occurred in the aftermath of slavery are difficult to obtain, but the Freedman's Bureau kept detailed accounting of the murders and "outrages" that African Americans reported to it during Reconstruction. Those are accessible to researchers at the Freedmen's Bureau Online (www.freedmensbureau.com).

70. Tanner receives able biographical treatment in William Seraile, *Fire in His Heart: Benjamin Tucker Tanner and the A.M.E. Church* (Knoxville: University of Tennessee Press, 1998).

71. *Proceedings of the National Convention of the Colored Men of America* (Washington, DC: Great Republic Book and Job Printing Establishment, 1869), 24.

72. *Christian Recorder*, January 30, 1869.

73. *Christian Recorder*, January 30, 1869.

74. *Christian Recorder*, January 30, 1869; *Genius of Universal Emancipation* 3, no. 4 (June 1824).

75. See Miller, *Search for a Black Nationality*; Dixon, *African America and Haiti*; Fanning, *Caribbean Crossing;* and Bourhis-Mariotti, *L'Union fait la force.*

76. "Hayti at Dominica," *Christian Recorder*, February 13, 1869.

77. "Hayti at Dominica."

78. David Blight, *Race and Reunion: The Civil War in American Memory* (Cambridge, MA: Belknap Press of Harvard University Press, 2001), 28. On the emergence of black expressions of U.S. nationalism during the Civil War and Reconstruction, see Eric Foner, *Reconstruction.*

79. Octavius V. Catto and J. O. White, *Our Alma Mater: Notes on an Address Delivered at Concert Hall on the Occasion of the Twelfth Annual Commencement of the Institute for Colored Youth, May 10th, 1864* (Philadelphia: C. Sherman, Son, 1864), in the Daniel Alexander Payne Murray Pamphlets Collection, Rare Book and Special Collections Division, Library of Congress, https://www.loc.gov/item/918981481.

80. See Teal, *Hero of Hispaniola* for biographical information on Bassett.

81. Teal, *Hero of Hispaniola*, 49.

82. Ebenezer Bassett to William Seward, in Letters of Application and Recommendation During the Administration of Andrew Johnson, National Archives Microfilm Publication M650.

83. John Mercer Langston, *From the Virginia Plantation to the National Capitol or the First and Only Negro Representative in Congress from the Old Dominion* (Hartford, CT: American Publishing Company, 1894), 276. In fact, Langston also rejected Johnson's offer to replace Oliver Otis Howard as the commissioner of the Freedmen's Bureau. It seems that Langston correctly assessed the intentions of Johnson who, knowing that many of the bureau's white employees harbored racist attitudes, sought to undermine it by placing a black man in a position of leadership.

84. Annette Gordon-Reed, *Andrew Johnson* (New York: Henry Holt, 2011), 2.

85. Republican Committee of Baltimore, Maryland to Ulysses S. Grant, May 1869, in Letters of Application and Recommendation During the Administration of Ulysses S. Grant, National Archives Microfilm Publication M968 (hereafter cited as Letters of Application).

86. "Washington," *New York Times*, April 13, 1869.

87. The National Executive Committee of Colored Men to Ulysses S. Grant, March 15, 1869 in Letters of Application.

88. Ebenezer Don Carlos Bassett to Ulysses S. Grant, March 17, 1869, in Letters of Application.

89. "City Items," *Christian Recorder*, May 1, 1869; Charles Spencer Smith, *A History of the African Methodist Episcopal Church* (Philadelphia: Book Concern of the AME Church, 1922), 87; "Public Reception of the Hon. Ebenezer D. Bassett, Minister and Consul General to Hayti, at Shiloh Church New York," *National Anti-Slavery Standard*, June 19, 1869. An account from the *New York Tribune* places the New York ceremonies at the Mother African Methodist Episcopal Zion Church. I have located it, as the *Standard* does, at Shiloh Presbyterian Church for two reasons. First, the *Standard*'s account is, by far, the most extensive even though it was published a month after the event. Second, Aaron M. Powell, editor of the *Standard*, was invited to the event by William P. Powell. It stands to reason that he would have known where it took place.

90. "Public Reception of the Hon. Ebenezer D. Bassett." A portion of Powell's remarks appear in "Our Consul-General to Hayti," *Tribune*, May 26, 1869. While the *Tribune*'s quotations match those of the *Standard*, the New York paper did mischaracterize Powell as "Powers." It also refers to Charles B. Ray, a prominent abolitionist in his own right, as "Wm. Wray."

91. "Public Reception of the Hon. Ebenezer D. Bassett."

92. "Public Reception of the Hon. Ebenezer D. Bassett." Here, the *Standard* and the *Tribune* are in complete accordance. A much shorter portion of Zuille's remarks also appears in "Colored Diplomacy," *Commercial Advertiser*, May 26, 1869.

93. "Public Reception of the Hon. Ebenezer D. Bassett." Again, the *Standard* and the *Tribune* are in complete accordance with the *Commercial Advertiser*.

94. "Public Reception of the Hon. Ebenezer D. Bassett"; "Our Consul-General to Hayti."

95. "Public Reception of the Hon. Ebenezer D. Bassett."

96. "The Island of San Domingo, or Hayti," *Daily Central City Register*, December 4, 1869.

97. "Interview of the New Minister to Hayti with the President," *National Republican*, June 2, 1869.

98. "Interview of the New Minister to Hayti with the President."

99. "Public Reception of the Hon. Ebenezer D. Bassett."

100. "Public Reception of the Hon. Ebenezer D. Bassett."

101. "Public Reception of the Hon. Ebenezer D. Bassett."

102. Dennis Hidalgo, "Charles Sumner and the Annexation of the Dominican Republic," *Itinerario* 21, no. 2 (July 1997): 58–59.

103. "Constitution Tinkering," *Mobile* Register, February 18, 1869; Eric T. L. Love examines how racism served as a limiting force as well as a motivation for U.S. imperial pursuits in his *Race over Empire: Racism and U.S. Imperialism, 1865–1900* (Chapel Hill: University of North Carolina Press, 2004).

104. Ebenezer Don Carlos Bassett to Frederick Douglass, July 3, 1869, in FDP, LOC.

105. W. H. H., "The Negro in a New Attitude," *Elevator*, July 16, 1869.

106. "Hayti and Its Beauties," *Crisis*, December 15, 1869.

107. "Frederick Douglass," *Chicago Tribune*, December 30, 1871, quoted in Millery Polyné, "Expansion Now!: Haiti, 'Santo Domingo,' and Frederick Douglass at the Intersection of U.S. and Caribbean Pan-Americanism," *Caribbean Studies* 34, no. 2 (July–December 2006): 5. On Douglass and Dominican annexation, also see Juliet Hooker, *Theorizing Race in the Americas: Douglass, Sarmiento, Du Bois, and Vasconcelos* (New York: Oxford University Press, 2017), 25–66.

108. Douglass, "Santo Domingo," in FDP, LOC.

109. "Gen. Grant: What He Says About a Third Term—The St. Domingo Question," *Chicago Tribune*, July 26, 1878.

110. "Sad State of Hayti," *Chicago Tribune*, June 15, 1873. On White's career, see Joseph Logsdon, *Horace White, Nineteenth Century Liberal* (Westport, CT: Greenwood Press, 1971).

111. Thomas S. Malcolm, "The Republic of Haiti," *Christian Recorder*, May 8, 1873.

112. Michael P. Young, *Bearing Witness Against Sin: The Evangelical Birth of the American Social Movement* (Chicago: University of Chicago Press, 2006).

113. Gaines expounds on these limitations of racial uplift during the Jim Crow era in *Uplifting the Race.*

114. Jewett Washington Allen, "The African Methodist Episcopal Church in the Island Republic of Haiti: A Study to Determine the Adaptability of the African Methodist Episcopal Church to the Needs of the Haitian People" (M.A. thesis, Oberlin College, 1951), 106–116.

115. David M. Dean, *Defender of the Race: James Theodore Holly, Black Nationalist Bishop* (Boston: Lambeth Press, 1979) and Brandon R. Byrd, "Fabre Geffrard, the Holly Family, and the Construction of a 'Civilized' Haiti," in Celucien L. Joseph and Nixon S. Cleophat, eds., *Vodou in Haitian Memory: The Idea and Representation of Vodou in Haitian Imagination* (Lanham, MD: Lexington Books, 2016), 1–20.

116. Smith, *History of the African Methodist Episcopal Church,* 444.

117. On the mixed success of the AME's missions to the freedmen and freedwomen of the South during and after the Civil War, see Clarence E. Walker, *A Rock in a Weary Land: The African Methodist Episcopal Church During the Civil War and Reconstruction* (Baton Rouge: Louisiana State University Press, 1982).

118. "Our Mission Work," *Christian Recorder*, February 13, 1869. On the wider rise of Protestant foreign missions, see William R. Hutchison, *Errand to the World: American Protestant Thought and Foreign Missions* (Chicago: University of Chicago Press, 1987).

119. "Our Missionary Work," *Christian Recorder*, May 11, 1872.

120. William Seraile, *Voice of Dissent: Theophilus Gould Steward (1843–1924) and Black America* (Brooklyn: Carlson Publishing, 1991), 49.

121. Theophilus Gould Steward, *Fifty Years in the Gospel Ministry* (Philadelphia: AME Book Concern, 1921), 378.

122. The rendering of this greeting in French says much about Steward's political project. It is far more likely that non-elite Haitians would have greeted him in Kreyòl, with *bonjou, mesye.*

123. Theophilus Gould Steward, "The Message of San Domingo for the African Race," in *Papers of the American Negro Academy*, vol. 18–19 (Washington, DC: American Negro Academy, 1916), 25–47.

124. Theophilus Gould Steward, *Journal of the Voyage to Port-au-Prince from New York,* June 14–16, 1873, in Theophilus Gould Steward Papers, Schomburg Center for Research in Black Culture, New York Public Library.

125. Steward, *Journal of the Voyage*, June 15, June 20–23, July 1–4, July 5–8, 1873.

126. On black intellectuals' perceptions of civilization and Africa, see especially Wilson J. Moses, *The Golden Age of Black Nationalism* (Hamden, CT: Archon Books, 1978).

127. Theophilus Gould Steward, "A Card from Rev. T. G. Steward," *Christian Recorder*, February 26, 1874.

128. Steward, *Fifty Years*, 149–150.

129. Bettye Collier-Thomas, *Jesus, Jobs, and Justice: African American Women and Religion* (New York: Alfred A. Knopf, 2010), 152–154. On the WPMMS, see also Brandon Byrd, "The Transnational Work of Moral Elevation: African American Women and the Reformation of Haiti, 1870–1950," *Palimpsest: A Journal on Women, Gender, and the Black International* 5, no. 2 (2016): 128–150.

130. "An Open Letter," *Christian Recorder*, May 14, 1874.

131. Mary A. Campbell, "An Address to the Auxiliary Mite Societies and the Women in General of the A.M.E. Church," *Christian Recorder*, June 29, 1876; Richard R. Wright, *Centennial Encyclopaedia of the African Methodist Episcopal Church* (Philadelphia: Book Concern of the AME Church, 1916), 59.

132. On the rise of AME's South African missions, see James T. Campbell, *Songs of Zion: The African Methodist Episcopal Church in the United States and South Africa* (Chapel Hill: University of North Carolina Press, 1998).

133. Collier-Thomas, *Jesus, Jobs, and Justice*, 188–190.

134. T. A. Cuff, "Temperance," *Christian Recorder*, November 12, 1874.

135. *Christian Recorder*, June 11, 1874; "Quit You Like Men," *Christian Recorder*, November 4, 1875.

136. Isabella Noel, "The Letter from Port-au-Prince Hayti," *Christian Recorder*, October 5, 1876.

137. Daniel Alexander Payne, *History of the African Methodist Episcopal Church* (Nashville, TN: Publishing House of the AME Sunday School Union, 1891), 479.

138. Charles W. Mossell, "Haiti," *Christian Recorder*, February 1, 1877.

139. Payne, *History of the African Methodist Episcopal Church*, 479.

140. *Christian Recorder*, August 16, 1877.

141. James Theodore Holly, Triennial Report for the Haitian Mission for the Years Ending August 1875–1877, Archives of the Episcopal Church, Record Group 68, Haiti Mission Records, 1855–1967 (hereafter cited as Haiti Mission Records).

142. Julien Alexandre, Annual Report, Church of the Good Shepherd Cabaret Quatre, May 12, 1869, in Haiti Mission Records.

143. *Christian Recorder*, August 16, 1877.

Chapter 2

1. Philip S. Foner, "Black Participation in the Centennial of 1876," *Phylon* 39, no. 4 (Winter 1978): 283–296.

2. *Liberator*, December 1, 1832.

3. Preamble to the Declaration of Independence.

4. John Hope Franklin, *George Washington Williams: A Biography* (Durham, NC: Duke University Press, 1998).

5. George Washington Williams, *Centennial, The American Negro, From 1776 to 1876. Oration Delivered July 4, 1876, at Avondale, Ohio, by Rev. Geo. W. Williams* (Cincinnati: Robert Clarke, 1876), 25 in The African American Experience in Ohio, 1850–1920, Ohio Historical Society Archives/Library Pamphlet Collection, http://www.ohiohistory.org/africanam. Here, Williams drew from his earlier lectures on Toussaint Louverture. See Franklin, *George Washington Williams*, 35, 38.

6. Williams, *Centennial*, 25.

7. Robert Randolph Robinson, *Robinson's Manual of the Constitution and Regulations of National Colored Protective Association, U.S.A.* (Jacksonville, FL: R. R. Robinson, 1917), 3.

8. *Commercial* (Cincinnati), August 19 and 22, 1876, quoted in Franklin, *George Washington Williams*, 39.

9. *Nation*, July 6, 1871, quoted in Nell Irvin Painter, *Standing at Armageddon: A Grassroots History of the Progressive Era* (New York: W. W. Norton, 2008), 3. On the end of Reconstruction, see also Eric Foner, *Reconstruction*, 564–601.

10. "The Mass Meeting at Black's Station," *Yorkville Enquirer*, October 12, 1876.

11. J. R. Ralls, *The Negro Problem: An Essay on the Industrial, Political and Moral Aspects of the Negro Race in the Southern States as Presented Under the Late Amendments to the Federal Constitution* (Atlanta: Jas. P. Harrison, 1877), 13, 15–16.

12. Ralls, *Negro Problem*, 12.

13. Ralls, *Negro Problem*, 78.

14. Ralls, *Negro Problem*, 74.

15. "Personals," *Christian Recorder*, December 21, 1876.

16. "General Mention," *Christian Recorder*, July 12, 1877.

17. The best work on Langston, by William Cheek and Aimee Lee Cheek, *John Mercer Langston and the Fight for Black Freedom, 1829–1865* (Urbana: University of Illinois Press, 1996), stops before Langston arrives in Port-au-Prince. Langston's diplomatic tenure in Haiti receives its fullest treatment in John Dirk Fulton, "John Mercer Langston, United States Minister to Haiti, 1877–1885" (M.A. thesis, University of Nebraska at Omaha, 1969).

18. Langston, *From the Virginia Plantation*, 355–356, 358.

19. "Washington Letter," *Weekly Louisianan*, November 3, 1877.

20. *Inter-Ocean*, October 24, 1877; Richard Theodore Greener, "'Our Honored Guest'—Read at the Banquet given by the Citizens of Washington, D.C., October 24, 1877, to Hon. John M. Langston," in John Mercer Langston Collection, Howard University, Moorland-Spingarn Research Center, Manuscript Division (hereafter cited as Langston Collection).

21. Greener, "'Our Honored Guest.'"

22. Langston, *From the Virginia Plantation*, 359–360.

23. Langston, *From the Virginia Plantation*, 371–372. Langston likely knew that part of Sumner's appeal to Haitians was due to the deceased senator's introduction of the bill calling for the diplomatic recognition of Haiti.

24. Langston, *From the Virginia Plantation*, 372.

25. Langston, *From the Virginia Plantation*, 400.

26. *Nashville Banner*, October, 1880, Langston Collection.

27. Langston, *From the Virginia Plantation*, 385. On the other hand, as some of Langston's contemporaries and the historian Rayford Logan noted, the practice of granting asylum to Haitians during periods of revolution could reflect a humanitarian desire "to protect Haitians from Haitian mobs rather than any wish to interfere in Haitian political affairs." Logan, *Diplomatic Relations*, 365.

28. Emphasis mine; "Washington Letter: Grand banquet to Hon. John Mercer Langston," *New York Globe*, October 7, 1882.

29. "The Black Republic," *Washington Post*, September 8, 1883; "Mr. Langston on Hayti," *Washington Post*, August 15, 1881.

30. "Minister Langston," *Chicago Tribune*, September 12, 1883; "A Rosy View of Hayti," *Baltimore Sun*, September 9, 1885.

31. Langston, *From the Virginia Plantation*, 400.

32. "Mr. Langston on Hayti," *Washington Post*, August 15, 1881.

33. Carnegie is quoted in T. J. Jackson Lears, *No Place of Grace: Antimodernism and the Transformation of American Culture, 1880–1920* (Chicago: University of Chicago Press, 1981), 8; "Mr. Langston on Hayti."

34. "Mr. Langston on Hayti."

35. Langston, *From the Virginia Plantation*, 358.

36. Henry Adams, *Senate Report 693*, II: 104, quoted in Nell Irvin Painter, *Exodusters: Black Migration to Kansas after Reconstruction* (New York: W. W. Norton, 1976), 84. On the Exodusters, also see Mitchell, *Righteous Propagation*, 16–50.

37. My definition of racial destiny draws primarily from Mitchell, *Righteous Propagation*, 7–9.

38. *Pine and Palm*, October 12, 1861.

39. Elise A. Guyette, *Discovering Black Vermont: African American Farmers in Hinesburgh, 1790–1890* (Burlington, VT: University of Vermont Press, 2010), 147–150.

40. Louden S. Langley, "Hayti," *Christian Recorder*, January 22, 1880.

41. Louden S. Langley, "Hayti," *Christian Recorder*, January 29, 1880.

42. The best treatment of sectional reconciliation, which began in 1865 and coalesced in the early twentieth century, is in Blight, *Race and Reunion*.

43. Langley, "Hayti," January 29, 1880.

44. Langley, "Hayti," January 22, 1880.

45. Langley, "Hayti," January 22, 1880.

46. Langley, "Hayti," January 29, 1880.

47. Langley, "Hayti," *Christian Recorder*, March 11, 1880.

48. Langley, "Hayti," January 22, 1880.

49. James Theodore Holly, "Emigration to Hayti," *Christian Recorder*, February 10, 1881.

50. Langston, *From the Virginia Plantation*, 400.

51. Guyette, *Discovering Black Vermont*, 151.

52. Mary Ella Mossell, "Father Forgive Them, For They Know Not What They Do," *Christian Recorder*, May 16, 1878.

53. David Michel, "Mary Ella Mossell," in Henry Louis Gates, Jr., and Evelyn Brooks Higginbotham, eds., *African American National Biography* (New York: Oxford University Press, 2008).

54. G. B. Reid, "Hayti—Our Church and School," *Christian Recorder*, March 31, 1881; and Carter Wright, "The Haytien Mission," *Christian Recorder*, October 27, 1881.

55. *Christian Recorder*, July 7, 1881; "Springfield Items," *Christian Recorder*, June 30, 188; and James Townsend, "Missionary Correspondence," *Christian Recorder*, July 14, 1881.

56. Mary Ella Mossell, "Domestic Life in Hayti," *A.M.E. Church Review* (1887): 393–398. On these prevailing notions of domesticity, civilization, and self-government, see Gail Bederman, *Manliness and Civilization: A Cultural History of Gender and Race in the United States, 1880–1917* (Chicago: University of Chicago Press, 1995), 25, 31–35.

57. "Arrival of Our Missionary," *Christian Recorder*, October 17, 1878; "Appointments of Rev. C. W. Mossell, Missionary from Hayti," *Christian Recorder*, December 12, 1878.

58. Charles W. Mossell, "Will We Succeed," *Christian Recorder*, March 10, 1881.

59. Benjamin F. Lee, "University News," *Christian Recorder*, March 10, 1881. "1883–1884 Educational Department: Wilberforce University," in Benjamin W. Arnett, ed., *The AME Budget* (Dayton, OH: Christian Publishing House Print, 1883), 103–104.

60. Charles W. Mossell, "Haytian Work," in Arnett, *The AME Budget*, 99, 103.

61. Mossell, "Haytian Work," 100–101.

62. Mossell, "Haytian Work."

63. Emily J. Cooper, "Communications," *Christian Recorder*, February 3, 1881.

64. Cooper, "Communications."

65. "Springfield Items," *Christian Recorder*, June 30, 1881.

66. On the history of the American Colonization Society, see especially P. J. Staudenraus, *The African Colonization Movement, 1816–1865* (New York: Columbia University Press, 1961); Eric Burin, *Slavery and the Peculiar Solution: A History of the American Colonization Society* (Gainesville: University Press of Florida, 2005); Beverly C. Tomek, *Colonization and Its Discontents: Emancipation, Emigration, and Antislavery in Antebellum Pennsylvania* (New York: New York University Press, 2011); and Beverly C. Tomek and Matthew J. Hetrick, eds., *New Directions in the Study of African American Recolonization* (Gainesville: University of Florida Press, 2017).

67. Charles Harris to William Coppinger, August 28, 1877, in the American Colonization Society Papers, quoted in Eric Foner, *Reconstruction*, 601.

68. Nathaniel Southgate Shaler, "The Negro Problem," *Atlantic Monthly* 54 (1884): 699, 707. On Shaler and emerging theories of black criminality in the late nineteenth-century, see Khalil Gibran Muhammad, *The Condemnation of Blackness: Race, Crime, and the Making of Modern Urban America* (Cambridge, MA: Harvard University Press, 2010), 15–20.

69. Shaler, "Negro Problem," 698.

70. Sir Spenser St. John, *Hayti; or, The Black Republic* (London: Smith, Elder, 1884), viii.

71. St. John, *Hayti*, 134. On the impact of St. John's work, see James Leyburn, *The Haitian People* (New Haven, CT: Yale University Press, 1966), 132, 334.

72. St. John, *Hayti*, 131–132.

73. M. W. H., "The Black Republic: A Terrible Arraignment of Haytien Life," *Atlanta Constitution*, November 24, 1884.

74. "Hayti: The Fairest and Richest Island in the World in the Hands of Vaudoux Savages," *Chicago Tribune*, December 13, 1884.

75. "The Negro in Hayti: A Study of His Life and Government by an Impartial Witness," *Atlanta Constitution*, February 2, 1885.

76. Herbert S. Fairall, *The World's Industrial and Cotton Centennial Exposition New Orleans, 1884–85* (Iowa City: Republican Publishing, 1885), 380. See also *Practical Common Sense Guide Book Through the World's Industrial and Cotton Centennial Exposition at New Orleans* (Harrisburg, PA: L. S. Hart, 1885), 44.

77. Fairall, *World's Industrial and Cotton Centennial Exposition.*

78. Lydia Maria Francis Child, *The Freedmen's Book* (Boston: Ticknor and Fields, 1866), 33–83.

79. 1880 United States Census, Washington, District of Columbia, National Archives and Records Administration (NARA) microfilm publication T9, 1,454 rolls, digital image, Ancestry.com, https://www.ancestry.com. Shimm was also a frequent contributor to newspapers, including the Washington, D.C.–based *National Republican*. Her published letters on topics ranging from proper infant care to politics appear under the pen name of "Faith Lichen."

80. Child, *Freedmen's Book*, 83.

81. "A Wonderful Sofa," *Cleveland Gazette*, January 10, 1885.

82. On public spheres and black counterpublic spheres, see Catherine Squires, "Rethinking the Black Public Sphere: An Alternative Vocabulary for Multiple Public Spheres," *Communication Theory* 12, no. 4 (November 2002): 446–468.

83. During the antebellum era, black activists had drawn parallels between their fight against slavery and Kossuth's role in the Hungarian struggle against Austrian rule. See Richard J. M. Blackett, *Building an Antislavery Wall: Black Americans in the Atlantic Abolitionist Movement, 1830–1860* (Baton Rouge: Louisiana State University Press, 1983), 10–11.

84. *Appeal*, July 4, 1885.

85. "The New Haytian Minister," *New York Freeman*, August 15, 1885, translated from *Le Moniteur*, July 4, 1885, in Langston Collection.

86. "New Haytian Minister."

87. Dean, *Defender of the Race*, 83; *London Guardian*, February 18, 1885.

88. Alonzo P. Holly, "Haytians Not Cannibals," *New York Freeman*, August 28, 1886.

89. T. Thomas Fortune, "Browbeating Hayti," *New York Freeman*, April 23, 1887. In 1884, the *New York Globe* changed its name to *New York Freeman*. In the fall of 1887, it again changed name, this time to the *New York Age*.

90. On the transnational, civilizationist dialogue that linked African Americans to Haitian elites, see Byrd, "Fabre Geffrard."

91. Mossell, "Domestic Life in Hayti," 400, 392.

92. Mosell, "Domestic Life in Hayti."

93. On the black press, see especially Armistead Scott Pride and Clint C. Wilson, *A History of the Black Press* (Washington, DC: Howard University Press, 1997); and Todd Vogel, *The Black Press: New Literary and Historical* Essays (New Brunswick, NJ: Rutgers University Press, 2001).

94. "Labor Demonstration," *New York Freeman*, March 20, 1886.

95. "An Awful Story: Man-Eaters Within Two Days Journey of Our Coast," *Atlanta Constitution*, December 10, 1886; and "Cannibalism in Hayti: Man-Eaters Within Two Days Journey of Our Coast," *Chicago Daily Tribune*, December 16, 1886.

96. "Cannibalism in Hayti," *Chicago Daily Tribune*, February 13, 1887.

97. "A Retrograding Population," *Baltimore Sun*, March 15, 1888.

98. Spenser St. John, *Hayti; or, The Black Republic* 2nd ed. (New York: Scribner & Welford, 1889).

99. Dubois, *Haiti*, 184–185; Logan, *Diplomatic Relations*, 397–400.

100. Logan, *Diplomatic Relations*, 398–399.

101. "President of Hayti," *Aberdeen Daily News*, August 31, 1888.

102. *Cleveland Gazette*, September 29, 1888.

103. On testimonies of racial violence in the post-Reconstruction era, see Kidada Williams, *They Left Great Marks on Me*, 55–100. I draw my understanding and use of epistemic violence from Gayatri Chakravorty Spivak, "Can the Subaltern Speak?," in Cary Nelson and Lawrence Grossberg, eds., *Marxism and the Interpretation of Culture* (London: MacMillan, 1988), 271–313.

104. Dubois, *Haiti*, 184–186; Logan, *Diplomatic Relations*, 398–400.

105. *Philadelphia Inquirer*, December 8, 1888; "The Republic of Hayti," *New York Times*, December 1, 1888.

106. "The Black Republic: Full Description of Hayti, Its People and Wars," *Chicago Tribune*, December 16, 1888.

107. *Columbus (Georgia) Enquirer-Sun*, December 8, 1888.

108. "Didn't Want a War with Hayti," *Washington Bee*, November 10, 1888. On African Americans and Harrison's campaign, see George Sinkler, "Benjamin Harrison and the Matter of Race," *Indiana Magazine of History* 65, no. 3 (September 1969): 197–213.

109. Logan, *Diplomatic Relations*, 400.

110. "Cleveland vs. Hayti," *Washington Bee*, December 15, 1888. The incident referred to by Chase occurred on March 17, 1886, and is covered in Rick Ward, "The Carroll County Courthouse Massacre, 1886: A Cold Case File," Mississippi History Now, May 2012, http://mshistorynow.mdah.state.ms.us/articles/381/the-carroll-county-courthouse-massacre-1886-a-cold-case-file.

111. "The Haytien Trouble," *Cleveland Gazette*, January 5, 1889.

112. "Haytien Trouble."

113. "Haytien Trouble."

Chapter 3

1. *St. Louis Public Schools. Printed Record of the Board of President and Directors, Vol. VII. July 1, 1889 to July 1, 1892* (St. Louis: Nixon-Jones Printing, 1892), 376–377, 391–392, 413, 429.

2. "Named for Negroes, and the Great Anti-Slavery Leaders Left Unremembered," *St. Louis Post-Dispatch*, December 10, 1890. See, also, John Aaron Wright, *Discovering African American St. Louis: A Guide to Historic Sites*, 2nd ed. (St. Louis: Missouri Historical Society Press, 2002).

3. *St. Louis Public Schools*, 461.

4. "Named for Negroes."

5. Bryan M. Jack, *The St. Louis African American Community and the Exodusters* (Columbia: University of Missouri Press, 2007); Clarence Lang, *Grassroots at the Gateway: Class Politics and Black Freedom Struggle in St. Louis, 1936–1975* (Ann Arbor: University of Michigan Press, 2009); Priscilla A. Dowden-White, *Groping Toward Democracy: African American Social Welfare Reform in St. Louis, 1910–1949* (Columbia: University of Missouri Press, 2011).

6. "White Folks and Christians in Hayti," *American Citizen*, January 25, 1889.

7. "White Folks and Christians in Hayti."

8. Paul M. Kennedy, *The Samoan Tangle: A Study in Anglo-German-American Relations, 1878–1900* (New York: Barnes & Noble, 1974); and Stuart Anderson, "'Pacific Destiny' and American Policy in Samoa, 1872–1899," *Hawaiian Journal of History* 12 (1978): 45–60.

9. *American Citizen*, January 18, 1889.

10. *Huntsville Gazette*, January 26, 1889.

11. Irvine Garland Penn, *The Afro-American Press and Its Editors* (Springfield, MA: Wiley, 1891); and Rashey B. Moten, Jr., "The Negro Press of Kansas" (M.A. thesis, University of Kansas, 1936).

12. Jay-Kay, "American Diplomacy," *Washington Bee*, February 9, 1889.

13. "America—Hayti—Samoa," *Cleveland Gazette*, February 23, 1889.

14. Norma Brown, ed., *A Black Diplomat in Haiti: The Diplomatic Correspondence of U.S. Minister Frederick Douglass from Haiti, 1889–1891* (Salisbury, NC: Documentary Publications, 1977), 41–42.

15. Brown, *Black Diplomat in Haiti.*

16. Brown, *Black Diplomat in Haiti*, 255.

17. Dubois, *Haiti*, 187.

18. Alonzo P. Holly, "What Hayti Has Done," *New York Age*, July 27, 1889.

19. *Freeman*, July 20, 1889.

20. *Cleveland Gazette*, July 6, 1889.

21. *Leavenworth Advocate*, July 6, 1889.

22. *American Citizen*, July 5, 1889.

23. "'The Black Republic.' Minister Douglass Has Faith in the Future of Hayti," *Washington Post*, July 4, 1889.

24. "Frederick Douglass and Hayti," *New York Morning Journal*, July 26, 1889, FDP, LOC.

25. "'Black Republic.'" The allegation that Douglass "favored the policy of coercion" appears in "Our Haytian Policy," *Washington Post*, July 3, 1889.

26. "'Black Republic.'"

27. " 'Black Republic.' "

28. "American Protectorate for Hayti," *Chicago Tribune*, October 18, 1889.

29. "American Protectorate for Hayti."

30. "American Protectorate for Hayti."

31. "Hayti's Deliverance," *Freeman*, October 12, 1889.

32. *Plaindealer*, October 11, 1889.

33. Logan, *Diplomatic Relations*, 420.

34. Frederick Douglass, "Haïti and the United States: Inside History of the Negotiations for the Môle St. Nicolas, II," *North American Review* 153 (October 1891): 456–457.

35. Logan, *Diplomatic Relations*, 411–414. Mahan published his influential book *The Influence of Sea Power upon History, 1660–1783* in 1890. It attributes the rise of the British Empire to the dominance of British sea power.

36. Myra Himelhoch, "Frederick Douglass and Haiti's Mole St. Nicolas," *Journal of Negro History* 56, no. 3 (July 1971): 161.

37. *Cleveland Gazette*, February 15 and March 29, 1890.

38. *Plaindealer*, August 8, 1890.

39. W. H. H. J., "His Pet Plan," *Plaindealer*, January 11, 1890.

40. "Hayti and the South," *Biddeford Daily Journal*, August 16, 1890, FDP, LOC; "Hayti Getting Better," *Boston Daily Globe*, August 19, 1890, FDP, LOC; "Fred Douglass Heard From," *Torchlight Appeal*, February 22, 1890; *Plaindealer*, April 18, 1890; *Washington Bee*, August 2, 1890.

41. *Cleveland Gazette*, August 2, 1890.

42. Along with Rayford Logan's foundational work, this transition receives excellent treatment in Chantalle F. Verna, *Haiti and the Uses of America: Post–U.S. Occupation Promises* (New Brunswick, NJ: Rutgers University Press, 2017), 20–41.

43. "He Was Not Snubbed," *Pittsburgh Dispatch*, July 27, 1890.

44. " 'Thrifty Americans' and Hayti," *New York Age*, August 2, 1890.

45. Rael, "Black Theodicy."

46. "Hayti in America," *New York Age*, May 9, 1891.

47. Omar H. Ali, *In the Lion's Mouth: Black Populism in the New South, 1886–1900* (Jackson: University Press of Mississippi, 2010).

48. William Henry Harrison Hart to Frederick Douglass, February 14, 1890, FDP, LOC.

49. "Haytian Troubles," *New York Age*, February 8, 1890; "Clippings, Here & There," *Freeman*, December 6, 1890; "News of Interest," *Washington Bee*, December 20, 1890.

50. Brown, *Black Diplomat in Haiti*, 58.

51. Anténor Firmin, *The Equality of the Human Races*, trans. Asselin Charles (Urbana: University of Illinois Press, 2002).

52. Logan, *Diplomatic Relations*, 438–439; Frederick Douglass to James G. Blaine, January 6, 1891, in Philip Foner, ed., *The Life and Writings of Frederick Douglass*, vol. 4 (New York: International Publishers, 1955), 460.

53. C. H. Hollister to William H. Seward, September 7, 1868, in *Papers Relating to Foreign Affairs* (Washington: U.S. Government Printing Office, 1869), part 2, p. 362.

54. Logan, *Diplomatic Relations*, 440–441; William S. McFeely, *Frederick Douglass* (New York: W. W. Norton, 1991), 348–349; Frederick Douglass, "Haïti and the United States: Inside History of the Negotiations for the Môle St. Nicolas, I," *North American Review* 153 (September 1891): 343–344.

55. Douglass. "Haïti and the United States, I," 344–345.

56. McFeely, *Frederick Douglas*, 350–351; Logan, *Diplomatic Relations*, 442–451.

57. "American Interference in the Affairs of Haiti," *New York Age*, January 4, 1890.

58. "The Haytian Complication," *Chicago Daily Tribune*, April 18, 1891.

59. E. L. Thornton, "Mr. Douglass on Hayti," *New York Age*, July 11, 1891.

60. *Cleveland Gazette*, June 13, 1891.

61. "News of the Week," Springfield *State Capitol*, May 2, 1891.

62. "Minister Douglass Insulted," *Cleveland Gazette*, April 18, 1891.

63. "Mole St. Nicolas," *Huntsville Gazette*, May 16, 1891.

64. *Appeal*, May 28, 1891.

65. Douglass, "Haïti and the United States, I," 338–340.

66. Douglass, "Haïti and the United States, II," 452–453; Douglass, "Haïti and the United States, I," 340.

67. Thornton, "Mr. Douglass on Hayti."

68. Thornton, "Mr. Douglass on Hayti."

69. Laura Langer Cohen and Jordan Alexander Stein, eds., *Early African American Print Culture* (Philadelphia: University of Pennsylvania Press, 2012).

70. Roche Grellier, *Haïti: Son Passé, Son Avenir* (Paris: Arthur Rousseau, 1891); Grellier, *Études Économiques sur Haïti* (Arthur Rousseau, 1891); Paul Drayton, "Hayti's Past and Future," *New York Age*, July 11, 1891; Drayton, "Haytian Economic Studies," *New York Age*, August 29, 1891; "The Truth About Hayti," *New York Age*, July 11, 1891; "Personal and Pertinent," *New York Age*, June 20, 1891; Fortune, "Men Worth Talking About," *New York Age*, January 2, 1892.

71. Solomon Porter Hood, "Haiti: Paper I," *AME Church Review* 8 (July 1891): 11.

72. Solomon Porter Hood, "Haiti: Paper II," *AME Church Review* 9 (July 1892): 35.

73. "The Record of Shame: Appalling List of Victims Lynched Last Year," *Plaindealer*, February 3, 1893; "A Terrible Example: Will the Government Persist in Refusing to Defend and Protect Its Citizens," *Plaindealer*, April 8, 1892.

74. *Plaindealer*, June 19, 1891.

75. *Plaindealer*, September, 4, 1891.

76. "Hayti in America," *New York Age*, May 9, 1891.

77. "Hayti and the South Compared," *New York Age*, June 21, 1891.

78. "European Intervention in Hayti," *New York Age*, June 27, 1891.

79. "We Have Enough to Do At Home," *New York Age*, July 11, 1891.

80. Sumner Welles, *Naboth's Vineyard: The Dominican Republic 1844–1924* (New York: Payson & Clarke, 1928), 467.

81. Rick Warwick, email to author, May 6, 2017; Williamson County Deed Book 11, p. 283, January 1, 1884 in Rick Warwick, *Williamson County in Black and White* (Franklin, TN: Williamson County Historical Society, 2000), 246–247.

82. "Our National Holiday," *Historic Times*, August 1, 1891.

83. "Mr. Douglass in Delaware," *New York Age*, July 9, 1892.

84. Jacqueline Bacon, *Freedom's Journal: The First African-American Newspaper* (Lanham, MD: Lexington Books, 2007).

85. Benjamin Fagan, *The Black Newspaper and the Chosen Nation* (Athens: University of Georgia Press, 2016).

86. J. Montague Simpson, *Six Months in Port-au-Prince* (Philadelphia: G. S. Ferguson, 1905), 78; *Freeman*, October 3, 1891; "Port-au-Prince, Hayti," *Freeman*, October 24, 1891.

87. "President Hyppolite," *Freeman*, July 9, 1892.

88. "A Gala Day in Hayti," *Freeman*, May 21, 1892; "Port-au-Prince, Hayti," *Freeman*, October 24, 1891; "The Freeman in Hayti," *Freeman*, April 9, 1892.

89. Reid R. Badger. *The Great American Fair: The World's Columbian Exposition and American Culture* (Chicago: N. Hall, 1979); and Neil Harris, Wim de Wit, James Gilbert, and Robert Rydell, *Grand Illusions: Chicago's World's Fair of 1893* (Chicago: Chicago Historical Society, 1993).

90. On black participation at the Chicago World's Fair, see Christopher Robert Reed, *"All the World Is Here!" The Black Presence at White City* (Bloomington: Indiana University Press, 2000).

91. Thomas J. Bell, "The Chicago Fair," *Bulletin of Atlanta University* (July 1893), 4.

92. Bell, "Chicago Fair."

93. Alfreda M. Duster, ed., *Crusade for Justice: The Autobiography of Ida B. Wells* (Chicago: University of Chicago Press, 1970), 115. On Wells, see Mia Bay, *To Tell the Truth Freely: The Life of Ida B. Wells* (New York: Hill and Wang, 2009).

94. Robert W. Rydell, *All the World's a Fair: Visions of Empire and American International Expositions* (Chicago: University of Chicago Press, 1987), 38–72. On the significance of Haiti's participation at the World's Fair, see especially Karen N. Salt, *The Unfinished Revolution: Haiti, Black Sovereignty and Power in the Nineteenth-Century Atlantic World* (Liverpool: Liverpool University Press, 2019).

95. *Savannah Tribune*, March 12, 1892.

96. "Hayti at the World's Fair," *Wisconsin Afro-American*, August 13, 1892; "Hayti at the Fair," *Plaindealer*, August 19, 1892; *Washington Bee*, January 14, 1893; "News and Sentiment," *Huntsville Gazette*, January 21, 1893.

97. "Deadlocked by a Negro," *Freeman*, August 20, 1892.

98. "Hayti's Pavilion," *Huntsville Gazette*, January 7, 1893.

99. James Weldon Johnson, "At the World's Fair," *Bulletin of Atlanta University* (May 1893): 3.

100. Reed, *"All the World Is Here!"*, appendix III.

101. Reed, *"All the World Is Here!"*, 155.

102. Ida B. Wells, Frederick Douglass, Irvine Garland Penn, and Ferdinand L. Barnett, *The Reason Why the Colored American Is Not at the World's Columbian Exposition: The Afro-American's Contribution to Columbian Literature*, ed. Robert W. Rydell (Urbana: University of Illinois Press, 1999), 13.

103. A comprehensive description of the Haitian Pavilion is found in Rossiter Johnson, ed., *A History of the World's Columbian Exposition*, vol. II (New York: D. Appleton, 1897), 422–423.

104. Renée Larrier, "DuSable, Douglass, and *Dessalines*: The Haytian Pavilion and the Narrative of History," in Marie-Agnès Sourieau and Kathleen M. Balutansky, eds., *Ecrire en pays assiégé: Writing Under Siege* (Amsterdam: Rodopi, 2004), 47–48. On Haiti's similar self-presentation at other nineteenth-century world expositions, see Hadassah St. Hubert, "We Are Part of the Civilised World: Haitian Representation in Late Nineteenth Century Expositions," *Caribbean Quarterly* 64, no. 2 (2018): 229–253.

105. Ida B. Wells, *Crusade for Justice: The Autobiography of Ida B. Wells*, in Alfreda Duster, ed. (Chicago: University of Chicago Press, 1970), 116. On African Americans' use of the Haitian Pavilion, see Reed, *"All the World Is Here!"*, 172–179; Larrier, "DuSable, Douglass, and *Dessalines*," 39–56; and Barbara J. Ballard, "African-American Protest and the Role of the Haitian

Pavilion at the 1893 Chicago World's Fair," in C. James Trotman, ed., *Multiculturalism: Roots and Realities* (Bloomington: Indiana University Press, 2002), 108–120.

106. "Remarks of Mr. Douglass on the Occasion of the Opening of the Haitian Pavilion at the World's Columbian Exposition in Chicago," FDP, LOC.

107. Frederick Douglass, "Lecture on Haiti," 9–10, FDP, LOC. On Douglass's two speeches, see Glen McLish, "Frederick Douglass and the Consequences of Rhetoric: The Interpretive Framing and Publication History of the 2 January 1893 Haiti Speeches," *Rhetorica: A Journal of the History of Rhetoric* 30, no. 1 (Winter 2012): 37–73.

108. Douglass, "Lecture on Haiti," 12.

109. Douglass, "Lecture on Haiti," 43–44.

110. *Chicago Inter Ocean*, August 16, 1893; *Chicago Times*, August 16, 1893; "Africa at the Columbian Exposition," *Our Day: A Record and Review of Current Reform* 9, no. 59 (November 1892): 774. Another contemporary account of the Congress appears in "The Chicago Congress on Africa," *Our Day* 10, no. 70 (October 1893): 284–293; Reed, *"All the World Is Here!"*, 179–191.

111. "Liberians at the Fair," *Cleveland Gazette*, April 29, 1893; "How Liberia Came to the World's Fair," *Cleveland Gazette*, September 16, 1893; "Chicago Congress on Africa," 290–293.

112. These transformations are captured in Bederman, *Manliness and Civilization*, 1–45.

113. Kristin L. Hoganson, *Fighting for American Manhood: How Gender Politics Provoked the Spanish-American and Philippine-American Wars* (New Haven, CT: Yale University Press, 1998).

114. For an excellent treatment of race, manhood, and imperialism in black discourse, see Mitchell, *Righteous Propagation*, 51–75. On ideas of black manliness and respectability, also see Martin Summers, *Manliness and Its Discontents: The Black Middle Class and the Transformation of Masculinity, 1900–1930* (Chapel Hill: University of North Carolina Press, 2004) and D'Weston Haywood, *Let Us Make Men: The Twentieth-Century Black Press and a Manly Vision for Racial Advancement* (Chapel Hill: University of North Carolina Press, 2018).

115. "Theatrical Gossip," *Daily Inter Ocean*, August 27, 1893.

116. "Theatrical Gossip," 117.

117. Literary scholars and art historians have contributed most analyses of *Dessalines*. See especially Robert J. Fehrenbach, "William Edgar Easton's Dessalines: A Nineteenth-Century Drama of Black Pride," *CLA Journal* 19, no. 1 (September 1975): 75–89; Dickson D. Bruce, Jr., *Black American Writing from the Nadir: The Evolution of a Literary Tradition, 1877–1915* (Baton Rouge: Louisiana State University Press, 1989), 28–29; Lindsay J. Twa, *Visualizing Haiti in U.S. Culture, 1910–1950* (Burlington, VT: Ashgate, 2014), 166–167.

118. William Edgar Easton, *Dessalines: A Dramatic Tale. A Single Chapter From Haiti's History* (Galveston, TX: J.W. Burson, 1893), iv, 13.

119. Letter from William Edgar Easton to Paul Laurence Dunbar, May 12, 1894 in Paul Laurence Dunbar Papers, microfilm edition, Ohio Historical Society, Columbus, Ohio.

120. *Freeman*, July 15, 1893.

121. "Dessalines," *Freeman*, April 15, 1893.

122. Ruben Ray, "What Does it Mean," *Freeman*, April 4, 1896.

123. Michael S. Sweeney, "Julius F. Taylor and the *Broad Ax* of Salt Lake City," *Utah Historical Quarterly* 77, no. 3 (Summer 2009): 205; *Broad Ax*, March 27, 1897.

124. "Toussaint L'Ouverture and the Republic of Hayti," *Broad Ax*, May 15, 1897.

125. For instance, see *Freeman*, March 10, 1894. Companies that sold similar engravings of Louverture included the Colored American Novelty Company.

126. H. L. Price, "Will the Negro Be a Man? What He Has Achieved as a Soldier and a Citizen," *Freeman*, August 29, 1896.

127. "Liliuokalani," *Washington Bee*, December 19, 1896.

128. John Hurst, "Hayti and the United States I," AME *Church Review* (1896): 436–439.

129. Charles Remond Douglass, "The Negro in the West Indies," *Parsons Weekly Blade*, January 5, 1895.

130. Robert E. Anderson, *Washington Bee*, October 28, 1893.

131. "Our Freedom," *Washington Bee*, April 24, 1897.

132. Kidada Williams, *They Left Great Marks on Me*.

133. Solon Ménos, *L'Affaire Luders*, 2nd ed. (Port-au-Prince: J. Verrollot, 1898).

134. "Poor Hayti," *Washington Bee*, December 11, 1897.

135. *Savannah Tribune*, December 11, 1897; "Germany Defiant," *Freeman*, December 11, 1897.

136. "Hayti," *Freeman*, December 18, 1897. See Willard B. Gatewood, Jr., ed., *Slave and Freeman: The Autobiography of George L. Knox* (Lexington: University Press of Kentucky, 1979), 32.

137. "They May Be Needed," *Washington Bee*, December 11, 1897.

138. *Biographical and Historical Memoirs of Pulaski, Jefferson, Lonoke, Faulkner, Grant, Saline, Perry, Garland and Hot Spring Counties, Arkansas* (Chicago: Goodspeed, 1889), 803–804.

139. "A. M. Middlebrooks," *Freeman*, December 17, 1898.

140. Gatewood, *Slave and Freeman*, 36.

141. "A. M. Middlebrooks."

Chapter 4

1. Louis R. Harlan, *Booker T. Washington: The Making of a Black Leader, 1856–1901* (London: Oxford University Press, 1972), 238–243; Robert J. Norrell, *Up from History: The Life of Booker T. Washington* (Cambridge, MA: Belknap Press of Harvard University Press, 2009), 173–179.

2. The Haitian government made at least two attempts to recover Louverture's remains during Washington's lifetime. Each time, the French government refused to comply. Excuses ranged from uncertainty about the location of Louverture's body to an inability to authenticate bones thought to belong to Louverture. See Dannelle Gutarra, "Toussaint Louverture's Captivity at Fort de Joux," *Journal of Caribbean History* 49, no. 2 (2015): 150–151; and Charles Forsdick, "The Panthéon's Empty Plinth: Commemorating Slavery in Contemporary France," *Atlantic Studies* 9, no. 3 (2012): 279–297.

3. Booker T. Washington, "On the Paris Boulevards," *New York Age*, July 13, 1899.

4. Washington, "On the Paris Boulevards."

5. Muhammad, *Condemnation of Blackness*.

6. Gaines, "Black Americans' Racial Uplift Ideology."

7. See, for instance, Michael O. West, "The Tuskegee Model of Development in Africa: Another Dimension of the African/African American Connection," *Diplomatic History: The Journal of the Society for Historians of American Foreign Relations* 16 (Summer 1992): 371–387.

My definition of Pan-Africanism derives mainly from Hakim Adi and Marika Sherwood, *Pan-African History: Political Figures from Africa and the Diaspora Since 1787* (New York: Routledge, 2003).

8. Norrell, *Up from History*, 115–135.

9. "The Standard Printed Version of the Atlanta Exposition Address," in Louis R. Harlan, ed., *The Booker T. Washington Papers, Volume 3: 1889–95* (Urbana: University of Illinois Press, 1974), 583–587.

10. W. E. B. Du Bois to Booker T. Washington, September 24, 1895, in Herbert Aptheker, ed., *The Correspondence of W. E. B. Du Bois: Volume I, Selections, 1877–1934* (Amherst: University of Massachusetts Press, 1973), 39.

11. W. E. B. Du Bois, *Dusk of Dawn: An Essay Toward an Autobiography of a Race Concept*, ed. Henry Louis Gates, Jr. (New York: Oxford University Press, 2007), 28.

12. Gaines, *Uplifting the Race.*

13. "Standard Printed Version of the Atlanta Exposition Address."

14. Booker T. Washington, Norman Barton Wood, and Fannie Barrier Williams, *A New Negro for a New Century: An Accurate and Up-to-Date Record of the Upward Struggles of the Negro Race* (Chicago: American Publishing House, 1900), 3.

15. Henry Louis Gates, Jr., "The Trope of a New Negro and the Reconstruction of the Image of the Black," in "America Reconstructed, 1840–1940," special issue, *Representations* 24 (Autumn 1988): 129–155.

16. Booker T. Washington, *The Future of the American Negro*, 2nd ed. (Boston: Small, Maynard & Company, 1900), 69.

17. Washington, *Future of the American Negro*, 70.

18. Washington, *Future of the American Negro*. Besides "On the Paris Boulevards," Washington made similar claims about Haiti in his "Sunday Evening Talk" delivered from Tuskegee on October 2, 1898. See Washington, "How to Build a Race," in Louis R. Harlan, ed., *The Booker T. Washington Papers Volume 4, 1895–1898* (Urbana: University of Illinois Press, 1975), 480–481.

19. Washington, *Future of the American Negro*, 70.

20. *Freeman*, August 9, 1902.

21. Tuskegee was not alone in attracting international students, of course. On the broader history and perceived benefits of international students in the United States, see Paul A. Kramer, "Is the World Our Campus? International Students and U.S. Global Power in the Long Twentieth Century," *Diplomatic History* 33, no. 5 (November 2009): 775–806.

22. Andrew Zimmerman provides an excellent treatment of Washington's work with German imperialists in West Africa in *Alabama in Africa: Booker T. Washington, the German Empire, & the Globalization of the New South* (Princeton, NJ: Princeton University Press, 2010). Frank Andre Guridy does the same for the Tuskegee-Cuba connection in *Forging Diaspora: Afro-Cubans and African Americans in a World of Empire and Jim Crow* (Chapel Hill: University of North Carolina Press, 2010), 17–60.

23. *Freeman*, June 8, 1901.

24. Booker T. Washington, "The Negro in the New World," *Journal of the African Society* 10 (January 1911): 174–175.

25. Washington, "Negro in the New World," 176.

26. On debates about education and national development among the Haitian elite, see Patrick Bellegarde-Smith, *In the Shadow of Powers: Dantès Bellegarde in Haitian Social Thought*, 2nd ed. (Nashville: Vanderbilt University Press, 2019).

27. Magdaline W. Shannon, *Jean Price-Mars, the Haitian Elite, and the American Occupation, 1915–35* (New York: St. Martin's Press, 1996), 19–20.

28. *Freeman*, October 31, 1903. The annual catalogue for 1903–1904 shows twelve Haitians among sixty-seven foreign students, which seems to have been the high point of Haitian enrollment for at least the next decade. See *Twenty-Third Annual Catalogue of the Tuskegee Normal and Industrial Institute* (Tuskegee, AL: Tuskegee Institute Press, 1904).

29. *Twenty-Third Annual Catalogue.*

30. Charles W. Pierce, "How Electricity Is Taught at Tuskegee," *Technical World Magazine* 1, no. 2 (April 1904): 426.

31. Guridy provides excellent analysis of the expectations of Afro-Cuban students in *Forging Diaspora*, 17–60.

32. Athanase M. Auguste to Booker T. Washington, November 11, 1902, Papers of Booker T. Washington, Library of Congress MSS 18,185.1, reel no. 191.

33. Auguste to Washington. On Janvier, see especially Marlene L. Daut, "Caribbean 'Race Men': Louis Joseph Janvier, Demesvar Delorme, and the Haitian Atlantic," *L'Espirit Créateur* 56, no. 1 (Spring 2016): 9–23.

34. Auguste to Washington.

35. *Freeman*, April 25, 1903.

36. Rayford Logan, *The Negro in American Life and Thought: The Nadir, 1877–1901* (New York: Dial Press, 1954).

37. Washington, "Negro in the New World," 174–175.

38. Frederick Ludwig Hoffman, *Race Traits and Tendencies of the American Negro* (New York: MacMillan, 1896), 329. On turn of the century ideas about black potential and the "Negro Problem," see Norrell, *Up from History*, 115–134.

39. James Creelman, *On the Great Highway: The Wanderings and Adventures of a Special Correspondent* (Boston: Lothrop, Lee & Shepard), 379–380.

40. Pan-African Association, "To the Nations of the World," 1900, W. E. B. Du Bois Papers, MS 312, Special Collections and University Archives, University of Massachusetts Amherst Libraries (hereafter cited as Du Bois Papers). On the Pan-African Conference, see Alexander Walters, *My Life and Work* (New York: Fleming H. Revell, 1917), 253–264; J. R. Hooker, "The Pan-African Conference 1900," *Transition* 46 (1974): 20–24; and Adi, *Pan-Africanism: A History* (London: Bloomsbury, 2018).

41. On assimilationism in the era of the so-called Negro problem, see Kendi, *Stamped from the Beginning*, 269–307.

42. William F. Powell, "Hayti as a Refuge," *Cleveland Gazette*, April 6, 1901.

43. Powell, "Hayti as a Refuge."

44. Powell, "Hayti as a Refuge." On Haitian diplomacy, see Brenda Gayle Plummer, "The Metropolitan Connection: Foreign and Semiforeign Elites in Haiti, 1900–1915," *Latin American Research Review* 19, no. 2 (1984): 119–142; and Plummer, *Haiti and the Great Powers, 1902–1915* (Baton Rouge: Louisiana State University Press, 1988).

45. Powell, "Hayti as a Refuge."

46. Powell, "Hayti as a Refuge."

47. "Home for Blacks," *Louisville Courier Journal*, May 12, 1901; "Afro-Americans' Destiny," *Los Angeles Times*, May 12, 1901; "Favor Hayti for Negro Colonies," *Chicago Tribune*, May 12, 1901.

48. Mitchell, *Righteous Propagation*, 51–75.

49. "Home for Blacks."

50. Monroe N. Work, "Negro Emigration from America," *Chicago Daily Tribune*, May 26, 1901.

51. Work, "Negro Emigration from America."

52. W. E. B. Du Bois, "The Talented Tenth," in *The Negro Problem: A Series of Articles by Representative American Negroes of To-Day* (New York: J. Pott, 1903), 31–76.

53. Charles Spencer Smith, "The Negro Is by Nature Harmless," *Colored American*, June 6, 1901.

54. Dubois, *Haiti*, 196–197.

55. Dubois, *Haiti*, 197–199.

56. Dubois, *Haiti*, 200–201.

57. *Broad Ax*, July 12, 1902.

58. "Volunteers for the Front," *Broad Ax*, November 6, 1902.

59. John S. Durham, *To Teach the Negro History: A Suggestion* (Philadelphia: David McKay, 1897), 41, 47.

60. John S. Durham to Charles W. Chesnutt, September 14, 1909, in Charles W. Chesnutt Collection, Fisk University Library Special Collections.

61. John S. Durham, "Diane, Priestess of Haïti," *Lippincott's Monthly Magazine* (April 1902): 387–467.

62. Durham, "Diane, Priestess of Haïti," 400.

63. Durham, "Diane, Priestess of Haïti," 391.

64. Haitian nationalist literature published at the turn of the twentieth century also reflected the impact of imperialism, most notably in its negative portrayals of Germans in Haiti. Shanna Jean-Baptist, "Writing the Fin de Siècle Nation: Haitian National Identity in Fernand Hibbert's *Les Thazar* and 'Le marriage d'Otto,'" paper presented at the Modern Language Association Conference (Chicago, January 2019).

65. William Pickens, *The Heir of Slaves* (Boston: Pilgrim Press, 1911), 122, 124.

66. William Pickens, "Hayti," *Yale Literary Magazine* 68, no.7 (April 1903): 232.

67. Pickens, "Hayti," 232–233.

68. Pickens, "Hayti," 234.

69. The trope of the loyal slave was central to the mythology of the Old South. On Washington's appropriation of it, see Booker T. Washington, *Up from Slavery*, ed. W. Fitzhugh Brundage (Boston: Bedford/St. Martins, 2003), 45–46.

70. Pickens, *Hayti*, 234–235.

71. Pickens, *Hayti*, 234–235.

72. Pickens, *Hayti*, 236.

73. Pickens, *Hayti*, 237.

74. Washington, *Up from Slavery*, 76–82.

75. Pickens, *Hayti*, 237.

76. Pickens, *Hayti*, 238.

77. Pickens, *Heir of Slaves*, 125–126.

78. "Juniors' Oratorical Champion Worked for His Board and Saved His Tuition," *Colored American*, April 18, 1903.

79. Census, immigration, and shipping records show a few Haitian Guilbauds living in New York City at the outset of the twentieth century. One, an Emanuel Joseph Guilbaud,

submitted a naturalization petition to the New York County Supreme Court in 1911. He is likely the Guilbaud who wrote to the *Sun*.

80. Emmanuel Th. Guilbaud, "A Haytian on the Pickens Oration," *Sun*, April 11, 1903.

81. Guilbaud, "Haytian on the Pickens Oration."

82. Guilbaud, "Haytian on the Pickens Oration."

83. Guilbaud, "Haytian on the Pickens Oration."

84. W. E. B. Du Bois, *The Souls of Black Folk*, intro. Randall Kenan (New York: Signet Classic, 1995), 87–88.

85. Niagara Movement, "Constitution and By-Laws of the Niagara Movement: As Adopted July 12 and 13, 1905 at Buffalo, N.Y.," 1905, Du Bois Papers. The dispute between the so-called Niagarites and Bookerites is well documented. See especially Norrell, *Up from History*, 263–287. The best treatment of black civil rights activism in this era is Shawn Leigh Alexander, *An Army of Lions: The Civil Rights Struggle Before the NAACP* (Philadelphia: University of Pennsylvania Press, 2012).

86. William Seraile, *Bruce Grit: The Black Nationalist Writings of John Edward Bruce* (Knoxville: University of Tennessee Press, 2003).

87. "Bruce Grit's Melange," *Colored American*, April 18, 1903.

88. "Bruce Grit's Melange."

89. On the emergence of cultural relativism and its relationship with racial theories, see Painter, *History of White People*, 228–244.

90. "Won Ten Eyck Prize," *Guardian*, May 9, 1903.

91. "Honors Again at Yale," *Guardian*, May 9, 1903.

92. "Pickens to Be in Cambridge," *Guardian*, May 23, 1903.

93. See Sheldon Avery, *Up from Washington: William Pickens and the Negro Struggle for Equality, 1900–1954* (Newark: University of Delaware Press, 1989), 16–18.

94. Trotter's reproach of Pickens coheres with his later opposition to the U.S. occupation of Haiti and his criticism of European colonialism in Africa at the Paris Peace Conference following World War I. Further reading on Trotter includes Charles W. Puttkammer and Ruth Worthy, "William Monroe Trotter, 1872–1934," *Journal of Negro History* 43, no. 4 (October 1958): 298–316; Stephen Fox, *The Guardian of Boston: William Monroe Trotter* (New York Atheneum Press, 1970); and Mark R. Schneider, *Boston Confronts Jim Crow, 1890–1902* (Boston: Northeastern University Press, 1997).

95. 1900 United States Federal Census, Sturgis, Union County, Kentucky, NARA microfilm publication T623, 1,854 rolls, digital image, Ancestry.com, https://ancestry.com; 1910 United States Federal Census, Sturgis, Union County, Kentucky, NARA microfilm publication T624, 1,178 rolls, digital image, Ancestry.com, https://ancestry.com.

96. Negroes Plan to Establish Black State," *Atlanta Constitution*, May 17, 1903.

97. "William Pickens, Yale Orator, Seeks to Lead Dissatisfied Colored Men of United States on Expedition to Establish New Republic in Hayti of the Colored Race," *Boston Post*, May 17, 1903.

98. "Plan a Negro Empire in Hayti," *New York Tribune*, June 7, 1903.

99. "Form a Republic for the Negroes," *Tennessean*, May 5, 1903.

100. "Would Conquer Hayti," *Seattle Republican*, May 15, 1903.

101. "Plan a Negro Empire in Hayti."

102. Pickens, *Heir of Slaves*, 127.

103. "Reporters Had Their Troubles Trying to Interview Mr. Booker T. Washington," *Detroit Free Press*, May 6, 1903.

104. "An Afro-American Republic," *Colored Citizen*, May 23, 1903.

105. *Journal of the Senate of the United States of America, Being the Second Session of the Fifty-Eighth Congress, Begun and Held in the City of Washington, December 7, 1903, in the One Hundred and Twenty-Eighth Year of the Independence of the United States* (Washington: Government Printing Office, 1903), 33, 593.

106. "More Annexation Madness," *Houston Post*, January 10, 1904.

107. "Another San Domingo Case," *Atlanta Constitution*, December 24, 1903.

108. "Another San Domingo Case."

109. Rosalvo Bobo, "À Propos de la Fête du Centenaire," in Michel Soukar, ed., *Écrits Politiques* (Pétion-Ville, Haïti: C3 Éditions, 2013).

110. David Howard Pitney, *The African American Jeremiad: Appeals for Justice in America* (Philadelphia: Temple University Press, 2005), 5.

111. Bobo, "À Propos."

112. *Voice of the Negro* 1, no. 3 (March 1904): Advertisements.

113. *Voice of the Negro.*

114. T. Thomas Fortune, "Haytian Revolutions," *Voice of the Negro* 1, no. 4 (April 1904): 139, 142.

115. William Pickens, "The Ten Eyck Prize Essay," *Voice of the Negro* 1, no. 4 (April 1904): 149.

116. John S. Durham, "The Hidden Wealth of Hayti," *Voice of the Negro* 1, no. 4 (April 1904): 143.

117. On discourses of primitive manliness, see Bederman, *Manliness and Civilization*, 170–216.

118. Durham, "Hidden Wealth of Hayti," 144.

119. The historian Linda Kerber has produced excellent scholarship on the concept of republican motherhood in the U.S. context. See *Toward an Intellectual History of Women: Essays by Linda K. Kerber* (Chapel Hill: University of North Carolina Press, 1997).

120. Durham, "Hidden Wealth of Hayti," 145.

121. Evelyn Brooks Higginbotham coined the phrase "politics of respectability" in *Righteous Discontent: The Women's Movement in the Black Baptist Church, 1880–1920* (Cambridge, MA: Harvard University Press, 1994). My understanding of respectability politics draws primarily from Higginbotham but is also influenced by Mitchell, *Righteous Propagation* and Brittney C. Cooper, *Beyond Respectability: The Intellectual Thought of Race Women* (Urbana: University of Illinois Press, 2017).

122. Durham, "Hidden Wealth of Hayti," 146. The Haitian Revolution led to what the leading scholar of Haitian history and culture Jean Casimir called the "counter-plantation" system. The small plots of land that independent farmers and families cultivated would became the basis of land tenure, social organization, and cultural tradition. See Jean Casimir, *La Culture Opprimée* (Delmas, Haïti: Imprimerie Lakay, 2001).

123. Teal, *Hero of Hispaniola*, 131–146.

124. Ebenezer Don Carlos Bassett, "Should Haiti Be Annexed to the United States?," *Voice of the Negro* 1 (May 1904): 192.

125. On Bassett's defense of Haiti and black sovereignty, see Karen Salt, "The Language of Politics in the Literary Archive of Black Sovereignty," *J19: The Journal of Nineteenth Century Americanists* 3, no. 2 (Fall 2015): 392–399.

126. Bassett, "Should Haiti be Annexed?," 197–198.

127. "Notes," *Journal of Negro History* 15, no. 3 (July 1930): 384–387.

128. "Rev. John Hurst Guest at Banquet," *Baltimore Afro-American*, September 25, 1909.

129. "Rev. John Hurst Guest at Banquet."

130. "Rev. John Hurst Guest at Banquet."

131. "Rev. John Hurst Guest at Banquet."

132. Véronique Hélénon, *French Caribbeans in Africa: Diasporic Connections and Colonial Administration, 1880–1939* (New York: Palgrave Macmillan, 2011).

133. "Rev. John Hurst Guest at Banquet."

134. Edwards, *Practice of Diaspora*.

135. "The Status of Haiti," *Freeman*, September 2, 1911.

136. "Hayti Misrepresented," *Freeman*, August 22, 1914.

137. "Hayti Misrepresented."

138. As Peter James Hudson shows, Roger Farnham, vice president of the National City Bank of New York, would become an architect of the U.S. occupation of Haiti. His bank, today's Citibank, supervised the National Bank of the Republic of Haiti and oversaw the transfer of its treasury reserves to New York. See Hudson, "The National City Bank of New York and Haiti, 1909–1922," *Radical History Review* 115 (2013): 91–114; and Hudson, *Bankers and Empire: How Wall Street Colonized the Caribbean* (Chicago: University of Chicago Press, 2017).

139. Dubois, *Haiti*, 204–205. On the buildup to the occupation, see Jeffrey Sommers, *Race, Reality, and Realpolitik: U.S.—Haiti Relations in the Lead Up to the 1915 Occupation* (Lanham, MD: Lexington Books, 2016).

140. Dubois, *Haiti*, 209–210.

141. Dubois, *Haiti*, 213–215.

142. Booker T. Washington, "Dr. Booker T. Washington on American Occupation of Haiti," *New York Age*, October 21, 1915, in Louis R. Harlan and Raymond W. Smock, eds., *The Booker T. Washington Papers, Volume 13, 1914–15* (Urbana: University of Illinois Press, 1984), 395–397.

143. Washington, "Dr. Booker T. Washington on American Occupation of Haiti," 398–399.

144. Washington, "Dr. Booker T. Washington on American Occupation of Haiti," 399–401.

145. Washington, "Dr. Booker T. Washington on American Occupation of Haiti," 401.

Chapter 5

1. "A Red-Stained 'Republic,'" *World*, July 29, 1915.

2. George Foster Peabody to Oswald Garrison Villard, July 30, 1915, Du Bois Papers.

3. Historians have paid scant attention to Du Bois's complex views on the U.S. occupation of Haiti. David Levering Lewis's biography of Du Bois cites one *Crisis* editorial as proof that "howls" about the occupation came from that publication. Brenda Gayle Plummer's article on the African American response to the occupation states briefly that Du Bois's *Crisis* "condemned intervention from the beginning." An article by Leon D. Pamphile on the NAACP's reaction to the occupation does not mention Du Bois. See Brenda Gayle Plummer, "The Afro-American Response to the U.S. Occupation of Haiti, 1915–1934," *Phylon* 43, no. 2 (2nd qtr., 1982): 131; Leon D. Pamphile, "The NAACP and the American Occupation of Haiti,"

Phylon 47, no. 1 (1st qtr., 1986): 91–100; and David Levering Lewis, *W. E. B. Du Bois: A Biography* (New York: Henry Holt, 2009), 342–343.

4. "Transcript of the Diary of Alexander Du Bois, 1856–1861," Du Bois Papers.

5. Most details about the Du Bois family come from W. E. B. Du Bois himself, particularly in his autobiography. See Du Bois, *The Autobiography of W. E. B. Du Bois: A Soliloquy on Viewing My Life from the Last Decade of Its First Century* (New York: International Publishers, 1968), 61–77. The best synopsis of this family history comes in Lewis, *Biography*, 11–46.

6. W. E. B. Du Bois, *The Suppression of the African Slave-Trade to the United States of America, 1638–1870*, Vol. I, Harvard Historical Studies (New York: Longmans, Green, 1896), 75.

7. Copy of extract from Jacques Léger, *Haiti: Her History and Her Detractors* (1907), Du Bois Papers.

8. Alfred E. Dubois to W. E. B. Du Bois, May 16, 1914, Du Bois Papers.

9. W. E. B. Du Bois to George Foster Peabody, August 3, 1915, Du Bois Papers.

10. Bates became a rather prolific travel writer, too. His books include *The Russian Road to China* (Boston: Houghton Mifflin, 1910) and *The Path of the Conquistadores, Trinidad and Venezuelan Guiana* (Boston: Houghton Mifflin, 1912).

11. Du Bois to Peabody. The most notable biography of Woodrow Wilson is John Milton Cooper, Jr., *Woodrow Wilson: A Biography* (New York: Vintage Books, 2011).

12. W. E. B. Du Bois to President Woodrow Wilson, August 3, 1915, Du Bois Papers.

13. Du Bois to Wilson.

14. The best treatment of U.S.-Cuban relations in this period remains Louis A. Pérez, Jr., *Cuba Under the Platt Amendment, 1902–1934* (Pittsburgh, PA: University of Pittsburgh Press, 1986).

15. On the U.S. invasion of Veracruz and its broader involvement in the Mexican Revolution, see John S. D. Eisenhower, *Intervention! The United States and the Mexican Revolution, 1913–1917* (New York: W. W. Norton, 1993).

16. U.S. imperialism in Latin America during this era receives excellent treatment in Jason Colby, *The Business of Empire: United Fruit, Race, and US Expansion in Central America* (Ithaca, NY: Cornell University Press, 2011).

17. "Mexico," *Crisis* 8, no. 2 (June 1914): 79.

18. Du Bois would recount the infamous episode between Wilson and a delegation of the National Independent Equal Rights League led by William Monroe Trotter in the January 1915 edition of the *Crisis*. See *Crisis* 9, no. 3 (January 1915): 119–127. The "humiliating" quote appears there and has since become emblematic of Wilson's racism. The phrase does not appear in Christine A. Lunardini, "Standing Firm: William Monroe Trotter's Meetings with Woodrow Wilson, 1913–1914," *Journal of Negro History* 64, no. 3 (Summer 1979): 244–264, an article produced from transcripts found in the Wilson Papers at the Library of Congress.

19. Du Bois to Wilson.

20. Lewis, *Biography*, 342.

21. Lawrie Balfour examines the implications of *Souls* and *Black Reconstruction* for the African American case for reparations in "Unreconstructed Democracy: W. E. B. Du Bois and the Case for Reparations," *American Political Science Review* 97, no. 1 (February 2003): 33–44.

22. Du Bois to Wilson.

23. Du Bois to Wilson. In his letter to Walters, Wilson concluded by assuring the AME Bishop that "my sympathy with them is of long standing, and I want to assure them through

you that should I become President of the United States, they may count upon me for absolute fair dealing and for everything by which I could assist in advancing the interests of their race in the United States." Woodrow Wilson to Bishop Alexander Walters, October 16, 1912, Du Bois Papers.

24. Du Bois to Wilson.

25. Its most notable target was Callie House, leader of the National Ex-Slave Mutual Relief, Bounty and Pension Association. On House and her movement to gain reparations for former slaves, see Mary Frances Berry, *My Face Is Black Is True: Callie House and the Struggle for Ex-Slave Reparations* (New York: Knopf, 2005).

26. W. E. B. Du Bois, "Another Open Letter to Woodrow Wilson," *Crisis* 6, no. 5 (September 1913): 233.

27. As Walter Rucker notes, much of Du Bois's writings at the turn of the twentieth century capture not only his integrationism but also an attendant aversion to the rise of Booker T. Washington. He interpreted calls for self-help as concessions to and "approval of the ongoing attempts to erode and deny black civil rights." See Rucker, "'A Negro Nation Within the Nation': W. E. B. Du Bois and the Creation of a Revolutionary Pan-Africanist Tradition, 1903–1947," *Black Scholar* 32, nos. 3–4 (Fall/Winter 2002): 42.

28. [W. E. B. Du Bois], "Hayti," *Crisis* 10, no. 5 (September 1915): 232.

29. [Du Bois], "Hayti," *Crisis* 10, no. 5.

30. [Du Bois], "Hayti," *Crisis* 10, no. 5.

31. The historian Henry Lewis Suggs argued that excitement for the presidential election of 1916 surpassed public interest in Haiti and alluded to another scholar who noted that "heavy criticism" of the occupation was rare in black newspapers in the early years of the occupation. See Suggs, "The Response of the African American Press to the United States Occupation of Haiti, 1915–1934," *Journal of Negro History* 73, no. 1/4 (Winter–Autumn, 1988): 34.

32. Plummer, "Afro-American Response," 128.

33. Plummer, "Afro-American Response," 127.

34. Dubois, *Haiti*, 217–219. Despite the censorship, a robust Haitian oppositional press emerged during the occupation. See Shearon Roberts, "Then and Now: Haitian Journalism as Resistance to US Occupation and US-Led Reconstruction," *Journal of Haitian Studies* 21, no. 2 (Fall 2015): 241–268.

35. Ernest Chauvet to Woodrow Wilson, quoted in "Pleads Haiti's Cause," *Brooklyn Daily Eagle*, September 19, 1915. For an earlier example of Chauvet's thoughts on U.S. interventionism, see "A Haytian's Views," *Brooklyn Daily Eagle*, December 4, 1908.

36. Chauvet to Wilson.

37. "Haitien Editor Says U.S. Proposal Unfair," *Fort Worth Star-Telegram*, September 16, 1915; "Haitians in Protest," *Washington Post*, September 17, 1915.

38. "Haitian President Recognized by U.S.," *Evening Star* (Washington, D.C.), September 18, 1915. Similar quotations appear in "The Haitian Treaty," *Outlook* 111 (September–December 1915): 245–246.

39. Roger Gaillard, *Premier écrasement du cacoïsme* (Port-au-Prince: R. Gaillard, 1981), 113, quoted in Dubois, *Haiti*, 220.

40. [W. E. B. Du Bois], "Hayti," *Crisis* 10, no. 6 (October 1915): 291.

41. [Du Bois], "Hayti," *Crisis* 10, no. 6.

42. [Du Bois], "Hayti," *Crisis* 10, no. 6.

43. Charles F. Dole, "To the Secretary of State," *Crisis* 11, no. 1 (November 1915): 32.

44. J. C., "Haitian and Other Savages," *Crisis* 11, no. 1 (November 1915): 31–32.

45. Du Bois ensured that most of the opinions on the occupation presented in the *Crisis* reflected his own views. That was in complete accord with his broader editorial tenure, during which he kept close control over what material made it into his magazine.

46. Alonzo Holly to W. E. B. Du Bois, January 4, 1916, Du Bois Papers.

47. Holly to Du Bois, January 4, 1916. After the sinking of the RMS *Lusitania*, Wilson promised Germany that the United States would consider any similar aggressions "deliberately unfriendly acts." A few months later, Lansing informed the Austro-Hungarian government that the United States believed that its sinking of an Italian ocean liner involved the "wanton slaughter of defenceless no-combatants." Background on European naval aggressions and the U.S. entry into World War I can be found in Justus D. Doenecke, *Nothing Less Than War: A New History of America's Entry into World War I* (Lexington: University Press of Kentucky, 2011).

48. Holly to Du Bois, January 4, 1916.

49. Holly to Du Bois, January 4, 1916.

50. Holly to Du Bois, January 4, 1916.

51. Alonzo Holly to W. E. B. Du Bois, March 3, 1916, Du Bois Papers.

52. W. E. B. Du Bois to Alonzo Holly, March 10, 1916, Du Bois Papers.

53. "Bleeding Haiti," *Crisis* 11, no. 2 (December 1915): 77.

54. "Editorial from *Le Nouvelliste*, Port-au-Prince, Haiti," *Crisis* 11, no. 3 (January 1916): 133.

55. Along with Suggs, "Response of the African American Press," see John W. Blassingame, "The Press and American Intervention in Haiti and the Dominican Republic, 1904–1920," *Caribbean Studies* 9, no. 2 (July 1969): 27–43, on the press and the U.S. occupation of Haiti.

56. On the Great Migration, see James M. Gregory, *The Southern Diaspora: How the Great Migrations of Black and White Southerners Transformed America* (Chapel Hill: University of North Carolina Press, 2005); and Isabel Wilkerson, *The Warmth of Other Suns: The Epic Story of America's Great Migration* (New York: Random House, 2010).

57. Erez Manela, *The Wilsonian Moment: Self-Determination and the International Origins of Anticolonial Nationalism* (New York: Oxford University Press, 2007).

58. My use of martial citizenship draws from Francine D'Amico, "Citizen-Soldier? Class, Race, Gender, Sexuality and the US Military," in Susie Jacobs, Ruth Jacobson, and Jennifer Marchbank, eds., *States of Conflict: Gender, Violence and Resistance* (London: Zed Books, 2000), 105–122.

59. The best treatments of the black military experience in World War I are Adriane Lentz-Smith, *Freedom Struggles: African Americans & World War I* (Cambridge, MA: Harvard University Press, 2009); and Chad L. Williams, *Torchbearers of Democracy: African American Soldiers in the World War I Era* (Chapel Hill: University of North Carolina Press, 2010).

60. James Preston Spencer, Virginia War Historical Commission Questionnaire, Library of Virginia, http://www.virginiamemory.com/blogs/out_of_the_box/2018/01/17/true-son-of-freedom-the-world-war-i-experience-of-james-preston-spencer/.

61. Anonymous to W. E. B. Du Bois, July 28, 1918, quoted in Williams, *Torchbearers of Democracy*, 3.

62. W. E. B. Du Bois, "Close Ranks," *Crisis* 16, no. 3 (July 1918): 111.

63. Hubert Harrison, "The Descent of Dr. Du Bois," *Voice*, July 25, 1918. Mark Ellis persuasively supports this accusation in "'Closing Ranks' and 'Seeking Honors': W. E. B. Du Bois in World War I," *Journal of American History* 79, no. 1 (June 1992): 96–124.

64. Williams, *Torchbearers of Democracy*, 75–77.

65. Jeffrey B. Perry, *Hubert Harrison: The Voice of Harlem Radicalism, 1883–1918* (New York: Columbia University Press, 2009).

66. *Messenger*, July 1918.

67. Jan Voogd, *Race Riots and Resistance: The Red Summer of 1919* (New York: Peter Lang, 2008).

68. Lewis, *Biography*, 367–382. Du Bois articulated this desire for what he called the future of Africa in a number of his writings leading up to the Pan-African Congress. For example, see W. E. B. Du Bois, "The Future of Africa," *Crisis* 17 (June 1919): 119–120.

69. See especially George Padmore, ed., *History of the Pan-African Congress: Colonial and Coloured Unity, a Programme of Action* (Manchester: Pan-African Federation, 1945); Elliott P. Skinner, *African Americans and U.S. Policy Toward Africa, 1850–1924* (Washington, D.C.: Howard University Press, 1992), 381–422; Manning Marable, *W .E. B. Du Bois: Black Radical Democrat*, updated ed. (New York: Routledge, 2016), 99–120.

70. Eliézer Cadet to the UNIA, April 19, 1919, in *The Marcus Garvey and Universal Negro Improvement Association Papers, Volume I, 1826–August 1919*, ed., Robert A. Hill (Berkeley: University of California Press, 1983), 408–410.

71. Isaac Beton to W. E. B. Du Bois, January 28, 1919, Du Bois Papers.

72. Pan-African Congress Resolutions, February 21, 1919, Du Bois Papers.

73. Firmin, *Equality of the Human Races*, 306.

74. Beton to Du Bois.

75. W. E. B. Du Bois to Blaise Diagne, memorandum, January 1, 1919, Du Bois Papers.

76. Hill, *Marcus Garvey*, 308n2; Brenda Gayle Plummer, "Garveyism in Haiti During the US Occupation," *Journal of Haitian Studies* 21, no. 2 (Fall 2015): 71.

77. "Postal Censorship Report," January 1919, from Eliézer Cadet to Hénec Dorsinville, January 13, 1919, in Hill, *Marcus Garvey*, 359. I have been unable to locate an extant copy of Cadet's letter to the editor.

78. I use this term in the sense offered in Adam Ewing, *The Age of Garvey: How a Jamaican Activist Created a Mass Movement & Changed Global Black Politics* (Princeton, NJ: Princeton University Press, 2014), 132.

79. "Postal Censorship Report," December 1918, from Cadet to Marcel Herard, December 2, 1918, in Hill, *Marcus*, 319.

80. "Addresses Denouncing W. E. B. Du Bois," from *Negro World*, April 5, 1919, in Hill, *Marcus Garvey*, 378.

81. "Eliézer Cadet to the UNIA," April 19, 1919, in Hill, *Marcus*, 409.

82. "Eliézer Cadet to the UNIA," March 13, 1919, in Hill, *Marcus*, 387.

83. *Negro World*, April 5, 1919, in Hill, *Marcus*, n. 399.

84. "Address Denouncing W. E. B. Du Bois," in Hill, *Marcus Garvey*, n. 395.

85. Domingo's "Clothed Faces" is a sardonic reference to Du Bois's "Close Ranks." Hill, *Marcus Garvey*, 399.

86. W. E. B. Du Bois, *Crisis* 20 (December 1920): 58–60.

87. "Postal Censorship Report," January 1919.

88. "Eliézer Cadet to L'Essor," June 19, 1919, in Hill, *Marcus Garvey*, 417.

89. "Address Denouncing W. E. B. Du Bois," in Hill, *Marcus Garvey*, n. 400.

90. On *caco* resistance to the occupation, see Roger Gaillard, *Charlemagne Péralte le caco* (Port-au-Prince: R. Gaillard, 1982); Yveline Alexis, "Remembering Charlemagne Péralte & His Defense of Haiti's Revolution," in Millery Polyné, ed., *The Idea of Haiti: History, Development and the Creation of New Narratives* (Minneapolis, MN: University of Minnesota Press, 2013), 51–68; and Yveline Alexis, "*Mwen Pas Connait* as Resistance: Haitians' Silence Against a Violent US State," *Journal of Haitian Studies* 21, no. 2 (Fall 2015): 269–289.

91. Suggs, "Response of the African American Press," 35.

92. Suggs, "Response of the African American Press," 35; "The Civilizing of Haiti," *Crisis* 21, no. 1 (November 1920): 38.

93. "America . . ." and "shameful" quotations from W. E. B. Du Bois, "Returning Soldiers," *Crisis* 18, no. 1 (May 1919). "At war . . ." from W. E. B. Du Bois, "Haiti," *Crisis* 19, no. 6 (April 1920): 297–298.

94. Du Bois, "Haiti," *Crisis* 19, no. 6.

95. Du Bois, "Haiti," *Crisis* 19, no. 6.

96. W. E. B. Du Bois, "Presidential Candidates," *Crisis* 20, no. 2 (June 1920): 69.

97. Du Bois, "Presidential Candidates."

98. Johnson was right. See Hudson, *Bankers and Empire*.

99. The articles were then published in a pamphlet from which these quotations are taken: James Weldon Johnson, *Self-Determining Haiti* (New York: Nation, 1920), 11. On Johnson's condemnation of the occupation and its impact, see Rayford W. Logan, "James Weldon Johnson and Haiti," *Phylon* 32, no. 4 (4th qtr., 1971): 396–402.

100. Johnson, *Self-Determining Haiti*, 12, 18.

101. Logan, "James Weldon Johnson and Haiti," 396. See also David Nicholls, "Idéologie et mouvements politiques en Haïti, 1915–1946," *Annales. Économies. Sociétés. Civilisations* 30, no. 4 (1975): 654–679.

102. W. E. B. Du Bois to H. L. Stone c/o *Outing Magazine*, July 24, 1920, Du Bois Papers.

103. Brett Fairbairn, *The Meaning of Rochdale: The Rochdale Pioneers and the Co-operative Principles* (Center for the Study of Co-operatives: University of Saskatchewan, 1994).

104. Du Bois to Mrs. Curtis, memo, 1920, Du Bois Papers.

105. [W. E. B. Du Bois], "Investigation of Haiti," *Crisis* 20, no. 6 (October 1920), 278.

106. [W. E. B. Du Bois], "Haiti," *Crisis* 20, no. 6 (October 1920): 261.

107. [Du Bois], "Haiti," *Crisis* 20, no. 6.

108. "Following the Advice of the 'Old Crowd' Negro," *Messenger* 2 (June 1919): 16.

109. "The 'New Crowd Negro' Making America Safe for Himself," *Messenger* 2 (July 1919): 17.

110. U.S. Senate, 66th Congress, 1st Session, May 19–November 19, 1919, Senate Documents 12, Investigation Activities of Department of Justice (Washington, D.C.: Government Printing Office, 1919), 180–181.

111. Edwards, *Practice of Diaspora*.

112. On black internationalism in interwar Harlem, see especially Makalani, *In the Cause of Freedom*. Of course, these changes were not limited to New York. The emergence of the New Negro outside of that city receives excellent coverage in Davarian L. Baldwin and Minkah

Makalani, eds., *Escape from New York: The New Negro Renaissance Beyond Harlem* (Minneapolis: University of Minnesota Press, 2013). The foundational works on Caribbean migration to the interwar United States include Winston James, *Holding Aloft the Banner of Ethiopia: Caribbean Radicalism in Early Twentieth-Century America* (New York: Verso, 1998); and Lara Putnam, *Radical Moves: Caribbean Migrants and the Politics of Race in the Jazz Age* (Chapel Hill: University of North Carolina Press, 2013).

113. Cyril Briggs, "Duplicating Belgium in Hayti," *Colored American* Review 1, no. 2 (October 15, 1915), quoted in Dalleo, *American Imperialism's Undead*, 49. On Briggs and the *Crusader*, see Robert A. Hill, "Racial and Radical: Cyril V. Briggs, *The Crusader* Magazine, and the African Blood Brotherhood, 1918–1922," introduction to *The Crusader*, vol. I (New York: Garland, 1987), v–lxvi; James, *Holding Aloft the Banner*; and Glenda Gilmore, *Defying Dixie: The Radical Roots of Civil Rights, 1919–1950* (New York: W. W. Norton, 2008).

114. Cyril Briggs, "American Kultur in the Island of Haiti," *Crusader*, October 1920.

115. Cyril Briggs, "President Harding and Haiti," *Crusader*, May 1921.

116. Mary Jackson McCrorey to Margaret Murray Washington, May 16, 1924, Mary Church Terrell Papers, Moorland-Spingarn Research Center, Howard University (hereafter cited as the Terrell Papers), quoted in Brandon R. Byrd, " 'To Start Something to Help These People': African American Women and the Occupation of Haiti, 1915–1934," *Journal of Haitian Studies* 21, no. 2 (Fall 2015): 154–180.

117. Grace Louise Sanders provides particularly useful insights into the collaboration between elite black women in Haiti and the United States in Sanders in "La Voix des Femmes: Haitian Women's Rights, National Politics, and Black Activism in Port-au-Prince and Montreal, 1934–1986" (Ph.D. diss., University of Michigan, 2013), 80–94.

118. Emily H. Williams to Margaret Murray Washington, December 12, 1922, Terrell Papers, quoted in Byrd, "Transnational Work of Moral Elevation."

119. Addie Hunton and Emily G. Balch, "Race Relations," in Emily G. Balch, ed., *Occupied Haiti* (New York: Writers, 1927), quoted in Byrd, " 'To Start Something to Help These People.' "

120. David Levering Lewis, *W. E. B. Du Bois: The Fight for Equality and the American Century, 1919–1963* (New York: Henry Holt, 2000), 208–211.

121. *Crisis* 32 (October 1926): 284.

122. "Negro Congress to Meet Here," *New York Times*, August 14, 1927. Lewis has argued that this article was "almost certainly written by Du Bois." I agree. See Lewis, *Fight for Equality*, 209.

123. Richard B. Moore, *Caribbean Militant in Harlem: Collected Writings, 1920–1972*, eds., W. Burghardt Turner and Joyce Moore Turner (Bloomington: Indiana University Press, 1988), 53.

124. Lewis, *Fight for Equality*, 208.

125. A particularly useful source for understanding the Fourth Pan-African Congress in historical perspective is George Padmore, ed., *Colonial and Coloured Unity: A Programme of Action; History of the Pan-African Congress* (London: Hammersmith Bookshop, 1947).

126. "The Pan-African Congresses," *Crisis*, October 1927, 264; and W. E. B. Du Bois, "Pan-Africa, 1927," c. 1927, Du Bois Papers. On Huiswood's impact on black thought and politics at the congress and in this era, see Makalani, *In the Cause of Freedom*.

127. Richard Moore, "Pan-African Congress Resolution," 1927, Du Bois Papers; "Negro Congress Told 'Race' Isn't Cause of Woes," *New York Herald Tribune*, August 22, 1927; William

Pickens, "The Brussels Congress," address to the Fourth Pan-African Congress, New York, August 21, 1927, William Pickens Papers (Additions), Schomburg Center for Research in Black Culture.

128. Circle for Peace and Foreign Relations, "Foreign Invitations Sent," March 1927, Du Bois Papers.

129. Du Bois, "Pan-Africa, 1927."

130. Report from the Fourth Pan-African Congress, c. 1927, Du Bois Papers.

131. W. E. B. Du Bois to Raymond L. Buell, May 28, 1929, Du Bois Papers.

132. Cumberland served as the financial advisor of Haiti from 1924 to 1927, a position in which he held far more power than the Haitian president. Marshall had just left a clerkship at the U.S. legation in Port-au-Prince, where he had been the only black member of the occupation government.

133. W. E. B. Du Bois, "Haiti," transcript of radio broadcast, December 21, 1929, Du Bois Papers.

134. Du Bois, "Haiti," transcript of radio broadcast.

135. Du Bois, "Haiti," transcript of radio broadcast.

136. Dubois, *Haiti*, 210.

137. Du Bois, "Haiti," transcript of radio broadcast.

138. Du Bois, "Haiti," transcript of radio broadcast. The Sixth Congress of the Communist International adopted its "Resolution on the Negro Question in the United States," which characterized black southerners as an oppressed nation that possessed an inherent right to self-determination. Robin D. G. Kelley demonstrates the grassroots expression of this idea in Kelley, *Hammer and Hoe: Alabama Communists During the Great Depression*, 25th anniversary ed. (Chapel Hill: University of North Carolina Press, 2015).

139. Du Bois, "Haiti," transcript of radio broadcast.

140. Sténio Vincent to Roy Wilkins, September 16, 1934, printed in *Crisis* 41, no. 10 (October 1934): 292.

141. Polyné, *From Douglass to Duvalier*, 89–130.

142. Foundational texts on black internationalism, black activism, and the Cold War include Brenda Gayle Plummer, *Rising Wind: Black Americans and U.S. Foreign Affairs, 1935–1960* (Chapel Hill: University of North Carolina Press, 1996); Penny M. Von Eschen, *Race Against Empire: Black Americans and Anticolonialism, 1937–1957* (Ithaca, NY: Cornell University Press, 1997); Mary L. Dudziak, *Cold War Civil Rights: Race and the Image of American Democracy* (Princeton, NJ: Princeton University Press, 2000); Carol Anderson, *Eyes Off the Prize: The United Nations and the African American Struggle for Human Rights, 1944–1955* (New York: Cambridge University Press, 2003); Nikhil Pal Singh, *Black Is a Country: Race and the Unfinished Struggle for Democracy* (Cambridge, MA: Harvard University Press, 2005); Penny M. Von Eschen, *Satchmo Blows Up the World: Jazz Ambassadors Play the Cold War* (Cambridge, MA: Harvard University Press, 2004); Kevin Gaines, "E. Franklin Frazier's Revenge: Anticolonialism, Nonalignment, and Black Intellectuals' Critiques of Western Culture," *American Literary History* 17, no. 3 (Autumn 2005): 506–529; Kevin Gaines, *American Africans in Ghana: Black Expatriates and the Civil Rights Era* (Chapel Hill: University of North Carolina Press, 2006); Gerald Horne, *Cold War in a Hot Zone: The United States Confronts Labor and Independence Struggles in the British West Indies* (Philadelphia: Temple University Press, 2007); Carol Boyce Davies, *Left of Karl Marx: The Political Life of Black Communist*

Claudia Jones (Durham, NC: Duke University Press, 2008); Gerald Horne, *Black Revolutionary: William Patterson and the Globalization of the African American Freedom Struggle* (Urbana: University of Illinois Press, 2013).

143. Matthew J. Smith, *Red & Black in Haiti: Radicalism, Conflict, and Political Change, 1934–1957* (Chapel Hill: University of North Carolina Press, 2009), 149–186.

144. W. E. B. Du Bois, "Haiti," April 1955, Du Bois Papers.

145. Du Bois, "Haiti," April 1955.

Epilogue

1. I wrote about this experience after returning to the United States and elaborate on some of those initial thoughts here. See Brandon Byrd, "White Folks and Christians in Haiti," H-Haiti, https://networks.h-net.org/node/116721/blog/h-haiti-blog/131170/white-folks-and-christians-haiti.

2. "White Folks and Christians in Hayti," *American Citizen*, January 25, 1889.

3. Excellent treatment of the failure of foreign aid in Haiti is found in Jonathan M. Katz, *The Big Truck That Went By: How the World Came to Save Haiti and Left Behind a Disaster* (New York: St. Martin's Press, 2013).

4. "White Folks and Christians in Hayti," *American Citizen.*

5. "White Folks and Christians in Hayti," *American Citizen.*

6. See Ulysse, *Why Haiti Needs New Narratives*; and Laurent Dubois and Kaima L. Glover, eds., "New Narratives of Haiti," special issue, *Transition* 111 (2013).

7. Kevin Walters, "Franklin's Historic African-American Cemetery Gets Attention," *Tennessean*, September 18, 2014, http://www.tennessean.com/story/news/local/williamson/franklin/2014/09/18/franklins-historic-african-american-cemetery-gets-attention/15851311/.

8. On Lumumba's life, death, and legacy, see Emmanuel Gerard and Bruce Kuklick, *Death in the Congo: Murdering Patrice Lumumba* (Cambridge, MA: Harvard University Press, 2015).

9. Foundational and recent works on the Duvalier dictatorship include Michel-Rolph Trouillot, *Les racines historiques de l'État Duvalierien* (Port-au-Prince: Henri Deschamps, 1987); Trouillot, *Haiti*;; James Ferguson, *Papa Doc, Baby Doc: Haiti and the Duvaliers* (Oxford: B. Blackwell, 1988); Bernard Diederich, *L'Héritier* (Port-au-Prince: Henri Deschamps, 2011); and Claire Antone Payton, "The City and the State: Construction and the Politics of Dictatorship in Haiti (1957–1986)," (PhD diss., Duke University, 2018).

10. See Camille Kuyu, *Les Haïtiens au Congo* (Paris: L'Harmattan, 2006). Peck's two works on Lumumba are *Lumumba: La mort du prophète* (1992) and *Lumumba* (2000).

11. The esteemed historian John Hope Franklin later wrote that, following the Italian invasion of Ethiopia, "almost overnight even the most provincial among Negro Americans became international minded." Franklin, *From Slavery to Freedom: A History of Negro Americans* (New York: Knopf, 1988), 385. Foundational and more recent scholarship on this trend include Robert Weisbrod, "British West Indian Reaction to the Italian-Ethiopian War, an Episode in Pan-Africanism," *Caribbean Studies* 10, no. 1 (April 1970): 34–41; William R. Scott, *The Sons of Sheba's Race: African Americans and the Italo-Ethiopian War, 1935–1941* (Bloomington: Indiana University Press, 1993); Joseph E. Harris, *African-American Reactions to War in Ethiopia, 1936–1941* (Baton Rouge: Louisiana State University Press, 1994); and James H. Meriwether, *Proudly We Can Be Africans: Black Americans and Africa, 1935–1961* (Chapel Hill: University of North Carolina Press, 2002), 27–56.

12. On Selassie and Ethiopian politics during his life, see Anothony Mockler, *Haile Selassie's War* (London: Oxford University Press, 1984).

13. Martin Luther King, Jr., "The Birth of a New Nation," April 7, 1957 in Documents, King Encyclopedia: Martin Luther King Jr. and the Global Black Freedom Struggle, Martin Luther King Jr. Research and education Institute, Stanford University, https://kinginstitute.stanford.edu/king-papers/documents/birth-new-nation-sermon-delivered-dexter-avenue-baptist-church.

14. The sociologist Roderick Bush provides an excellent contextualization and analysis of King's internationalism in *The End of White World Supremacy: Black Internationalism and the Problem of the Color Line* (Philadelphia: Temple University Press, 2009), 176–220.

15. Polynè contextualizes these silences in *From Douglass to Duvalier*, 180–208.

16. François Duvalier, *A Tribute to the Martyred Leader of Non-Violence, Reverend Dr. Martin Luther King Jr.*, translated from the French by John E. Pickering (Port-au-Prince: Presses Nationales, 1968), 23. On Duvalier and King, see Brandon Byrd, "François Duvalier and the Misuse of Martin Luther King, Jr.," *Black Perspectives,* January 15, 2018, https://www.aaihs.org/francois-duvalier-and-the-misuse-of-martin-luther-king-jr/.

17. Dubois, *Haiti*, 348.

18. Duvalier, *Tribute to the Martyred Leader*, 30. I have used a pseudonym for Samuel.

19. On January 14, 2017, Trump tweeted that U.S. congressman John Lewis, a vocal critic of his administration, "should spend more time on fixing and helping his district, which is in horrible shape and falling apart." A little less than a year later, on January 11, 2017, Trump fumed during a meeting on immigration with members of Congress that the United States did not want African and Haitian immigrants from "shithole countries."

20. Trump's rhetorical question about Haiti came at the January 11, 2017, meeting, one held just after he proclaimed that Haitians "all have AIDS." He asked black voters, "What do you have to lose?" throughout his 2016 presidential campaign.

21. Ta-Nehisi Coates, "The Case for Reparations," *Atlantic*, June 2014, https://www.theatlantic.com/magazine/archive/2014/06/the-case-for-reparations/361631/; Westenley Alcenat, "The Case for Haitian Reparations," *Jacobin*, January 14, 2017, https://www.jacobinmag.com/2017/01/haiti-reparations-france-slavery-colonialism-debt/.

22. Frédérick Mangonès, "The Citadel as Site of Haitian Memory," "Haitian Literature and Culture, Part 2," special issue, *Callaloo* 15, no. 3 (Summer 1992): 857–861.

23. W. E. B. Du Bois, "Haiti," April 1955, Du Bois Papers.

INDEX

ACKNOWLEDGMENTS

"To our future historian, we wish you love and success always, Mom & Dad, December 2005." In countless ways, the inscription inside my well-worn copy of John Hope Franklin's autobiography explains how this book came to be. It certainly captures why these acknowledgments have to begin with my parents. In their own ways, my mom and dad each emphasized the importance of education and the relevance of our history. I am eternally grateful to them for nurturing a passion that has become a career.

Along with my parents, siblings, and other family members who have been lifelong models of success and sources of strength, I am most grateful for the love and support of my wife, Rachel. Since meeting, we've had several graduations, a few moves, and two additions to our family. Throughout it all, Rachel has epitomized compassion, love, happiness, and drive. I'm grateful for the standard of professional success and familial commitment she sets every day.

As the Prologue suggests, this book would not have been possible without the formative influence of my professors at Davidson College. In particular, I am thankful to Daniel Aldridge, Jane Mangan, and Michael Guasco for encouraging my historical interests, advising my research projects, and offering invaluable advice while applying to graduate school. It made and continues to make a world of difference to have faculty who believed in me.

I have numerous people to thank from graduate school, too. At William & Mary, where I first developed my ideas about and interest in African Americans and Haiti, Robert Trent Vinson and Kimberly Phillips were ideal advisors. They asked probing questions of the material, offered important suggestions for further reading, and encouraged me to think deeper about black internationalism.

I received equally invaluable support at UNC. There, Fitz Brundage was the consummate advisor. He consistently made time to offer critical feedback on my writing and discuss my progress. Just as important, he encouraged me to develop this project in my own way and become the scholar that I wanted to be. The same can be said for Laurent Dubois, Jerma A. Jackson, Lisa A. Lindsay, and Heather A. Williams. I am grateful to all of them for reading several drafts and offering critical feedback that has helped turn this project into a book.

Without question, this book has benefited from the assistance, kind support, and critical feedback of a wide community of scholars. In particular, I owe special thanks to Patrick Bellegarde-Smith, Richard Blackett, Andrew Kahrl, Stephen Middleton, and Tiffany Ruby Patterson. At various stops on my professional journey, these colleagues and friends have listened to me talk through my hopes for and challenges with this book, read earlier versions of parts or even all of it, and offered invaluable suggestions for improved writing, argumentation, and further research.

There is no question that this book also reflects the unwavering support of Keisha Blain, Chris Cameron, Ashley Farmer, and all of my friends and colleagues at the African American Intellectual History Society (AAIHS). Since Chris invited me to be a part of his nascent organization, the AAIHS has provided an essential source of laughter, joy, friendship, and, of course, rigorous scholarship and intellectual sustenance. It is my community in what can otherwise be a solitary profession.

Throughout this process, various professional organizations and academic institutions have provided research funding. Special thanks to the College of William & Mary, the University of North Carolina at Chapel Hill, the Society for Historians of American Foreign Relations, Marquette University, the University of Massachusetts Amherst, the American Philosophical Society, Mississippi State University, and Vanderbilt University for their financial assistance. It has been essential in getting to the archives, procuring research materials, and publishing "Black Republicans, Black Republic: African-Americans, Haiti, and the Promise of Reconstruction," my *Slavery & Abolition* article that became the foundation of this book's first chapter.

Besides funding, this book also required the support and faith of Bob Lockhart, Steven Hahn, and everyone at the University of Pennsylvania Press. Thankfully, Bob has been enthusiastic about my project from our first meeting, given close, critical readings to chapter drafts throughout the revision process, and secured anonymous reviewers who helped improve the book with their insightful comments and critiques. I could not have asked for a better, more professional, or more caring editor.

Last but most important, I have to thank the newest additions to my life, Savannah Seay and Miles Powell. Savannah entered the world when I was making the final revisions to the manuscript, a time when sleep was optional but her laughter and love was essential. I hope this book makes her and her baby brother proud.